d Study Sample

	Aspects of the innovation			
ear began project	Status (as initially assessed)	Program type	Program name or initials[b]	Program content
1978	Expanding	Add-on	EPSF	Early childhood
1979	Expanding	Pull-out	Catch-Up	Reading/math
1979	Expanding	Add-on	IPLE	Law and government
1978	Ongoing	Drop-in	Matteson 4D	Reading
1977	Expanding	Add-on	IPA	Individualized educational planning[c]
1977	Dwindling	Add-on	Eskimo Studies	Social studies[c]
1976	Dwindling	Add-on	KARE	Environment
1978	Ongoing	Drop-in	ECRI	Language arts[c]
1977	Ongoing	Subsystem	EBCE	Career education
1976	Ongoing	Subsystem	Bentley Center	Alternative school
1977	Dwindling	Pull-out	CEP	Vocational education
1976	Ongoing	Drop-in	Tindale Reading Model	Reading

INNOVATION UP CLOSE

How School Improvement Works

ENVIRONMENT, DEVELOPMENT, AND PUBLIC POLICY
A series of volumes under the general editorship of
Lawrence Susskind, *Massachusetts Institute of Technology, Cambridge, Massachusetts*

PUBLIC POLICY AND SOCIAL SERVICES
Series Editor:
Gary Marx, *Massachusetts Institute of Technology, Cambridge, Massachusetts*

STABILITY AND CHANGE: Innovation in an Educational Context
Sheila Rosenblum and Karen Seashore Louis

FATAL REMEDIES: The Ironies of Social Intervention
Sam D. Sieber

OSHA AND THE POLITICS OF HEALTH REGULATION
David P. McCaffrey

INNOVATION UP CLOSE: How School Improvement Works
A. Michael Huberman and Matthew B. Miles

Other subseries:

ENVIRONMENTAL POLICY AND PLANNING
Series Editor:
Lawrence Susskind, *Massachusetts Institute of Technology, Cambridge, Massachusetts*

CITIES AND DEVELOPMENT
Series Editor:
Lloyd Rodwin, *Massachusetts Institute of Technology, Cambridge, Massachusetts*

INNOVATION UP CLOSE
How School Improvement Works

A. Michael Huberman
University of Geneva
Geneva, Switzerland

and

Matthew B. Miles
Center for Policy Research
New York, New York

PLENUM PRESS • NEW YORK AND LONDON

Library of Congress Cataloging in Publication Data

Huberman, A. M.
  Innovation up close.

  (Environment, development, and public policy. Public policy and social services)
  Bibliography: p.
  Includes index.
  1. Educational innovations. 2. Educational innovations—United States—Case
Studies. 3. School management and organization—United States—Case studies. 4.
Educational surveys—United States. I. Miles, Matthew B. II. Title. III. Series.
LB1027.H778   1984   371.2'07   84-13795
ISBN 0-306-41693-X

© 1984 Plenum Press, New York
A Division of Plenum Publishing Corporation
233 Spring Street, New York, N.Y. 10013

Printed in the United States of America

Preface

School improvement, like motherhood, has many advocates. Everyone is for it, without having to campaign actively on its behalf. And just as the 100% of people who have had mothers think they know how mothering could be done better, so the (nearly) 100% of people who have been pupils in schools, or have even taught in or managed them, think they know how schools can be improved. More precisely, they are sure that schools *ought* to be improved. The trouble is that they propose a staggering, conflicting range of methods of improving the schools, from "back to the woodshed" to teacher merit pay, a stiffer curriculum, a stronger tax base, reorganization, a more humane climate, "teacher-proof" innovations, community involvement—the list is nearly endless.

Furthermore, the issues are not merely technical, but normative and political. The term *improvement* is itself problematic. One person's version of improvement is another's version of wastefulness or even of worsening the schools. Furthermore, the versions that win out in any particular school are not necessarily technically "best." *Improvement* sometimes turns out to be merely a code word for the directives that administrators have successfully put into place, or for the agreements that teachers have lobbied into being.

How much do we really know about school improvement? The available research literature is quite substantial, but not as helpful as it might be. We have at our disposal a series of knowledge compilations, general syntheses, readers, quantitative surveys, and single-site case studies. Each has advantages and drawbacks. Knowledge compilations and general syntheses perform the useful function of retrieving information from a wide range of studies, but these studies are often not comparable and are of varying validity. Readers are stimulating, but often lack a coherent conceptual core. Quantitative surveys are systematic but often shallow, and they rarely show changes over time. Single-case studies are rich and provocative, but they are subject to all the limitations of looking at only one star in a cosmos of galaxies.

In this book, we have tried to atone for some of the sins of each approach, while still standing on the shoulders of what previous work has taught us. The knowledge compilations and syntheses have provided the conceptual frame-

v

work for our study. The anthologies have pointed out for us which factors appear to matter most and how they are likely to look in the field. The cases examined in this book are sampled from a nationwide, statistical survey of the educational innovation process, including 146 school districts. Finally, we have placed most of our emphasis on documenting and illuminating just how the educational change process plays out over time at the local level, in district offices and school buildings—but we have looked for systematic patterns beyond single sites.

Hence our title. We believe that the process of school improvement can only be understood "up close," in a rich and detailed way. Yet individual case studies of school efforts, to be useful, must be integrated so that the determinants of success and failure in school improvement merge cleanly and coherently.

In this book, the reader will find a concrete, systematic analysis of how significant educational changes were attempted in 12 elementary and secondary schools around the United States. Based on three years of data collection and analysis, the book seeks to show just *what happened* in the course of these school improvement efforts, to explain *why* it happened, and to suggest the *implications* for changes that may be undertaken elsewhere.

AUDIENCES

We have aimed the book at the full range of audiences who are involved with understanding, managing, and supporting educational improvement. These include educational *researchers* (professional, professorial, and student); the *federal and state agency* personnel responsible for policymaking and funding in the school improvement domain; the *state and regional agency* personnel responsible for assistance to schools; and *local school-district* people who, like those who appear in our case studies, are suffering *and* succeeding with planned-change efforts in their schools. The book was written to offer these audiences an intelligible view of school improvement processes, with detailed supporting material. It should be useful in guiding further *research*, in *training* change agents and local school personnel, and in outlining appropriate *policy* to guide school improvement activities.

GENESIS OF THE BOOK

This book was one component of a larger project, the Study of Dissemination Efforts Supporting School Improvement. (For other reports of the larger study, see the 10 volumes of D. P. Crandall and associates, *People, Policies and Practices: Examining the Chain of School Improvement.* Andover, MA: The Network, Inc., 1983. See also the reference section in this book.) The enterprise was a colossal one, into which we were first gradually drawn, then fully submerged. In coordination with four other research centers, The Network, Inc., undertook a three-year project to analyze federally supported educational innovations throughout the country, and to trace the school improvement process from the federal level down through the state level, and then to some 146 school districts. This was one of the larger, more complex "dissemination" studies ever undertaken, and it is likely to be the last of its breed for several years, if only because of the expense and the lack of manageability of such ventures. It involved over 5,000 respondents, four dozen researchers, several waves and multiple modes of data collection, and mountains of information to be distilled. And as with other mammoth research projects, its members' hopes for a breakthrough in understanding of the educational change process were constantly endangered by the demands of complexity, coordination, and scale. Nevertheless, we believe that the study, and the part of it reported in this book, achieved substantial advances in what is known about school improvement.

Our original role in the dissemination study was advisory. The study design had contemplated an "ethnographic" component that would enrich and deepen the conclusions drawn from the quantitative survey. As planning progressed it became clear that the qualitative fieldwork could also serve to validate and test such conclusions, and to suggest further avenues to be followed in the survey data. So the project was one of a newly emerging species: a multisite, multimethod study with the potential of combining and formulating the power of survey and field study approaches. We found ourselves encouraging a thoughtful approach to the field study work, then fleshing out its design for the people who would carry it out—and then, perhaps predictably, being urged to take it on ourselves. So we did.

IMPROVING QUALITATIVE RESEARCH

From the start, we were fascinated by the problems of doing qualitative research in a systematic way. Whereas quantitative research is a technology, qualitative research has traditionally been something like an art form, with very uncertain reliability and validity. Both of us had had rewarding and frustrating experiences in previous qualitative research, and we entered this study determined to break new ground, and to show that qualitative field research can be rigorous and systematic, yet still yield the contextual juice and grit that case studies render so well. We also wanted to develop a replicable methodology of moving from single-case to multiple-case analysis without converting words to numbers or otherwise butchering the meaning of each setting as it is clustered with another.

During the data analysis phase of our work, we were enormously helped by a National Institute of Education grant supporting our methodological innovation and inquiry. That work has continued to the present and has resulted in what we feel are strong contributions to a practicable, trustworthy methodology of qualitative data analysis. (See M. B. Miles and A. M. Huberman, *Qualitative Data Analysis: A Sourcebook of New Methods.* Beverly Hills, CA.: Sage, 1984.)

CHAPTER OVERVIEW

The first chapter is a general introduction. Chapter 2 provides brief case histories of the 12 school settings. Chapter 3 describes the sites prior to the time of actual implementation and outlines the innovations that were adopted.

With Chapter 4, we begin the systematic analysis of the process of change, starting with adoption, and moving through the experiences of early implementation, the several stages of mastering (or botching) a new educational practice, the role of assistance, and the sequence of later implementation and stabilization. Chapter 5 is devoted to the "transformations" taking place along the way: changes in the innovation itself, in the teachers using it, and in the operations of the schools involved.

Chapter 6 reviews and elaborates on the causes for the relative success of the 12 innovations. By *success*, we mean how stabilized the innovation was, how widely it was used in its district, how well "built in" it was, how much it enhanced teachers' professional skills, how strongly it affected pupils, and how teachers' and administrators' careers were affected. Chapter 7 is a reflective summary pulling the different explanatory strands together.

FORMAT

Each section moves from specific *descriptions* of particular sites to an integrated *overview* of what happend, in more conceptual terms. The overview is followed by systematic *explanations* of why things happened as they did, using specific, concrete material from sites to ground the generalizations being made. Information is presented in concentrated form in charts, matrices, and diagrams, and fleshed out with narrative text that tells the story.

We have profoundly enjoyed the process of deepening our understanding of school improvement, seen up close. We wish the reader similar excitement, and we look forward to whatever dialogue may ensue.

Acknowledgments

This book is an abridged version of a three-year field study funded by the U.S. Department of Education and published as Volume 4 of a 10-volume study report, *People, Policies and Practices: Examining the Chain of School Improvement* (Andover, MA: The Network, Inc., 1982).

Enterprises like ours, emerging from a gigantic research project, then honed down into a smaller, more easily digestible product, are more like movies than books. Listing all the key actors, supporting cast, and crew would fill up the screen for several minutes. Let us express our general indebtedness to all our colleagues associated with the Study of Dissemination Efforts Supporting School Improvement (U.S. Department of Education Contract 300-78-0527), then thank a few people who were especially helpful.

In the field study, we were joined by Beverly Loy Taylor and Jo Ann Goldberg as coinvestigators. Their competent fieldwork and masterful case reports were the foundation for much of the analysis provided in this volume.

Our strong thanks go to David Crandall of The Network, Inc., who directed the dissemination study, for his steady support and advice; and to Ann Bezdek Weinheimer, project officer at the U.S. Department of Education, for emphasizing the field study component and providing thoughtful commentary along the way.

The new methods that we developed for analysis of qualitative data came from a concurrent inquiry supported by National Institute of Education grant G1-81-0018. Rolf Lehming was our thoughtful and stimulating project officer.

We also profited from collegial feedback and suggestions on the part of the dissemination study staff, in particular from Joyce Bauchner, Pat Cox, Gene Hall, Ronald Havelock, Susan Heck, Susan Loucks, Glenn Shive, and Charles Thompson.

We benefited from fine-grained, capable critiques of draft sections by Michael Fullan, Rolf Lehming, Charles Thompson again, Rein van der Vegt, and Robert Wenkert. Gary Marx made useful suggestions for converting the original technical report into its present form in this book.

We are grateful to Sage Publications for permission to reprint several charts and figures from M. B. Miles and A. M. Huberman's *Qualitative Data Analysis: A Sourcebook of New Methods* (1984).

The Center for Policy Research and the Knowledge Transfer Institute of American University supplied basic and indispensable administrative services; our special appreciation goes to Sophie Sa, Marcia Kroll, Ann MacDonald, Debbie Roaden, and Nanette Levinson. The final manuscript was competently produced by Judy Woolcock; the art was provided by Estela Morales.

Finally, as the magic formula goes, the ideas presented here, many of them controversial, do not necessarily reflect the views or policies of the U.S. Department of Education or the National Institute of Education—at least, not yet. But we are nonetheless grateful for their sponsorship of our work, and grateful, too, for their having thrown us together into a collaboration that we can no longer think of ending.

A.M.H.
M.B.M.

Contents

List of Tables

List of Figures

CHAPTER 1

Introduction

Just another dumb program they were trying to shove down our throats. (Teacher, Proville site)

I like to tinker with the organization, see things happen. Our greatest enemy is social inertia. People are mostly uncomfortable with change. (Superintendent, Burton site)

We were so damn excited, we would have a meeting at six in the morning, or start at four, and go to seven, eight, or nine at night. We thought we really had it. Measurable outcomes would happen. (Counselor, Carson site)

I had nine kids who were really tough. They felt the success. For some of them, it was probably the first time. They were really gung-ho. They wanted to get those tests done. (Teacher, Masepa site)

Which of these quotes best serves as an epigraph for our study of the way school improvement works? No single one does—and all do. School improvement is a messy, rich process full of coercion and shared struggle, indifference and heavy involvement, uncertain results and real payoffs. That process, deeply conditioned by local history, takes place over a long period of time—usually several years—in a uniquely defined context that includes a specific district. The process unwinds in its own terms, mocking standard frameworks, and challenging the researcher to make a coherent summary from the welter of observed and reported events. And even when the story of the implementation process has emerged, there is still another challenge: developing explanations, a reasonable web of causal influences that helps us understand, not just *that* a school improvement effort worked or failed in the special circumstances at Plummet, Burton, Carson, or Masepa, but *why* it did.

This volume reports our study of 12 efforts to improve schools, carried out in rural, urban, and suburban settings in 10 states from Maine to California. We chose them from the larger sample of 146 schools studied by survey methods, and we visited them repeatedly, talking to teachers, administrators, students, and parents; watching classrooms, meetings, and life in the teachers' lounge; and reading documents from project proposals to notices sent home to parents. Using a standard format, we prepared 12 case reports, each of which described the context, processes, and outcomes of the school improvement effort in detail.[1] The reports totaled nearly a thousand pages, so—as rich and fascinating as they are—we do not include them here in their entirety.

This volume represents a distillation and analysis of the 12 site reports; it seeks to preserve both the particularity and the earthiness of the original reports, and to draw systematic, well-founded conclusions about the processes and outcomes of school improvement.

In addition, this text is an abridged version of the original technical report submitted to the U.S. Department of Education (Huberman & Miles, 1983b). Periodically, we shall refer the reader to that report for additional details, notably on more technical points, which were left out here to enhance readability.

OVERVIEW OF THIS VOLUME

We begin with the background of the field study, describing our reasons for the study, the way the sites were chosen, our data collection methods, our conceptual scheme, and our methods of data analysis.

Chapter 2 gives a short history of what happened at each site. Then we turn to our findings. The format for the chapters and major sections begins with an overview and a brief summary, then turns to the substance, and ends with the final conclusions.

Chapter 3 describes the local site contexts and the innovations that were being implemented in them. Chapter 4 is devoted to the processes occurring during school improvement: the decision to adopt or begin work, initial implementation, the sorts of assistance provided, and the results of later implementation.

Implementation always brought about changes to some degree—in the innovation itself, in those who used it, and in the school and the district as organizations. Chapter 5 discusses these "transformations" and offers systematically derived explanations about why they occurred.

---

[1]The case reports are available at cost from The Network, Inc., 290 South Main St., Andover, Mass. 01810. The 12 titles (site names are pseudonyms): Astoria (NDN): J. A. Goldberg, *Early Prevention of School Failure, Astoria, Southeast* (programs at these sites were sponsored by the National Diffusion Network). Banestown (NDN): A. M. Huberman, *Project Catch-Up, Banestown, Northeast.* Burton (NDN): B. L. Taylor, *IPLE (Institute for Political and Legal Education), Burton, Midwest.* Calston (NDN): J. A. Goldberg, *Matteson 4-D Reading, Calston, Midwest.* Carson (IV-C): M. B. Miles, *IPA (Individual Planning Approach), Carson, Plains* (programs at these sites were supported by Title IV-C development grants). Dun Hollow (IV-C): B. L. Taylor, *Eskimo American People's Culture Curriculum, Dun Hollow, Northeast.* Lido (NDN): B. L. Taylor, *KARE (Knowledgeable Action to Restore Environment), Lido, Northeast,* Masepa (NDN): A. M. Huberman, *ECRI (Exemplary Center for Reading Instruction), Masepa, Plains,* Perry-Parkdale (NDN): M. B. Miles, *EBCE (Experience-Based Career Education), Perry-Parkdale, Midwest.* Plummet (IV-C): J. A. Goldberg, *Bentley Alternative Education Center, Plummet, Southwest.* Proville (IV-C): J. A. Goldberg, *Vacational Intern Program, Proville, Southwest.* Tindale (IV-C): B. L. Taylor, *Tindale Reading Model, Tindale, Midwest.*

Then we move in Chapter 6 to the question of outcomes, showing how much final change occurred in terms of stabilized use of the innovation, spread of the innovation throughout the school and district, degree of institutionalization ("built-in-ness"), impact on students, improved teaching capacities, and changes in teachers' and administrator's careers. Here, too, we seek for causal explanations.

The final chapter provides a reflective, integrated summary of the study's findings.

Readers, like researchers, vary. Some want a complete and thorough warm-up on a study's aims and methods, right at the start. Others are impatient to get to the *story*, the substantive findings. For clarity, we provide background here on the reasons for the study, our sample of sites, the way we collected data, the conceptual scheme underlying our work, and our data analysis methods. The reader aching for substance can skim this section, or skip to the "Summary" (p. 16) and move on from there.

BACKGROUND

Reasons for the Field Study

Our field study was designed to complement data from the survey component of the Study of Dissemination Efforts Supporting School Improvement. Survey methods, using both interview and questionnaire data, can provide rapidly collected, systematic data that are comparable across a large number of representative school districts; such data can be easily machine-processed and analyzed with descriptive and inferential methods. But such an approach also carries with it a set of limitations: predesigned instrumentation, one "snapshot" pass at the site and its informants, difficulties in unraveling the longitudinal process by which innovations are adopted and implemented, and the discovery of unanticipated or equivocal findings that cannot be resolved within the data set itself.

To compensate for those inherent limitations, we designed a field study for a subset of 12 cases within the larger sample of 146 sites, drawing on ethnographic methods. Ethnographies typically entail a detailed, long-term descriptive account of individual and social behavior in a bounded cultural context (a village, a family, or a school). The strength of this approach lies in the continuous and unobtrusive presence of a researcher who observes naturally occurring events in a setting and gradually isolates the characteristics of the individuals and the setting that appear with regularity and that exert a directional influence on behavior. These "organizing contexts" can then account for the ways in which local actors make sense of their own and others' actions, can reveal what matters most to the actors in the setting, and can adequately explain how and why these actors respond to changes in their everyday environment. Such an approach can be adapted readily to the study of a local school as it creates or responds to changes in its curriculum, its administrative structures, or its working arrangements. Ethnographic methods are seeing more and more use in education (cf. Mulhauser, 1975; Wolcott, 1975; Wilson, 1977; Goetz & LeCompte, 1981).

Ethnographic methods are also valuable for their flexibility: One can compensate for weaknesses in survey designs by progressively reconstructing data-gathering methods in response to site characteristics, by making several passes at key informants, by observing the chaining of events over time, and by resolving ambiguities or puzzles as they emerge.

We designed the filed study component to strengthen and complement the survey component by:

1. Identifying typical patterns of outcomes and relationships that were obtained at local sites (i.e., "telling the story")
2. Identifying the causes or determinants of the process by which new practices were generated, adopted, implemented, and, in some cases, institutionalized
3. Validating or at least giving persuasive plausibility to the findings derived from the survey's cross-sectional analysis
4. Aiding with the interpretation of puzzling, equivocal, or nonobvious findings from the statistical analysis of survey data
5. Illustrating the relationships that emerged from the analysis of cross-sectional data, through documented instances

As it turned out, the field study also complemented the survey component in several other ways. First, there was its *orientation*, or focus. The survey leaned toward identifying the characteristics of *innovations* and *program* types and strategies that accounted for successful implementation outcomes; the field study component focused more on the everyday, taken-for-granted properites of the *site* and how they changed, and were changed by, the *process* of implementing new products and practices.

Second, the tendency of survey respondents to give an "official," noncontroversial, or disinterested rendering of the implementation process could be countered by focus during fieldwork on *latent issues*, agendas, and outcomes: career enhancement, personal mobility, and the achievement of other assorted individual and group interests. For example, 87% of the innovation users said on a survey item that they were using the innovation because they "wanted to," not because they "had to." That figure was clarified considerably through closeup interviewing in the field study. We found that administrative pressure was a strong fact of life in innovation adoption for nearly two-thirds of all users ("I didn't know I had a choice to refuse. The principal asked me to do it, and that's it"). And a range of still other motivations was reported:

> It will look good on my résumé. (Teacher, Calston site)

> I took the training for recertification credit. After all that, I had to follow through. (Teacher, Masepa site)

It sounded like an interesting idea and I'd never written curriculum before. They were
going to pay me for the summer, which is always important. And I had free time.
(Teacher, Tindale site)

Third, the fieldwork also uncovered the site-specific *effects of salient events*
unconnected to but affecting the innovation process, such as teacher strikes,
central office intrigues, or impending legislation. Finally, the survey analysis
could look only discretely or additively at interactions among the innovation,
the properties of the site, and the characteristics of key actors; the field study
could look at these interactions over time as a series of transactions or
institutional negotiations resulting in changes in the innovation, in the
practices of teachers and administrators, and, in some cases, in organizational
structures or procedures.

In brief, we wished to complement the standardized, extensive, snapshot
nature of the survey data with context-respecting, intensive, longitudinal data
from the field study. The strengths of each approach could complement the
weaknesses of the other.

To realize these hopes, it was necessary to relax the constraints on the
conduct of classic ethnographic research. A "classic" ethnography could have
been carried out at only three or four sites, thereby defeating the purpose of
getting a reasonable match with the diverse traits of the larger population of
146 schools. Trading off depth of inquiry against generalizability, we selected a
stratified sample of 12 schools, each to be visited for a total of 8–12 days during
the school year, along with intermittent telephone contact.

We also could not afford to be fully inductive, as in the classic ethnography.
We prespecified a general conceptual model underlying our work (see p. 11) and
derived from it a set of 34 systematic research questions that would guide our
local inquiries, while still leaving us open to "what the site had to tell us."[2]

The field study was thus an integrated multiple-case analysis, using
techniques of nonparticipant observation, informal and structured interviewing, and document review. On balance, the data collection methodology lies
closer to the domain of intensive investigative reporting (cf. Douglas, 1976)
than to that of traditional ethnographic fieldwork. Our data *analysis* methods,
many of which we invented during the course of the study, represent, we
believe, advances over currently used methods of qualitative data analysis
(Miles & Huberman, 1984); we explain them more fully below.

Choosing the Sample of Sites

The choice of the 12 sites was dictated by two general concerns. We
wanted sites that would be roughly *representative* of the larger population of 146
sites in the survey sample. And we wanted a *diversity* of sites that were at
different points in the implementation process, enjoying different rates of
success and posing different implementation requirements at the classroom
and school levels.

[2]The full set of research questions appears in the technical report (Huberman & Miles, 1983b) as
  Appendix A.

In order to meet these criteria, the final sample varied along the seven following dimensions: *program sponsorship* (NDN/IV-C); *geographic region* (Northeast, Midwest, Plains, Southeast, Southwest); *setting* (rural, small city, suburban, "urban sprawl," center city); *year of initial implementation* (1976 through 1979); *current status* (ongoing, expanding, dwindling); *program types* (see p. 7); and *program content*. Characteristics of the final sample are given in Table 1 (which also appears in the front end papers for easy reference). Several comments are in order. For program *sponsors*, we chose only NDN and IV-C, to enable cross-program comparisons within our sample, and to focus on the issues of locally generated (IV-C) versus externally introduced (NDN) innovations. Our sample includes 9% of the NDN sites in the larger study and 21% of the IV-C sites.

Our sample fits well with that of the larger study on the counts of *region* and *setting*. We used *urban sprawl* to refer to outlying—but nonsuburban—areas near large cities, where Midas Muffler shops and McDonalds' hamburgers are rife.

Considering *year of implementation*, we wanted to see projects that were at different points in their life history, since we believed that core issues, site dynamics, and outcomes would vary accordingly. We were able to include two first-year projects (Banestown and Burton); they were added to the larger survey sample.

The project's developmental *status*, as assessed by the survey research staff, also seemed important. In most cases, their judgments were correct (though it turned out that work at Masepa, believed to be "ongoing," was, in fact, expanding throughout the district, and that Proville, which was supposedly "dwindling," had, in fact, discontinued the innovation).

We expected that *program* type would make different sorts of demands on sites during the implementation process. We defined four and were able to sample them representatively. A *drop-in* program often involved the substitution of new materials (e.g., in reading and math) that could be easily incorporated into practice by the users. A *pull-out* program often took the form of a resource center or a remedial lab, where the pupils went from their regular classroom. *Add-on* programs enriched the regular curriculum with new content and activities, sometimes including experience outside school. Finally, *subsystems* were more ambitious attempts to create semiautonomous programs, usually with their own space, curriculum, staff, and students. Note, by the way, that most of the programs we studied entailed few organizational changes; they were mostly modest, manageable, content-oriented efforts.

The *content* emphasis appears in the last column on Table 1. We found, after constituting the sample, that at least half of the projects were addressed to *low-achieving or marginal* student populations. That tended to be true for the total IV-C and NDN project population as well.

We considered some additional sampling dimensions, but discarded them as less promising and as making systematic comparisons more difficult. They included the degree of assistance required to implement the program, the degree of developer prescriptiveness, school level, the district stance toward innovative programs (cautious/energetic), and the impetus for program adop-

TABLE 1. Characteristics of Field Study Sample

Site	Program sponsorship[a]	Site context		Year began project	Status (as initially assessed)	Aspects of the innovation		
		U.S. region	Setting			Program type	Program name or initials[b]	Program content
Astoria	NDN	Southeast	Small city	1978	Expanding	Add-on	EPSF	Early childhood
Banestown	NDN	Southeast	Rural	1979	Expanding	Pull-out	Catch-Up	Reading/math
Burton	NDN	Midwest	Suburban	1979	Expanding	Add-on	IPLE	Law and government
Calston	NDN	Midwest	Center city	1978	Ongoing	Drop-in	Matteson 4D	Reading
Carson	IV-C	Plains	Rural	1977	Expanding	Add-on	IPA	Individualized educational planning[c]
Dun Hollow	IV-C	Northeast	Urban sprawl	1977	Dwindling	Add-on	Eskimo Studies	Social studies[c]
Lido	NDN	Northeast	Rural	1976	Dwindling	Add-on	KARE	Environment
Masepa	NDN	Plains	Rural	1978	Ongoing	Drop-in	ECRI	Language arts[c]
Perry-Parkdale	NDN	Midwest	Suburban	1977	Ongoing	Subsystem	EBCE	Career education
Plummet	IV-C	Southwest	Center city	1976	Ongoing	Subsystem	Bentley Center	Alternative school
Proville	IV-C	Southwest	Urban sprawl	1977	Dwindling	Pull-out	CEP	Vocational education
Tindale	IV-C	Midwest	Urban sprawl	1976	Ongoing	Drop-in	Tindale Reading Model	Reading

[a]NDN = National Diffusion Network; IV-C = Title IV-C.
[b]IV-C program names have been given pseudonyms, to avoid identifying specific sites.
[c]Program was used at this site with a comprehensive sample of learners, rather than with low-achieving or marginal populations.

tion (from the building/from the central office). All these dimensions were, of course, attended to during data collection and analysis.

Using seven sampling dimensions for 12 sites made it likely that any given site would be unique in its sampling profile. How could we generalize with validity? There was a reasonably good similarity between our sample as a *whole* and the survey population; beyond this, we should note that the meaningful sampling unit was probably *episodes*, events occurring during adoption, implementation, and institutionalization, rather than "sites" as such. We had dozens of such "treatment" episodes, enough to result in good within-sample analysis and sample-to-survey comparisons.

Site Access

Once the site had agreed to become part of the larger study and had had survey staff visits for interview and questionnaire data-collection, we made contact with the 12 sites chosen for the field study component and arranged an introductory site visit, with the understanding that final confirmation of our working relationship would be reached at the end of that visit. Most sites had few reservations about our presence, probably because they had already agreed to be subjects of study for the larger project. In a few cases (e.g., Masepa), the principal simply agreed to the entire idea on the telephone. In one case (Carson), there was a good deal of initial hesitancy, resolved after the first site visit.

One site, a suburban district in the Northeast, in the—apparently stressful—process of implementing an NDN comprehensive language-arts program (ILA), decided not to participate after our initial visit. We replaced the site with another Northeast NDN site (Lido).

Data Collection Methods

The main corpus of data was generated from field notes taken during site visits spaced throughout the school year. During and after the site visit, the researcher dictated a full account, drawing from the field notes; these were transcribed as a "write-up" and later coded. Some visits were scheduled to correspond with a decisive event on the site (a district office meeting, a staff planning session, a visit of external consultants or trainers). A site was typically visited three or four times for two to three days, with interim contact by telephone. We collected data through interviews, on-site observations, and documents relating to the project or the institution.

Interviews

These were of two sorts. First, we used a semistructured interview developed after early site visits, with a schedule covering the principal research questions.[3]

---

[3]See the technical report (Huberman & Miles, 1983b), Appendix C, for this interview schedule.

The interview had items like:

- "What were you doing before you came here?"
- "What was this school like, before [the innovation] entered the picture?"
- "When you first heard about [the innovation], what did you think it might be like to use it?"

Second, we had many informal interviews, in empty classrooms, hallways, teachers' lounges, cars, cafés, offices, and homes. The questions depended on the person at hand and the state of our knowledge, and they ranged widely: "How come you decided to take that new job?"; "I heard that some people resent the way the decision to try the program was made. Is that so?"; "Was that meeting yesterday a typical one?" Informal interviews (really talks, discussions, and chats) often yielded additional "backstage" information about the users'[4] views of the innovation, relationships within the school, and the actions of building and central office administrators.

Observations

These were typically unstructured, though the researcher often had specific things to look for. They took place in settings ranging from steering-group meetings to the principal's office to classrooms and playgrounds, and they resulted in written-up field notes like these:

> Paul [the superintendent] went on to what was apparently another standard procedure: reviewing the items from the last meeting, on which action decisions had been made, to see if everything was OK. Very rapid fire. "Pancake tickets, OK. Furnace duplex, OK. Drivers, emergency people? Peggy, Arnie, and Wendy will be willing to help." (Field notes, Carson site)

> Lucille [turnkey trainer] starts with the directives—Read, spell and read, proof and correct (3 times), sound and read, make a sentence, read the sentence on the transparency, etc. I notice that she is almost literally snapping out the instructions. Not maliciously, but somewhat mechanically. (Field notes, Masepa site)

Documents

Whenever a piece of paper that looked or sounded significant came to our attention, we asked to look at it, and/or to have a copy made. Our sites varied considerably in their attention to documents. Some sites had notebooks four inches thick for each year of the program; in others, the paper trail was almost nonexistent. We abstracted the content of each document and noted its significance. For example:

> Daily report of absences, and activities announcements (high school).
> Significance: note that details of excused absences are given at a very micro level— implies close control, knowledge of students, sanctions for nonexcused absences. (Document file, Carson site)

---

[4]*User* means persons directly involved in carrying out the innovation with students. These were usually teachers, but also roles such as aide or program coordinator.

Survey Data

We also examined data collected from the 12 sites by the survey researchers, including taped interviews with users and administrators, user and administrator questionnaires, an external agent interview and questionnaire, building work-climate questionnaires, configuration checklists for the project and for users, level-of-use rating sheets, and demographic information sheets for the building and the district.

The field researchers used a variety of verification procedures to assure the credibility of their interview data, including cross-checking informants' accounts with other informants, matching interview data with observations, matching interview data with survey data, careful sampling of informants (main actors, a variety of users, nonusers, dissidents, former program personnel, pupils, and users and administrators in other buildings), and, occasionally, more confrontational devices, such as challenging the account of events given by an informant.

The details of the data collection effort and the methods for the 12 sites are given in Appendix A.

The Conceptual Scheme

Initial Flow Model

Before we began data collection, our study design contained a dynamic model of the implementation process. The model (see Figure 1) includes six variable sets, which interact over time to produce three types of outcome. In the model, the adopting school is seen as a "host" or active recipient of an *innovative program* (one that is new to the school, at least initially) and of *assistance* tied to the program. The *contextual press* from the surrounding community and the district office also has an impact within the school. (In several instances in our study, for example, changes in statewide legislation were funneled into the school through the central office and were connected to an innovative program designed to work in the direction of the mandate.)

The adopting school, then, assimilates the innovative program as a function of its *demographics;* its *prior history of innovative practices;* its *organizational practices, procedures, and norms;* and its *user purposes and assumptions.* The *decision to adopt,* as well as a preliminary *plan for implementation* and *support* services, follow from a series of negotiations—often tacit—beween district administrators, school personnel, and developers or advocates of the innovative program.

During early and later implementation, users interact with the new program under existing organizational arrangements. Through a series of accommodative transformations, the *innovation* is adjusted through user and organizational pressure (for example, its parts are simplified, bent in various ways, left out, or supplemented). Implementing the innovation also changes *users'* perceptions and *practices* (for example, they become more skilled at individualization, feel closer to the students, and understand mastery learning

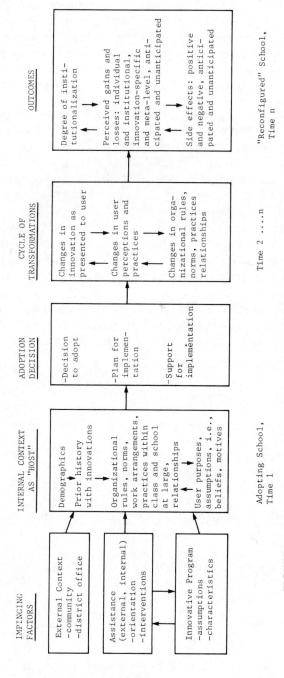

FIGURE 1. Field-study conceptual flowchart. (From Miles & Huberman, 1984. Reprinted by permission.)

methods better). And implementation also brings about *organizational shifts* (for example, when projects entail cross-age grouping, cross-disciplinary teams of teachers, new evaluation procedures, or redelegations of authority).

The model assumes that these transformations produce distinct *outcomes*, most perceived as gains and losses at the individual and institutional levels. These outcomes may or may not (note *side effects*) correspond to those specified by the program developers; many may also have been unanticipated.

In a later iteration of this model, six outcomes are specified in more detail:

1. Stabilization of use: the degree of practice mastery and "settledness" of the new practice in the users' instructional repertoire.
2. Percentage of use: the number of users in a school or a district in proportion to the number of eligible or possible users.
3. Institutionalization: the degree to which the innovation is "built in"—incorporated into the ordinary structures and procedures of the school and its surrounding district.
4. Student impact: achievement, affective, and behavioral changes in students as a result of exposure to the innovation.
5. User capacity change: changes in users' knowledge, attitudes, or skills that are of general professional value, beyond the immediate innovation's requirements.
6. Job mobility: movement of school personnel to new positions inside their schools or districts (down, sideways, or up); to new positions outside their districts; or out of education altogether.

In short, our study was driven by the idea of following out the contextual consequences of *an* innovation in a school setting. We did not aim to look at all innovative behavior in our schools.

Research Questions

We used the model to generate a list of 34 research questions, each with subqueries. They covered six main categories:

1. The characteristics or properties of the innovation
2. The context of the school as a social organization, prior to implementation
3. The adoption decision
4. Site dynamics during implementation
5. Role of internal and external assistance
6. Outcomes and reconfigurations in school practice

The complete set of research questions appears as Appendix A in the original technical report (Huberman & Miles, 1983b).

Core Variables

As we worked on our causal analyses for each site, we gradually developed a total of 31 "core variables" within the six boxes of the model, from our

TABLE 2. List of Antecedent, Mediating, and Outcome Variables

Antecedent or start variables	Mediating variables	Outcomes
Internal funds	External funds	Stabilization of use
Career advancement	Program adoption (NDN)	Percentage of use
motivation	Program concept initiative	Student impact
Assessed adequacy of local	(IV-C)	User capacity change
performance	Program development (IV-C)	Institutionalization
Environmental turbulence	District endorsement	Job mobility
	Building endorsement	
	Influence of innovation	
	advocate	
	Implementation requirements	
	Adequacy of initial user	
	preparation	
	Program–district fit	
	Program–building fit	
	Program–user fit	
	Assistance	
	User commitment	
	User skill	
	Program transformation	
	Teacher–administrator	
	harmony	
	Validation effort (IV-C)	
	Stability of program leadership	
	Stability of program staff	
	Organizational transformation	

Note: From Miles & Huberman (1984). Reprinted by permission.

original research questions, and from what turned out to be important at our sites. These variables enabled us to make systematic comparisons across all 12 sites, as we struggled with the task of comparing the 12 "causal networks," which were qualitatively derived path analyses.[5] The 31 core variables were organized according to *antecedent* or start variables existing before the implementation process began, *mediating* variables occurring during implementation, and *outcomes*. Here we simply list them without further explanation (Table 2); their meaning will become clear as we proceed.

Final Recasting of the Model

As might be expected, the process of cross-site analysis that resulted in this volume led to one more iteration of the model, with a number of new variables added to the 31. It will have much more meaning to the reader once our findings are clearly in mind. It appears on page 190.

[5]The procedures used to generate core variables and to elaborate within-site and cross-site causal networks are described in detail in Miles and Huberman (1984).

Data Analysis Methods

As we have pointed out elsewhere (Huberman & Miles, 1983a), methods of qualitative data analysis are not well codified and are often left vague or implicit in research reports. We want to provide enough clarity about our methods to be reassuring, without drowning the reader in arcane methodological detail.[6]

We were naturally concerned about developing descriptions and explanations that could be reasonably comparable across 12 diverse sites, produced by four different field workers/analysts. The first solution to this problem has already been described: the set of research questions, keyed to the interview schedule that we used during later fieldwork.

Second, working from the research questions, we developed an exhaustive list of codes, which we could use to categorize and sort events and statements in our field notes. These codes were of two sorts. *Descriptive* codes were used in the margin of field notes to characterize a "chunk" of the notes. For example, the code AP-MOT (adoption process—motives) was applied to this piece of the Tindale field notes:

> I asked him what the need for the new program was, and he responded that the students coming into the ninth grade were two years below grade level, and that the old curriculum was ineffective. Through testing (the Nelson Reading Test) it was determined that students were growing academically only five to six months during the ten-month school year.

The second kind of code—actually, a metacode—was *explanatory*. Such codes emerged from our experience with the sites and were usually *leitmotivs* (repeated themes) or causal explanations of outcomes that were offered by site people or that emerged from our own musings. For example, the explanatory code CL-EXPL (causal link—explanation) was applied to this segment of the Banestown field notes:

> But he [Mr. Walt] says that he does not know that much about what is exactly involved in the catch-up program. He thinks that "it is a combination of a lot of things." The resource lab appears to be used in the morning for the FACILE program, which Mr. Walt knows a great deal more about. . . . In the afternoon, Mrs. Hampshire uses the lab for catch-up purposes. Mr. Walt says that this is a different program, and therefore, it is a different use.

This apparently innocuous statement, we learned very early in our Banestown contacts, reflected a long and acute power struggle between two factions in the central office, in one of which Mr. Walt was active. The CL-EXPL code was applied to other instances of this struggle, and we used the subhead "Teams" to signify factions. The CL-EXPL code was also applied to many other causal links, with appropriate subheads. For a complete list of our codes and their definitions, see Appendix B.

A field researcher typically coded each set of transcribed field notes before returning to the site. We attended in particular to explanatory codes that our

[6]The reader with strong methodological interests should consult Huberman and Miles (1983a,b) and Miles and Huberman (1984).

discussions showed were emerging at other sites, with an eye to cross-site comparability. Our coding system stabilized fairly soon after the first round of site visits, so a minimum of back recording was required.

Writing Case Reports

Before proceeding to the cross-site analysis reported in this volume, we needed to understand the dynamics at each site thoroughly, and to have basic data for the site available in one place. We wrote up the data from each site as a case, using a common framework. The case structure included the following sections:

1. Overview/abstract of the site report
2. Geographic and contextual features of the community, the school district, and the adopting school
3. Organizational chart showing key actors, authority relationships, stance toward the innovation, users, and nonusers[7]
4. Description of the data base (numbers of visits, interviews, observations, documents, phone calls, and size of corpus of notes)
5. Brief chronology of events, including "event listings" for each phase of the innovation process[7] and a chart showing the progression over time in numbers of users or pupils (a growth gradient)[7]
6. Responses to the full set of 34 research questions, including for each a statement of the findings, a display of the data backing up the findings (typically in matrix or tabular form), and an assessment of confidence in the findings
7. Event–state network, showing the principal events transpiring at the site and connecting them to the "states" (of the school, or of key individuals) that resulted in the course of implementation[7]
8. Causal network, using the 31 core variables, plus site-unique variables in a path-analytic flow from antecedent variables to mediating variables to outcomes (see Appendix C for an example, with associated text)

In assembling the site report, the researchers retrieved pertinent material by scanning the body of field notes for the appropriate codes. The coded segments were then collected and analyzed. In most cases, the coded material was reduced to short phrases and inserted in the appropriate cell of a descriptive or analytical matrix; most of the responses to the research questions are contained in matrix or diagram form (see pp. 46 and 208 for examples of site-level data displays).

Methods of Cross-Site Analysis

Given a thorough understanding of what had happened at each site and why, we needed to develop integrated, well-founded generalizations. What

[7]See the appendixes of the technical report (Huberman & Miles, 1983b) for illustrations.

patterns of variables, or families of sites, could we see, and what general causes seemed to be at work? The data-reductive and data-displaying devices in the site reports were an immense help. Each section of the site report contained one or more graphs or matrices that boiled down the data for careful review. The 12 graphs or matrices could be extracted from the site reports and could be compared for common and contrasting profiles.

Our usual way of proceeding was first to assemble a *descriptive metamatrix*, which displayed the data from all 12 sites on a particular issue. For example, Table 15 (pp. 62–63) shows a metamatrix with the data on the "Initial Assessments of the Innovation." Looking down the columns of the metamatrix helped us draw generalizations about what was important, across sites. Then we typically developed another type of metamatrix, a *predictor-outcome matrix*, where we could array the sites by high to low amounts of some variable, such as rough or smooth early implementation. Table 18 (p. 84) is an example. Using it, we could see, for example, that the sites trying innovations that caused a good deal of change in users' practice had a rougher time of it, while the sites with minor changes had a smooth start.

The third step in our analysis was often the creation of a *cross-site causal network*, showing a comprehensive explanation that seemed applicable to all sites. For example, see Figure 10 (p. 185), which shows our explanations of what led to greater amounts of organizational change at our sites as a result of the implementation effort.

The causal networks developed for each site were also useful in cross-site analysis. We were able to sort them into *scenarios* where the causal dynamics were similar. For example, Figure 32 (p. 228) shows an example of the "weak commitment" scenario, where the indifference of administrators ultimately led to a very low amount of final student impact.[8]

Summary

We designed the field study using modified ethnographic methods that would provide intensive, longitudinal data, drawn from the contexts of 12 school sites. The sites had a wide geographic range and varied in their community settings, in the amount of time they had been implementing the innovations, and in type of program. Seven were NDN-sponsored, and five were working with Title IV-C funding. We collected data during three or four visits of two to three days each, using semistructured and informal interviews, observation, and available documents. Survey data from the larger study were also available.

Our conceptual model, which generated 34 focused research questions, emphasized the initial effects of the local context, the properties of the innovation itself, and the nature of the assistance provided to sites as affecting a process that began with adoption; proceeded through "transformations" in

---

[8]All the techniques mentioned on the preceding pages are described in detail in Miles and Huberman (1984).

the innovation, the people, and the local school organization; and resulted in outcomes ranging from "stabilization of use" to student impact and job mobility of local personnel. Our conceptual model evolved and developed over time as we learned more about site dynamics, and it provided the basis for coding the field notes.

The data analysis continued with the preparation of 12 structured site reports, each with tables, charts, and narrative text focused on the research questions. Our cross-site analysis, which is reported in this volume, used cross-site matrices—large charts displaying data from all 12 sites—to develop generalizations, culminating in "causal networks" that gave systematic explanations of the implementation process and its outcomes.

CHAPTER 2

Twelve Brief Case Histories

Here we offer brief capsule accounts of what happened at each of our sites. The aim is to provide a warm-up and an integrated account to serve as a base for the cross-site analyses that follow.

EARLY PREVENTION OF SCHOOL FAILURE: MITCHELL ELEMENTARY SCHOOL, ASTORIA, SOUTHEAST

I give the overall direction. How EPSF is implemented is determined by the local school. (Coordinator of curriculum)

Astoria is a seaport that has retained much of its patrician eighteenth-century architecture. It is primarily a middle- to upper-middle-class community, with residents from the upper levels of the military hierarchy and the state government, as well as professionals, who commute to a larger urban area some 40 miles away.

Mitchell, as a parochial primary school, draws from the more affluent and educated social membership of the city. The student population typically scores above state means on achievement batteries; the teachers characterize the pupils as privileged and academically motivated.

In 1977, at the request of the principals of the 97 schools in the parochial regional district, a post of curriculum coordinator was created in the district to review existing content areas, with the aim of outlining a unified curriculum. A special committee was activated to study kindergarten-level programs. One of the programs studied, Early Prevention of School Failure (EPSF), available through NDN, was recommended to the curriculum coordinator by the NDN state facilitator; it was this program that the committee recommended. Shortly thereafter, the district superintendent called for districtwide, mandatory implementation of EPSF in all kindergartens and in first-grade classes of schools without kindergartens, as was the case at Mitchell.

EPSF requires careful testing of incoming children, the providing intensive, individualized remedial work in speech, language, audition, motor coordination, and socioemotional development. After initial training in March 1979,

18

the Mitchell team of first-grade teachers was impressed by the kindergarten program but questioned its suitability for their first-grade pupils, most of whom had already achieved the program's objectives. These doubts remained discreetly within the school. The staff proceeded dutifully with the initial screening and diagnostic batteries in May, but found that the pupils weakest in the five components of EPSF were already scheduled for supplemental assistance under Title I. To use EPSF as designed, it was felt, would be superfluous and would entail reorganizing the entire basal program. As a result, with the approval of the vice-principal, substantial adaptation ensued. The implementation procedure consisted of dividing up the components and farming the remedial work out to volunteer teachers and teacher's aides, outside the classroom, with minor reinforcement of the existing first-grade curriculum. There were virtually no modifications in ongoing classroom practice.

Three months after the 1979–1980 school year had begun, all but one or two of the participating first-grade pupils had completed the EPSF program. The curriculum coordinator, having visited the school, was pleased with the results. The program is now written into the district curriculum. At the last site visit, Mitchell was preparing its screening procedures for the new cohort of first-graders.

PROJECT CATCH-UP: BANESTOWN, SOUTHEAST

> I don't know. Maybe we got into it too fast. Maybe I should have slowed down a little. But I told [the teachers], "You just start going when you feel ready and let me know what you need." (Elementary supervisor)

Banestown is a rural, conservative town lying in a chain of small towns and villages separated by homesteads running through a picturesque valley between two mountain ranges. Education is an important, but not essential, component of social and cultural life, which revolves around farming and livestock. The district office is perceived as conservative and loosely administered, although, at the elementary level, a small group of dynamic women vie for visibility and influence.

As is the case throughout the state, district schools feel the hot breath of a state-mandated program to meet minimal competency levels in the "basics." District officials were thus alarmed in the fall of 1978 when they learned from a delegation of fourth-grade teachers that some 40% of their pupils were from one to three grade-levels behind and would not normally be graduated to the two local middle schools. Officials began to look around for solutions and learned of an upcoming NDN awareness fair, at which they discovered and immediately adopted a pull-out remedial lab using a variety of commercial materials for intensive daily work in reading and mathematics. The groups are small, averaging five pupils for each lab teacher and aide. The skills are broken into small components, which pupils progressively master on a schedule of near-complete success, with systematic positive reinforcement.

The initial training and preparation were extremely rapid; the lab was operational and funded four months after the 1978 awareness fair. The program was then extended to the two middle schools and to two other elementary schools in the fall of 1979. At the target school, the formula was perfected during the second year, although one crucial component—regular coordination with classroom teachers—was not put in place. There were central office factions struggling for power, and the original innovation advocate lost control over the program, moving back into a secondary role.

The testimony from lab teachers, classroom teachers, students, and central office personnel was positive; initial analyses of test scores showed clear gains in reading and mathematics. The lab teachers also reported a number of personal capacity changes following the experience of mastering an individualized diagnostic-prescriptive instructional program.

Unexpected budget cuts from both county and external sources were announced in May 1980 for the following year. Through budgetary manipulations at the district office, Catch-Up was temporarily salvaged under a transitonal soft money arrangement, requiring the reassignment of lab teachers and shifts in the pupil population. Its longer term future is uncertain.

IPLE (INSTITUTE FOR POLITICAL AND LEGAL EDUCATION): BURTON, MIDWEST

> I don't view this year as implementation. It's more experimentation, letting teachers try out some of the activities and approaches in the program, with no pressure from me. I'll help any way I can, but it's up to them right now. Next year will be implementation. (Social studies coordinator)

The Burton district lies in a sprawling suburb outside a major urban center, where land goes for $20,000 an acre. The population is of mixed ethnicity, with WASP, Italian, Polish, Mexican-American, and black families, and it ranges widely in social class from professionals to welfare recipients. A new superintendent is attempting to jostle what has been a rather traditional district by rotating administrators into new jobs; three of the four high-school principals are new in their jobs, and there is a new director of instruction.

In 1978, after a social-studies needs assessment, the central office coordinator for social studies began searching for a legal/governmental program and located IPLE, which was appealing because of its active learning approach. He got state funds for an awareness workshop; with the interest that developed, he got district encouragement to seek IV-C funds to support training and materials for an adapted version of IPLE for the district.

IPLE is an NDN-brokered social studies program that gives high-school students practical experience and understanding in political, governmental, and legal processes, with units on voter education; government at the state, county, and local levels; and individual rights. It stresses knowledge and skill acquisition, via active student participation, both in the classroom (role plays, games) and in the community at local and state agencies. The ultimate aim is to give students the chance to initiate and carry out projects that affect the community positively.

Burton received funding for IPLE materials and training in September 1979. A workshop for all social studies teachers took place in October. Potential users were told they had the option of experimenting with the materials—or ignoring them. Most ignored them. Four teachers at three different high schools used portions of the materials, and one integrated a good many of the classroom materials into his existing curriculum. But *no* user engaged students in community activities, a feature seen as essential by the developer.

IPLE is marginal in the schools and the district, being treated so far as an optional supplement. The coordinator hoped to get portions of it written into the social studies curriculum through committee work that began in the spring of 1980. Some IPLE users are on these committees and might support that hope. But Burton is a traditional district, with many traditional, high-seniority teachers. The most likely scenario is that some of the more familiar, easily integrated classroom activities will be written in to enliven teachers' lectures, and that the idea of community activities will not appear at all in Burton teachers' practice. IPLE has certainly not been seriously implemented at Burton, much less institutionalized.

INDIVIDUAL PLANNING APPROACH: CARSON, PLAINS

We were so damn excited, we would have a meeting at six in the morning, or start at four, and go to seven, eight or nine at night. We thought we really *had* it. Measurable outcomes would happen. (Counselor)

Everything in the program is looking good, but it has to be implemented. . . . There are many loose ends. Many teachers are still grappling with implementation. (Program coordinator)

It would only disappear if there were a change of administration from top to bottom and/or some community dissatisfaction. Now, if you had to choose between IPA and football, that would be a different matter. (Teacher)

Carson is set in a major river's flood plain west of a large city. It is really three communities: old-time town residents and those farming corn and wheat; working-class people in a decaying riverside village; and wealthy, commuting professionals in a new resort development.

The school district, which contains only one elementary and one high school, has changed a great deal recently. In 1975, a new, humanistically oriented superintendent was hired to improve a system seen as conflict-ridden and stagnant. Most respondents felt that his hiring of new principals and teachers, together with his style, ideology, and practices, had led to a more innovative, considerate, collaborative, and student-oriented climate.

In 1976, a teacher and a counselor, with support from the new high-school principal and the superintendent, and with strong help from an external consultant, initiated work on the program that came to be called IPA. Essentially, it took a highly individualized approach to student needs, interests, and career intentions. It included diagnostic testing of students; three-way conferences among parents, teachers, and students; the development of individualized growth plans; and special activities ranging from trips to observatories to units on dinosaurs to the visit of a famous football player. The whole project has a full-time coordinator, is steered by a teacher–administrator management team, has been carefully evaluated with the aid of the same external consultant, and is approved for dissemination throughout the state.

Early volunteer users had much enthusiasm for the program and worked intensely with it. But the decision to mandate the program for all teachers in the third year brought less committed teachers, students, and parents, and the program was simplified and less fully implemented. It became, in effect, a set of "enrichment" activities for younger students and a course-advisory system in the high school. The coordinator's work load of evaluation and "validation" activities meant that she could not supply as much assistance to the users as they really needed.

Even so, the IPA program seems to have increased the teachers' awareness of the students as individuals and as family members; to have changed some classroom practice; and to have increased student achievement, self-concept, attitudes toward school, and friendliness. Organizationally, it brought about changes such as the management team structure, new scheduling, systematic in-service work, and more elementary-secondary school interaction. Carson was probably the site that changed its organizational functioning most among our 12.

By the spring of 1980, IPA was moderately well institutionalized and would probably survive the departure of the coordinator and the high-school principal, who had taken new jobs. As one teacher said, "Even done poorly, it can't go wrong."

MATTESON 4D READING PROGRAM: DISTRICT 5, CALSTON, MIDWEST

> The beauty of the program was that there was an excellent correlation between the strands of the [existing] Calston reading program and 4D . . . it seemed to me that in the hands of the right teachers this would do it. (District coordinator of instruction)

> You almost feel penalized for wanting to increase your professional activity. If you are going to implement a new program, you have to suffer the consequences. (Teacher)

The Calston subdistrict is located in a large midwestern city nine miles from the affluent lakeside section. The community is predominantly white, multiethnic, and blue collar, with older, well-maintained two-story brick residential dwellings. As is typical of this area, the neighborhoods are flanked by major boulevards lined with small businesses and grocery and hardware stores. The demographics of the community are changing, as upwardly mobile Latinos are integrated into the predominantly white population.

The growing bilingual population had made it difficult to maintain and upgrade reading scores within the district, a source of concern for local teachers and administrators, who operated under an accountability system in which salary "merit" increases were tied to reading achievement scores. In 1976, the district coordinator of instruction attended an NDN fair in Calston, where she discovered Matteson 4D, a drop-in, individualized reading program for students at normal ability levels in Grades 4–8. The program's appeal lay in its stress on word attack skills and appreciation of literature, areas in which district schools had been performing poorly. In addition, Matteson 4D correlated well with the ongoing language-arts curriculum.

During the following year, the coordinator invited two district principals to look over the program at another NDN fair. Both expressed interest. In September 1978, each principal recruited teachers in her respective school; in-service training was held in October at the district office.

Implementation was not smooth, owing to delays in the arrival of materials, to teacher overload from other new programs, and to illness among the program staff. Gradually, the requisite materials arrived, and the teachers settled into progressive mastery of the program. With one exception, the teachers were enthusiastic, although none was certain of the program's effectiveness, and all felt that the administrative support and assistance had been inadequate.

In its second year, the program continued to receive endorsement from district office personnel and school principals. Its continuation, however, has been compromised by a recent budgetary crisis within the Calston school system. Because of the crisis, the advocate of the program at the district office has been reassigned; two of the three current users may not be rehired because of low seniority; and the third is considering a job outside public education. Further dissemination of Matteson 4D, originally planned, has been curtailed. More budgetary cuts are expected. Program continuation is uncertain.

THE ESKIMO PEOPLES' CULTURE CURRICULUM: DUN HOLLOW AREA SCHOOL DISTRICT, NORTHEAST

> The curriculum took too much work, and while I enjoyed putting meat on the bones, it just got to be too time-consuming. I'm suspicious of the Eskimos trying to sell material to the district that they haven't even created yet [to get state funding]. And most of all I'm annoyed with the ESC [Education Service Center]. They stopped asking and started saying, "You *will* prepare a lesson, you *will* evaluate each lesson." (Teacher)

The Dun Hollow Area School District is located just 10 miles from the commercial and industrial center of a large city. Its nearly all-white population is divided among six different municipalities: three lowland working-class towns and three in the hills, two being upper middle class, and the other poor and rural. The district (and school) population ranges from corporation presidents to miners and welfare recipients, as well as a subgroup of Alaskan Eskimos.

In 1976, the Council of Still Waters Eskimo Center moved its headquarters to the immediate proximity of a Dun Hollow elementary school. This was the impetus for the design and the field test of an Eskimo-American culture curriculum in the winter of 1978.

The Eskimos first approached the state regarding the problem of stereotyping and worked subsequently with a local intermediate educational center's curriculum unit with IV-C funding. The resulting project was designed as a drop-in supplement to a social studies curriculum, with the aims of (1) eliminating stereotypes and (2) increasing the knowledge of the history, customs, and current practices of Alaskan Americans. The units included printed material supplemented with transparencies, cutouts, drawings, and slides to be used by the regular classroom teacher.

The field test "decision" appears to have been slid into, rather than firmly made. Only the developer, based outside the district, advocated the use of the program. The initial training was cursory, as were the implementation and evaluation workshops. Revisions of the materials, which were judged to be poor and excessively demanding, were based on teachers' input. But the changes were described by district personnel as inadequate and disappointing.

Over the three years of its existence, the program involved only three users, in two schools. It did have some impact on the participating teachers, who spent time and energy developing materials and activities. The administrators, on the other hand, tended to ignore the program and its users' troubles, and they appeared to be increasingly disenchanted with it. All respondents, with the sole exception of the superintendent, leaned toward nonadoption of the program, beyond the field test, unless it were written into the regular social studies curriculum. The program is unlikely to be continued.

KARE (KNOWLEDGEABLE ACTION TO RESTORE OUR ENVIRONMENT): LIDO, NORTHEAST

A program like this should be more than just happy faces in the woods, and busy hands. (Teacher)

The Lido school district is located in a small, oceanside town midway between two large seaports. The town is one of the six wealthiest in the state and is mostly WASP. Several years ago, Harrison Park was given to the town by the granddaughter of its namesake, and a committee was established to oversee its maintenance. This park provided the setting for an off-campus science program begun by a science teacher before KARE funds were available in 1976.

Operating with considerable support from the high-school principal, the teacher developed a marine biology course that utilized Harrison Park; the course also received the support of the superintendent because it helped to alleviate the overcrowded conditions at the old high school, by getting students out of the building and freeing up space. In the following year, two science teachers created an off-campus forestry–ecology program. Through NDN, they chose to adopt KARE, essentially as a means of expanding the off-campus programs by providing the needed finances to purchase equipment and supplies, and getting training in hands-on, discovery-oriented instruction for one of the science teachers.

The KARE program consists of interdisciplinary learning activities that encourage students to confront real environmental problems, such as water pollution and air contamination, in action-oriented tasks outside the classroom. Booklets give many ideas for activities and teaching techniques, and it is intended that teachers select what they want from the program materials. In other words, KARE is not a full-fledged, step-by-step curriculum; it is an approach to teaching that can be used with many different courses and subject matters.

Funds of $6,100, received in the summer of 1976, were spent by the two science teachers on tools for building their own equipment, sampling kits, instruments for measurement, and materials. Training was limited to an initial three-day workshop and was effective in motivating the teacher who was unfamiliar with the teaching approach. There was one follow-up visit the next spring and several phone calls throughout the year between developers and program users. Users also conducted several environmental workshops for other districts on the hands-on approach.

A change in high-school principals and the move to a more spacious new high school led to reduced administrative support for the off-campus program. The program went from a popular option for high and low achievers to a shrunken dumping ground for discipline problems. There were a total of three users, although one of them did not use the program in 1979–1980 because of a scheduling mix-up that caused the cancellation of the marine biology course. Each off-campus course had space for 14 students, the number that a minibus can transport to sites.

The program was not central in the school or the district, though it enjoyed community support. The teachers themselves were committed to off-campus programs, and KARE "made it all possible." There was considerable discontent in the science department, based on the current lack of administrative support, the poor salaries, and the lack of recognition. The principal and the "lame-duck" superintendent had extremely limited knowledge of the KARE program and less interest in discussing it, though they both thought it would be around in its present form for a "couple of years." The fate of the off-campus program, and KARE within it, depends on whether the science teachers stay in education, the policies of the new superintendent, and whether the principal will become more accommodating.

ECRI (EXEMPLARY CENTER FOR READING INSTRUCTION): MASEPA, PLAINS

[ECRI] *was* something, especially in the first years, but it wasn't any big thing. And everything was positive about it; that helps. . . . Most of the vibes have been real good.

> But it was nowhere near the investment of time it takes to negotiate one contract with a teacher. (Assistant superintendent)

> All those cards, all those definitions, having all my sentences ready, having all the materials ready, placing them in groups, there was a whole lot there. I didn't see how I was going to get it all done. (Teacher)

Masepa is a small, relatively poor city of 14,000, lying in the middle of a massive, unfertile plain stretching across the central and eastern parts of the state. The local economy derives from dirt farming, small-scale industry, local and federal civil service, and a large meat-packing plant on the city's outskirts. The city is culturally active, with a multitude of service clubs, adult education programs, and cultural events. Education, in particular, seems to be an important and well-supported sector in Masepa.

The chronology of events stretches from 1975 to 1980. After an initial exposure to ECRI at a national NDN conference, the curriculum coordinator arranged for an awareness session in Masepa. There followed a "miraculous" pilot implementation by a local teacher, who then teamed with another teacher and the curriculum coordinator to disseminate the program throughout the district.

ECRI is, in the words of its developer, a "highly regimented and task-oriented behavior modification teaching strategy." As an integrated language-arts curriculum, it provides teachers with highly scripted instructional sequences in word recognition and comprehension, study skills, spelling, penmanship, dictation, and creative writing. The program runs all morning in three successive "cycles": a drill cycle, an independent pupil-work cycle, and a "backup" or review cycle. It represents a near-total modification of instructional practices by users.

The 17 teachers who first implemented ECRI in 1977–1978 were beset with problems of inadequate materials and a lack of initial preparation, yet they reported positive results. Some 13 additional teachers implemented the program in the following year, extending ECRI from Grades 2 through 7. As support improved and the number of volunteers rose, the central office decided midway in the year 1979–1980 to mandate the program.

One of the six elementary schools, Humphrey, was quick to spread the use of ECRI across Grade 2–6, under the supportive but pressure-exerting direction of the principal, who returned from ECRI training a strong believer in the merits of the program.

Most local and district teachers found ECRI effective but overly prescriptive. Their continued use came from perceived results, from the generous provision of on-site technical assistance and of instructional materials, and from sustained, teacher-responsive central-office support for the program. The experience of implementing ECRI proved to transform teachers' practices more than was the case in any of our twelve sites, and organizational changes were substantial as well.

EBCE (EXPERIENCE-BASED CAREER EDUCATION): PERRY-PARKDALE SCHOOLS, MIDWEST

You can do things on your own. The teacher is not breathing down your throat. The staff is fantastic, they care. . . . Here you learn stuff you really need to know. It prepares you to go out there. (Student)

It's hard to swallow, not having control of the kids. Here your basic trust is your control. (Staff member)

It's a good program. It works for kids, parents like it, employers like it . . . but senior-high-school principals are very autonomous and very powerful here. [He] is not sure we should be the delivery system for career learning. (Program director)

The Perry-Parkdale school district lies in a lower-middle-class suburb in a sprawling urban area, 20 miles from a large city. Most residents work in the city at a nearby automotive plant; the economic picture is currently grim.

The school district is known for "hustling," getting a quarter of its financial support from federal and other soft-money grants, but its administration is currently in a state of turbulence and turnover.

Driven by state mandate and by a sensed need for improvement in local career-education offerings, central office administrators sought out and adopted an NDN-available version of Experience-Based Career Education, a work experience program that brings students directly into the world of work and seeks to improve not only job knowledge but also the skills of self-assessment and decision making. The students spend the majority of the school day in the program, working on basic skills, "life skills" and "life competencies" (e.g., income tax forms), and carrying out independent learning projects at job sites. The program also brought the district some $300,000 in extra funds over three years through Vocational Education Part D auspices.

The training and materials were received from the Northwest Regional Educational Laboratory (NWRL), and were adapted with minor changes to the Perry-Parkdale setting. There was good central-office support but weak endorsement by school principals and counselors. The program was implemented with fidelity to the NWRL model but drifted toward a population of lower-performing, more alienated students. There were also drifts toward greater routinization, less individualization, more achievement emphasis, and increased control over students. Although it established a modest niche for itself, the program brought about little change in the two sending high schools, from which it remained isolated. The program also received IV-C funds for dissemination purposes in the state.

By late 1980, the program appeared to have been reasonably effective in aiding its 60-70 students to connect with the world of work, to stay in school, to become somewhat more mature, and to communicate more freely with adults. It was, however, not well institutionalized. District support for 1980-1981 was to be cut to 25 students and one staff member plus an aide. This outcome was attributable to weak endorsement by building principals and counselors and was exacerbated by acute financial pressures (declining enrollments, staff cutbacks, and the end to external funding for the program).

BENTLEY ALTERNATIVE CENTER FOR EDUCATION, PLUMMET UNION HIGH SCHOOL DISTRICT: PLUMMET, SOUTHWEST

> In a way we got into a partnership with the Plummet Union High School System. We told them we needed help with the kids and that we were willing to help with funding if they handled the kids. We would be the pipeline that would provide the student population. The district would set up the program and we would back out. (Probation department officer)

> We've been allowed to operate autonomously. We've been allowed to experiment. (Teacher)

Plummet, a rapidly growing Sunbelt city, lies on flat desert plains. In the southern and central areas of the city, one commonly encounters poor Indian and Mexican families strolling or lounging in public areas, a reflection of the city's original inhabitants. Moving northward, one sees evidence of the flight of the city's affluent middle and upper middle class to newly completed tract homes and condominiums. The Bentley Alternative Center—the "innovation" created through IV-C and other funds—lies in a lower-class, industrial section of Plummet, surrounded by a scrap-metal yard, low-income homes, and a collection of industrial plants.

In 1975, leaders of Plummet youth service organizations met to express growing concern over the district dropout rate (13.2%) and the increasing number of referrals of high-school students to juvenile courts. From this and a subsequent conference emerged the concept of a "transition school" for hardcore dropouts, with the goal of returning adjudicated adolescents to their regular high schools within 90 days. Strong backing came from the local school board, the courts, the superintendent of schools, and the probation department. Initial funding of $300,000 came from the department of court services through the Law Enforcement Administration Act (LEAA); the school system provided the facility, the equipment, and the materials; and additional funds were raised through the Career Education and Training Act (CETA), special education, and Title IV-C.

A project director was hired in June 1976 and proceeded to recruit a staff of 15 teachers and counselors with experience in alternative or experimental schooling for dropouts. The initial implementation of the new school in 1976–1977 was uneven, mainly because of continuous shifts in the student population. The school underwent a series of reorganizations and redirections in the two succeeding years, ending up with three departments (academic, general education, and "life skills") corresponding roughly to the three subgroups of its student population. These shifts were managed under a loosely structured, collegial administration, headed by a charismatic director. At the end of the second year, the school survived the skeptical scrutiny of the budgetary review committee, which foresaw the imminent end of external funding.

Still another reorganization was under way in the fourth year of operations, as the notion of an "alternative" rather than a "transition" school hardened. Although the budget was picked up by local district monies, there were substantial changes in orientation and in school management likely as a result of the departure of the director and the probable replacement of program staff.

THE CAREER EXPERIENCE PROGRAM, PROVILLE UNIFIED SCHOOL DISTRICT: PROVILLE, SOUTHWEST

Just another dumb program they were trying to shove down our throats. (Principal)

Jack Tweed [the superintendent] was getting old . . . they would do what he said when he said it, but it was a different story behind his back. (Program coordinator)

There were so many places where the program could go wrong. There could be problems with the principals, the voc. ed. teachers, the classified personnel, and the students. I recall Coles [the coordinator] getting a lot of static from the teachers about scheduling and that classified personnel weren't given enough training. (Central office project writer)

The population of Proville is predominantly made up of conservative, white-collar, middle- and upper-middle-class suburbanites, many of whom were drawn to the area through jobs with aerospace engineering firms. The city has expanded rapidly in the last 10 years as a result of the population shifts and the economic growth characteristic of the Southwest. Three of Proville's four high schools had been built within the past 10 years to meet its expanding student population.

In 1975, an industrial arts teacher at one of the high schools conceived of a plan to provide vocational education seniors with on-the-job experience in the school district itself, under the supervision of certified employees. The teacher conveyed his concept to the superintendent, who, the following year, offered him the administrative position of coordinator of career and vocational education and encouraged him to develop and implement what came to be known as the career experience program (CEP).

Through the intervention of the superintendent, initial funding was provided by the local school board, then through a first-year operations grant from Title IV-C. The new funds allowed the district to hire a full-time project director and to expand participation to 100 students per year.

In September 1976, the principals of the four high schools, along with the vocational education teachers and the directors of maintenance and personnel, were informed of the program and asked to identify students. Initial recruitment was low (16 out of 281 eligible students), ostensibly because class schedules had already been established. In the second semester, 32 students were recruited. From the start, however, both principals and teachers had felt pressured to participate in a program in which they had little interest, and which some perceived as a district office initiative with the aim of providing jobs for the superintendent's "loyalists."

In the second year, 1977–1978, CEP lapsed for six months when the project director left the district. The new director attempted to reduce building-level resentment and to clarify implementation procedures. Participation increased modestly.

During the third year, the original developer moved up to a more senior position in the district office, and the new program director became the coordinator of career and vocational education, with many tasks other than CEP. Though up to 40 students got involved, most of them came at the urging of a single teacher in one high school; everywhere else, CEP was ignored. By year's end, the project was completely terminated, with some minor segments included in the special-education program.

TINDALE READING MODEL: TINDALE SCHOOL DISTRICT, MIDWEST

We *had* to succeed because the program wasn't leaving. If it didn't work, the people would have to leave instead. *We* were supposed to change. (Teacher)

The two target high schools are located in a sprawling suburb of a major urban center. Tindale has a melting-pot population, divided into ethnic pockets, and a 60% minority (black and Hispanic) student population. Reading achievement had dropped to an average of two levels below grade, which led the district administration to mount a reading-program development effort for the high-school level.

By the use of IV-C funds, a new set of courses—the Tindale Reading Model, replacing the old basic English curriculum for the freshman through senior years—was designed by three local administrators: the director of curriculum and two English department chairs. They selected teachers to write the curriculum and other teachers to implement it.

The model starts with the freshman year (where it includes math fundamentals and general science) and goes through the senior year, aimed at remediating reading skills through linking reading, graphics, composition, and language structure. Students completing a level successfully are often "mainstreamed" back into regular classes.

Heavy monitoring and evaluation were used to keep teachers on track and to discourage deviation from the prescribed curriculum. One teacher characterized changing an objective as a "moral sin" and changing an activity as a "venial sin." The users first experienced a loss of freedom, resentment, and stress, but they gradually reached a level of tolerance, if not comfort, with the model, noting that no preparation was needed and that most of the practical bugs had been eliminated.

The model is currently being used by 29 teachers in three disciplines (English, science, and math) at Tindale East High School and has a "settled-in" feeling. There has been measured improvement in student reading skills and attitudes toward reading. During the fourth year of implementation (1979–1980), additional Title IV-C funds were received for disseminating the program to other schools in the state.

CHAPTER 3

Before Implementation

The 12 short stories presented in Chapter 2 provide a general idea of the course of the implementation process and its varied outcomes. Before we return to the details of implementation, we should describe the school contexts (the *where* of implementation) and the innovations (the *what*). Here is a short summary of the contexts in which implementation was to take place, and of the innovations that were about to enter, or to be developed in, those contexts.

As we shall see, the general picture is of middle-class, moderately innovative districts, working in fairly stable environments to implement what turned out to be nontrivial innovations, for an increasing percentage of the student population. There were, of course, many specific exceptions to these general trends.

THE LOCAL CONTEXTS

Structural Properties

A look at Table 3 gives a clearer picture of our sample. The table assembles information on aspects of the local school contexts that we call *structural*. These include the geographic area and the setting; the size of the district (as indicated by the number of schools and the number of pupils); the number of schools and pupils involved in adoption at the beginning of the process, as well as later on; and the socioeconomic level of students in the district and the schools.

Some general comments may help the reader draw meaning from Table 3 and prevent information overload. As we have already noted, the distributions of geographic area and settings are fully representative of the range of sites in the larger study. District size, as indicated by the number of schools, also shows a substantial range, from the 2 schools in rural Carson to the 28 in suburban Perry-Parkdale to the 29 in urban Calston. The adopting elementary schools tended toward the small: most were under 400, with the exception of the two Calston schools and one Banestown school. The high schools showed a very wide range in size, from Carson's 354 to the 3,250 in Tindale West.

Across all sites, the number of adopting schools began at an average of 3.0

and moved to 9.8. But those figures are bent substantially by the mandated district adoption in Astoria's parochial system. If Astoria's figures are removed, the averages are 2.9 schools at the start and 2.9 at the end of our study: no net shift. However, the number of pupils involved did increase markedly: If we use an arbitrary figure of 25 for each classroom, the start mean is 116.4 pupils, and the end mean is 280.1, so increased spread was occurring within schools.

Finally, district socioeconomic status (SES) levels ranged substantially, as Table 4 shows. Note that the districts at (average) position 4 on the scale include some with a full SES range (upper middle to lower: Burton, Dun Hollow, and Tindale) and others with a narrow range (middle to lower middle: Masepa and Banestown). We had no districts that were predominantly lower class, though we did have one such school (Tindale East).

Summary

The size of the districts and of the high schools that we studied ranged very widely. Most of the elementary schools were small. On the average, about three schools per district were using the innovation, and the number of students involved showed a substantial increase over the implementation period. Though the socioeconomic status of students varied widely within and across districts, the most frequent levels were middle to lower middle.

Functional Properties

We also wanted to know how our sample's districts actually functioned or operated, before and during implementation. Here we picked a series of variables that seemed like obvious, plausible things that one might like to know about a district just launching an improvement effort. They included what the *accountability* setup was like; where the innovation's *advocates* were located; what the *history of innovation* was like in the district and the target schools; and how much environmental *turbulence* was present. We also noted other salient district-specific characteristics that did not fall into these categories.

Table 5, which shows the data, is even more complex than Table 3, and we do not encourage more than browsing in it, unless the reader is voracious for background data. Rather, we summarize here the main trends in Table 5 and leave it for later reference.

In seven districts, the *accountability* pattern was traditional or "classic": the teachers reported through the building principals to the central-office curriculum specialists. But in five others, the picture was different: In Burton, Banestown, and Tindale the line went directly to the central office, bypassing the principals either officially or unofficially (Banestown). In Perry-Parkdale and Plummet, the innovation was a separate subsystem, with direct accountability to the district office. We should note that even in the "classic" districts there was, practically speaking, a good deal of decentralization, also known as "loose coupling" (Weick, 1976).

The early *advocates* of the innovation tended to be (at 10 of the 12 sites) in

TABLE 3. Local Contexts:

Site	Geographic area	Setting	Number of schools in district	Number of pupils in target schools
Astoria	Northeast	Small city	1 elementary 1 jr.-sr. HS (both parochial)	270—Mitchell
Banestown	Southeast	Rural	3 elementary 2 middle 1 high school	850—Smithson 215—Carington 550—Banestown middle
Burton	Midwest	Suburban	12 elementary 5 middle 4 high schools	1,150—Queen HS 1,100—Taylor HS 1,138—Burton HS
Calston	Midwest	Urban center	25 elementary & jr. highs 4 high schools	500—Lyles 500—Reston
Lido	Northeast	Rural	1 elementary 1 middle 1 high school	585—Lido HS
Masepa	Plains	Rural	6 elementary 1 jr.-sr. HS	247—Jefferson
Perry-Parkdale	Midwest	Suburban	22 elementary 4 jr. highs 2 high schools	2,300—Aldrin HS 2,300—Perry HS
Carson	Plains	Rural	1 elementary 1 jr.-sr. HS	314—Elementary 354—High School
Dun Hollow	Northeast	Urban sprawl	7 elementary 2 jr. highs 1 high school	380—Tortoise Area 283—Carr
Plummet	Southwest	Urban center	11 high schools	550—Bentley
Proville	Southwest	Urban sprawl	13 elementary & jr. HS 4 high schools	2,100—Endrosas HS 1,900—Elencots HS 250—Elburroes HS ?—Vacville HS
Tindale	Midwest	Urban sprawl	17 elementary & jr. HS 2 high schools	3,090—East 3,250—West

*Boldface shows majority level, if present.

Structural Properties

Adopting schools		Pupils involved		SES level[a]	
Start	End	Start	End	District	School
10 (in archdiocese)	92 (in archdiocese)	70	70	**middle** to upper middle	**middle** to upper middle
1	4	30	95	middle to lower middle	middle to lower middle
3	3	4 classrooms	6 classrooms	upper middle to lower	upper middle to lower
2	2	4 classrooms	3 classrooms	lower middle	lower middle
1	1	4 classes 56 students	2 classes 28 students	**upper middle** to lower middle	**upper middle** to lower middle
6	6	17 classrooms	36 classrooms	middle to lower middle	lower middle to lower
2	2	32	50	**lower middle** to lower	**lower middle** to lower
2	2	60–65	668	upper middle to lower	upper middle to lower
2	2	2 classrooms	2 classrooms	upper middle to lower	upper middle to lower
1	1	228	550	lower middle to lower	lower middle to lower
4	0	16	0	**middle** to upper middle	**middle** to upper middle
2	2	9 classrooms (Tindale East only)	29 classrooms (Tindale East only)	middle to lower middle	East-lower; West-lower middle to lower

TABLE 4. SES Levels of Districts in Sample

Mainly upper middle	1—	Lido
	2—	
Middle	3—	Astoria, Proville
	4—	Burton, Masepa,ᵃ Banestown, Dun Hollow, Carson, Tindaleᵃ
Mainly lower middle	5—	Calston, Perry-Parkdale
	6—	Plummet
Lower	7—	

ᵃMasepa *school* was lower middle to lower; Tindale schools were (1) lower; (2) lower middle to lower. Other school levels were identical with district.

the district office; they were sometimes accompanied by teachers (5 sites), building principals (2 sites), or people in external agencies (3 sites). During later implementation, the pattern was similar, except that, as might be expected, more building administrators became advocates (4), and at two sites, new roles (helping teacher and reading adviser) came into play.

As far as *past innovative history* is concerned, most of the districts had had at least a moderate past interest in new programs; only four districts qualified as low, and there were six that were moderate-high to high. However, the picture at the building level was much more traditional: 6 of our 12 sites were low or low-moderate, and none at all appeared on the moderate-high to high end of the scale. This finding is congruent with the more vigorous presence of central office people as advocates.

Environmental turbulence was low at most (8) of our sites. During the 1979–1980 school year, when we were at the sites, Calston was going through a citywide budget crisis; Banestown and Perry-Parkdale had local budget cuts and loss of federal funds; and Plummet was going through severe budgetary problems and reductions in force. So turbulence where it existed, was primarily economic, not the result of community conflict.

We will not attempt to summarize the "other" characteristics (they will be reviewed more carefully in our later section on organizational change), but a scan down the column will repay the reader's curiosity and will underline the district-idiosyncratic nature of key contextual features, ranging from old-boy networks to accountability pressure and lame-duck superintendents.

Summary

The accountability structures at our sites were nearly evenly split between "classic" ones (teacher to principal to central office) and others where teachers were directly accountable to the central office, at least for purposes of the innovation. Not surprisingly, central office people were usually the early advocates of the innovation. Most of the districts had a moderate to high past innovative history; we are not talking about innovative "laggards." The school buildings, however, had a somewhat more conservative past history. Finally, most of the districts existed in a relatively stable, nonturbulent environment.

THE INNOVATIONS

What sorts of innovations were destined to be implemented in the contexts that we have just outlined? Table 6 provides a capsule description of each and describes some key properties: the general *type* of innovation involved, the extent of its *implementation* requirements, the characteristics of the *population* it was suited for, and whether the innovation was *externally or locally* generated. As in the preceding section, we provide only a brief overview: aspects of the innovation and how it changed during implementation are discussed in depth later.

Summarizing Table 6, we note that the *implementation requirements* were at least moderate for nine sites; only Burton's IPLE program, Dun Hollow's Eskimo curriculum, and Proville's CEP (work experience) program had low to moderate implementation requirements. (And, as we shall see, even these ran into implementation difficulties.) In brief, the innovations being attempted were usually not minor in terms of what they demanded of users. Some, like the Masepa implementation of ECRI, were tremendously demanding. The Plummet alternative school led, like many such efforts, to staff burnout; the Carson system of parent-student-teacher conferences in individualized planning meant role changes for everyone.

The implementation requirements cannot be easily deduced from the *program type:* the heavy ECRI program at Masepa was a "drop-in" program, and "add-on" programs could be relatively easy to implement (Burton) or difficult (Carson), depending on how much they asked of the users and the administrators.

In terms of *school level,* the 12 innovations included 5 that were at the high-school level, 4 at the elementary level, 1 kindergarten through ninth grade, and 2 that covered the full range from kindergarten or first grade through twelfth grade.

In *ability level,* half the programs were defined as appropriate for lower-ability students; the other half had no restrictions. Four of the low-ability programs were also aimed at students with other, often associated characteristics—alienated, disruptive, dropping-out, or vocational-track students.

In terms of *innovation source,* all seven of the NDN programs, by definition, came from outside the adopting district. (That is, they had been developed by other school districts or agencies and were being introduced by "developer/ demonstrators.") The picture for IV-C programs was not, however, the opposite. The Dun Hollow Eskimo curriculum was developed outside the "adopting" district, as the IV-C funds went to an intermediate educational service unit. And in Tindale and Proville, though the programs were "locally" developed "inside" the district, the work was essentially done at the central office level, so that the innovation was *external* to the local schools. Only Carson and Plummet followed the classic IV-C pattern, where district and schools alike participate in program development.

We will not attempt to summarize the innovation description column, but

TABLE 5. Local Contexts:

Site	Accountability	Location of innovation advocates	
		Early	Later
NDN			
Astoria	Classic: centralized, but vice principal has high *de facto* control and autonomy.	District office curriculum coordinator State facilitator	
Banestown	Program staff reports directly to district office; building admin. is bypassed.	District office: elem. supervisor, reading supervisor	
Burton	Departmental "building reps" report directly to district office coordinator; principals uninvolved in curriculum.	District office—social studies coordinator	
Calston	Classic: teachers report to district office coord. via bldg. admin.	District off. curric. coord.	Dist. off. bldg. admin.
Lido	Classic: supt. through HS principal to dept. chair to teachers.	HS principal	Teacher
Masepa	Classic: decentralized; bldg. admin. has high *de facto* control.	District off. teachers (2)	Dist. off., bldg. admin., "helping" teacher
Perry-Parkdale	Separate subsystem; program director reports to district off.—building admins. largely bypassed.	Dist. off. prog. dir., teacher	Prog. dir., prog. staff
IV-C			
Carson	Classic: close collaboration among supt., el. principal, HS principal, and A.P. as team.	Supt., HS principal, teachers, counselor	Supt, both principals, prog. dir.
Dun Hollow	Three units involved: schools, Eskimo Center, intermediate educational service center. Within district, classic accountability.	Intermediate unit (educational service center), program developer	
Plummet	Separate institution; director reports to district office.	School bd., supt., juvenile court, dept. probation	Bldg. admin., district office, juvenile ct., dept. probation
Proville	Classic: teachers report via principals to prog. dir. in district office.	Dist. off. (2), including supt.	Dist. off. (1)
Tindale	Departmental chairpersons in schools report directly to district office; building admins. bypassed.	Dist. off. (2), dept. chairpersons	Dist. off. (1) dept. chairpersons, reading advisers

˙MD = missing data; NA = not applicable.

Functional Properties

Innovation history		Environmental turbulence	Other site characteristics
District	Building[a]		
NDN			
Low	Low	Low	Highly centralized, disciplined administration. No state aid.
Low	Low	High in 1979–80	Conservative inbred community. Loose district control; internal power struggle. 30% Title I pop. Much external fund seeking. State accountability pressure.
Past: low Recent: mod to high	Low	Low	New supt.; many job shifts, new programs, curriculum overhaul.
Mod	Mod–low	High in 1979–80	Innovativeness driven by accountability systems. Funds tight (district ineligible for poverty $).
Low	Low–mod	Low	"Lame-duck" sup't. Tight financial picture. Tight high school space; available off-site facility.
High	Mod	Low	Strong community emphasis on service/ education. Good school-district relations—frequent communication. Many Title I children.
Mod–high	Aldrin HS: high Perry HS: mod	High in 1979–80	High unemployment, enrollment declines. Many key relationships with state dept., univ., other districts doing the program.
IV-C			
Past: low Recent: high	Elem: mod HS: high	Low since 1977	Influx of middle-class professionals. District has achieved substantial recent improvement. Small-scale, informal working style. Strong humanistic ideology.
High	Mod	Low	Central office admins. remote from school; wish to maintain relations with intermediate unit.
Mod	NA	High in 1979–80	High dropout, juvenile crime rates. Collab. between courts, schools, CETA, Teacher Corps.
High	MD	Low	Population expansion—3 of 4 HS built in last 10 yrs. Supt. as "godfather"—old-boy network in district office. Recession—shortage of outside jobs for students. Much external fund seeking.
Low	Low	Low	Middle-class flight, ethnic pockets. Longevity of district admins.—old-boy network. History of local teacher-driven curriculum development.

TABLE 6. The

Site	Innovation type	Implementation req'ts	School level
NDN			
Astoria	Add-on	Moderate	Kindg.
Banestown	Pull-out	Moderate	3–6
Burton	Add-on[a]	Low–mod	9–12
Calston	Drop-in	Moderate	4–8
Lido	Add-on[a]	Moderate	K–12
Masepa	Drop-in	High	K–9
Perry-Parkdale	Subsystem	Mod–high	9–12
IV-C			
Carson	Add-on	High	1–12
Dun Hollow	Add-on[a]	Low–mod	1–6
Plummet	Subsystem	High	9–12
Proville	Pull-out	Low–mod	12
Tindale	Drop-in (Quasi subsystem)	Mod–high	9–12

[a]These innovations could also be (and were) treated as displacing existing practice.

General description of innovation
NDN
Developmentally oriented, diagnostic-intervention program for kindergarten, with screening and daily remedial work (20–30 min) in *speech, language, audition, motor coordination, and emotional-social development.*
Diagnostic-prescriptive remedial laboratory using commercial materials for individualized remedial work in *reading* and *mathematics.* Daily (30–45 min.) instruction using graduated difficulty, instant error correction, positive reinforcement.
Student-centered, participatory approach to learning about *voter education, state government, and individual rights.* Work experience and projects in local community. In-class methods include simulations, role plays, and inquiry methods.
Teacher-managed, individualized supplemental *reading* program, with series of learning packets keyed to 108 behavioral objectives. On-task time divided between independent work on sequentially arranged skill cards and sustained silent reading.
Environmental studies program stressing "hands-on," interdisciplinary projects in local communities. Uses "process education" and student-centered techniques, outside school space and schedule. Community members and agencies involved.
Highly regimented, task-oriented behavior-modification instructional program in *language arts.* Teachers use scripted formats for word recognition and phonetics; pupils work independently through mastery tests in reading comprehension and vocabulary; composition practice daily.
Individualized, community-based *career education* program with work experience and three classroom components: basic skills, "life skills" (e.g., career decisions), and "life competencies" (e.g., income tax forms). Pupils work with minimal supervision carrying out projects at job sites in the community.
IV-C
Program for developing and implementing *individualized educational plans* for normal children. Based on student profile data and teacher–student–parent conferences, learning goals and activities (both in school and community) are specified and monitored for each child. Steered by representative teacher–administrator group.
Supplementary *social studies* curriculum designed to eliminate stereotypes and increase knowledge of Alaskan American history and customs. Units included family living, dance and music, historical and contemporary tribes, arts.
Alternative school for dropouts and delinquent youth, reintegrating pupils into high school after 1–3 months of intensive, individualized remedial instruction, comprehensive student and parent counseling, and vocational training.
Program providing *vocational*-track high-school seniors with on-the-job experience for one day a week under supervision of district classified employee who monitors and evaluates job performance. Students gain school credit, earn minimum wage.
Comprehensive *reading* intervention program replacing basic English curriculum with remedial skill instruction through linear and visual (e.g., film) reading, composition, and identification of language structures and conventions. The program is used in *English* and in *science-math* classes.

we suggest a brief reader scan for the complete range of what was being considered for implementation.

Summary

The innovations being attempted were not minor; most had moderately demanding implementation requirements. They focused on the high-school level (five) and the elementary level (four), with the three remaining aimed at both. About half the innovations were aimed at low-ability students. Nearly all the innovations came from outside the district, the school, or both; only two sites (IV-C) had locally developed innovations with full school involvement.

Table 6 is printed as the back endpapers so that the reader can refer to it quickly as we proceed and can keep the identities of 12 diverse sites clear.

CHAPTER 4

The Implementation Process

Now we turn to what happened as innovations came into school contexts. First, this chapter explores the motives and attitudes centering on adoption of the innovation and describes people's initial perceptions and assessments of the practices that they would be implementing. Then, in turn, we examine the early implementation, the assistance provided to users, and the process of later implementation.

ADOPTION OF THE INNOVATION

Introduction

As our model indicates, educational innovations are not introduced into a vacuum. School people have gradually built up a history of relationships among themselves, and with the institutions they work in. Each educator builds on that history as a function of his or her personal set of goals and career trajectory. This process makes for a complex, sometimes tangled web of relationships initially invisible to the outsider. That web can be intensified or shifted when an innovation enters the scene. With the innovation often come added funds, possibilities for promotion, opportunities to resolve nagging problems, chances for professional growth, and revision in patterns of institutional influence.

In interviews and observations at the field sites, we focused on making the web of relationships and motives visible. What were the teachers' and the administrators' main reasons for adopting the innovations? Why, how, and with whom did they get involved? Was there any relationship to their career goals? Were they initially favorable to or skeptical of the new practice? How central was the innovation to their day-to-day work in the classroom, the principal's office, or the district office?[1]

---

[1]Most of these data are low-inference in character. That is, we recorded what people told us, after checking against what others were saying and with other things that the respondents did or said in subsequent interviews. In one case, however, that of career interests linked to the innovation, we often had to probe deeper or infer motives from the full set of remarks made by a respondent. Such inferences were also checked carefully against other sources.

We will also review in this section the question of who advocated the adoption and made the key decisions that led to adoption, along with a discussion of the relative influence of central office administrators, building administrators, and teachers. Finally, we will survey the timelines at the 12 field sites from the moment when the local staff first became aware of the innovation to the date of initial implementation.

Motives

In most cases, users'[2] and administrators' incentives for adopting the new practices were multiple. In particular, the motives were often—but not always—linked to career plans, to the importance given to the innovation, and to initial attitudes toward it. Table 7 is an array of these themes for one of the field sites, Masepa.

Table 7 gives us an idea of the web of local motives. Note first that users' motives (first column) are *multiple,* that *social influence* (e.g., hearing about the success of a colleague) is prominent throughout, and that there are some *shifts* in responses between early and recent users—slightly more pressure to adopt is felt. (Multiple motives and increases in the administrative pressure exerted on later users were typical at our field sites. Often, the early users were courted. Later, when the practice was being generalized in the school or the district, there was more strong-arming.) The administrators' motives at the Masepa site were more functional; the practice *met a need* or *was an improvement* over current practices.

There were *career incentives* for three of seven users, and possibly for one administrator. The *centrality* of the innovation was high for nearly everyone, though it loomed less large for administrators more distant from the school. In terms of *attitude,* the users were ambivalent about the program introduced at Masepa, because of its complexity (a totally new language-arts curriculum) and the administrative pressure to execute it. The administrators themselves were neutral to favorable.

Finally, some of the local site dynamics around the adoption of the innovation come through in the table: the obvious *advocacy* by the curriculum coordinator, the *pressure* exerted on later users by the principal, and the undercurrents of *resistance* reflected in the responses of the nonuser and L. Brent.

Users' Motives

With the profile from Masepa as a backdrop, let us survey the 12 sites as a whole. First, for users, Table 8 shows the motives expressed for the adoption of the new practice, in order of decreasing frequency.

Table 8 should be interpreted cautiously, as there was an unequal number

[2]We define *users* as those staff members, usually teachers, who were directly involved in using the innovation with students. *Administrators* are defined as others (usually principals or central office personnel) involved in managing or aiding implementation.

of respondents at local sites. There was also some retrospective infiltration: The respondents sometimes invoked incentives that came *after* the initial implementation. Some respondents gave two or three motives, others only one. Deeper probing often produced multiple motives. An example, including "novelty," "extra money," and "constraint," is this:

> It sounded like an interesting idea, and I'd never written curriculum before. They said I'd be teaching it in the fall, and they were going to pay me for the summer, which is always important. And I had the free time. (Teacher at Tindale site)

In other cases, there were several motives, but one *leitmotiv*:

> I can add it to my résumé. The children are learning more skills. I get to meet people like you [field researcher]. That's about all. You grow—that's the answer. You grow. (Calston site)

But with these caveats, what jumps out of Table 8 is the *degree of administrative pressure*. This motive appeared at all 7 NDN sites and at 4 of the 5 IV-C sites. It was mentioned more frequently by the later users than by the pioneers. The lone site with all volunteers involved the creation of a new institution—and alternative school—in which all staff members had *applied* for the job.

Clearly, the users were more *targets* than initiators. This interpretation also gets support from an analysis of the innovation advocates and the key decision-makers at the 12 sites. At 11 sites, the primary initiators and decision makers were central office administrators, most often an assistant administrator for curriculum or the equivalent. At the twelfth site, the school principal and the department chair were the prime movers. When school-level personnel were also active in adoption, they were almost always building principals and/or department chairs. At only two of the sites were teachers with no administrative responsibilities active participants in the adoption decision. It is worth noting, however, that of the 4 sites at which school-level practitioners (including departmental chairs and teachers) *were* primary participants in the adoption process, 3 turned out to be the most successful projects in the sample in terms of the outcomes attained and the relative smoothness of project execution.

There were degrees of administrative pressure. In projects just under way, teachers reported that they were "strongly encouraged" to volunteer. One respondent put this concisely: "The principal wanted it in; we got the message." There was sometimes an element of seduction at this phase, but underneath it was the clear understanding that demands for compliance could not be countermanded. Below is an excerpt showing this between-role alchemy:

> She [the assistant superintendent for curriculum] was really excited about it; she really wanted me to take it. But I guess I really didn't have any choice. (Teacher at Banestown site)

But just as frequently, a new practice required—and got—compliance, even without an expressed order:

TABLE 7. Motives and Attitudes of Users, Nonusers, and Administrators at Masepa

	Motives	Career relevance	Centrality	Initial attitude toward program
Early users: 1977–78				
R. Quint	*Self-improvement:* "To get better, I had to change." . . . "Maybe I wasn't teaching the best ways." *Pressure:* "They wanted us to do it." *Social influence:* "Everybody was saying what Gail's doing is great."	None—improvement of practice	*High:* "Biggest thing I've ever done that somebody else told me to do."	*Neutral:* "There wasn't any appeal. They said it worked so I was going to try it."
L. Bayeis	*Observation:* Saw G. Norris do it and "was impressed." *Fit to personal style:* "I like structure." *Practice improvement:* "Looking around for a different way to teach reading." *Novelty:* "You get tired of always doing the same old thing."	Vehicle to turnkey trainer role; also became Title I coordinator	*High:* "Most important thing I've been involved with."	*Favorable*
Second generation: 1978–79				
F. Morelly	*Social influence:* Heard from several friends about program *Opportunity, effort justification:* "I took the training for recertification credit. After all that, I had to follow through." *Pressure:* "He (Weeling) is the reason we do it here. He's so enthusiastic about it."	None—possibly stabilizing her job at the school	*High:* "This is the only new thing I've done since I've been out of school . . . I had to invest so much."	*Neutral:* Apprehensive
L. Brent	*Social opinion, influence:* "I heard how good it was." *Pressure:* ((Weelling) was really sold on it. They really want it in." *Conformity:* Most doing it or planning to in the school; "it's what's coming." *Self-improvement:* Occasion to "keep growing."	None, possibly fear	*High:* "It's been a nightmare."	*Unfavorable:* Once training began
Recent users: 1979–80				
V. Sharpert	*Obligation:* Requirement to obtain teaching post: "I didn't have a choice." *Practice-improvement:* Complementing preservice training.	Ticket to teaching job in the district	*High:* "My first job."	*Neutral:* Apprehensive

A. Olkin	Social influence: "Heard it was good" . . . "a good friend liked it." Pressure: "Strongly encouraged" by Weelling and Dahloff. Observation, modeling: Saw G. Norrist: "She really impressed me."	None: felt obligated by administration	High: "This was really the big one for me."	Neutral: Mixed feelings
S. Sorels	Observation: "It was so good for my own kids . . . tremendous change in reading, spelling, work habits."	Ticket to full-time teaching position	High: "This was really a big step for me—a big move . . . [nothing else] as high as this in my career."	Favorable: "I was excited about it."
Nonuser				
C. Shinder	Relative disadvantage: "My program was better." Poor fit with personal style: "Too scholastic . . . too programmed."	None	Not applicable	Unfavorable
Administrators				
K. Weelling, Principal	Met need: "I was looking for a highly structured, skill-oriented reading program." Novelty, promise of practical improvement: Intrigued by reading about mastery learning; wanted to see it in operation.	None at first; later, appreciated the visibility	High: "Largest investment I've ever made."	Neutral: then favorable
J. Dahloff, Curriculum coordinator	Relative advantage, face validity of program: "Well organized"; could be used for other subject matters. Social influence: "Impressed" that outstanding teachers favored the program. Practice improvement: beginning teachers ill prepared in reading: "We didn't know what to do with them. . . They just had to learn on the job."	Another in a series of implementations	Moderate: "It was one thing among a lot of things I was working on."	Favorable
W. Paisly, Asst. Superintendent	Social influence: "Talked into it" by J. Dahloff.	None	Low: "It was no big deal."	Neutral

Note. From Miles & Huberman (1984). Reprinted by permission.

TABLE 8. Reasons Given for Adoption by Users ($N = 56$)

Reasons/motives	No. of respondents mentioning item
Administrative pressure, constraint	35
Improves classroom practice (new resources, relative advantage over current practice)	16
Novelty value, challenge	10
Social (usually peer influence)	9[a]
Opportunity to shape projects	5
Professional growth	5
Gives better working conditions	3
Solves problems	2
Provides extra money	1
Total	86

Note. From Miles & Huberman (1984). Reprinted by permission.
[a] Seven mentions were from one site.

> I didn't know I had a choice to refuse. The principal asked me to do it, so that's it. She tells me she's got an intermediate program and that we are committed to using it. Can I say no? (Teacher at Calston site)

Sites varied on the salience of the pressure. At one extreme was an NDN site (Astoria) where the users mentioned *only* administrative pressure. As it turned out here, the innovation was later mandated in a similarly top-down mode, although, in fact, the teachers were using only small segments of the practice. At most other sites, pressure was a dominant or a frequent response, but not the only motive given. At only three sites was pressure infrequently mentioned. At one (Burton), the innovation was in its first year and was regarded by the administrators as a pilot. In the other two cases (Carson and Plummet), interestingly enough, there was a strong ideological theme driving adoption to which both administrators and teachers subscribed.[3]

Another noteworthy phenomenon in Table 8 is the low salience of *problem-solving motives.* The users were saying not that they expected the innovation to solve chronic or severe instructional problems, but that it had the potential to improve classroom practice: add resources, enrich curricula, work better than the practice they were using, and improve working conditions in the classroom. There was little evidence of strongly felt user *need* or problem driving adoption. Rather, the innovation looked like something "better" and was being supported by administrators—and so it was agreed to in good faith.[4] Here again, users

[3] To some readers, the word *pressure* may mean coercion, and may somehow imply that users would not have adopted the innovation if left to their own devices. We simply mean the direct exercise of administrative influence, pushing, energizing. As we have noted, teachers had many other reasons of their own for adoption: they were not just being pushed around from above.
[4] This picture differs considerably from that proposed by Zaltman *et al.* (1973), who believe that a "performance gap" or an unsolved problem of some sort drives the adoption decision. As we shall see in a moment, such a relatively rationalistic justification for adoption may be present for some administrators, but the Table 8 data suggest its irrelevance for users.

come through as *consumers* of the practice rather than as active agents. The brief phrases in the first column of Table 7 for Masepa capture this general emphasis well.

The final set of motives in Table 8 can be loosely grouped under the rubric of *professional growth*. The respondents thought that these innovations could counter professional stagnation through their novelty value, could stretch existing instructional repertoires, could add to professional qualifications, and could put teachers in the role of curriculum developers. Were these items grouped (challenge, opportunity to shape project, and professional growth), they would exceed the frequency of practice improvement motives. This fact underscores the need to broaden perspectives when we look at incentives and rewards. Although innovations were supposedly often introduced for instrumental reasons (e.g., to improve achievement scores) they were not necessarily construed this way at the classroom level in our sample. For example, no teacher mentioned "achievement gains" as a motive for adoption. On the other hand, professional growth was a *strong* motive in many cases and acted as a catalyst for the introduction of new practices that *did*, in fact, improve academic performance.

Administrators' Motives

Table 9 shows the profile for administrators and repeats, for purposes of comparison, the users' distribution.

Administrators gave more diverse reasons and configured them differently from users. Pressure was far less frequently reported but was still present, notably among principals, and sometimes had a sharp bite. At the Proville (IV-

TABLE 9. Reasons Given for Adoption by Administrators, and Comparison with Users' Reasons

Reasons	Administrators ($N = 41$)[a]	Users ($N = 56$)[a]
Improves classroom instruction	21 (51%)	16 (29%)
Improves school capacity	10 (24%)	—
Solves problems	7 (17%)	2 (4%)
Access to funds	6 (15%)	1 (2%)
Improves teacher capacity	4 (10%)	5 (9%)
Administrative pressure	4 (10%)	35 (62%)
Helps meet goals, follows philosophy	3 (7%)	—
Enhances own professional image	3 (7%)	—
Meets external demands	2 (5%)	—
Increases own power/authority	2 (5%)	—
Novelty value, challenge	1 (2%)	10 (19%)
Improves achievement scores	1 (2%)	—
Social influence (teachers spoke well of it)	1 (2%)	9 (16%)
Good politics	1 (2%)	—
Opportunity to shape projects	—	5 (9%)
Gets better working conditions	—	3 (5%)

[a]Percentages add to more than 100% because of multiple responses.

C) site, for example, one principal called the innovation "another dumb program that was being shoved down our throats." Another commented that "for a principal to cross the district openly is almost like suicide." (Data from the survey are instructive: 94% of the superintendents, 94% of the principals, and 87% of the users said that they "wanted" to adopt the innovation (as contrasted with "had to"). The figures for "wanted to" are undoubtedly inflated, if only because they can include the situation where one "wants" to do the innovation because of superiors' expectations. But the cross-role trend of the survey data clearly fits with the field study results: The users were more constrained than the principals or the superintendents.)

The administrators' responses also indicate that instructional and school-wide improvement were salient motives: the new practice "had merits"; it "was a good alternative"; it "could be used elsewhere" in the system at a later stage. Note here again that local problem-solving, though more frequently than for the users, was not a dominant theme (nor was it more prevalent at IV-C sites than at NDN sites). Nor was there—except for one administrator—explicit expectation that achievement scores (or any specific student outcome) would improve as a result of program adoption. The accent, not suprisingly, was on the school-capacity–enhancing characteristics of the innovation (e.g., enriching curriculum or providing remedial materials), which the administrators felt could mean achievement gains further down the line.

It is of some interest to note the teachers' greater growth motivation (novelty value, challenge, and opportunity to shape projects) and the role of social influence, in comparison to the administrators/responses.

At only two of the sites (Perry-Parkdale and Lido) was access to funds, as such, an explicit motive. But at a more latent level, it seemed clear that virtually all the sites were interested in the added resources that the new programs provided: new materials, free training, salaries for aides, and administrative slots for friends and protégés whom the central office administrators were bringing along, into either a principalship or a central office job. For administrators, funding could even become an end in itself, often with clear career implications:

> One's job depends on how many projects one gets funded. (Central office administrator at Perry-Parkdale)

> Outside dollars are irresistible. But I don't write for grants unless I'm wired. (Central office administrator at Burton)

Like the teachers, the administrators had multiple motives. Obviously, the greater the number of incentives and their relative importance to a key administrative actor, the more assertive and consequential the decision to adopt. And the closer we got to the full agendas of principals and central office personnel, the more numerous and various were the incentives. Here is an illustration from the field notes:

> Summary of explicit and inferred motivations for the elementary education director: resolves local problem of low achievement, competes with elementary-level rival in

central office, increases relative clout of elementary ed. sector, meets emotional needs (attention to disadvantaged pupils), enhances professional image, responds to pressures external to the district. . . . All of roughly equal importance to her. (Banestown)

Career Relevance of Motives

In making available new resources while adding to the infrastructure of a school district, an innovation often alters career opportunities. First, it frequently *creates new roles*, facilitating upward mobility. Teachers can become local trainers. Administrators are appointed program directors. Second, innovations also attract attention: those involved in their execution freqently get higher *visibility* than in their conventional work, and higher visibility can enhance professional advancement. Finally, since central office administrators were active advocates of most of the new practices that we studied, they came into more direct contact with principals and teachers, thereby multiplying the opportunities for school-level personnel to forge useful *interpersonal links*. In short, innovations can accelerate promotions or other career shifts for both teachers and administrators.

We saw a good many career-related incentives for adopting innovations at the 12 field sites. But we should be careful. At only one site was career advancement the paramount motive for adoption; usually, it was one of several reasons for adoption. Also, career incentives were not always obvious at the time of adoption; they materialized later, when the local actors saw more clearly what the institutional implications of the new practice were. So local personnel were neither overly cynical nor Machiavellian; they simply looked out for themselves and capitalized on the opportunities crossing their paths. The important thing to remember is that the paths existed.

What kinds of career shifts did the site informants mention? We chose to sort out these motives as being derived from what we called *trajectories*. School people may have been going nowhere or going someplace in their career progression, so the innovation was an asylum, a way station, a vehicle, or a final destination. Logically enough, there were four gross trajectories: the innovation provided an opportunity to *move in* (for example, from a prolonged leave or from a distasteful job elsewhere); to *stay in* (securing or solidifying a new role, or avoiding demotion); to *move up* (e.g., from aide to teacher, from teacher to principal, or from principal to central office administrator); or to *move away* (to a lateral job, or to another line of work). Table 10 is a more differentiated breakdown of the trajectories being followed by users and administrators.

Roughly half of the administrators and the teachers for whom there were data had no discernible career motive. Either they were not interested in changing roles, did not see the innovation as a good vehicle for career shifts, or simply focused fully on the contribution of the new practice to their immediate setting without regard to their own career progression. The remaining half had plans. For both teachers and administrators, these plans involved promotions more often than other kinds of shifts, but the teachers' career motives were quite varied, whereas the administrators seemed to be either setting up a promotion or solidifying one. For the most part, our informants spoke to us openly

TABLE 10. Dominant Career Incentives for Users and Administrators

Direction	Career motive	Users (N = 56)	Administrators (N = 41)
No career motive apparent		23 (41%)	21 (51%)
Moving in	Getting back in after a leave.	2 (4%)	0
	Getting away from a distasteful job.	2 (4%)	0
Staying in	Holding on to a job, securing one's status.	4 (7%)	6 (15%)
Getting ready to move up	Getting positioned for later promotion.	4 (7%)	4 (10%)
Moving up	Within the district.	6 (11%)	7 (17%)
	Elsewhere.	1 (2%)	1 (2%)
Moving away	To a private sector job.	1 (2%)	0
	Laterally (another teaching or admin. job).	3 (5%)	0
Moving someone else in	As a replacement.	0	1 (2%)
Unknown		10 (19%)	1 (2%)
Totals		56	41

about these plans, but they were often discreet in their formulations, speaking of the innovation as "an intermediate step" or "a way to get more responsibility."[5] Sometimes, there were two-step trajectories:

> I figured it was a good way to get back in after my leave. The program had a good reputation and I liked the one-on-one work in it. . . . It was an interesting job while I was waiting to get my own class. (Teacher at Banestown)

"Moving someone else in" was a dominant motive at only one site, but a *sub rosa* one at two others. In two cases (Proville and Banestown), this motive led to intense jockeying that took its toll on program execution. The innovations did not create these perturbations but amplified interpersonal tensions already present, adding noise and friction to the system. In contrast, at three of the five sites where administrative careerism was low (Carson, Masepa, and Tindale), implementation was smoother: more task-focused, more collaborative between central office administrators and building-level personnel, and less perturbed when staff turned over. But the two other sites (Dun Hollow and Lido) seemed to *suffer* from the lack of central office investment, which might have been stronger if a career motive had been present. In the seven remaining sites, administrative careerism was strong, without being manic or exploitive; it appeared to inject energy into the adoption process by accelerating the time line, mobilizing resources, and, in some cases, generating enthusiasm at the school-building level.

---

[5]In almost all cases, teachers were well aware of the career plans of one another and of their principals, as were principals of the central office personnel's career plans.

Attitudes

Centrality and Initial Attitudes

We tried to determine how large the innovation had loomed in the daily life of teachers and administrators at the time of adoption, asking them, "Compared to the kinds of things that matter for you . . . how much did this one really count, back then?" We also asked the respondents whether they were initially favorable to the new practice. Table 11 gives a tabulation of responses from the 12 field sites.

Most users initially saw the innovation as central to their classroom life and were favorable to it, but many were neutral or had reservations. Centrality was high in the early stages of program execution, especially if the innovation was complex or demanding for the users. In these cases, the teachers spoke of "a big step" or "the biggest thing I've done." Initial attitudes were more favorable when there was a strong advocate in the building, such as a principal or—even better—a department chair or a respected peer. But there was clearly a wait-and-see attitude on the part of many, as if people were saying, "Let's see how it works initially," or "Let's get a better look at this program that the principal or the curriculum coordinator is so eager for us to try out."

Centrality was lower for administrators, and their initial attitudes were more favorable. The principals were often as much the targets or the consumers of the project as were the teachers, so their initial commitment was not always high. Also, many of the projects were organizationally modest, affecting only a few classrooms. Even in the case of central office advocates, the project was often one of many that they were serving as patrons for. That the administrators' initial attitudes were highly positive seemed often the result of central office advocacy and of the perception by principals that these innovations were improvements on current practices without being institutionally disruptive.

Are the innovations more central when they are bound up with users' careers? Table 12 shows that they are, to some extent. The relationship would be still stronger if we controlled for constraint and complexity; almost all the cases of high centrality and low career relevance involved projects imposed by central office administrators and perceived by teachers as initially complex and demanding.

The relationship is just as strong for administrators (Table 13). Note

TABLE 11. Centrality and Attitudes at the Time of Adoption

| | Centrality | | | Attitudes | | |
	Low	Moderate	High	Negative/ skeptical	Neutral	Positive
Users (N = 56)	4 (7%)	19 (34%)	33 (59%)	4 (7%)	22 (39%)	30 (54%)
Administrators (N = 41)	10 (24%)	11 (27%)	22 (54%)	2 (5%)	5 (12%)	34 (83%)

TABLE 12. Centrality and Career Relevance for Users $(N = 56)^a$

	Centrality		
	High	Moderate	Low
Career-linked	18 (82%)	4 (18%)	0
Career not a key factor	10 (42%)	12 (50%)	2 (8%)

^{a} Data missing: 10.

TABLE 13. Centrality and Career Relevance for Administrators
$(N = 41)^a$

	Centrality		
	High	Moderate	Low
Career-linked	16 (80%)	4 (20%)	0
Career not a key factor	4 (20%)	6 (30%)	10 (50%)

^{a} Data missing: 1.

something else: Decoupling career plans from the adoption of an innovation seems to deenergize administrators more than it does teachers. The four deviant cases of high centrality/low career relevance come from (1) estimates of early centrality (the innovation was a big item at the time of adoption, then consumed little energy) and/or (2) complex and demanding projects.

When we relate centrality to initial attitudes, a strong positive relationship emerges. Most respondents initially liked projects that were very central, that is, that would require a lot of personal investment. There is clear social-psychological theory and research supporting the idea of "effort justification": We love that for which we have suffered (Lawrence & Festinger, 1962). Here, the justification seems to be anticipatory; if we have decided to do a difficult innovation, it must be something we like. (The exception here, of course, is those who felt that they were being strong-armed into adoption.)

Adoption Timelines

One can also analyze the adoption process by viewing it over time, as a succession of decision points. If we look at the individual chronologies between initial "awareness" of the innovation (when the NDN sites learned that the innovation existed and the IV-C project idea germinated) and the moment of "adoption" (when there was notification of funding), our 12 sites varied widely and did so for different reasons. Overall, however, it seemed to take longer at the typical IV-C site (abut 17 months) than at the NDN sites (about 14 months) to get from the actual decision to adopt or develop the innovation to the moment of first use with students.[6]

[6]For a fuller discussion and cross-case analysis of adoption timelines, see the technical report (Huberman & Miles, 1983b, pp. 75-77).

The *location of key decision-makers,* who were usually the project's advocates, affected the time from awareness to adoption. If they were in the central office, things often moved rapidly. At Banestown, it was only a matter of a week or two before the central office coordinator decided to proceed with the Catch-up program she had heard about. The Dun Hollow superintendent moved briskly to tell the elementary education head to proceed with implementing the Eskimo curriculum. Conversely, as at Masepa, when teachers had influence in the early decision-making, the decision to proceed with an adoption agreement came more gradually. The same was true at Proville, where the idea of the project was originated by a teacher. Until he was moved into the central office, things went slowly.

Most advocates were in key positions in the educational hierarchy; they needed few authorizations and few resources beyond external seed money, and they could command local resources (in-service training funds, annual procurements of materials and equipment, and deployment of aides and substitute teachers) so that a strong case for adoption could be made.

In most cases, the *decision to adopt* was made solely by a central office administrator, usually someone in a substantive role, like an assistant superintendent for curriculum. At smaller sites, the head of elementary or secondary education played this role. In some cases, school building principals were consulted, but summarily. Seldom were teachers decisive in the decision to adopt. As we noted earlier, however, when teachers or department chairs *were* active here (Masepa, Lido, Tindale, and Carson), the ultimate results were, in three of the cases, very positive. But the chain leading from styles of local decision-making to ultimate outcomes was long and tangled; collegial decision-making appeared at most to heighten initial commitment—though this had the nontrivial consequence of carrying the project intact through the first serious barriers encountered during program execution.

To better ground these remarks, let us look at Table 14, which shows the roles played by the local actors in the adoption decision.

The findings are quite clear. Central office administrators were at the locus of decision making in 11 of the 12 cases. Because Lido was a small-scale rural site, the district superintendent was consulted before the decision to adopt was made. At a larger site, it would have been conceivable for a low-wattage innovation like the one at Lido to be adopted without central office involvement.

Building principals were more often consulted (6 cases) than directly included in decision making (2 cases) or wholly absent from it (3 cases). In all 6 cases of prior consultation, central office staff would probably have forged ahead with the innovation without building-level approval, unless they had run into a barrage of resistance, an unlikely event. The simple fact that the central office was promoting the project was a clear message for principals to get into line, even if they had some reservations (Calston, Masepa, Dun Hollow, and Proville).

When department chairs were present as decision makers, they played key roles in the adoption decision by "working" both the teaching staff and the

TABLE 14 Roles Played in the Adoption Decision by Central Office Administrators, Building Administrators, and Teachers

| Program/ site | Cent. office administrators | Building admin. | | Teachers |
		Principal	Dept. head	
Astoria (NDN)	Made decision	Absent— "informed"	NA	Absent
Banestown (NDN)	Made decision	Consulted	NA	Consulted
Burton (NDN)	Made decision	Consulted	NA	Consulted
Calston (NDN)	Made decision	Consulted	NA	Absent
Lido (NDN)	Consulted— "approved"	Made decision	Made decision	Consulted
Masepa (NDN)	Made decision	Consulted	NA	Made decision
Perry- Parkdale (NDN)	Made decision	Consulted	Absent	Consulted
Carson (IV-C)	Made decision	Made decision	NA	Made decision
Dun Hollow (IV-C)	Made decision	Absent	NA	Absent
Plummet (IV-C)	Made decision	NA[a]	NA[a]	NA[a]
Proville (IV-C)	Made decision	Absent	NA	Absent
Tindale (IV-C)	Made decision	Consulted	Made decision	Absent
Modal role:	Made decision	Was consulted		Was absent

[a]No staff present at time of adoption, as project entailed creating a new institution. NA = not applicable.

building principal. At both Lido and Tindale, department heads were active advocates of the innovation and drew on their boundary-spanning roles to obtain local support.

Teachers were absent from the decision to adopt in 5 of the 11 possible cases, were consulted in 4 instances, and were actively involved in 2. At Masepa, the teacher was a pioneer in the use of the new language-arts program; it was she, in fact, who urged the central office administrator to make a district-level adoption. At Carson, local teachers were an integral part of the collectively enthusiastic team that developed the individualized instructional and guidance plan.

But looking just at the formal decision-making process is not only myopic but also possibly misleading. For example, at several sites (e.g., Tindale and Burton), there were informal meetings or workshops during which administrators and teachers looked into the concept of the new program or exchanged some initial information about a promising product that was later to be formally adopted by central office administrators alone. A project was often run around, in schematic form, among the various constituencies, before the formal decision was made. Of the 12 cases, there were only 2 (Astoria and Dun Hollow) where a decision to adopt was made in the central office with virtually no prior consultation. Even at those sites, there was evidence of prior working groups (Astoria) or informal contact (Dun Hollow) involving building-level staff.

Adoption to Implementation

Things happened quickly after the adoption decision—sometimes too quickly. If we consider the six sites where implementation began four months or less after funding was received, four of these (Calston, Banestown, Masepa, and Plummet) ran into serious problems at the start from lack of needed training or materials, overload, or all three. The other two (Burton and Proville) were more modest add-on programs that were easier to space out and slow down.

In general, the sites where the transition from the adoption decision to implementation was longer had a more successful time of it, except where the projects were excessively large and complex.

Conclusions

Users, like administrators, had multiple motives for adopting an innovation. In nearly two-thirds of the cases, the prime motive for *users'* adoption was *administrative pressure*, varying from strong encouragement to raw power. This pressure often put teachers in the role of consumers or "targets" of the new practice, although most were neutral or favorable to it at the outset. Adopting the innovation to "solve local problems" was *not* a salient motive; rather, teachers felt that the new practice would *add* resources, enrich curriculum, or outperform existing practices. Another cluster of incentives turned around *professional growth;* implementation of the innovation was seen as a vehicle for becoming a stronger, more resourceful professional, almost independently of the merits of the project itself.

Administrators focused on the potential of the innovation to *improve classroom instruction* and schoolwide *management*. Here again, problem solving was not a strong item. An implicit incentive was that of gaining *access to funds* via adoption—funds that provided new materials, free training, recruitment of aides, and new supervisory posts.

Incentives were, for about half the sample, tied up with *career plans*. Local actors had more-or-less clear career trajectories in mind, and the innovation was a vehicle for moving in, moving up, staying in, or moving away. For both users and administrators, the modal trajectory was securing their *present status* (staying in) or *getting ready to move up*. Too many career-driven incentives impeded successful adoption and implementation, but too few were equally a handicap. Career incentives galvanized local actors, teachers, and administrators alike, to move more quickly, to bypass regulations, and to mobilize in-service and procurement funds for the project.

For most users, the innovation was *important;* it loomed large in their daily life. Initial attitudes were *neutral to positive*. For administrators, the project was often one of several that they were working on, so centrality was lower, but initial attitudes were largely positive, in part because the new practice was perceived as an improvement on current practices that did not disrupt existing working arrangements.

There was a fairly strong relationship for users between the centrality of the project to them and its career relevance; people saw career-relevant practices as more important. Where career issues were *not* a key factor, administrators downrated project centrality more than teachers did. For both groups, centrality was related to initial attitudes; people liked innovations that they saw as important in their daily work.

The *length of the adoption process* varied by site. At some sites, people moved from a first awareness of the innovation to a decision to adopt in a few months; others took over a year. The adoption-to-implementation cycle was faster. In 8 of 12 cases, it took less than six months, once funding was approved. In fact, many of these quick starters got into trouble during early implementation because of having hurried the project into execution.

There were almost invariably key *innovation advocates* in the central office, most of whom made the actual decision to adopt, usually after some consultation with building administrators and teachers.

VIEWS OF THE INNOVATION: INITIAL PERCEPTIONS AND ASSESSMENTS

Introduction

Our sample comprises only sites at which an innovation was actually adopted and implemented in some measurable way. Although we have cases in which such implementation was uneven, unsuccessful, or largely ceremonial, we have no nonstarters. In fact, when we look over the data from the 12 sites, the adoption decision[7] itself seems to have been noncontroversial (a finding echoed in the survey data from the larger study). Either all parties were favorable, or unfavorable parties had little *de facto* power to dissent. There is another possibility: Initial doubt or resistance was negotiated out of the way before implementation. This last option was common among our sample, notably among the NDN projects, where it was often a finished "product" that was being implemented, and much of the bargaining had to do with the degree of freedom given the users to modify that product. For example, the adoption process at Burton, Calston, and Lido included a cascade of negotiations about the *conditions* of local use that began at the level of the program designer (the developer/demonstrator), flowed through the central office, and ended with explicit (Burton) or implicit (Calston) agreements between the principals and the end users on how much of the project was to be implemented. In short, the adoption process was a political one.

The process was a fascinating one at our sites, where the central office administrators were usually champions or strong advocates of the new practice. They had the power to impose adoption on local principals and users,

---

[7]The reader is reminded that for the NDN sites, the adoption decision was whether to *use* the innovation in the district. For the IC-C sites, the "adoption" decision was whether to proceed actively with the *development* work that would be required before "use" was possible.

and some did precisely that (e.g., at Astoria and Tindale). Others bargained. The bargain was usually for a fair trial at the school or classroom level. This was the scenario, for instance, at Burton (NDN), Calston (NDN), and Dun Hollow (IV-C). Sometimes, administrators made their offer more attractive by promising additional resources or consultant services throughout the first year (e.g., at Banestown and Calston). In most cases, however, users had little room to maneuver; they were confronting offers that they could not refuse, and they usually assented while the negotiations had some semblance of symmetry, that is, before the administrators resorted to raw power.

In this section, we survey several aspects of the adoption process, focusing on two variable clusters: (1) users' and administrators' *initial perceptions or assessments* of the innovation—how the project looked to them when first proposed—and (2) the informants' *estimates of the changes implied* by the new practice at the classroom and the organizational levels.

Chronologically, these perceptions, assessments, and estimates of demanded change occurred in a sort of gray area. In some cases, the adoption decision had, for all practical purposes, already been made, and the prospective users were viewing the innovation in the perspective of preimplementation; in other cases, these early assessments were made before the actual "adoption" decision. In all cases, we are talking of users' retrospective views of the just-encountered innovation.

First, a *caveat:* Our data are weaker here than in the sections dealing with implementation, in part because of the retrospective bias operating when we asked our informants to recall events that were sometimes three or four years old. Like others before them, our informants probably sinned in recalling selectively, streamlining what had probably been an unruly adoption process, and confounding their preadoption impressions with their postadoption experiences. In other cases, we were diverted from our line of questioning; for example, a question about the perceived difficulty of implementing might lead into a response about the relative merits of the new practice. Diversions of this sort translated into a sizable amount of missing data. In addition, since our concern in this section is with the initial decision to adopt, we report only on the data collected from first-year users, regardless of how long the innovation had been around at the site. There were three to five such users per site (average 3.8).

We collected data on six variables of interest:

1. *Salient features* striking users and administrators
2. *Initial sizing up* of the innovation by users and administrators (strengths, weaknesses, probable implementation problems, and so on)
3. *Goodness of fit* with users' operating philosophies or teaching styles
4. *Perceived changes anticipated* in implementing the innovation *at the classroom level*
5. *Perceived changes anticipated at the organization level*
6. Overall *goodness of organizational fit,* as inferred by researchers from administrators' assessments

For purposes of cross-site analysis, the "salience" variable was dropped, as it yielded only site-specific responses. But we added a general category, *other variables influencing the adoption decision,* along with an overall *estimate of approval* on the part of the users, the principals, and the central office administrators.

Illustrative Data

Before moving to the cross-site level of analysis, it is worth mentioning how some of these variables fit together at the site level.[8] When we scan the responses for a particular informant, there is often a central "theme" or message. For example, one teacher at Masepa was struck by the prescriptiveness of the new program and its attendant instructional complexity. It seemed boring, yet overwhelming, and that theme is repeated throughout her responses to the six research questions in this set.

Another common strand is that virtually all informants seem to be assessing the new project in the light of how easy or difficult they anticipate its implementation to be—how well they feel they can *cope.* Intellectualism is low. The assessment of the innovation is made less on its merits than on the estimate of how much anticipated practice change is involved and how confident the individual actors feel of bridging that gap. These findings fit with Hall's work with the Stages of Concern (SoC) (1976) instrument, showing that users are initially self-preoccupied.

Looking across the 12 Sites

Table 15 displays data collected across all sites. The first four columns focus on the users' initial perceptions (initial sizing up, personal fit, and implied changes at classroom level), with a single administrator measure (sizing up by principals and central office staff). The next two columns, anticipated organizational changes and organizational fit, display the administrators' responses.[9] For each site, the responses of individuals have been pooled to make a "mean" site-level assessment. The seventh column lists other variables that contributed to the decision to adopt the innovation, as seen by the users or the administrators.

As there were no obviously meaningful subgroups among the individual sites, they are arranged alphabetically within NDN and IV-C.

There are several cases with missing data, some sites for which the case report did not provide responses in the categories used for analysis, and four cases in which classroom-level change was not a key issue.

Table 15 probably looks complex and forbidding at first. To help it come alive for the reader, we will make a vertical analysis, discussing the columns one by one. We do this to help the reader see what conclusions we reached and how we reached them.

[8]For a detailed discussion of responses for two illustrative sites, see the technical report (Huberman & Miles, 1983b, pp. 86–87).
[9]From two to five administrators were involved at each site (average 3.1).

Initial Size-Up of the Innovation

As the double column 1 shows, we asked our informants to choose between two poles of four scales often employed to determine how "usable" people judge an innovation to be when they first assess it. The dominant user and administrator responses for each site are shown in boldface.

Overall, these judgments could be described as daunting, especially on the users' part. Most saw the new practice as *complex*, in the sense of having many parts or involving several different skills. More users were "unclear" than "clear" about the program's objectives, features, and workings. This was especially true at sites where the innovation had already been adopted at the level of the central office, for example, at Banestown, Calston, and Tindale. As the Calston site report put it, most users were at best "dimly aware" of what they were being asked to do. In our analysis of early implementation (see pp. 72 ff.), we find that the users' understanding remained fairly muddy well into the initial six months, and that some users (e.g., at Banestown) who had *thought* they understood how the project worked found out that they had only a global sense of what was actually involved operationally. The gist of these data seems to be that many users tacitly *postponed* (or avoided) the achievement of clarity until they actually got their hands on the materials under classroom conditions, on the apparently correct premise that clarity would emerge progressively from hands-on experience.

Sometimes, levels of complexity and clarity were simply a function of the scale or scope of the innovation; bigger projects were more unfathomable than small ones. For example, users at Lido and Dun Hollow felt that they had a good fix on the add-on curriculum that they were to implement, whereas the more mystified users at Plummet and Carson were looking at the creation of a subsystem, or a far-reaching change in teacher, student, and parent roles.

At *all* sites providing a response, users said that they anticipated that the innovation would be *hard to do*. Sometimes, the fault lay in the design of the practice. At Dun Hollow, for instance, the program was judged hard to do because users saw it as badly flawed, with too few experiential activities and an instructional format adjusted to older pupils than theirs. But in most cases, users were wondering whether they were equal to the task. Here are two representative comments from sites in this category:

> This was big, almost bordering on the overwhelming. We had to deliver if the parents wouldn't. It jacked us up. (Teacher at Carson)

> [My doubt was that] I didn't know how to handle the two programs [the innovation and the current reading curriculum] at once. It was difficult to correlate the two programs. It meant a good deal more work, and for what? (Teacher at Calston)

Finally, most of the new practices were judged to be *flexible*, the exceptions being Astoria, Masepa, and Tindale, where the program depended largely on a highly scripted instructional sequence. Most informants appreciated the flexibility and complained about the prescriptiveness, but there were several exceptions. For example, some users at Masepa had actively sought a prescriptive

TABLE 15. Initial Assessments of the Innovation at 12 Field Sites

NDN sites	1. Size-up[a]		2. Goodness of user fit	3. Level of anticipated classroom level change	4. Level of anticipated organization level change	5. Goodness of organizational fit	6. Other key variables
	Users	Administrators					
Astoria	Simple—**complex**[b] **Clear**—unclear Easy to do—**hard to do** Flexible—**prescriptive**	MD **Clear**—unclear MD Flexible—**prescriptive**	Good	High	Moderate–high	Poor	Admin. pressure Appeal of program segments Local obedience Admin. latitude
Banestown	**Simple**—complex Clear—**unclear** Easy to do—**hard to do** **Flexible**—prescriptive	**Simple**—complex **Clear**—unclear **Easy to do**—hard to do **Flexible**—prescriptive	Good	Low[c]	Low–moderate	Fair–good	Problem solution Admin. pressure Minimal disruption
Barton	**Flexible**—prescriptive MD	**Flexible**—prescriptive MD	Fair	High	Moderate	Poor–fair	Appeal of materials "Trial" status Admin. latitude Admin. pressure
Calston	MD Clear—**unclear** Easy to do—**hard to do** **Flexible**—prescriptive	MD Easy to do—**hard to do**	Good	Moderate	Low	Fair–good	Appeal of program Admin. pressure Admin. latitude Problem solution
Lido	Simple—**complex** **Clear**—unclear **Flexible**—prescriptive MD	MD	Fair	Moderate	Low	Fair–good	Appeal of materials Appeal of funds
Masepa	Simple—**complex** Clear—**unclear** Easy to do—**hard to do** Flexible—**prescriptive**	Simple—**complex** **Clear**—unclear "Manageable" **Prescriptive**—flexible	Fair–poor	High	Moderate	Fair	Admin. pressure Peer pressure Reputation of program

Site							
Perry-Parkdale	**Clear**—unclear[b] Easy to do—**Hard to do** **Flexible**—prescriptive MD	MD	Good	Low[c]	Moderate	Fair–good	Appeal of program Appeal of funds Problem solution
IV-C sites							
Carson	Simple—**complex** Clear—**unclear** Easy to do—**Hard to do** **Flexible**—prescriptive	MD	Fair	High	High	Fair–good	Ideological core System renewal Admin. pressure (moderate)
Dun Hollow	**Simple**—complex[b] **Clear**—unclear Easy to do—**Hard to do** **Flexible**—prescriptive	MD	Poor	Low	Low	Fair–good	"Trial status Topicality of project Admin. pressure
Plummet	Simple—**complex**[b] Clear—**unclear** Easy to do—**Hard to do** **Flexible**—prescriptive	MD	Good	High	High	Good	Problem solution Ideological core
Proville	MD	MD	Good	Low[c]	Moderate	Fair	Admin. careerism Admin. pressure "Face validity" of project
Tindale	Simple—**complex** Clear—**unclear** **Easy to do**—hard to do Flexible—**prescriptive**	**Simple**—complex **Clear**—unclear Easy to do—**hard to do** **Flexible**—prescriptive	Fair	Moderate	Low– moderate	Fair–good	Satisfaction with project design Problem solution Admin. pressure

[a]Boldface indicates dominant user and administrator responses. MD indicates missing data.
[b]Inferences from case report data.
[c]Few classroom-level components in program.

language-arts program, and all four users at Banestown saw the innovation as *too* flexible. One said this:

> I knew what kinds of things I wanted to get across to the children, but I didn't know
> how to do it and the program didn't tell you at all how to do it . . . it was all very loose.
> (Teacher at Banestown)

One final remark on the sizing-up process as shown in Column 1 on Table 15: Note that where we have a full set of data for administrators, there are some sharp differences between their initial perceptions and those of the users. Banestown, Masepa, and Tindale are cases in point. For central office administrators notably, the innovations looked simple, clear, and manageable, in some instances, because the administrators, as partisans of the new practice, had studied it more closely. But it was probably more the case that new practices looked simpler and more tractable to people who would not themselves have to carry them out. (Had the innovation been chiefly an *administrative* change, we would probably have had inverse assessments from users and administrators.) The data from the initial phase of program execution at these three sites (see the following section) show that the users' assessments turned out to be more accurate than the administrators': Early implementation was "rough", or "very rough."

There is also clear evidence at these three sites and others (e.g., Calston) that administrators tried to convince users that their fears were groundless. This occurred during what we might call the seduction phase, when potential users were being recruited for a project that the administrators had decided to adopt. Teachers looked at the project and balked; administrators reassured them, sometimes a little misleadingly. In these cases, there was bitterness on the part of users after a rocky period of initial use, often resulting in a new wave of reassurances coupled with more resources, such as the provision of consultants. This scenario (which occurred, for example, at Banestown, Calston, and Masepa) is discussed later.

Sometimes, both administrators and users were misled. Here is a vignette from Banestown:

> There are indications that the people who visited the developer's site came away with
> a deceptively sanguine view of the innovation; it looked straightforward, clear,
> flexible, perhaps a little complex in getting the correct fit between the wealth of
> materials and the diagnosed skill difficulties in reading and math. [One of the lab
> teachers] explains that, as soon as the program began, her view changed dramati-
> cally. . . . [It] was complex and [seemed] impossible to individualize for 30 children
> coming in 30-minute waves with no transition or planning time between each group.
> This latter perspective was shared by first-year teachers who had *not* been to the
> developer's site. Their first look told them it was complex, unclear, difficult to master,
> and disjointedly flexible. (Field notes)

The point here is not that the program developers deceived future users, but that novices had come to observe a program that had been progressively debugged and stabilized, and that thus looked deceptively effortless.

Goodness of Personal Fit (Column 2)

Users warmed to this question. There was, in effect, a very quick assessment of the innovation when the users first saw or heard of it—a sort of "trying on" of the requisite skills and materials, much as one mentally "tries on" a dress or a suit in a store window. More careful appraisals came later, but these early assessments were hard to shake. When the fit was a good one, the users spoke of it almost somatically: the practice "felt right" (Banestown); it was "like putting your hand in a new glove" (Carson). By contrast, a poor fit "wasn't me" or "didn't fit my style" (Masepa).

Behind these responses were three somewhat distinct judgments. First, users connected goodness of fit to congenial ways of *relating to pupils*. This point emerged more frequently when the fit was poor, often in cases of highly prescriptive innovations. The language used by disgruntled teachers at Masepa and Tindale was sometimes strong; people talked of being "stifled" or "violated." A second meaning related to the *familiarity* of the innovation. A good fit occurred when the project demanded skills that were "in my routine" (Astoria) or were already "under my belt" (Calston). Finally, there is a *normative* or philosophical dimension; goodness of fit meant it "sounded like what I believe in" (Carson) or "what these kids really need" (Plummet).

When we look across all 12 sites, goodness of personal fit was judged as fair to good. A site evaluation of "fair" often meant that some users felt comfortable with the new practice and others did not; it was common to find mixed reactions of this kind at a given site. But goodness of fit was not a strong predictor of later success; some apparently well-tailored sites ran into serious trouble from the start (e.g., Banestown, Calston, and Proville), and some fair to poor fits were associated with reasonably smooth program execution (e.g., Lido, Dun Hollow, and Burton). As we shall see, something else along with goodness of fit was at work.

A final point: Poor user fit was sometimes actively sought out by users. For instance, users at Banestown, Burton, Carson, and Lido saw the innovation as a pacer—a vehicle for growth or change in directions in which they wanted to go. In all cases, the challenge was to move from a more academic, classroom-based format to a field-based (Lido), inquiry-based (Burton), or child-centered (Carson and Banestown) approach. In brief, innovations can be vehicles for professional growth, almost independently of their hoped-for effects on pupils or schools.

Anticipated Classroom Change

Users were asked to recall how much change they had expected to result from the use of the innovation in their usual practices of grouping, evaluating, instructing, managing, or relating to pupils. Column 3 in Table 15 shows that the question was ill suited to innovations with few classroom-level components (Banestown, Perry-Parkdale, and Proville). In the remaining nine cases, anticipated classroom change tended to run high (five cases, with three others judged "moderate" and one "low"). Also, if we redefine classroom change more broadly as the amount of practice change required of the users in their new setting, whether it was inside or outside a classroom, the anticipated levels were high at both Banestown and Perry-Parkdale, thus swelling the ranks of the high-anticipated-change sites to over half the sample.

In general, anticipated changes could cover every aspect of classroom life: different materials, new instructional sequences, revamped curricula, new evaluation and supervisory modes, the loss of familiar props (such as teachers' manuals and workbooks), or the deletion of competing units. Some of these changes were welcome, and others looked foreboding. All looked as if they would require more work than the present arrangement. Some users felt that the local administrators underestimated both the added risks and the investment facing the adopting teachers. Here is an illustrative remark by a first-year prospective user at Calston:

> Sure, I *want* to try it, but there must be a realistic commitment on the part of the administration. It's no good. All it is is taking you down for the third time. There's no sense of understanding of what it takes to implement it.

Let us stay for a moment with these four high-anticipated-change sites. At Astoria, the new program entailed a near-total reorganization of the classroom. As one user put it, "You'd have to be organized completely differently. . . . I'd have to throw out my basal program." At Burton, the innovation called for inquiry-based, field-centered, and student-run activities in largely conventional lecture-based, self-contained, and teacher-run classrooms. Thus, substantial structural changes were potentially likely at both sites. At Carson, changes in daily practice were yoked to attitudinal shifts; the program called for increased personal involvement and interpersonal closeness between teachers and pupils carrying out an individualized instructional and counseling plan. Some early users were skeptical, others were threatened; all felt overwhelmed by the commitment required. Finally, we labeled Masepa a *teacher-transforming site* to reflect the depth and scope of the within-classroom changes resulting from execution of the new practice. The principal at one of the Masepa schools captured it nicely:

> Teachers who've taught for years and years with a grammar they know backwards and forwards: they'll go through it page by page; they know all the workbooks; they've got worksheets for the children. Now all of a sudden they can't use that anymore. They've got to go to flip charts and mastery tests and creative writing sheets that they don't have any experience with, and a lot of this material they have to make by themselves . . . it's a lot to take on.

Anticipated Organizational Changes

Column 4 in Table 15 suggests that the local sites were about equally divided between high, moderate, and low levels of anticipated organizational change. Generally, the sites anticipating a lot of such change also expected strong classroom-level shifts. The most awesome case of anticipated organizational change was Plummet, where an entirely new institution was to be created as an alternative to conventional high schools in the city.

The contrast between organizationally ambitious and modest projects was striking. Whereas the actors at Carson were looking at schoolwide scheduling and far-ranging role and relational changes, the administrators at Lido and Calston had to resolve relatively trivial issues of transportation for one or two classes or increased inventories of books. Organizationally modest projects were for the most part small modules that could be plugged into, tied onto, or pulled out from existing classroom-based components.

Organizational changes, which are discussed more fully in Chapter 5, fell into three broad categories. *Structural* changes included the creation of a new, functionally separate unit, such as an in-service committee or management team or, in the case of Plummet, the creation of previously absent links between the high schools and the courts. A more potentially conflict-laden structural change could result from the fact that the new program came into competition with existing programs (for example, at Perry-Parkdale and Proville), drawing from the same, limited pool of students. For the most part, users and administrators saw these features before starting out, though they sometimes minimized their expected impact.

Most innovations entailed operational or *procedural changes*. There would be rescheduling, new evaluation and supervisory forms, increased coordination between teachers or administrators, revised class loads, or new teaming arrangements among teachers. Some of these were more consequential than others. For instance, shifting the schedule for physical education to accommodate the new language-arts curriculum (Masepa) was more trivial than team-teaching remedial reading classes (Tindale). Here again, with allowances for retrospective bias, most informants seemed to be aware of these changes prior to implementation.

Finally, site personnel could anticipate changes in the *organizational climate*. These often turned around the creation of new assumptions or norms (*schoolwide* exceptions or standards). For example, to carry out the remedial reading program at Tindale effectively, the teachers had to have a shared *belief* that low-achieving pupils could succeed and that a new approach to reading would achieve this end. At Carson, the individualized planning concept required the teachers to become advocates of their pupils and to accept out-of-school learning as legitimate. At Perry-Parkdale, pupil self-regulation and more egalitarian pupil–teacher relations were important premises of the career education program.

Climate changes were hard to anticipate before the local actors actually confronted them. Few were seen in advance, except in the form of personal concerns (e.g., worries among the Perry-Parkdale staff about the monitoring of pupils at job sites). Nor did our informants seem aware of the *links* between procedural and climate changes—how, for example, setting up a pull-out remedial lab (at Banestown) could result in one teacher's monitoring what another was doing in a school where the climate supported independence and isolation. Often, administrators lacked an overall vision of what they were undertaking. Rather, energy went into getting the new program on its feet, then resolving one problem at a time.

Here is an illustration of weak anticipation. At Banestown, the superintendent was unable to assimilate the idea that there could be different readers or math materials within a single reading and math program. Two central office administrators put it charitably: "He gets confused." Others had no difficulty with the idea of using diverse materials, and they proceeded that way. But *no one*, apparently, saw that using different materials from the math workbooks would transfer poorly when the pupils moved from classroom to lab or from lab to classroom.

Organizational Fit (Column 5)

To some degree, the administrators judged the goodness of organizational fit the way users judged the goodness of personal fit. But once again, the world views were somewhat different. The administrators seemed to factor in the *demandingness* of the new project on the school or school district in relation to the resilience or institutional slack available to meet the demands—a sort of stress ratio. For example, at Astoria, the vice-principal saw right away that the proposed—more precisely, the *imposed*—remedial preschool project would wreak havoc on the organization of the first-grade classrooms expected to use it. The amount of institutional change would be disproportionate to the likely rewards. The central office advocate, needing to be assured of "adoption" in the 92 schools of the district, was quick to allow local option in implementation, and the solution for this school was a largely ceremonial, decorative gesture: The program was eventually "implemented" in a pull-out, truncated form using aides, parents, and the local administrator.

The second judgment method used by administrators was a rapid *cost–benefit calculation:* How much did the innovation have going for it in institutional terms, and how much trouble was it likely to cause? Because all the innovations had appealing and unattractive features, the key criterion was the differential *weights* that the administrators put on the separate features. An illustration: The reading program at Calston was judged to be well designed, appropriately remedial, and strong in areas (literature) where existing curricula were weak. *But* it entailed extra work for teachers, was not wholly correlated with the rest of the reading curriculum, and looked tricky to implement, with its highly individualized format. For the central office administrator, some aspects (e.g., the literature component) were especially appealing and others (e.g., the individualization) less so. For the principals, on the other hand, the design and the remedial aspects were paramount, but the added work and individualization were worrisome. And the principals had to factor in the relative institutional weights of the pressure to adopt coming from the central office and the complaints coming from the teachers. These calculations were thus different for different role incumbents. But across the 12 sites, they were usually of the same *type,* had *similar weightings,* and gave way to a similar *process of intrainstitutional bargaining.*

Such calculations get still more convoluted when we recognize that changes in one part of the organization are likely to have effects elsewhere.

Administrators did not seem to make these kinds of analyses. But administrators did realize that these programs were double-edged, in that they *resolved* some troublesome institutional problems while *creating* some new ones. For example, the career education project at Perry-Parkdale was a good capstone to the existing network of vocational programs, was also a convenient "dumping ground" for apathetic or intractable students, and could run on outside funds, when inside funds were tight. The program could also function as a separate unit; no new administrative links were needed between the two participating high schools. As we saw earlier, however, some new problems were likely if the program were adopted: low supervision of pupils, competition with other projects, an overly nonacademic focus, and the necessity, probably sooner than later, of picking up the costs with local funds. But because the upshot of such trade-offs was formal adoption in all cases, the assessment of organizational fit was often skewed by the fact that administrators focused more on the benefits than on the costs—many of which they either did not want to see or were initially unable to see.

We noted a sort of "Scarlett O'Hara effect" among administrators that influenced their decision to adopt. For most, the project looked good; it came well recommended and, sometimes, well endowed. It seemed to resolve some gnawing problems or, alternatively, to promise to outperform existing practices. True, it also made for institutional complications. Some prospective users were lukewarm or openly hostile. There could be, in institutional terms, a messy day of reckoning in six months or a year, but that was far away, and there was plenty of time between now and then to straighten things out. All that could be worried about tomorrow, as Scarlett was fond of saying.

Column 5 in Table 15 shows that the 12 sites are evenly split between poor, fair, and good organizational fits, as judged by the administrators and pooled by the site researchers to make site-level estimates. There was a tendency, logically enough, for goodness of fit to relate directly to anticipated organizational change; bit changes put more stress on the system than small ones.

The two deviant cases are Plummet and Carson where the anticipated change was high, and the fit was expected to be good or nearly so. In Plummet (where the *actual* fit turned out to be poor),[10] it seemed that the wholly new school would encounter few existing structures to be modified. This assessment, along with other assets (strong central-office support, the serious teenage-delinquency problem to be solved, nearly full autonomy from citywide regulations, and a committed project staff with experience in reaching a disenfranchised student public) made almost all the signs look good, and others (e.g., skepticism on the part of some school-board members, no assessment of the real capacities of the incoming student public) look less ominous than they later turned out to be.

At Carson, it seemed that the ideological zeal of the program's designers

---

[10] The fit problems at Plummet were largely with the incoming student population, not with the structure or procedures of the district organization.

and volunteer users led them to minimize the far-reaching role changes (along with problems of scheduling, record keeping, and in-service training) that would be involved; this denial was stronger for the administrators, as we have noted elsewhere.

Other Key Variables

The five variables discussed so far in Table 15 represent our best guesses at what was important for users and administrators in thinking about the new practice that they were about to implement. In most cases, we guessed fairly well; these size-up, anticipated-change, and fit measures often turned out to be influential, and some, as we shall see, were decisive in guiding early implementation at the 12 field sites. But these are premeditated factors—variables we had fed into the study, before collecting data, drawing from other empirical and conceptual work on the change process. We were aware that more factors were likely to be in play during the adoption process, and we tried to keep our data-collection efforts open to their emergence.

Column 6 in Table 15 provides a site-by-site list of these additional variables. We tried to keep the list short—including only highly salient items—and to gauge the relative importance of each. This relationship is reflected for each site in the order in which the items are listed. Note that these variables are meant to capture influences *facilitating* or *obstructing* the local decision to adopt and implement.

The most frequent item is *administrative pressure*, usually exerted in a daisy chain from the central office through the principal to lukewarm or dubious teachers. This was not always the most important factor, but it is on the "short list" in Column 6 in 8 of the 12 cases; interestingly, it is present for four of the five IV-C sites. Of course, there were degrees of pressure: subtle at Carson, diplomatic at Dun Hollow, heavy-handed at Tindale. We saw earlier that central office administrators were strong advocates of the new practice at several sites and that, for most of these administrators, the next step in their career trajectory was tied up with the innovation. The users were usually well aware of this fact.

In five cases, there were *problems* to which the innovation appeared to be a remedy, if not a solution. The thesis that most innovations constitute responses to perceived problems was not upheld in our sample. If we look more closely at the five "problem-solution" sites, the acuteness of the problem is sharp only at 2 (Banestown and Plummet), moderately high at 1 (Tindale), and low at 2 (Calston and Perry-Parkdale).

The notion of the innovation's having a *relative advantage* over what the site informants had available at the time is somewhat problematic. Few people framed the adoption decision that explicitly. At 9 of the 12 sites (6 of them NDN), people focused on the project's appeal—its design or its materials—or simply said, "It looked good." The comparison to current practice was usually left implicit—and current practice was not usually seen as notably disappointing or dysfunctional.

TABLE 16. Summary: Attitudes by Role, at Time of First Implementation

	Users			Principals			Cent. office		
	Neg./ mixed	Neut.	Pos.	Neg./ mixed	Neut.	Pos.	Neg./ mixed	Neut.	Pos.
NDN (7)	1	0	6	1	2	4	0	1	6
IV-C (5)	3(1)[a]	0	1(1)[b]	1	2	2	0	0	5
Totals	4(1)	0	7(1)	2	4	6	0	1	11

[a]"Other teachers" at Carson.
[b]"Pioneers" at Carson.

Finally, at four sites, we get a glimpse of the *institutional negotiation* that often accompanied adoption. Our informants, usually principals and users, approved of the proposed project because they would have latitude to change it (Astoria and Burton), were using it only on a trial basis with no ultimate commitment (Burton and Dun Hollow), or were assured that its use would cause minimal disruption of the ongoing working arrangements (Banestown). The last two items were also important to nonusers, whose assent was often important.

Estimates of Approval Prior to Early Use

We can pull much of this material together by looking more globally at how the users, principals, and central office administrators felt about the innovation before actually starting in.[11] If we compare *initial* attitudes—the first confrontation with the innovation—and attitudes at the time of *first implementation*, there turn out to be few shifts; people tend to stay largely with their initial feelings. Also, the users are more extreme in their approval and disapproval, whereas the principals tend to be more neutral, and the central office administrators are favorable in 11 of 12 cases and enthusiastically so in 6.

Let us summarize these data, adding a few new findings. Table 16 shows that, although the profile for the principals and the central office staff is similar for both NDN and IV-C, the NDN users were more favorable at the outset. The neutrality of the principals also comes across more clearly; it reflects their often-passive role in the face of energetic, pressuring central-office administrators, virtually all of whom are favorable. Note, too, that the users are split: They either approve or disapprove. As the old union song goes, "They say in Harlan County/There are no neutrals there."

Conclusions

By the time these innovations were formally adopted, most of the parties concerned were favorable, although the teachers had been initially polarized between enthusiasts and skeptics. The initial bones of contention had ap-

[11]For a more detailed analysis, see the technical report (Huberman & Miles, pp. 105–106).

parently been negotiated away, notably by allowing users some latitude in the ways they could execute the project.

Whether the local actors initially liked or disliked the innovation and were inclined to put it into practice was a function of their initial perceptions—how it looked when first presented to them—and of their estimates of the changes implied by the new practice at the classroom and building levels. In their *initial sizing up* of the project, most users felt that it was complex, hard to do, unclear, and flexible—often too flexible. Administrators tended to see the same project as simpler, clearer, and more manageable, and they spent time reassuring the first generation of users. At NDN sites, both users and administrators were sometimes lulled into complacency by observing the apparent effortlessness with which the staff at the demonstration sites managed the new practice.

Initial attitudes were also a function of the *goodness of personal fit* for prospective users: how it "felt" at first blush, how it interacted with congenial ways of working with pupils, how familiar it was ("under my belt . . . in my routine"), and how well it corresponded to personal norms and values. The fit was judged to be fair to good overall.

Users at over half the sites initially *anticipated* high *classroom change:* different materials, instructional sequences, curricula, and evaluation formats, and the loss of familiar props, such as workbooks and teachers' manuals. Administrators, by contrast, saw varying amounts of *anticipated organizational change* resulting eventually from adoption. Some were trivial (e.g., transportation), others momentous (e.g., creating a new institution). Such changes were structural (e.g., creation of a new unit), procedural (e.g., rescheduling), or climate-related (e.g., different attitudes toward low-achieving pupils), the last type being hard to see before jumping in. The sites also varied on *goodness of organizational fit*, the demandingness or stress ratio of a proposed innovation. Administrators tended to overweight the potential benefits and underweight the potential drawbacks.

Other variables facilitating adoption included *administrative pressure, the perception that the practice solved a local problem*, the project's *relative advantage* ("it looked good"), and the *latitude* given users to make changes during execution.

EARLY IMPLEMENTATION

Introduction

One of the reasons that innovations are, almost by definition, exceptional is that innovating is often painful. Changing instructional and management practices frequently involves confusion, self-doubt, temporary setbacks, plateaus that seem to last forever, new procedures for daily work, shifts in institutional influence, and other uncertainty-arousing events that most people would rather not endure on a regular basis. We found that successful implementation usually entailed anticipating these events and taking measures to reduce their intensity or duration. Even if no particular steps were taken, innovations that made heavy demands on users' energy and tolerance for uncertainty usually wound down over time to a more energy-conserving, routinized, streamlined version (see Chapter 5, pp. 134–151 on changes in the innovation, and pp. 167–186 on organizational changes).

We tried to chart the course of early implementation by observing it where we could, and by asking local site people about their feelings and concerns during the first months, along with their day-to-day actions, their understanding of the project, and their difficulties in getting the new practice to work as they wanted it to. In reporting in some detail on our findings, we begin with an overview of the users' early attempts to master and understand the new practice, then survey teachers' salient concerns during early use. Finally, we look into the range of factors that account for the shape and the relative smoothness of early implementation.

Mastering the Innovation

Mastery is both a *process* (it has several stages or phases) and an *accomplishment* (later phases are more "masterful" than earlier ones). For some of our informants, the process was initially very long and the accomplishments meager. Two illustrations:

> I got into it. I fell down and I had to pick myself up. That happened a lot of times. I'm just beginning to walk. (Teacher at Masepa)

> Every day, one of us would say, "We'll never do *that* again," or "This works; we'd better keep this." And that's basically how we got through the year. That's what it was, too—getting through the year. (Teacher at Banestown)

Even at sites where the initial program execution had been relatively smooth, the same configuration of behaviors recurs, although less acutely: day-to-day coping, unsuccessful attempts to "make it work like it's supposed to," inability to get through a daily or weekly segment, successive cycles of trial and error, and difficulty in doing the new practice without sacrificing other core activities. This configuration was well captured by Loucks *et al.* (1975) in their levels-of-use sequence of innovation mastery, notably in their initial implementation phase, which they call "mechanical use":

> State in which the user focusses most effort on the short-term, day-to-day use of the innovation with little time for reflection. Changes in use are made more to meet user needs than client needs. The user is primarily engaged in a stepwise attempt to master the tasks required to use the innovation, often re-resulting in disjointed and superficial use. (p. 8)

Typical Difficulties

Reading through the users' comments at the field sites, one finds three typical mastery-related difficulties mentioned during initial program execution. First, there were too many, apparently simultaneous, tasks to do in the time available. The users were "overloaded" and complained of depleted energy, of "so much coming at me," and of not being able to keep up. Over time, as we see later, they resolved this problem by "chunking" together different segments, trimming difficult or time-consuming parts, and developing time-saving algorithms that worked something like this: *When only a week is left, select part x, combine y and z, and shorten a, b, and c.* Second, the users said that they couldn't anticipate the immediate consequences of their actions. Trying the same materials the same way for the same children turned out differently each time. This outcome led to repeated cycles of trial and error to see whether varying an instructional sequence or grouping children differently had any consistent effect. Gradually, consistencies did emerge, so that the users could predict the likely effects of their treatments and could build on the growing store of action algorithms, by adding several like this: *When I try x together with y, I can usually get z.* A related problem here was that the pupils' behavior was erratic, often as a result of the changes introduced in the classroom; this added to the general level of uncertainty and unpredictability. Gradually, the pupils were "grooved" into a new habit pattern, and the problem was largely resolved.

The third theme in the litany of early implementation difficulties involves lack of understanding. Users said that they didn't see how the project really worked, how the parts fit together. They talked of a "global," "vague," "jumbled," "confused," or "fuzzy" understanding of how one gets from the objectives to actual day-to-day organization, and from there to the desired outcomes:

> I didn't understand why I was doing what I was doing. . . . I didn't see how the whole thing came together. (Teacher at Masepa)

> I thought it was just a spelling program and there was something about commercial materials and "catching up," but that's about it. (Teacher at Banestown)

In cognitive terms, there are two things going on here. First, the users' understanding was *undifferentiated;* they had only a "vague" idea of what the new practice entailed; they knew only globally "what it's about." Second, their understanding was made up of *unintegrated* fragments; they saw several different parts that did not fit easily together. They were operating with a primitive mental road map that had only the major thoroughfares and contained several uncharted areas. As we have seen, their instructional or managerial behaviors related to the innovation were also primitive, partly as a function of their level of understanding. Later, as trial-and-error cycles turned up consistencies, some notions of what underlay those consistencies, and a large set of action algorithms, their road maps became far more detailed and interlocking, contributing in turn to more economical and effective results in day-to-day work. An important corollary here is that understanding of the innovation appears to be *achieved*—something that gradually emerges from doing it and making sense of what happens as a result—rather than something that comes before program execution. For example, several informants said that they *thought* they had understood the structure and procedures of the innovation—until they actually had to execute it and found out the extent of their misunderstanding. Our finding here is closely allied to Fullan's (1982) emphasis on the centrality of achieved *meaning* during the implementation process.

Feelings and Concerns during Early Use

Many of the initial concerns of users were a function of what was happening to them: their poor understanding of the practice, their stumbling through the day, or their inability to keep up with the prescribed or recommended program. So informants spoke, logically enough, of feelings of confusion, inadequacy, and exhaustion or discouragement. At a few sites, there was variability; some suffered less than others, and these people tended to be more experienced or to be playing more marginal roles in the project. But for the most part, the users' concerns and emotions were similar at the same site. Everyone muddled through.

When we look into the content of these concerns, we find, as did Hall, Loucks, Rutherford, and Newlove (1975), that much of it was self-centered. It was as if the users were so flooded with the difficult experience of day-to-day coping that they had little attention available for the problems of pupils or peers. Strictly speaking, of course, these concerns overlapped and fed one another. For instance, it was often *because* the pupils did not seem to be taking to the innovation that the teachers felt anxious and vulnerable. But the direct object of their worries, as it were, was themselves. When the teachers were troubled, for example, about sections of the standard curriculum that they were leaving out as a result of the time needed to do the new program, they talked less about the effects on their pupils than about how "it could get me in trouble."

It is not easy to catalogue these early concerns without some conceptual force-fitting. Perhaps the most straightforward procedure is to give a general idea of what the users were worried about, how this worry was expressed, and what kind of emotion it appeared to evoke. If we take only the items mentioned at at least three sites, here is a summary:

Area of Concern	How Expressed	Chief Emotion
Professional adequacy	"Am I doing it right?" "Can I deliver . . . am I up to it?" "What do the others think of me?"	Apprehension, inadequacy
Flaws in the innovation or in its execution	"It wasn't working the way it did at the trainer's site." "The kids didn't like it . . . weren't adjusting to it."	Confusion, anxiety
Bad institutional fallout	"Shabby kids could get us into trouble." "I had to sacrifice two reading periods; I couldn't keep doing that."	Apprehension

Area of Concern	How Expressed	Chief Emotion
Stamina	"Barely hanging on" . . . "Too much work" . . . "Couldn't keep it up." "Thought I was never going to get on top of it."	Distress, discouragement, exhaustion

More of the flavor and density of these concerns comes through when we see them in an untruncated form. From within one site (Banestown), here are excerpts from different teachers on three of the above-mentioned areas of concern:

1. *Adequacy.* "I was afraid [that] the children would go out and tell what they were doing and it wouldn't be good, and [about] what some of the other teachers and aides would think."
2. *Flaws.* "I wanted it to be like it was supposed to be and I don't think it was [during the first year]. I couldn't get it. They [at the training site] were so individualized, and they were so sure of what they were doing. Everything went so smooothly [for them]."
3. *Stamina:* "I didn't think I could get it done. How to keep my head above water? [But] when I see kids, I can do it. You gotta do it."

Footnotes to the Experience of Initial Use

Before moving on to the factors facilitating and impeding early implementation, three brief addenda are in order:

1. First-time users in successive years had an easier experience than first-time users in the initial year of implementation. In the interim, users and administrators had debugged the most egregious flaws and, in some cases, had caught up with the project in terms of infrastructure and supporting resources. The trade-off was that the second-generation users were often less committed than the "pioneers."
2. The number and gravity of the initial difficulties took their toll on the organizational climate (see pp. 168–170 on transitory organizational changes); at some sites, the project staff became defensive and accusatory toward one another.
3. Administrators saw fewer and less serious problems during initial use than did users, *unless* the thrust of the innovation was primarily administrative (e.g., the creation of a subsystem, or the rescheduling and reallocation of pupils and staff).

Factors Contributing to Successful Early Use

When our informants were asked to explain why their early experience had been rough or smooth, they usually mentioned the adequacy of their own preparation or of logistical arrangements at the local site. The main message was that something had been rushed, wasn't ready, wasn't well designed, wasn't available when needed, or couldn't be done as expected (because it was rushed or poorly designed). We tried to unbundle the several components of preparedness and asked the informants about the extent to which, in retrospect, each component had been in place prior to project execution or, in some cases (e.g., debugging, consulting, and reviewing progress), was provided during early use. Table 17 arrays these responses, aggregated to the site level, by category and adequacy of preparedness, and breaks them down according to the relative smoothness of early use.

We shall look at Table 17 piece by piece. Note first that the majority of sites had a rough start-up phase. Note next that all five IV-C projects were rough beginners, while the NDN sites had an easier time overall. This is an interesting finding. Theoretically, IV-C projects have a separate "development" phase during which local developers (usually administrators and teachers) work to develop the innovation and ready it for local use. Presumably, this phase secures the necessary commitment, support, and understanding, even if all the logistics are not worked out. But the table (see the "preparedness" score) shows IV-C projects—perhaps because they were still being "developed"—to be *less well* prepared than the NDN projects. Although the IV-C projects were equal to or slightly better than the NDN projects in the commitment–support–understanding categories, they were far weaker in the resource–skill–training–debugging categories. So lack of *technical readiness* seemed to hurt more than the presence of *attitudinal or cognitive readiness* helped, at least in the initial phase. That NDN projects were better geared up technically attests to the relative sophistication of the delivery mechanisms in the National Diffusion Network: generating awareness, arranging for training and site visiting, emphasizing teacher-usuable materials, and making provisions for follow-up consulting or turnkey-training. To judge from Table 17, the delivery mechanisms in most cases heightened local preparedness and facilitated early implementation.[12]

Is a rough start fatal? To anticipate our later discussion of outcomes (see pp. 187 ff.), the answer is "yes and no." The most successful projects, as judged by our several impact and institutionalization measures, were *all* rough starters: Masepa, Plummet, and Tindale. Two of them (Masepa and Tindale) were also poorly prepared. On the other hand, the two most unsuccessful innovations (at Dun Hollow and Proville) were *also* rough starters and poorly prepared. Clearly, we need to look at more predictors.

Relative Degree of Preparedness

Move now to the final two columns of Table 17, where we have done some rudimentary computations to see whether smoothness of early use is related to

---

[12]Other factors may have been at work here, too. The IV-C innovations tended to be bigger and more demanding than the NDN ones, on the average (see p. 245); the very fact that local development was occurring may have kicked up more personal and political issues than when an existing "package" from outside was being implemented.

TABLE 17. Degree of Preparedness as Related to Ease of Early Implementation at Field Sites (First Generation of Users)[a]

Ease of early use, by sites[b]	Commitment			Understanding			Resources/ materials	Skills	Training	Preparedness score[c]	Group median	Ongoing aid/ in-service	Building-level support
	Users	Building principal	Central office admin.	Users	Building principal	Central office admin.							
Smooth early use													
Astoria (NDN)	▲[F]	▲	▲	▲	▲	▲	▲	▲	▲	19		▲	▲
Burton (NDN)		▲	▲*[F]	▲	—	▲*[F]	▲*[F]	▲	▲	17	18	▲	▲
Mostly smooth													
Lido (NDN)	▲*[F]	▲	?	▲	▲	?	▲*[F]	▲	▲	17	17	—	▲*[F]
Mixed[d]													
Calston (NDN)	▲*[F]	▲	▲*[F]	▲	▲	▲	—*[B]	▲*[F]	▲	16		▲*[B]	▲
Perry-Parkdale (NDN)	▲*[F]	—	▲[F]	▲	—	▲	▲	▲*[B]	▲	15	15.5	▲	▲
Rough													
Banestown (NDN)	▲[F]	▲	▲[F]	—*[B]	—	▲	▲[B]	▲*[B]	▲[B]	12		▲[F]	▲
Masepa (NDN)	▲[F]	▲[F]	▲[F]	▲*[F]	▲	▲	—[B]	—*[B]	▲[B]	8		▲[F]	▲
Carson (IV-C)	▲[F]	▲	▲	▲	▲	▲	▲[B]	▲*[B]	▲[B]	16		▲[F]	▲
Dun Hollow (IV-C)	▲*	▲*	▲	▲	▲▲	▲	▲[B]	▲*[F]	▲	14		▲	▲
Plummet (IV-C)	▲*[B]	▲*[B]	▲*[F]	▲	▲*[B]	▲*[B]	▲[B]	▲[F]	—	14		▲	▲
Proville (IV-C)	—*[B]	▲[F]	▲[F/B]	▲	▲	▲	▲	▲	▲	10		▲	▲
Tindale (IV-C)	—[B]	▲[F]	▲*[F/B]	▲	▲	▲	▲[F/B]	▲	▲	13	13	▲[F/B]	▲

Note. Adapted, with permission from Miles & Huberman (1984).

[a] ▲ = fully in place; ▲ = partly in place; — = mostly absent, missing; ? = missing data; * = field researcher estimate that factor was decisive in affecting ease of early use; F = factor facilitated early use; B = factor was barrier to successful early use.

[b] Field researcher judgment from users' responses and/or from observation of practice in use.

[c] Computed in the following way: ▲ = 2 pts.; ▲ = 1 pt.; — = 0 pts.; ▲ = 1 pt.; F = +1 pt.; B = −1 pt.

[d] Smooth for some users, rough for others.

degree of preparedness. This scorecard seems to say that there is a linear relationship—smoothness goes with preparedness—although we have few cases overall and there are some mavericks (e.g., Carson). Also, the "commit- ment-support" scores are probably overweighted (they make up one-third of the total items)—which is, incidentally, how Carson got a relatively high preparedness score. The predictive value of the preparedness measure looks even better if we refine the scores within the "rough" group. If we separate the rough starters (Carson, Dun Hollow, and Tindale) from the very rough—as one user put it, "nightmarish"—starters (Banestown, Masepa, Plummet, and Proville), the first group median is 14 and the second is 11. So we have a gross ordinal scale of preparedness corresponding closely to a similarly rough index of facility of early use.[13]

Early Experience and the Components of Preparedness

Let us now examine in turn, in Table 17, each of the factors that we considered a part of "preparedness."

Commitment

Levels of commitment for all three categories of informant were, for the most part, adequate. Note that the levels of user commitment were fairly similar to the levels of the building administrators, and that both were lower than for the central office administrators. Here is still another indication that many of these innovations—and, according to Table 17, NDN projects in particular—were being championed by the central office administrators and offered to, sold to, or forced on the principals and the teachers.

There was also a tendency for commitment on the part of all three informant categories to matter more when the early implementation was rough. Note the numerous asterisks, signifying the informants' and the site researchers' estimates that the presence or absence of local engagement strongly influenced the smoothness of early implementation. When initial use was difficult, strong commitment expressed itself in two ways: (1) by carrying users through the rough spots as they "kept the faith," and (2) by galvanizing the building principals and the central office staff to provide more support. This was the scenario at Banestown, Masepa, Carson, and Plummet—especially in the latter two cases, where the innovation had a strong ideological core. At Proville, low levels of user and principal commitment crippled the innovation from the start, despite the efforts of the local developer in the central office. Tindale was a more complex case. Teachers were forced to use the program by resolute administrators convinced of its merits. Strong-arming recalcitrant early users created ill will, which was in part assuaged by administrative support when users ran into trouble. So commitment is an important factor.

---

[13]Detailed illustrations of early implementation experience at a "smooth-starting" and a "rough- starting" site are in the technical report (Huberman & Miles, 1983b, pp. 120–121).

Understanding

Table 17 shows, as we hinted earlier, that few site personnel knew what they were in for before they got into the innovation on a daily basis. Here again, the central office administrators had as good—or as poor—an understanding as the users, and a clearer vision than the building administrators. *Understanding* draws few asterisks. Having more of it did not seem to facilitate the course of early implementation, although having less did appear to make things worse for the sites already in trouble. General bewilderment about how the new practice actually worked increased the levels of confusion and anxiety at Carson and Masepa. At Plummet and Proville, the key administrators only very gradually got a clear idea of what they wanted to happen; this uncertainty disoriented users in the participating schools.

Resources and Materials

The presence or absence of resources and materials affected initial use decisively at 7 of the 12 sites. Moreover, this variable does better than most in discriminating between the smooth beginners, where it facilitates early efforts, and the rough beginners, where lack of it is a handicap. We should remember that many of these new practices were heavily materials-centered—packages, curricula, testing and diagnostic devices—so that successful use depended on the materials' quality and availability. At Burton and Lido, the materials were both good and available when needed. At Calston and Masepa, they were satisfactory but unavailable or insufficient in number. At Banestown, Dun Hollow, and Plummet, the materials did not work well; because virtually the entire project—especially at Banestown and Dun Hollow—hung on their quality, early implementation was compromised, with few alternatives at hand. To illustrate with a teacher's remarks at Dun Hollow:

> It was as though they picked some arbitrary point in history. It had no beginning or end, and there was no connection between the eighteenth and twentieth centuries.... The focus wasn't clear, and we began to wonder if it was really worth all of this time.

Finally, Tindale was again a more convoluted case. Most of the materials were good, but there are too many of them. Since users were expected to use them all, early efforts led to overload, resentment, and some randomness in instructional sequencing.

Skills and Training

Skills and training are related both conceptually and empirically so we will look at them together. Table 17 indicates that the NDN sites geared up users better than did the IV-C sites, and that both factors made more of a difference in the rough-starting projects than in the smooth-starting ones. At two sites, weak training and low skill levels served as barriers to smooth implementation. The training at Banestown consisted of a breathless hit-and-run visit to the program developer's site, and the users at Carson felt that they had been inadequately prepared to take on the complex and many-faceted program they found themselves contending with during the initial months. In both cases, lack of formal initial preparation got the sites into trouble.

But training as such, curiously enough, seemed *not* to affect strongly the relative smoothness of early implementation at all the other sites. What seemed to matter more was the preexisting instructional or managerial *skills repertoire* of those using the program. Calston, Dun Hollow, and Plummet might all have closed down after three months had local staff not been so skilled as a result of earlier or cumulative experience in the same area. For instance, the innovation at Dun Hollow was poorly designed; the local teachers trimmed, added to, and reconfigured it on the fly and, at the same time, meshed it with the conventional social-studies curriculum. At Calston, the materials arrived late, crowded out other segments of the language arts curriculum, and fragmented the teachers' monitoring of seatwork. But the staff coped resonably well, largely because, as one teacher put it, "I have a lot of these types of programs under my belt."

So training was, surprisingly, a minor contributor by itself to the relative smoothness of early experience at both NDN and IV-C sites. It operated more influentially *in conjunction* with other, more influential variables, notably prior skills. As we just saw, high levels of instructional skill can compensate for inadequate initial training (e.g., at Plummet and Dun Hollow). What about *low* levels of prior instructional skills? Table 17 shows that inadequate skills created problems in early use at Banestown, Masepa, Perry-Parkdale, and Carson. The data from these sites show, however, that the users were not lacking in teaching experience nor in general instructional mastery, but that their existing repertoires were *inappropriate*. The degree and kind of practice change required to use the innovation successfully were substantial. For example, the teachers at Masepa were used to teachers' manuals, workbooks, and worksheets and to whole-group instruction. As they began to implement the new language-arts program, they found themselves without any of these props, and with a highly individualized, pupil-run pacing that seemed, at first, unmanageable. Skimpy preparation exacerbated similar problems at Banestown, Masepa, and Carson, but more training at that point would not necessarily have resolved them, judging from Table 17.

On balance, it is not unreasonable to find that preimplementation training is only a weak determinant of successful early use. Across these projects, the actual time and effort invested in training was modest. Also, some of the projects were so complex or ambitious (e.g., Plummet, Carson, and Masepa) that formal preparation could only have provided a taste of what was to come— and might even have added to the confusion and ambivalence that, as we have seen, was a normal accompaniment of significant change. Other innovations (those, for example, at Dun Hollow, Lido, and Burton) were modest add-on or drop-in programs from which users could pick and choose at discretion, so that training was largely superfluous. Note that we have already run through half of the 12 projects. When we add the remaining 6 sites, it would probably be more accurate to talk about initial "exposure" than about formal training. In most cases, users got a global understanding of the program components. Anxiety levels were lowered. Users could gauge the overall scope of practice change that the innovation required of them. In the best cases, the trainers modeled some of the teaching behaviors. Plans for the first weeks or months were drawn up. And users found out how much ongoing help they could count on, and where to request it from. There was a general perception at most sites, which trainers also shared, that the course of early implementation was largely unpredictable, and that needs for assistance would become much clearer in a few months' time. This perception shifted the mental "set" of the actors at the site from *preparing* for the innovation to *debugging* it.

Ongoing Aid/In-Service Training

However, Table 17 shows that the actual amount of such debugging was also modest. In other words, the site personnel may well have stressed the *need* for ongoing assistance but did not, in 9 of the 12 cases, *provide* very much of it— often becuse they had not put it in the implementation plan. In 6 of the 9 cases, weak ongoing assistance did not appear to have made much difference. Smoothly implementing sites were not hurt by the lack of ongoing assistance (with the exception of Calston, where assistance from trainers that had been *promised* and *planned* was not delivered when needed). Roughly implementing sites fall into two categories: places where the lack of ongoing aid was not a strongly contributing cause (Perry-Parkdale, Dun Hollow, Plummet, and Pro-ville) and places where provisions for debugging markedly facilitated early use (Banestown, Masepa, and Carson).

At Masepa, and to a slightly lesser extent at Carson, the presence of an ongoing monitoring–support–debugging function helped to salvage an innovation that otherwise might have gone under after a rocky start. At Masepa, for example, teachers were ready to give up after the initial two months. The program survived, according to virtually all informants, because local administrators were supportive and because a part-time "helping teacher" made materials, held weekly meetings, held hands, encouraged the teachers to stay with whatever seemed to work for them, and authorized the bootlegging of workbooks and worksheets back into the reading program. One of the first-generation users rendered the experience well:

> They kept saying, "We'll help you, we'll help you." We kept saying, "I'm never going to be able to do it." But, you know, you attack it and you do it. (Teacher at Masepa)

Tindale, Masepa, and Carson are illuminating in that they all began roughly but provided consistent and many-pronged assistance that gradually turned into a well-oiled, integrated infrastructure consisting of periodic meetings, in-service training, continuous monitoring, yearly updating and revisions, and occasional recourse to outside consultants. One consequence was that the second-generation users had a far smoother initial experience. And as the program became locally institutionalized, the support structure remained largely intact, so that the project enjoyed some institutional "slack" and could attend to its ongoing improvement. The presence of a durable support structure may be one of the prime factors accounting for the ultimate success of the innovations at these three sites.

Building-Level Support

Table 17 shows that, in the initial phase of these projects, building-level support was spotty. The ratings of smoothly-beginning projects are no different from the others, and in only one case—Lido—did such support shape the course of early implementation. This instance is instructive; Lido is the only case where the energy for both adopting and implementing the innovation came from within the school building, rather than being initiated in or propelled out of the central office. At Lido, active support from the principal helped the science teachers to make the transition from an academic to a more experimental curriculum. Elsewhere, the modal attitude of principals at the start was often that of benign neglect or casual benevolence—helping out by using the resources at hand through authorizations, materials, and released time.

Other Influences in Early Implementation

So far, we do not have very decisive explanations. If we take the total pool of readiness indices (132), only about a third (42) have asterisks in Table 17 as being strong influences on the course of early use. In a gross way, it looks as if initial "preparedness," plus (possibly) ongoing assistance, aided early smoothness. But we don't get a good picture of how this aid was working. Furthermore, being well geared up somehow did not seem to help as much as being poorly geared-up could hurt the process. At "smooth" sites (Astoria, Burton, and Lido), something else must have been at work (note that, for Astoria, not one of the 11 predictive factors was a strong determinant of smoothness). So we must look elsewhere to develop a fuller explanation for the success of early implementation.

Table 18 tries to do just that by listing other determining factors during early implementation that were identified by informants and field researchers. Let us first define and survey briefly the variables in the column headings.

Users Volunteered versus Pressured

This variable is an estimate of the degree to which first-generation users were willing or conscripted parties to the innovation. (Recall that there was more conscription among the second-generation users.) Note that, in general, volunteerism is a facilitator and pressure a barrier, although for half the cases this variable was not judged a decisive one.

Where pressure was a decisive factor, there appeared to be several scenarios. At smoothly implementing sites, like Burton and Lido, users' volunteerism involved negotiations with the administrators to permit changes in the innovation (latitude) that would ease early use.

TABLE 18. Additional Factors Related to Early Implementation[a]

Ease of early use, by sites	Users (1st generation) volunteered or pressured	Actual classroom/ organizational fit	Actual degree of practice change	Latitude for making changes	Actual size/scope of innovation[b]
Smooth early use[c]					
Astoria (NDN)	Pressured	**Good**$_F$	**Minor**$_F$	**High**$_F$	Small
Burton (NDN)	**Pressured**$_F$	**Good**$_F$	**Minor**$_F$	**High**$_F$	**Small**$_F$
Mostly smooth					
Lido (NDN)	**Pressured**$_F$	**Moderate**$_B$	**Moderate**$_B$	**High**$_F$	Small–moderate
Mixed[d]					
Calston (NDN)	Pressured	**Poor**$_B$	**Moderate**$_B$	**Mod–high**$_B$	Small
Perry-Parkdale (NDN)	Volunteered	Moderate	**Moderate**$_B$	**High**$_F$	Moderate
Rough					
Banestown (NDN)	Pressured	Moderate	**Major**$_B$	**High**$_F$	Small–moderate
Masepa (NDN)	Volunteered	Good	**Major**$_B$	**Low**$_B$	Large
Carson (IV-C)	**Volunteered**$_F$	Moderate	**Major**$_B$	**High–mod**$_F$	**Large**$_B$
Dun Hollow (IV-C)	Volunteered	**Poor**$_B$	**Minor**$_F$	Moderate	**Small**$_F$
Plummet (IV-C)	**Volunteered**$_F$	**Poor**$_B$	**Moderate–major**$_B$	**High**$_F$	**Large**$_B$
Proville (IV-C)	**Pressured**$_B$	Moderate	Minor	High	Moderate[e]
Tindale (IV-C)	**Pressured**$_B$	**Moderate**$_B$	**Major**$_B$	**Low**$_B$	Moderate–large

Note. From Miles & Huberman (1984). Reprinted by permission.

[a] F = factor facilitated early use; B = factor was a barrier to successful early use; boldface signifies researcher estimate that factor was decisive in affecting ease of early use.

[b] As contrasted with preimplementation size and scope. For comparison, see Table 6, "Implementation requirements."

[c] Field researcher judgment from users' responses and/or from observation of practice in use.

[d] Smooth for some users, rough for others.

[e] Substantial role changes, but for limited populations.

At sites with early roughness, there were two "pressure" scenarios. At Tindale, forced compliance simply meant that most users were using a new practice that they abhorred. They resisted passively, making things harder for themselves, as administrators gave little latitude, insisting on orthodox use from the start. And at Proville, passive resistance led to spotty and somewhat chaotic early implementation, as the building administrators made only ceremonial attempt to recruit participating teachers.

Finally, at Carson and Plummet, volunteerism seemed to heighten the commitment of early users, enabling them to keep going through the rocky period of initial use.

Actual Classroom/Organizational Fit

This variable refers to problems encountered early by users who were trying to integrate the innovation into ongoing working arrangements. For example, at the Calston site, the new reading program, if used as designed, tended to squeeze out parts of the core language-arts curriculum. Note here that, logically enough, good fit was better: Relatively good fit contributed to smoothness of early execution at Astoria and Burton, moderate or poor fit caused problems, notably at three of the seven rough-starting sites.

Actual Degree of Practice Change

How much were the users trying something new and different, in comparison with their prior practice? We estimated this variable by a second-order analysis of users' and field researchers' descriptions of early experience. In scanning the column, this looks to be the single most influential variable. Minor practice change facilitated, and major change impeded; the rough-starting sites had comparatively more major changes to contend with than the smooth-starting sites. The degree of practice change was judged an important predictor of early experience at all sites except Proville.

Note, too, that the IV-C sites experienced more severe fit problems and a greater magnitude of practice change than did the NDN sites.

At some of the rough-starting sites, the required changes in everyday classroom or schoolwide practices were stark and immediate. For example, one user at Banestown said that she was "so used to getting instructions; I don't know what to do on my own [with this project]." Another spoke of a "complete change" whereby she could no longer use workbooks, instructed the children for only 30 minutes ("They aren't *my* kids any more, just other teachers' kids coming to the lab"), and worked in a team with two other teachers ("I don't have my kids, I don't have my class the way I used to").

Latitude for Making Changes

This variable refers to the degrees of freedom given to users by building-level and central office administrators for "bending" the innovation to fit personal styles and perceived local-fit problems. This variable is discussed in greater detail in Chapter 5, in relation to changes in the innovation during implementation. For our purposes here, it is noteworthy that moderate or high latitude was a facilitator, and low latitude was an impediment of early use at 10 of the 12 sites.

Size and Scope of the Innovation

Here we were concerned with the number of parts and the organizational complexitiy of the innovation. For example, the program at Burton was a minor add-on to the existing social studies program, whereas the innovation at Plummet was the creation of a complete alternative secondary school. Here as well, more was worse; for five of the sites at which this factor was influential, smallness was a blessing and large scale a bane.

Summary Analysis

Stepping back a moment, how can we characterize *smoothly implementing* sites, and how do they differ from the sites with more problems? (Keep in mind that smooth or rough early use does not necessarily predict final implementation success.) If we start with the family of smooth early users, Astoria, Burton, and Lido were all characterized by relative smallness of scale, low to moderate degrees of practice change, good organizational fit, and wide latitude for making changes. These were "midget" innovations in terms of their scope and demands, when we contrast them with the teacher-transforming or institution-transforming innovations at Masepa, Carson, and Plummet. They were not free of initial bugs; the users at all three "smooth" sites reported problems—chiefly in relation to local fit and practice change—but saw them as transitory or minor difficulties. For example, users at Astoria complained of increased record-keeping and new groupings of pupils. At Burton, there was lack of necessary time for copying handouts, planning activities, pretesting, and tailoring the program to personal instructional styles. One user at Lido found it hard to loosen up "my authoritarian style"; another had difficulties working with high- and low-achieving pupils in the same group. But no one said, "How did I get into this?" or spoke of "struggling to keep up" or of "barely hanging on," as did users at Banestown, Masepa, and Carson.

There is an overriding reason that the smoothly implementing sites were, in operational terms, midgets making few local demands: The users got to shape them that way. These programs could have been giants—or at least basketball-player size. Had the full innovation-as-designed been implemented at Astoria, Burton, and Lido, these sites would probably have joined the ranks of the rough-starting sites. To execute the remedial skills program fully at Astoria would have meant, in the words of one user, being "organized completely differently; I'd have to throw out my basal program." Similarly, the program at Burton, if used integrally, would have obliged the users to use "active" teaching techniques that were not in their repertoire, and to send pupils out and bring community people in, for which neither the school nor the users were prepared. Full use of the environmental science modules at Lido would have had similar consequences. In all three cases, local administrators colluded with users to scale down the project to easily manageable (and, as we shall see, less impactful) proportions. The users at Burton and Lido picked and chose at will from the program as a whole; the users at Astoria implemented a small fraction of the project and shipped much of that to aides, parents, and administrators outside the regular classroom. Classroom or organizational constraints were minor because the innovation was closely accommodated to existing arrangements. Users essentially did as much or as little as they desired, drawing on the discretionary latitude given them by the principals or the central office staff. In fact, the explicit (Burton and Lido) or implicit (Astoria) agreement between users and administrators prior to implementation was that the program as designed would be bent to fit the users' requirements.

By contrast, the *roughly implementing* sites were, for the most part, the locus of ambitious, change-inducing, and organizationally difficult programs with variable latitude for user-level modifications. The users were doing something sharply different from what they normally did, while confronting a poor fit between the classroom or school and the heavy demands of the innovation. Some (Masepa and Tindale) had no authorization in the initial phases to ease these demands. And most, as we saw earlier, were ill prepared to take on an enterprise of this magnitude. In fact, the severity of the fit problems (incompatibility with classroom or schoolwide procedures) and of the effective degree of practice change probably accounted in part for users' retrospective perception that they were not prepared prior to implementation.

Not all roughly starting sites were organizationally and instructionally demanding. At Dun Hollow, implementation ran into early trouble because the program was poorly designed. The modest ambitions of the program made it easy for the users to recast it while executing it. At Proville, incomplete design, strong local resistance, and fairly cavalier administrative leadership all conspired to compromise early success.

Conclusions

Only 3 of the 12 field sites experienced a smooth early execution; over half, including all 5 IV-C sites, had a troublesome time. At the classroom level, teachers complained of day-to-day coping, unsuccessful attempts to "make it work like it's supposed to," continuous cycles of trial and error, inability to get through daily or weekly segments, and the sacrifice of other core activities. Overall, the difficulties were related to the overflow of apparently simultaneous tasks ("so much coming at me"), to unpredictability ("sometimes a treatment works, sometimes it doesn't"), and to a lack of understanding (lack of differentiation and an unintegrated mental road map).

As other researchers have found, users were self-preoccupied; whether pupils were profiting from the practice was a secondary concern at this stage. There were widespread feelings of apprehension, confusion, and distress. The areas of concern included professional inadequacy ("not doing it right"), flaws in the innovation ("not working like it should"), bad institutional fallout, and exhaustion ("barely hanging on").

Several factors were identified that contributed to successful early use. The *general degree of preparedness* was influential but not decisive. Smooth-starting sites were helped by the provision of *resources and materials,* a key provision because so many of these innovations were materials-centered. Rough starters were hurt by *lack of user commitment* and *understanding of the practice,* by *lack of sufficient and available materials,* and by *inadequate skills and training.* Still, *training* was less crucial than prior experience—both its amount and its appropriateness to the demands of the innovation. *Ongoing aid and in-service training* were instrumental at rough-starting sites and seemed especially beneficial at sites that turned out later on to be the most change-inducing and the best institutionalized.

Other variables discriminating between smooth and rough early use included *administrative pressure* (which made things worse for rough starters), the actual *classroom/organizational fit* (better fit helped smooth use), the *actual degree of practice change* (more change meant more problems), *latitude* for making changes (a facilitator), and *project scale* (smallness went with smoothness). Overall, the smoothly implementing sites seemed to have got that way by reducing the scale, lowering the gradient of practice change, and thereby bettering the local fit. Such "midgetizing" eliminated most of the potential headaches but also threw out most of the potential rewards. By contrast, the roughly implementing sites remained ambitious, change-inducing, and ill fitting, with variable latitude, all of which resulted in difficult initial use.

Three questions arise from this portrayal of smooth and rough early experience: (1) What part does assistance of all sorts play in reducing roughness and aiding implementation? (2) Is later implementation smooth for the sites with a difficult early experience? (3) Are there differences in intermediate or ultimate outcomes between the "midget" and the more gargantuan projects: Is more gained when more is ventured? We turn now to Question 1, aiming to "unpack" the nature of the assistance provided at our sites. Question 2 is discussed in the following section (pp. 114–132), and Question 3 is discussed at several points in Chapters 5 and 6.

THE ROLE OF ASSISTANCE

Introduction

Though more than one user at our sites said, "We did it ourselves," the actual picture is not one of heroic, isolated users struggling toward personal mastery and practice stabilization on their own. In point of fact, the users—and the administrators—often received assistance in their efforts in a variety of forms: training, supportive materials, debugging, controlling/pressuring, trouble-shooting, and just plain hand-holding. Assistance was an important part of what we have just been looking at as "preparation"; it occurred during early implementation and, as we shall see, played a strong part in later implementation as well.

During our site visits, we were interested in such questions as who the receivers and the givers of help were, and where both were located within and/or outside the social structure of the school; what the general orientations or role perspectives of the assistance givers seemed to be; what specific types of assistance were supplied; when assistance came during the implementation process; how different types of assistance were coordinated or combined; what the receivers thought of assistance efforts; and what the consequences of assistance, both short- and long-term, appeared to be.

Our discussion of assistance begins with some sample displays from particular sites, to provide a flavor of the sort of data we were able to marshal on a site-by-site basis. Then, we turn to summarizing the *sources* and *amounts* of assistance received—and *by whom*—across the 12 sites. The next section examines the nature of assistance offered: what *types* of assistance were offered *at different stages*, before and during implementation. Next we reexamine the *effects* of assistance on the individuals and the schools. Finally, we look both at the *antecedents* of assistance—what caused it to appear in our sites—and its general *consequences* in terms of early and later implementation effectiveness.

Examples of Assistance at the Site Level

Our sites varied substantially in what we called the *presence*—the density or completeness—of the assistance provided. Figures 2 and 3 show what the assistance picture looked like at Carson, a site with a substantial assistance presence, and at Calston, where modest "front-end" assistance was supplied, with little support later on.

The Carson program, aimed at individualizing education for all district students, was steered by a management team or steering committee, had a special program coordinator, and used outside consultants liberally—especially an external evaluator ("We never could have done it without Kenn"), who supplied program design, training, and facilitative help not only to the steering committee and the coordinator, but also to the superintendent, the principals, and the early users of the program.

We can also see that the superintendent, principals, and counselors offered help to users, mostly in the form of "support" and "facilitation," and that the program steering committee and the coordinators were more broad-ranging, bringing to bear as well "training," "resource adding," "advocacy," "formative inquiry," "solution giving," and direct "control." Figure 2 only partially illustrates the fact that the types of assistance given varied according to time— during preimplementation, and early and late during program operations. We return to the question of the phasing of assistance efforts later. For a description of the meaning of each assistance type, see page 102.

Informal assistance also came from peers and from users' home situations. Materials were an important assistance source, especially for later users.

In addition to Kenn Mueller, there were other outside sources of assistance, ranging from an external training conference attended by the management team to in-service training supplied by a charismatic lecturer

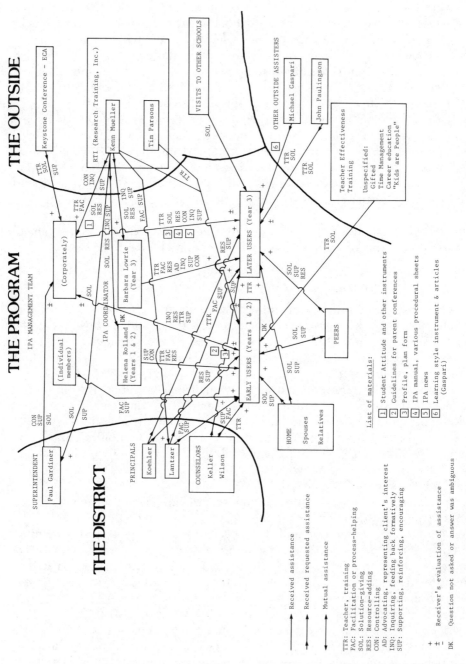

FIGURE 2. Location and orientation of assistance during planning and implementation, Carson site.

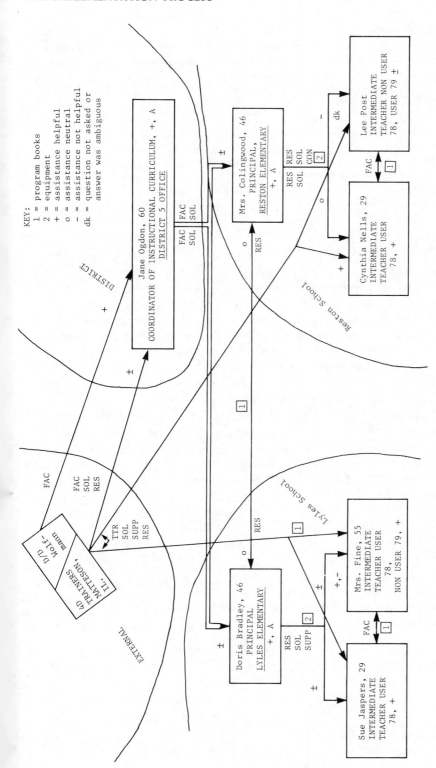

FIGURE 3. Location and orientation of assistance during planning and implementation, Calston site. → = received assistance; ⟶ = mutual assistance; ⟶⟶ = received requested assistance; ↦ = received assistance; ⤚→ = solution giving; RES = resource adding; CON = controlling; AD = advocating, representing client's interest; INQ = inquiring, feeding back formatively; SUP = supporting, reinforcing, encouraging.

KEY:
1 = program books
2 = equipment
+ = assistance helpful
o = assistance neutral
- = assistance not helpful
dk = question not asked or answer was ambiguous

(Michael Gaspari) on "learning styles" and by several other consultants on issues from discipline to teacher effectiveness. There seemed to be moderate to high coordination of assistance through the medium of the management team and of the evaluator's work with it and with the coordinator, the administrators, and the counselors.

We should note, however, this excerpt from the site report:

> Though Figure 2 looks dense with helping relationships, it should be said that some users—and the third-year coordinator—believed that assistance to users was insufficient. And in most cases episodic and continuing assistance were not particularly salient and mentioned only in response to questions by me. The exceptions were Mueller, who was extremely salient to Management Team members and the coordinators . . . and the charismatic Dr. Gaspari, who made a lasting impression on almost everyone I talked to.

Despite this disclaimer, Carson did have considerably more assistance presence than many other sites (it ranked third among our 12 sites). At the Calston site, Figure 3 shows us that a considerably more circumscribed reading program involved a more limited range of assistance roles and types. The developer/demonstrator (D/D) and trainers of the Matteson 4D program supplied "solutions," "resources" (in the form of materials), front-end "training," and "support" to the central office coordinator, who was the innovation's main advocate, and directly to users. The coordinator also aided the two principals, who in turn worked with teachers; the teachers' aid to each other was minimal. Materials were moderately important as an assistance source, but their delayed arrival slowed implementation seriously. There was one follow-up visit from the trainers. Generally speaking, the coordination among the various sources of assistance was moderate to low. Even so, we should note that the Calston assistance "presence" ranked approximately seventh across our 12 sites. The innovation, a focused "drop-in" program, presumably required much less assistance than the districtwide, role-changing program being attempted at Carson.

Two more tables may be useful to show something of the consequences of the varying amounts and types of assistance at our sites. Tables 19 and 20 review the specific, "uncategorized," ongoing assistance efforts that we noted at the Masepa and Dun Hollow sites, reporting the users' assessment of the usefulness of the assistance, and assessing their short-run and longer-term effects.

At Masepa, the site that had more assistance presence than any other, the analyst noted:

> The site is rich and various in ongoing assistance; almost all informants attribute the growth and durability of the program to the multiplicity of aid received in the initial years of implementation.

Table 19 documents this claim, reviewing in turn the vigorous presence of the building principal, the central office administration, the "helping teacher" (a specially trained internal consultant), meetings of users, the other teacher users in other schools as well as in the target school, and the "turnkey trainers"—teachers who had been specially trained to teach the methods to their peers.

Short-run and longer-run effects, though diverse, formed a coherent pattern; users were receiving a good working understanding of the ECRI program and support in carrying it out, knew that the program had strong, sustained central-office and principal backing, and developed strong commitment to the innovation.

In some contrast, Table 20 displays the types of ongoing assistance and the results achieved at Dun Hollow, which we ranked tenth of our 12 sites in assistance presence. Here, an external developer was "using" (in both senses of the word) the local school district as a field-testing site for newly prepared social studies materials on Alaskan Eskimos. Neither the central office nor the building administrators provided any ongoing assistance, so the teachers were on their own. The developer's efforts, which included a series of brief "orientation" and "implementation" workshops, were seen as ineffective and wasteful. The materials themselves were seen as incomplete and often excessively demanding. The only reliable assistance occurred in the third year of implementation, when two teachers who were already teamed for other purposes helped each other plan, shared materials, and provided mutual support.

Overall Assistance Presence

These examples provide some flavor of what the assistance picture looked like at a few of our sites, though they may have overly encouraged the view that assistance was either full, dense, and effective, or sparse and ineffective. That view warrants correction. If we sort all 12 sites in order of assistance presence, including both "event-linked" and "ongoing" types,[14] 6 of them reflect *substantial* assistance, both initially and in later stages (though it naturally decreased as the innovation stablized). Three others had modest *initial* assistance, but little or no follow-up or ongoing help. Finally, the last three sites had almost no real assistance except for brief start-up help.[15]

Sources and Receivers of Assistance

Table 21 is a summarizing count showing who *received* assistance from different sources without regard to intensity.

Table 21 is read as follows (see top row, left side): At 3 substantial-assistance sites, users received assistance from "external conferences." At 1 site, a program coordinator received assistance from this source. And at 5 of 6

---

[14]"Event-linked" assistance was specific, time-bounded assistance like workshops, visits, and meetings; "ongoing" assistance was supplied recurrently at many points in time by specific sources (administrators, peer users, materials, and so on). Naturally, event-linked and ongoing assistance were usually tied together in a characteristic pattern or configuration for the site.

[15]A chart documenting the sources, amounts, and recipients of assistance across the 12 sites is in the technical report (p. 146).

TABLE 19. Specific Types and Effects of Ongoing Assistance at Masepa Site

Location	User's assessment[a]	Types provided	Short-run effects (user's "state")	Longer-run consequences	Researcher explanations
Building admin.	++ ++ − +	1. Authorizes changes 2. Eases schedules, assigns aides 3. Controls fidelity 4. Consults, offers solutions	1. Relieves pressure, encourages 2. Helps early implementation 3. Feeling policed 4. Feeling backed up, substantially helped	Users are helped administratively and substantively, feel obliged to do ECRI with minor adaptations.	Admin. authority, servicing, availability, and flexibility lead to sustained, faithful implementation model.
Central office admin.	+ ++	1. Promotes ECRI 2. Answers building admin., trainers' requests	1. Pressures nonusers 2. Bldg. admins. have material, administrative support	Program is perceived as supported, assisted, "protected" by central office.	Central office able to push program and answer requests, yet not perceived as main actor by users.
Helping teacher	++ + ++ ++ ±	1. Provides materials 2. Demonstrates, models 3. Answers requests 4. Encourages 5. Circulates, controls	1. Reduces effort, increases repertoire 2. Trains, facilitates use 3. Problems solved rapidly 4. Maintains level of effort 5. Ambivalent: helped yet coerced	New, experienced users receive systematic instruction, follow-up, materials; stay with program and are careful about making changes in it.	Personalized in-service mechanism, with both training and assistance allows for mastery and spread of ECRI in "faithful" format.

	a				
User–helping teacher meetings	++ + + +	1. Comparing practices with others 2. Debugging, complaining 3. Learning about new parts 4. Encouragement	1. Encourages, regulates 2. Cathartic, solves short-run problems 3. Expands repertoire 4. Gets through rough moments	Creates reference group, gives users a voice, solves ongoing problems, and lowers anxiety.	Multipurpose forum that consolidates use and users, defuses opposition.
Teacher-users in other schools, target school	+ + +	1. Sharing materials 2. Exchanging tips, solutions 3. Comparing, encouraging	1. Increases stock 2. New ideas, practices; problems solved 3. Motivates, stimulates	Increases commitment, regulates use (decreases deviance).	Additional source of assistance, which increases as numbers of users grow.
Trainers in target school, other school	++ ++ + +	1. Tips for presentations 2. Solution to short-term problems 3. Encourages 4. Serves as successful model	1. Facilitates practice 2. Helps expand beyond core format 3. Maintains effort 4. Stimulates	Reliable, unthreatening backup provided in school.	Elaborate and effective lateral network; trainers seen as peers.

Note. From Miles & Huberman (1984). Reprinted by permission.
[a] ++ = very effective; + = effective; ± = mixed response; − = ineffective.

TABLE 20. Specific Types and Effects of Ongoing Assistance at Dun Hollow Site

Location	Users' assessment[a]	Types provided	Short-run effects ("state" of users)	Longer-run consequences (able/unable to do)	Researcher explanation
Central admin.	0	None	"We're alone"	Mastery on own	District norm
Bldg. admin.	0	None	"We're alone"	Mastery on own	District norm
Developer	–	Organized workshops	"Waste of time"	No effect	Poor developer–user relations made alliance unproductive
	–	Distributed units	"Where are activities?"	Developed own	
	–	Visited once yearly	"So what?"	No effect	
	–	Did revisions	"Same problems as last year"	Less time to curric. improvement	
Teammate	+	Helped with planning	How it could work	Improved each other's performance by sharing resources	Strengthened teamwork by calling on all their resources
	+	Gave ideas, sug'ns	Interesting input		
	+	Shared materials	Saved some time, effort		
	+	Gave encouragement, ear for griping	Not alone, making life easier		
Materials (units)	±	Course outline, content, teacher readings, activity sheets, slides	"Some good stuff here, but omigod, the stuff that's missing!"	Able to fill in the gaps, but probably not to own satisfaction	Too much resistance and anger for satisfaction to emerge

[a]+ = effective; ± = mixed response; – = ineffective; 0 = *no* assistance provided.

TABLE 21. Sources and Receivers of Assistance at High- and Low-Assistance Sites

| | At substantial-assistance sites (N = 6) | | | | At modest- to minimal-assistance sites (N = 6) | | | |
| | No. of sites that assisted | | | | No. of sites that assisted | | | |
Sources	User	Prog. coord.	Admin.	Key[a] source	User	Prog. coord.	Admin.	Key[a] source
Event-linked assistance								
External conference	3	1	5	0			1	0
Pre-startup training	4	2	1	1	6		1	3
Follow-up session	3	1	1	0	4		1	1
In-service meetings	6	1	0	0	1			0
Visit to other site	2	2	1	1	1			0
Committee meetings	3	2	4	1	1		1	0
Team/faculty mtgs.	5	2		0	1		2	0
Evaluation meeting	2	3	1	1	1		1	0
Ongoing assistance								
Materials	6	2	2	1	6			1
Program coordinator	4		1	3	1		1	0
Peer users	6			4	5			1
Bldg. administrator	3	1		1	4			1
Home	4	1		0				0
Central office	1	4	3	1	4	1	4	3
External indiv./agency		3	3	1	1			0
Other	5	3	0	3	2			0

[a]Number of sites where source was seen as "key" or crucial, according to respondents.

high-assistance sites, the administrators received assistance from external conferences. However, external conferences were not a "key source" at any of the high-assistance sites.

Among the modest-to-minimal assistance sites, at only 1 site did administrators receive help from external conferences, and it was not "key."

It is clear that at the high-assistance sites, *both* users and administrators received assistance more frequently (in the categories of "external conference," "in-service meetings," "committee meetings," "materials," and "external individual/agency") than did those at the low-assistance sites, where such assistance as occurred was directed more to users. Only for "central office" assistance do we note that more low sites got assistance than did the highs. Finally, we can see that, not coincidentally, four of the six high-assistance sites had a program coordinator—who not only gave but frequently received assistance. The coordinator at Proville—a low-assistance site—received almost no assistance and also gave little.

Event-Linked Assistance Sources

Let us turn to the sources of event-linked assistance in more detail, with emphasis on those that differentiated the high-assistance from the low-assistance sites and were "key."[16] We see that *external conferences* were present (though not "key") at five high-assistance sites: the intensive off-site conference that the Valley team attended, the Plummet planning sessions with local court services and the teacher corps, and the awareness conferences offered by NDN D/Ds for Masepa, Perry-Parkdale, and Banestown seem to have had both a "cosmopolitanizing" and supportive effect. At the low-assistance sites, there was only Calston's one-day awareness conference.

In-service meetings also show differences between high- and low-assistance sites. Their frequency was generally not more than two to four meetings a year (even intensive Tindale's near-weekly sessions dropped off substantially after early implementation), and they were not considered "key." But the low-assistance sites typically had no in-service assistance at all.

Visits, another cosmopolitanizing strategy, though rare, appeared only at high-assistance sites: The Perry-Parkdale staff's early scouting of an Experience-Based Career Education (EBCE) site whose program they did *not* adopt affected their final adoption decision. When Banestown personnel saw their innovative program in operation in a neighboring community (and when Perry-Parkdale saw it operating at the D/D site), the response was to feel reassured and encouraged:

> I feel like we've done more in the month since they came back from Millville than we got done all last year. It was really important to see a lab set up, even if we don't have the space to do it like they have. (Teacher at Banestown)

---

[16]We also drew on site reports to clarify the importance of particular assistance events. Note, however, that there are few bold-face numbers given for event-linked assistance (Table 21), and we therefore treat our generalizations with some caution.

Committee meetings were present at four high-assistance sites and two low-assistance ones. Typically, they appeared to perform a strong initial planning function (Plummet, Banestown, and Tindale), along with a later steering function (the management team at Carson and the "crisis" meetings at Banestown), and sometimes continued program development (Carson, and the summer writing sessions at Tindale). The presence of committees demonstrated the district's serious commitment to the innovation as something that required energy and operating support mechanisms *beyond* those ordinarily available. By contrast, the kindergarten program-search committee at Astoria served only to legitimize the adoption of the EPSF program, without helping the ongoing users, and the Goodrich Park committee at Lido monitored the use of the environmental teaching facility only generally, without helping the teachers with the sketchy implementation of the KARE program.

We note that *team and faculty meetings*, another indicator of serious commitment, were typical at the high-assistance sites (five of six); at the "low" sites, there were only a couple of principals' meetings, and one for Proville's vocational education teachers. But the weekly meetings of user teams and faculties that took place at Masepa, Plummet, Tindale, and Perry-Parkdale appear to have been primary settings for support, encouragement, problem solving, social regulation, coordination, and learning:

> It keeps you on your toes. . . . You find out what others are getting done and you're not and what you're doing wrong. (Teacher at Masepa)

> You go where you're safe and secure first, to gripe and complain. (Teacher at Tindale)

> Now I can't imagine being on a staff without having really good friends. You know, it's all that affective stuff that's getting popular everywhere, but it counts. (Teacher at Plummet)

Event-linked assistance tied to *evaluation meetings* was present at several high-assistance sites. The recurrent IV-C reporting required at Carson and at Perry-Parkdale aided in program clarification and systematization. More centrally, the main evaluator at Carson, Kenn Mueller, had also served as a basic program designer and continuing consultant; he developed a regularized system-check method that the management team used at all its meetings. At Tindale, "evaluation" had a different flavor, that of being monitored closely for faithful implementation by the department chair, who said:

> I have the power of assignment, which means I can take away favored courses and make schedules difficult for them if they don't cooperate.

It is instructive to look at event-linked assistance that did *not* discriminate between high- and low-assistance sites. Both sorts of sites had *pre-start-up training*, usually for at least three days. They also experienced brief *follow-up* sessions from the developer/demonstrator (all NDN sites except Burton, plus the Tindale IV-C planners). We note that the pre-start-up training was seen as especially key at Calston, Astoria, and Lido, where assistance largely dwindled thereafter. As we have already seen, these were sites attempting smaller scale innovations, with (for two of the three) plenty of administrative latitude that allowed for simplification and required minimal user learning.

Ongoing Assistance Sources

Turning to the bottom half of Table 21, and reviewing site-level data, we can add some conclusions.

First, as we might expect from noting the presence of start-up training, brief follow-up, and sporadic in-service sessions, ongoing assistance tended to *dwindle* over time, though less so for the high-assistance sites. The original technical report chart (Huberman & Miles, 1983b, p. 146) shows that for high-assistance sites, 50% of the assistance delivered, 42% stayed steady, and only 8% increased. For low-assistance sites, 75% of the assistance sources ($N = 20$) decreased, 20% stayed steady, and only 5% increased.

When we look at specific rows of Table 21, the differentiation between high and low sites at first seems less strong for ongoing than for even-linked assistance. For example, both high- and low-assistance sites mention *materials* as an assistance source. But materials presence is called "heavy" at three of the five high-assistance sites and at none of the low-assistance sites. So we can infer a real difference.

Help from *peer users* is also mentioned at high and low alike; but here, too, note that it is key or crucial at four high sites and at only one low site. Site-level analyses also show us that peer user assistance was absent to moderate at the low-assistance sites, and moderate to heavy at all the high-assistance sites. So we can believe quotes like these from the high sites:

> The teachers ask each other a lot. They don't come to me; they go to their next-door neighbor and ask, "Is this working for you?" Or, "I've got this problem." (Principal at Masepa)

> I have her, and she has me. (Teacher at Masepa)

> Guess we were helping each other. I was helping Jessica when we were deciding what to do. When we came to a test and didn't have any materials, we were helping each other decide where to go to get what. (Teacher at Banestown)

And ones like these from low sites:

> I don't offer help to Queen High School teachers because they've been teaching longer than I have. On the seniority scale, I'm on the bottom with only 10 years. At Taylor, the teachers are younger and are more likely to ask for help, but as a group we're all self-confident and we work on our own.

At both sorts of sites, it seems clear that peer user help was normatively regulated; there were shared ideas about the appropriateness or the inappropriateness of colleague support. Prior work has stressed the importance of such norms (Miles, 1972; Runkel *et al.*, 1980) in school change efforts more generally; here, we see direct effects on initial assistance.

There also appear to be differences between high- and low-assistance sites in regard to assistance received from *home*. Moderate help from spouses and others (including children and one's own parent) was mentioned at four "high" sites and at no "low" sites. Three of the four high sites (Banestown excepted) were working with especially demanding innovations, so we were not surprised to find spill-over to nonwork settings.

Ongoing assistance from *external individuals or agencies* is also more frequent at high-assistance sites. Cases in point are the "security blanket" offered the Carson schools by evaluator-cum-consultant, Kenn Mueller; the less strong but still salient role of evaluators and consultants at Perry-Parkdale; and the strong initial assistance provided in envisioning and designing the Plummet program by the city court system and teacher corps. Tindale used consulting help lightly in the design of its reading program and its evaluation. By contrast, at Dun Hollow, the developer sited in the nearby intermediate unit gave assistance that the teachers felt was infrequent *and* ineffective.

In the "Other" category, note that, at two high-assistance sites, there were key ongoing assistance efforts by *internal consultants:* the helping teacher and turnkey trainers at Masepa, and the peer reading consultants at Tindale. No such roles appeared at the low-assistance sites.

Note, too, that the *program coordinators,* who tended to combine line and staff functions, were seen as key assisters at three of the four high-assistance sites where they were present. By contrast, Proville's successive coordinators supplied moderate help at first, then pulled back radically as other job pressures intervened.

Finally, we should look at the role of line managers. The assistance provided by *building administrators* does not show a contrast between high- and low-assistance sites. Though the two principals at Carson and the Plummet program director gave quite vigorous energy to supporting users, there was decreasing principal involvement at Tindale and at Banestown over time, and none at all in Perry-Parkdale, where the principals were distant and variable in their attitudes to the EBCE program. Turning to the low-assistance sites, we can note the key role played by the Astoria vice-principal in ensuring implementation of the mandated EPSF program, along with the early moderate involvement of Calston's principals in blessing and supporting the new 4D reading program, and the Lido principal's championing of the KARE environmental education program. Perhaps, though, we might conclude that real absence of principal help (or negativism, as at Proville) is more likely at the low-assistance sites. Note, for example, the hands-off attitude of the Dun Hollow and Burton principals. Perhaps the only reason the Perry-Parkdale program succeeded in spite of principal indifference or opposition was that it was essentially isolated and free-standing, a sort of nonthreatening adjunct to the ordinary high-school program that principals could tolerate, if not encourage.

The role of *central office administrators* is, in a word, central. As we have already seen, central office pressure was a strong factor in the adoption of many of the programs we were studying. Here we note that central office involvement in assistance is initially heavy to moderate at *all* high-assistance sites and stays at least moderate at all sites except Tindale. It was initially heavy at three of the low-assistance sites, but absent to light at the other three (Lido, Dun Hollow, and Burton). At Calston and Astoria, central office initiation was a core reason for adoption; once the implementation was under way, and other administrators were picking up the assistance slack, the central office input dwindled. At Proville, the slack was never picked up when the superintendent lost power ("They would do what he said when he said it, but it was a different story behind his back"), and the central office turned its attention elsewhere. So we can conclude that the high-assistance sites had a nontrivial amount of continuing implementation assistance from the central office.

Generally speaking, then, the picture is that the high-assistance sites reported more frequent, more sustained ongoing help from nearly all sources in Table 21: materials, peers, external individuals and agencies, program coordinators, internal consultants, people at home, and central office administrators. The picture for building administrators is less clear; the high-assistance sites did not always have a high principal presence, though it appears that opposition or lack of principal support was more frequent at the low-assistance sites.

These findings also suggest that ongoing assistance was more crucial—or at least more consistent—than event-linked assistance.

Types of Assistance over Time

So far, we have been looking at sheer *amounts* of assistance. But what *sorts* of assistance were supplied to people at our sites, and did different sorts materialize at different points in the school improvement process?[17]

We developed a set of categories for what we called *assistance orientation:* what the assister, in general, seemed to be doing. Our codes were as follows:

1. CON (Control): The assister was exerting pressure aimed at making the receiver do something.
2. TTR (Teaching/training): The assister was explicitly transmitting information, developing receiver skill, and so on, usually in a structured way.
3. SOL (Solution giving): The assister was giving the receiver "answers," advice, solutions to problems.
4. RES (Resource adding): The assister was providing materials, money, time, or other resources needed by the receiver.
5. ADV (Advocacy): The assister was actively representing the interest of the receiver to some other audience (such as administrators or funders).
6. FAC (Facilitation): The assister was aiding the receiver to achieve goals, giving at-the-elbow assistance with the processes being used.
7. INQ (Inquiring): The assister was collecting data from the receiver, or from the implementation situation more generally, and feeding it back in a "formative evaluation" to aid in the next steps.
8. SUP (Support): The assister was providing encouragement, reinforcement, or emotional support to the receiver.

These codes draw on prior work on the role of "linking agents" (Nash & Culbertson, 1977) and consultants (Blake & Mouton, 1976). We have arranged them above along a general continuum that runs from more "directive" types of behavior to more "nondirective" ones. This continuum has been suggested by

---

[17]For a detailed analysis at the site level of assistance provided over time, see the technical report (pp. 158–160).

prior researchers on consultation (e.g., Lippitt & Lippitt, 1978; Schmidt & Johnston, 1977) and seems useful in our study, if only to highlight the degree to which assistance is, broadly speaking, user-centered as opposed to assister-centered (or innovation-centered).[18]

To understand such data across all 12 sites, we examined the site-level charts and assembled their data into an overall chart, which appears as Table 22. Because the site-level charts were bristling with complexity, we owe the reader a careful account of our "decision rules" for cross-site data reduction and categorization. In brief, given our interest in the ebb and flow of different assistance types over time:

1. The aim was to get a single estimate of the *maximum* strength of assistance of each type, regardless of its sources or the number of different sources providing it.
2. If the assistance sources varied in strength, more weight was given to the source *closer to the user* (for example, the building principal, peer users, and materials).
3. If the close-to-user sources varied in their strength, the "tilt" was toward the *"heavy"* side (e.g., in Masepa, where the building administrator gave moderate RES assistance, and the helping teacher gave heavy RES assistance, "heavy" RES was coded).

We thus maximized the likelihood that we could "see" a particular type of assistance, *if* it were present at any particular phase. Table 22 is not very useful as a measure of overall assistance *presence* or intensity, because one instance of "heavy" RES counts just as much as "heavy" RES supplied from five different sources. Even so, Table 22 does discriminate the 12 sites in almost exactly the same way as did the analysis of assistance presence in the technical report (Huberman & Miles, 1983b, p. 146).

How Assistance Looked in Different Phases

An overall look at Table 22 shows us that our six high-assistance sites are giving not just "more" assistance than the low-assistance sites, but more *diverse* assistance. Typically, seven of our eight types of assistance were present, especially during implementation, but even during final planning and pretraining. The picture, in effect, is one of full-fledged follow-up or "back-end" assistance, in some contrast with the initial or "front-end" assistance and the weak follow-up help that we can see at the low-assistance sites.

Let us proceed phase by phase. In the *planning–development–adoption* phase, we can see that the typical project seems to involve control, solution giving, and resource adding, regardless of whether it will turn out later to be a high- or a

---

[18]This ordering is conceptually plausible and can help us see general themes in our data. At any particular site, the degree of "directiveness" attached to any particular type of assistance did, of course, vary. For example, the "support" offered at a number of sites was not wholly "user-centered" but contained strong elements of persuasion and selling (e.g., Superintendent Tweed's role at Proville).

TABLE 22. Frequency and Orientation

Sites/Scale of assistance	Planning–development–adoption								Final planning–pretraining							
	CON	TTR	SOL	RES	ADV	FAC	INQ	SUP	CON	TTR	SOL	RES	ADV	FAC	INQ	SUP
Substantial assistance																
Masepa (NDN)	(missing data)								(TTR included in third column)							
Plummet (IV-C)			**SOL**	**RES**	**ADV**			SUP	*CON*		**SOL**	**RES**	**ADV**	FAC	INQ	SUP
Carson (IV-C)	**CON**		**SOL**	**RES**				SUP	*CON*	TTR	**SOL**	**RES**		FAC		SUP
Tindale (IV-C)	**CON**		**SOL**	**RES**						*TTR*	**SOL**	RES				
Perry-Parkdale (NDN)			**SOL**	**RES**		FAC		SUP		*TTR*	**SOL**	**RES**		FAC		SUP
Banestown (NDN)	(Included in second column)								**CON**	**TTR**	**SOL**	RES		FAC	INQ	*SUP*
Initial assistance, then minimal																
Lido (NDN)	(Included in second column)									TTR	**SOL**	RES	ADV	FAC		SUP
Astoria (NDN)	**CON**		SOL	RES		FAC			(Included in third column)							
Calston (NDN)	(Included in second column)									TTR	**SOL**	RES		FAC		SUP
Nearly none																
Dun Hollow (IV-C)	(not applicable)									*TTR*						
Proville (IV-C)	**CON**		**SOL**		ADV			SUP			*SOL*	*RES*		FAC		SUP
Burton (NDN)	(Included in second column)									*TTR*		RES				**SUP**

[a] Frequency of assistance: boldface = heavy; roman = moderate; italic = light; blank spaces = absent.
[b] For sites with two or more later implementation years: ↑ = increased; → = maintained; ↓ = decreased.
[c] Appeared only in second year.

low-assistance site. Support, however, does seem more visible during this early phase at the high-assistance sites. We can also note that assistance behaviors that are more "directive" (toward the left side of the continuum) are more typical than those toward the right, where we might infer that the support being given was a "pushing," "blessing," "entrepreneurial" support rather than a user-centered, socioemotional type.

The site reports tended to confirm this inference: At Carson, there was active mutual support among the superintendent, the principals, and the consultant as they pursued their intense planning; at Plummet, both the superintendent and the city court system were convinced of the need for a transition facility for delinquent youth and pushed the idea hard. In the Perry-Parkdale central office, both the charismatic Henry Jenkins and the more phlegmatic Dick O'Hara made the case for the needed new work-experience program. And at what turned out to be, later on, a low-assistance site, the Proville work-experience program was initially pushed hard and lengthily by Superintendent Tynes. Perhaps it is no coincidence that three of the four sites with strong early support were IV-C. And the Perry-Parkdale NDN innovation was a substantial one that turned out to involve IV-C funds as well. We should also note that three of the four sites with control during early planning were IV-C. Perhaps locally developed projects require both more direct influence and more pushing and blessing in the planning phase.

In the *final planning–pretraining* phase, as might be expected, we begin to see of Assistance, by Phase[a]

First year of implementation								Later implementation[b]							
CON	TTR	SOL	RES	ADV	FAC	INQ	SUP	CON	TTR	SOL	RES	ADV	FAC	INQ	SUP
	TTR	SOL	RES	ADV		INQ	SUP	CON→	TTR→	SOL→	RES→	ADV→		INQ→	SUP→
CON		SOL	RES	ADV	FAC	INQ	SUP	*CON→*		SOL↓	RES↓	ADV↓	FAC↓	INQ→	SUP↓
CON	TTR	SOL	RES		FAC	INQ	SUP	CON	TTR→	SOL→	RES↑	ADV↑	FAC→	INQ→	SUP→
CON	TTR	SOL	RES		FAC		SUP	CON↓		SOL→	RES→		FAC↓		SUP↓
CON	TTR	SOL	*RES*	*ADV*	FAC		SUP	*CON→*	TTR↓	SOL→	*RES↑*	*ADV↑*	FAC↓	INQ→	SUP→
	TTR	SOL	RES		FAC	*INQ*	SUP	CON	TTR	*SOL*	*RES*		**FAC**	INQ	SUP
		SOL	RES	ADV	*FAC*		SUP				RES→	ADV↓	FAC→		*SUP↓*
CON↓	TTR	**SOL**	*RES*		FAC		SUP			(not applicable)					
CON		SOL	RES		*FAC*		*SUP*								
	TTR		RES						TTR→	SOL[c]	RES↑		FAC[c]		SUP[c]
CON		*SOL*	*RES*		*FAC*		*SUP*			*SOL↓*	*RES↓*		FAC→		
		SOL	*RES*				*SUP*			(not applicable)					

more user-centered assistance behaviors (toward the right), and the differences between high- and low-assistance sites begin to sharpen. Though both kinds of sites offered training, the high-assistance sites did it more intensely. Solution giving was stronger at the high-assistance sites; so were resource adding and support. Facilitation was a bit stronger, too. But we also note some differences in kind: We note control at three high-assistance sites, and inquiry at two, though neither appears for any low-assistance sites. It is as if these high-assistance sites were "getting ready" for the controlling and inquiring that would turn out to be needed later on.

During the *first year of implementation*, the high-assistance sites did not seem to differ very much from the low-assistance ones as far as resource adding was concerned; and we can also see that the assistance behaviors of control, facilitation, and training were present in almost all the projects (two of the bottom three excepted). But it's clear that solution giving was more intense at the high sites; and that strong support was present at all of them, while being light or absent at five of the six low sites. We also see that advocacy and inquiry were present in several high sites and at no low ones. Even in the first year of implementation, the high-assistance sites were giving attention to user issues: advocating their interests to key decision-makers, collecting steering data on the progress of implementation and feeding it back, and providing strong support.

In the years of *later implementation*, the differences are even more striking.

The six high-assistance sites show a sustained pattern of comprehensive aid. The existing level of control (whether light, moderate, or heavy) continued, whereas it was clearly absent at the low sites. Training continued to be available; so did solution giving. Facilitation and support also continued, decreasing slightly, but not to "light" levels. And we note that the advocacy levels continue or increase, and that high to moderate levels of inquiry are maintained. The general picture is one of self-sustaining, user-oriented assistance processes.

The picture at the low-assistance sites is quite different. No control was exerted; there were no examples of inquiry. Training and advocacy occurred at only one site each. The working assumption seems to have been that little or no continued assistance was required. At some sites, this assumption was undoubtedly warranted. At Calston, the users had mastered the innovation, and the citywide fiscal crisis made further diffusion of the innovation unworkable. At Astoria, the arrangements for what promised to be a workable second-year implementation were well in place. At Burton, the first year's selective, adaptive use was supposedly a warm-up for later adoption. But at Lido, discouraged users, bitter at lack of support, were thinking about leaving; the Dun Hollow users, exhausted from having to develop materials and teaching practices themselves in the face of ineffective developer assistance, came out against the experimental social studies units. At Proville, the combination of near-invisible assistance and resentment from teachers and principals killed the innovation.

Table 22 leads us to the speculation that diverse, self-sustaining, intense assistance, especially late in the implementation process, may be essential for full-scale, stabilized use of innovations. Also, such assistance seems to reflect, above all, the presence of administrative commitment, as well as the existence of innovation requirements that demand something of users. We will look at the evidence for these speculations shortly. First, however, we should turn to the evidence on what assistance accomplished locally.

The Specific Effects of Assistance

What did these various assistance efforts do for those who received them— or more generally, for the progress of implementation in the school setting? We can best examine this issue by tabulating the specific effects of assistance and arraying this information against the amount of assistance provided.[19] If we simply list the principal effects, we come up with more than 50. Clearly, the assistance being provided was diverse and consequential—it had an impact on early and later execution.

The effects break out into three broad domains: effects on the *innovation* and its use, effects on *individuals*, and effects on the school as an *organization*. All sites had effects from assistance on the *innovation's* progress from facilitating

---

[19]Readers interested in the details of the assistance effects as well as in the first-level analysis of these data should consult the technical report (pp. 165–167).

planning to facilitating final dissemination; all sites showed effects (even more numerous) on *individuals*, from giving reassurance to increasing mastery and assuring personal continuation of the practice. All sites but two showed effects on the *organization* from conflict resolution to environmental linkage, though they were the least frequent type of effect. And a general scan across the 12 sites confirms our earlier analysis: there were many more diverse effects at the high-assistance than at the low-assistance sites. Finally, the low-assistance sites were much less likely to show assistance effects on the *innovation* and on *individuals* occurring late (such as "program continuation" or "routinization").

Table 23 enables us to substantiate these first impressions. The numbers show the total of effects across sites, in each category.

We can see in Table 23 the numbers that document the generalizations just made. We can also see that negative outcomes of assistance efforts on *individuals*—what might be called *backfiring*, along with simply ineffectual efforts—are more present at the low-assistance than at the high-assistance sites, amounting to a third or so of all effects noted. For example, for short-run effects of ongoing assistance on individuals at the low-assistance sites, there are 7 instances of negative effects out of the total of 19. Site-level analysis shows that most of these negative effects occurred at Dun Hollow (where users got more and more disenchanted with the developer's nonresponsiveness and lackadaisical help for the demanding social studies units that they were field-testing for her) and at Proville (where principals and vocational education

TABLE 23. Summary of Short- and Long-Term Effects of Assistance, by Assistance Domain[a]

Effects on	For high-assistance sites (N = 6)				For low-assistance sites (N = 6)			
	Ongoing		Event-linked		Ongoing		Event-linked	
	Short run	Long run	Short run	Long run	Short run	Long run	Short run	Long run
The innovation and its use	25 •	24 • • •	12	20 • •	11 •	16 • •	3 •	5 •
Individuals	39 • •	28 • • • •	17 • •	22 • • •	19 •• •• •• •	10 •	10 • • • • •	12 • • • •
The organization	12	11 • •	9	13	4 •	0	0	0

Note. Adapted, with permission, from Miles & Huberman, 1984.
[a]Cell totals are a simple count of effects (O1, O2, E1, E2), summed across all sites. • = negative or undesired effect (included in numerical totals).

teachers felt increasingly resentful of the pressure applied by the central office coordinator).

We also see that negative effects in the *innovation*-specific domain are just about as likely, proportionately speaking, at the high- as at the low-assistance sites. Comparisons for the *organization* effects domain are difficult, as the base rate of organization effects was almost nil for the low-assistance sites, where, as we have already noted, large-scale—thus, potentially organization-changing—innovations were usually not being attempted.

Table 23 also indicates that the bulk of assistance provided was judged positively. So users' feelings *at the time* about whether the assistance was effective, or a mixed bag, are not a very reliable guide to the positive effects, either short- or long-run, that can be noted by an analyst. However, clearly negative assessments can probably be trusted. For example, the negative assessment of the Dun Hollow developer's performance and of the Proville coordinator's pressuring tactics fit with the absence of positive outcomes. At Dun Hollow, the only positive assistance occurred among users; at Proville, early orientation meetings provided partial understanding but made no difference in the face of continuing resentment, resistance, and lack of support felt by the primary and secondary users.

The Content of Effects

Turning back to site-level charts for a minute, what can we learn about specific effects? Those that occurred at at least four of six sites in the *innovation* domain were

High-assistance sites	Low-assistance sites
Planning, developing	Planning, developing
Goals, direction, priority	
Aiding start-up	
Preparing and adding materials	
	Aiding good-quality implementation
Program adaptation	
Program maintenance	

The general picture of frequent effects at the high-assistance sites suggests thoroughgoing start-up planning and support, followed by assistance that aids adaptation and maintenance. The low-assistance sites also show effects on planning, but on little else; the "quality-aiding" finding is true only for the sites (Lido, Astoria, and Calston) with a small-scale innovation requiring little follow-up.

For the effects on *individuals*, we note, at at least four of six sites:

High-assistance sites	Low-assistance sites
Reducing anxiety	
Increasing understanding	Increasing understanding

High-assistance sites   *Low-assistance sites*
Increasing ownership   Increasing ownership
Feeling supported
Enlarging repertoire
Solving problems
                                  Increasing competence, confidence

The recurring emphasis across sites on understanding and ownership is consistent with Fullan's (1982) view that problems of *meaning* are the central issues as users approach an innovation. For the high-assistance sites, the effects noted also involved anxiety reduction and reassurance, strong support, and repertoire enlargement accompanied by problem solving. The latter two are consistent with our earlier finding that sustained assistance was more typical at the high-assistance sites.

Finally, we note that the most frequent type of *organizational* effect, occurring at five of the six high-assistance sites, is increasing cohesiveness and trust. We should also note a pattern of effects at the high-assistance sites (three sites each) that adds up to building a more interdependent, more tightly coupled set of structures: reducing isolation, building an implementation "team," building an assistance infrastructure, coordination, and improved collaboration. The message here is that sustained high assistance moves its client systems away from "loose coupling," strengthening their capacities beyond those needed simply to implement the innovation. Organizational effects at the low-assistance sites were rare and scattered.

Short- and Long-Term Effects

Table 23 shows us two things, at least. Long-term effects are at least as frequently mentioned as short-term effects and are usually *more* frequently mentioned in terms of innovation-specific and organization-changing effects. But for ongoing assistance to *individuals*, the reverse is true. It is as if immediate impacts on persons are easily discernible, but their long-term consequences more ambiguous, whereas the long-term effects are more visible at the more general (innovation or organization) level. This is perhaps natural in that many of the individual effects were on immediate attitudes and feelings (anxiety, resistance, ownership, and feeling supported); if there were a minimum of "backfires," and sustained assistance occurred, we would expect such assistance effects to be less needed, and assistance could concentrate on the innovation and the organization.

The Antecedents and Consequences of Assistance

What seems to have induced the varying levels of assistance that we have noted? And can we discern in a preliminary way what the general consequences seem to have been? Table 24 arrays our 12 sites in the usual way, by assistance presence, and identifies several possible "causal" factors. It also shows two

TABLE 24. Antecedents and Consequences of Assistance

Sites/Scale of assistance	Antecedent conditions								Consequences	
	Size–scope of innov.	Required practice change	Classroom–organizational fit	Implementation requirements[a]	Scale of funding	Central office commitment	Admin. latitude	OVERALL ASSISTANCE PRESENCE	Smoothness/roughness of early implementation	Practice–stabilization (later implementation)
Substantial assistance										
Masepa (NDN)	Large	Major	Mod-good	12	$30–50K	High	Low	HIGH	Very rough	Mod
Plummet (IV-C)	Large	Mod–major	Good–poor[b]	12	$300K	High	High	HIGH	Very rough	Mod
Carson (IV-C)	Large	Major	Mod–good	12	$96K	High	Mod	MOD–HIGH	Rough	Mod
Tindale (IV-C)	Large–mod	Major	Mod	12	$87K	High	Low	MOD–HIGH	Rough	High
Perry-Parkdale (NDN)	Mod	Mod–major	Mod	10	$300K	Mod	High	MOD–HIGH	Mixed	Mod–high
Banestown (NDN)	Small–mod	Major	Mod	10	$5.6K	High	High	MOD	Very rough[a]	Mod
Initial assistance, then minimal										
Lido (NDN)	Small	Mod	Mod	7	$6.1K	Low	High	LOW–MOD	Mostly smooth	Mod–high
Astoria (NDN)	Small	Minor	Good	3	None	High	High	LOW–MOD	Smooth	High
Calston (NDN)	Small	Mod	Poor	9	None	Mod–high	Mod–high	LOW–MOD	Mixed	Mod–high
Nearly none										
Dun Hollow (IV-C)	Small	Minor	Poor	7	None	Low	Mod	LOW	Rough	Low
Proville (IV-C)	Mod	Minor	Mod	7	$180K	High–low	High	LOW	Very rough	Low
Burton (NDN)	Small	Minor	Good	3	$3.1K	Mod–high	High	LOW	Smooth	Mod

Note. From Miles & Huberman (1984). Reprinted by permission.
[a]Weighted sum of three variables at left, scaled 1–5.
[b]Good at district level, poor for students.
[c]IV-C Funds, to adopt and disseminate NDN innovation.

general consequences of assistance: the smoothness or roughness of early implementation, and "stabilization of use," a variable that we discuss more fully in the next section.

Antecedents of Assistance

We expected that innovations that were of a larger *size or scope*, that required more *change* in users' practice, and that were a poor *fit* with the current classroom and organizational setup would be more likely to evoke a larger assistance presence.[20]

We computed a weighted index of the three in the fourth column of Table 24. Scanning the four columns and comparing them with the column marked "overall assistance presence" show that these indicators of implementation requirements do indeed predict the amount of assistance offered. More specifically, it appears that the real issues are *size and scope* and *required practice change*. The degree of classroom and organizational fit is not so critical: Note that Masepa's good fit and Carson's moderately good fit coexisted with high assistance presence; and conversely, that Calston's and Dun Hollow's poor fit went with low assistance presence.

We also thought that *scale of funding, central office commitment to change*, and *administrative latitude* might be relevant to how much assistance was mounted.[21] *Funding* would, of course, be larger with the typical large-scale innovation; funds would also enable more delivery of assistance, especially when special training events or outside assisters were involved. Broadly, we can see from Table 24 that more funding does indeed mean more assistance. There are two deviant cases: Masepa, where only moderate funds were available, but assistance was very high, probably as a result of the missionary zeal that developed during implementation[22]; and Proville, where a heavily funded program foundered through increasing central office indifference and building-level resistance.

Central office commitment was high at nearly all sites, and it indifferently predicts levels of assistance, although the low commitment at Lido and Dun Hollow is noteworthy.

We expected that *administrative latitude* (willingness to allow users to make changes in the innovation, rather than maintaining a prescriptive stance) might work *against* assistance giving; permitting energy-saving adaptations would mean that users would encounter fewer stresses and would need less help. Latitude might be another symptom, too, of low administrative commitment, as at Lido and perhaps Dun Hollow. We did see that moderate to high latitude at all the low-assistance sites goes with low to low-moderate assistance, as does

---

[20]These variables, which appear in the first three columns of Table 24, are discussed and explained more fully in our section on change in the innovation (pp. 134 ff.). Some have already been discussed in the section on early implementation.

[21]These three variables are reviewed in more detail in the sections on change in the innovation (pp. 134 ff.) and changes in the organization (pp. 167 ff.).

[22]Central office people at Masepa were also very good at finding special "pots" of money here and there in the state bureaucracy, and at working out barterlike arrangements that never appeared in formal budgets.

low latitude with moderate to high assistance (Masepa, Carson, and Tindale), so there is some support for our guess. But the relationship is not simple when we turn to other, larger-scope innovations. Plummet, Perry-Parkdale, and Banestown all had high latitude but moderate to high levels of assistance. A careful look back at site-level charts shows us that most of the assistance at those three sites came from the program coordinator (who, like the users, was closely involved with the work) and from users themselves; all three sites were also "special," marked-off, somewhat isolated programs, two of them being rather substantial subsystems. The "latitude" given was essentially freedom for the users to *build* and *manage* a demanding setup (an alternative school, a work experience program, and, at a smaller scale, a remedial lab)—not latitude to adapt the program out of existence.

Summary

So, in general, assistance seems to be more likely when large, practice-changing innovations are being attempted, with the support of moderate funds, and where users either have little latitude for change or use the latitude that they are given to supply vigorous, closeup assistance to each other. The central office commitment, as such, makes little difference in assistance.

Consequences of Assistance

What can be said about the effects of assistance? Generally speaking, large amounts of assistance could reasonably be expected to aid in smoother *early implementation*, and to result in more *stabilized practice*[23] later on. That, presumably, is what assistance is for. The last two columns of Table 24 show our judgments of roughness and smoothness (drawn from the preceding section) and of practice stabilization (drawn from the preceding section) and of practice stabilization (drawn from the section that follows). The data can be understood somewhat more easily by a look at Figure 4.

The left side of the figure shows us very clearly that sheer amounts of assistance do *not* make for smooth early implementation. Rather, it seems likely that larger innovations (as in Table 24) resulted in rougher early implementation, *regardless* (Cluster A in the upper-left-hand corner), and that smaller innovations made life easier (Cluster B). Cluster C involves assistance incompetence: the low amount of assistance for the weakly designed and potentially demanding innovation at Proville, and the ineffective attempts of the developer to "explain" the poorly designed and unexpectedly demanding Eskimo units to the field-testing teachers at Dun Hollow. So roughness in early implementation experience—as we saw in the preceding section—comes from trying big innovations, and assistance is relatively unavailing in the face of their

---

[23]Our measure of stabilization actually includes two parts: *practice mastery* (user skill in using the practice) and *program settledness* (the degree to which the innovation has stopped changing and shifting). (See pp. 126 ff.)

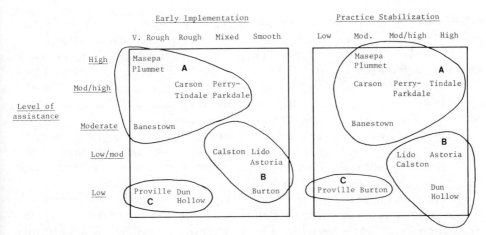

FIGURE 4. The consequences of assistance. (From Miles & Huberman, 1984. Reprinted by permission.)

demands. Little assistance is usually needed for the smaller innovations, which can probably be smoothly implemented anyway, *if* they are well designed.[24]

The right-hand side of Figure 4 shows us the picture for the eventual stabilization of practice at our sites. Here, too, there are three—almost identical—clusters. For the large-scale innovations in Cluster A—which had such a rough start—the more assistance, the more stabilization. As we have already seen, the issue was *sustaining* assistance during later stages. The Cluster B sites managed good stabilization with little assistance, a finding consistent with what we have already noted about the less demanding nature of the task. Even at Dun Hollow, things stabilized reasonably well, mainly because of the users' support of each other. The Proville site ended with low stabilization (actually, discontinuation of the innovative program), in part because of the very weak assistance provided to a potentially substantial program. At Burton, little assistance was provided, and users achieved only moderate mastery and moderate settledness (it was very uncertain which parts of the innovation would continue in use).

Conclusions

The sites giving high assistance did so with much more diversity—and with more sustained energy over the life of the implementation process—than the sites where the initial assistance disappeared or was weak and ineffective. Effective assistance was user-oriented rather than innovation- or assister-

---

[24]We do not attempt to differentiate among our innovations on the question of innovation quality. With the exception of Dun Hollow and Proville, where serious design flaws were evident, the remaining innovations were either well validated through the Joint Dissemination Review Panel or state dissemination panels. The only unvalidated innovations, at Plummet and Tindale, struck us as being very well worked out; also, both showed high student impact.

oriented and became more so over time. It achieved effects such as reassurance, support, repertoire expansion, problem solving, and increased interdependence.

The assistance *events* used more frequently at the high-assistance sites were external conferences, in-service training, visits, and meetings of committees, teams, and faculties. *Ongoing* assistance was more consistently supplied and came more frequently at the high-assistance sites from materials, peer users, relatives, external agents, and central office personnel.

Assistance was more frequent and intense when *large-scope, practice-changing* innovations were being attempted, with *moderate funding,* and when users either had little *administrative latitude* to change the innovation or used the latitude that they had to supply *peer support.*

Heavy assistance did not necessarily result in easier early implementation; it was not able to override or compensate for the sheer effects of the innovation's demands, where they were substantial. Of course, weak assistance could make for rougher implementation, especially if the innovation was somewhat demanding. But smaller innovations usually achieved smooth early implementation without much help. Larger innovations required continuing assistance for eventual practice stabilization, but small ones did not.

Next, we turn in more detail to the saga of later implementation.

LATER IMPLEMENTATION

Introduction

In this section, we take up the second major phase of the implementation chronicle as it was played out at the 12 field sites. First we focus on the *process of practice mastery* as it was achieved by individual users. We try to capture the successive stages or phases of the mastery process, along with the various changes in understanding, affect, and behavior that made up the process. We are interested here not only in the *sequence* of practice mastery, but also in the *links* between the different components that constituted that sequence—how, for example, users' understanding of what they were doing was related to their day-to-day activities in the classroom, laboratory, or field setting.

Components of User Practice Mastery

In the section on early implementation, we said that practice mastery was not an event but an accomplishment, gradually and often painfully achieved. That section, in fact, reads more like a litany of woes than a forward progression. When we survey our 12 sites, the good news is that most users at almost all sites attained what they and the local administrators judged to be a satisfactory level of expertise in the new practice within two years—in most cases, within 18 months. (And at the sites where the innovation had been scaled down to a modest effort, practice mastery came after five or six months.) After the achievement of reasonable practice mastery, energies went into refining, debugging, and extending core components. However, mastery was never complete, often because users went on to more challenging or ambitious tasks, and also because inputs (e.g., a new student population) changed or because resolving one problem led to a new, unresolved one. As the project director at Perry-Parkdale put it, "You think you're on top of it, then something happens."

If we break out the population of users in the moderate- or high-change sites with more than 18 months of experience with the innovation and set them against others with from three to six months' experience, the contrasts are striking. In general, insecurities gave way to securities, doubts to confidence, and vulnerabilities to a sense of being in control. Although we have thin data for some sites, in all cases there was a roughly similar profile of progression with respect to (1) main feelings; (2) levels of understanding of the practice; (3) catalogs of segments mastered and of parts that still felt shaky; (4) the main tasks and activities being carried out; and, with somewhat more dispersion among sites, (5) remaining problems or concerns. Let us review these modal patterns.

Feelings

The overall image here was one of self-efficacy. Users saw themselves as in the saddle, as operationally effective on a daily basis, and as increasingly successful in getting the results they were after. Being efficacious was celebrated in the following four ways:

1. *Being "comfortable."* Users said that they were "at ease" with the practice, that they felt "secure" and, usually, "relaxed." In virtually all cases, the "comfort" was the result of mastering the innovation *technically*, of getting better at doing it.

2. *Being confident.* A teacher at Banestown captured the general sentiment by saying, "Now I know I can deliver; before, I wasn't sure." Some users got slightly manic, like this teacher at Calston: "This year is a breeze. I feel like a hot-shot."

Confidence seemed to come from getting good results, and getting them consistently rather than randomly, as was often the case initially. This led to the next sentiment:

3. *Being in control.* The metaphors are instructive here. Users talked of "being on top of it," of "getting a handle on it," and of "getting it to go *my* way."

4. *Feeling gratified.* The obvious source of gratification was, presumably, successful results in terms of pupils' performance increments or attitudes. But the users at our sites were not chaining gratification to these summative indices; rather, they mentioned short-term rewards, such as "good days" and positive feedback from pupils. When "the kids say they like it"—especially the difficult, underachieving, or turned-off pupils making up the majority of the target public at our sites—their teachers "light up."

In all cases, informants said that they worked through to these sentiments, that these feelings were *achieved* or earned. This process can be shown inferentially. For example, no one talked of being "relieved," as would be the case if the problems simply went away or were easily resolved. Rather, being confident came gradually from being increasingly less insecure, and feeling gratified came after repeated instances of feeling overloaded or downtrodden.

There were also less-sanguine feelings. At Dun Hollow, and in the third year of use at Lido, users felt disappointed and discouraged, either because the program was ineffective or because external support had waned. There were also some pervasive sentiments of "burnout" at sites with complex innovations (e.g., Masepa, Carson, and Plummet). We will discuss more of this later. But even in these cases, users invoked and enjoyed the experience of having achieved practice mastery and of having "reached" their pupils.

Understanding

Our data are uneven here. At only six sites were the responses fully comparable. What data there are point to a sharper, more differentiated, and more inclusive understanding of how the new practice worked. Users at Banestown, for example, where we probed fairly deeply for cognitive changes, spoke of "seeing it as a system," "seeing how it all comes together," or "putting the pieces together" as a result of their experience with the remedial laboratory. Until the middle of the second year of implementation, these same informants had used images of nondifferentiation ("kind of a vague idea") and noninte- gration ("a hodgepodge"). They now had a better mental road map and were using it to get results more economically, to reconfigure the practice, or to trouble-shoot emerging problems. Learning about the innovation meant learn- ing what could be *done* with the innovation, and doing it resulted in a more differentiated and integrated vision of how it worked.

Parts Ready and Parts Unready

Here we have usable responses for eight sites. The overall assessment, by about midway into the second year of use, was that "things were falling into place" (Banestown), "a routine was consolidated" (Masepa), and procedures were "easier" (Carson) or "more streamlined" (Perry-Parkdale). If we pull these strands together, the dominant message is that the components of the innovation were securely in place.[25] Doing them was easier, went more quickly, had predictable effects, and "worked" progressively better. These results, were in turn, the fruits of successive approximations, of a better understanding of the practice, and—a key ingredient—of a parallel level of mastery and habituation on the part of pupils. Here are two excerpts on this last aspect:

> This year I have no problems with 4D. I know the placement tests . . . I know what to say to the student to get him right in the groove. (Teacher at Calston)

> It's . . . more streamlined. We know where the kids are; they know what the deal is. (Learning manager at Perry-Parkdale)

A caution here: As we suggested earlier, being on top of the program did not always mean that users *liked it*, although they usually did. Some users at Masepa, Tindale, and Dun Hollow, for example, found the innovations, as a Tindale teacher put it, "distasteful" but felt (and were observed by field researchers to be) pedagogically secure. Here is an illustrative opinion:

---

[25]This does not necessarily mean that the components as defined by the developer were in place; as we shall see shortly (pp. 133 ff.), what went into place was frequently an adapted, revised, bent version.

We know what we're doing and how to do it, but everyone's hoping we won't be doing it again next year. (Teacher at Dun Hollow)

Even after 18 months, there were usually components that had not been mastered, especially in the case of the more complex and demanding projects. Although users at Astoria could say they had few difficulties because "I'm doing very little differently from before," the practice change gradient was steeper at Carson, Masepa, and Plummet. Here, many users struggled to come to grips with the core components for two years, and some did so for three years.

The more complex parts of all the practices naturally took longer than the simpler ones. For example, teachers at Banestown had learned to set up daily remedial routines for groups of three to five pupils coming to the lab, but they were still unable to get beyond batching to the individualization of daily exercises. At Masepa, developing higher-order skills, such as analytical reading, called for a difficult integration of instructional procedures, whereas word recognition, a constituent part of analytical reading, was simple to program and monitor. And at Burton, we had another good example of the *hierarchical character* of practice mastery. Users were able at an early date to use selected parts of the new social studies curriculum. At first, they simply added these segments to others already in place. But accretion meant overbudgeting the available time. This led to a second phase, during which users trimmed some of the new materials and cut back more on the traditional lecture and discussion components. The two units then ran side by side. But this arrangement made for incoherence, since each unit had been coordinated with the parts that were now removed, but not with one another. So, near the end of the first year, users began to *integrate* the materials from the new and the old curricula to form a coordinated program that was more than the sum of its parts. Consequently, in the initial phase, users felt that their chief problem was lack of time; in the second, that their teaching was disjointed or scrabbled; and by the third phase, that an integrated program was in place but needed to be fine-tuned.

Main Tasks and Activities

What were users spending most of their time on during later implementation? If we define later implementation as after 6 months for low-change projects and after 18 months for the others, we can sort the responses into six categories.

1. *Reaching up.* Users were spending more time on the most complex parts of the project. In particular, they were moving from the basic routines to the more difficult and demanding segments. For example, we just saw that teachers at Masepa reported that they were getting to the "higher order (analytical) skills" only after having mastered the instruction for the basic skills of word recognition and spelling.

2. *Improving and debugging.* This activity was directly focused on the program's flaws. Having worked through the components and tested them thoroughly—in some cases, on at least two groups of pupils (first-year and second-year groups)—there was some closure about which components needed weeding out or

strengthening. For example, the lab teachers at Banestown began looking for new materials to replace what they found to be ineffective exercises within the Catch-up recommended set. Teachers at Dun Hollow scrapped most of the original Eskimo core materials in the project and made their own.

3. *Refining.* During the second year, teachers at Tindale began what they called "routinizing" procedures, which entailed both a codification (in manual or guideline form) of instructional routines for the reading program and a set of core exercises—a sort of "automatic pilot" repertoire—to be used for each component. A similar, school-level codification took place at Carson. At Astoria (after five months), users began to work with subgroups, differentiating treatments within the program for specific pupils.

4. *Integrating.* The earlier illustration from the Burton site shows how users moved beyond basic mastery to attempts to fold new materials into existing ones. Most of the add-on or drop-in innovations required such a phase. At Calston, for example, one of the more intractable problems was the meshing of the new 4D reading program with the district reading program.

5. *Adapting.* This category is instructive; it reminds us that the larger context surrounding these projects was not standing still. For example, at the start of the second year, users at Lido began to get a less responsive, lower-achieving student public, for whom the original program format was, in parts, ill designed. So revisions had to be made, then looked at again when virtually the entire pool of students in the third year turned out to be low achievers.

6. *Extending.* At some sites, we asked our informants to put names on the different phases of practice mastery as they saw them. One user at Banestown came up with a label that fits others' experiences well:

> Sort of like branching out, you know, trying some new things, putting the pieces together another way . . . now I've got it under control pretty much and I can look for other things to put in it.

Usually, branching out meant one of two things: looking outside the project for materials or exercises that could be incorporated into it or, alternatively, transferring components of the project to other segments of one's activity. For instance, a user at Lido began to elaborate a community-based project drawn from his fieldwork with high-school students.

There are more economical ways of describing this progression from initial to more consolidated practice mastery. For example, the six participles used above can be inserted in the progressive "levels of use of the innovation" identified by Hall *et al.* (1975). We saw before that early implementation corresponded to the difficult, disjointed *mechanical use* phase. The next notch up on the LoU scale is *routine use*, during which program execution is stabilized, with few, if any, changes made or envisaged. Users are essentially *"doing"* the innovation, with fair success and little stress. The next phase is *refinement*, in which users vary parts of the innovation in order to heighten its impact. Next is *integration*, when users are combining their own efforts with those of others in extending or refining the new practice. Finally, there is *renewal*, during which phase users seek or make major modifications in the practice.

There was no clear evidence at our field sites that one of the six activity types we have outlined was necessarily antecedent or superordinate to the others— that, for example, refining took place before or was a prerequisite to extending. Rather, these seemed to be *simultaneous* activities during later implementation. We have some data suggesting that "reaching up" to the more complex segments happened before "extending," as if the practice needed to be consolidated before users would look beyond it. But even here users seemed to be "extending" beyond *some parts* that they had mastered and at the same time "improving" *other parts* that they had not successfully come to grips with, while "refining" still other parts. In other words, the innovations were not monolithic. Implementation was like a sculpture in process, on which some parts of the body were rough-hewn, other parts already distinctive but in need of fine chisel work, and still other parts fully completed and integrated into the larger vision of the work as a whole. Users were moving from one part to another, depending on their energy, the responses of their pupils, the certainty of getting outcomes to correspond to treatments, and the environmental pressures exerted by key actors elsewhere in the school or district.

But the Hall *et al.* categories are more *inclusive* than ours, and thus, they are a useful boiling-down device. Note that we also had a measure of users' level of use of the innovation, taken from the survey data. We shall look at these results toward the end of this section (p. 127).

Problems and Concerns

Surveying the 12 field sites, we find a very mixed bag. For the most part, the problems line up well, logically enough, with the six principal tasks that we just listed. The obstacles met in accomplishing these tasks turned into perceived problems and concerns.

Table 25 orders and illustrates the relationship between problem areas and principal tasks in later implementation. The table also reminds us that, though later implementation was far smoother then early use, there were still some virulent bugs, loose ends, structural incompatibilities with existing arrange-ments, unsuccessful attempts to resolve many of these difficulties, or new problems emerging out of the resolution of old ones. And there were a number of sites (Masepa, Perry-Parkdale, Carson, and Plummet)—typically, but not ex-clusively, places with a high degree of practice change—where many users felt after two years that they were not fully on top of the project. Here, for example, is an assessment after two years:

> Everything in the program is looking good, but it has to be implemented. . . . Some teachers still don't feel comfortable with the plan form. There are many loose ends. Many teachers are still grappling with implementation. (Program director at Carson)

But the *constellation* of problems and concerns had changed from that seen in early implementation. For example, there were few laments over the personal or professional capacity to carry out the project. Those issues seemed to be settled, as was the concern over what others would think. This shift was rendered well by one of the lab teachers at Banestown:

TABLE 25. Problems and Concerns Stemming from Major Tasks of Later Implementation at Field Sites

Task/activity	Problem type	Illustrations
Reaching up	Difficulty in mastering more complex components	"Some parts just aren't working. They're harder than the first ones I did." (Teacher, Masepa) "I still can't monitor the children's progress . . . there are too many pupils to keep up with." (Teacher, Calston)
Improving, debugging	Solving specific problems, often connected to poor program design	"The bookkeeping is awful" (Teacher, Banestown). Paperwork (Perry-Parkdale, Carson). Scheduling problems (Banestown, Calston, Carson, and Proville). Pupils disturbing, interrupting each other (Perry-Parkdale). "Materials [that are] not right for this age" (Dun Hollow).
Refining	Differentiating, tailoring	"Needs tailoring . . . the time isn't there." (Teacher, Lido) Inability, despite repeated attempts, to break down groups into individual exercises. (Lab teachers, Banestown)
Integrating	Combining new project with regular curriculum	"Will this destroy my own curriculum? How can I fit it in?" (Teacher, Burton) Lack of time to do both old and new. (Calston, Dun Hollow, and Carson)
Adapting	Accommodating the project to new inputs	"The course is all floaters now . . . I get the burn-outs, who sit in a daze and are hard to reach." (Teacher, Lido) Changes in released time, budget decreases (Lido). New testing requirements (Banestown).
Extending	Using components elsewhere, reorganizing practice, bringing in other segments	Trying to bring back former "stuff that worked" (Masepa). Feeling "bored," looking for more stimulating materials (Tindale).

Note. From Miles & Huberman (1984). Reprinted by permission.

I was a lot more off myself and more on the kids. I wasn't thinking about myself so much, but I was asking and checking, "Is this material right for them? Is this going to work for each one of those kids?"

This shift—from onself to the task at hand—is a classic phenomenon in the research on adult learning and innovation implementation. Hall (1976) captured it well in his sequential model of "stages of concern" on the part of teachers executing a new practice. The later stages of that model describe economically the problem areas that we have just examined:

1. Concerns about efficient *management*, with paramount concerns turning around "organizing, managing, scheduling and time demands"
2. Concerns about student impact or *consequence*, i.e., for improving outcomes and making the changes enabling that
3. Concerns about *collaboration* with others, in relation to the innovation
4. Concerns for *refocusing*, with consideration of major changes, replacements, alternatives

Our evidence on whether there is a linear or ordinal progression through these stages of concern is mixed. We have already noted that a progression from self-centered to practice-centered concerns occurred at our sites. We also noted that "management" concerns seemed to be paired with hard-to-master components, and "consequence" concerns with the components under control. But by and large, though there was often a dominant concern, we could, like Hall and George (1978), usually see all types of concerns ongoing, side by side, within most of our sites, and within many of our users. For example, the longer-implementing sites (and users) were not necessarily more caught up in refocusing issues than were the newcomers. So there is probably not a hierarchical, orderly progression of concerns.

Darker and Broader Concerns

There is still more to the story of users' concerns during later implementation. Because we have fastened onto the process of *practice mastery* and what gets in its way, we have overplayed the technical or instrumental aspects of mastery over other problem areas. Up to now in this section, we have underattended to the pain, noise, friction, and organizational concerns of later implementation.

Many of these themes have been treated elsewhere in our report. For example, changes in the innovation are studied as responses to personal and organizational incompatibilities (see pp. 133 ff.), and user change is treated in part as a response to the demands of the innovation at the classroom and school levels (see pp. 151 ff.). In other words, the problems of early and later implementation led to transformations in the users, the innovation, and the organization. Here, we should limit ourselves to a brief summary of later-implementation concerns that were not directly practice- and mastery-connected, but that did take their toll on program execution as a whole. The summary appears in Table 26.

Note that only two sites escaped unscathed: Astoria and Burton, both places

TABLE 26. Later Implementation: Additional Individual and Institutional Concerns

Type of concern/Item	Sites at which item mentioned (N = 12)
Individual concerns	
Relational problems—friction among project staff	Banestown, Perry-Parkdale
Motivational problems (discouragement, disenchantment, "distaste" for the practice)	Calston, Lido, Masepa, Dun Hollow, Proville, Tindale
Stamina, exhaustion, excessive demands of the project	Masepa, Carson, Plummet
Institutional concerns	
Lower institutional or district-level priority of project (with attendant lessening of rewards)	Lido, Plummet
Poor overall functioning (project as a whole, or a component)	Perry-Parkdale, Dun Hollow, Proville
Resistance, obstruction, lack of support by other staff not on project	Banestown, Perry-Parkdale, Carson
Worry whether project will "deliver" on its promises or objectives	Banestown
Continuation the following year(s)	Banestown, Calston, Lido, Perry-Parkdale, Plummet

Note. From Miles & Huberman (1984). Reprinted by permission.

where the change effort was drastically scaled down from the program developer's version. Table 26 does not tell us anything about the gravity, the pervasiveness, or the real impact of the concerns—all of which varied from site to site. But it does show us several more general things. First, there were many nontechnical concerns during later implementation. These included at least one item ("stamina") where the concern was a carryover from early implemetnation and was still self-centered. Second, it is clear that the project staff had concerns during later implementation that were institutional worries, going well beyond practice mastery. At Lido, for example, the innovation's users were technically masterful, but the institutional support had eroded—for reasons largely independent of the merits or demerits of the program itself. So mastery may have assuaged institutional programs, but by no means resolved them, since political rather than technical factors were at play. More on this below.

The Process of Practice Mastery: A Summary

Keeping our earlier summaries in mind,[26] let us try a synthesized view of how practice mastery proceeds. It seems to follow a basic learning-theory paradigm, as applied to behavioral change in complex social settings. There are successive cycles of "practice → expand → practice," during which the users evolve first a set of practical decision rules, then "routines" or action algorithms for an increasing number and variety of situations. These increasingly well-rehearsed

[26]Readers will find a finer-grained profile of later implementation at the illustrative field sites in the technical report (pp. 191–196).

mental plans trigger responses that, over time, come automatically. We might compare, for someone learning to drive, how the complexity of braking, accelerating, changing gears, negotiating turns—sometimes all at once or in rapid succession—gradually becomes automatic. Once that happens, things go more quickly, less stressfully, and to better effect. The successive cycles of trial and error turn up procedures that work consistently. At the same time, seeing *how* these procedures work—by varying them, by seeing what *else* happens, by finding out under what conditions they *do not* work—gives users a more differentiated understanding of the project's structure. Then come refinements, for the segments already debugged, along with integrations and extensions, as users get a broader view of what this practice does in relation to the other things they are doing or would like to do.

Finally, getting better and seeing results tends to channel more energy into the progressive cycles of mastery, and to lend confidence for making small leaps to the next, or more difficult, parts.

We might usefully plot this progression on a classic learning or S curve, as in Figure 5. The progression on the curve follows the successive cycles of practice→ expansion→ practice that we have developed, with the caveat that users can be at different stages for different parts of the new practice in our analysis. We have tried to yoke cognitions and actions, so that low differentiation and poor conceptual integration go with fragmented use, and increasing cognitive mastery covaries with smoother execution. Finally, when the users have an elaborate mental road map and a series of well-grooved routines, they

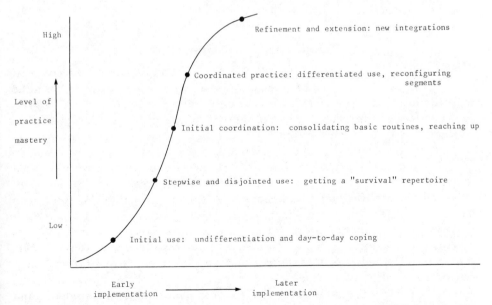

FIGURE 5. Practice mastery plotted as a learning curve. The reader is reminded that adequate mastery may take up to three years, so the steepness of the curve should only be taken as a schematic representation.

can then move on to conceive new configurations, including integrations with other parts of their work and extensions to new practices that seem like the logical next steps in classroom or school-level improvement. (As in other aspects of life, *can* and *will* are not identical. A user capable of moving on to a new level may not necessarily do so, depending on factors like commitment and supports for institutionalization.)

The figure also reminds us that the mastery is not linear; a more empirically faithful curve, in fact, would probably look more like a slowly ascending roller coaster. All informants spoke of setbacks, of plateaus, of reversions to prior practice, or of "freezing" the project for a few weeks while they gathered energy and rehearsed the parts that they considered crucial. Here is a description of the freezing process from one of the lab teachers at Banestown:

> I got overwhelmed, so I went back to the DISTAR stuff I used before I came to the lab. . . . I guess I was trying to gain time so I could figure out how to make the lab work right. I sort of had to slow things down so that I could get on top of it. So I went back to the things that I knew the kids would need and I knew how they would work, those materials, I mean.

Finally, let us try to assemble in one place (Table 27) the several components of practice mastery that we have covered in this section and the section on early implementation. Note that we begin "before the beginning" and trace how users conceptualized the practice, their cognitive attempts to determine how it "worked," their day-to-day actions, and their chief concerns. Also notable is the strong overlap between our findings and those of Hall *et al.*, which lends some additional external validity to both the "Levels of Use" and the "Stages of Concern" scales.

Stabilization and Continuation

In reviewing users' concerns during later implementation, we saw that school- and district-level factors began to intrude into users' plans to continue with the new practice. Recall from Table 26 that, at five sites, the users felt continuation was uncertain, at two of these (Lido and Plummet), lower district-level priority for the project meant that users could expect lowered assistance and support, even without a formal decision to end the project.

This finding is an important one, in that it displaces our focus from individual to institutional factors. Innovations can be technically mastered, perhaps even shown to be effective, but this does not ensure their continuation. We could even have the inverse relationship: Practices could be *poorly* mastered by users and *still* be continued by administrators, for political reasons. To be sure, if an instructionally effective practice outperformed its predecessors, the next reasonable step would be for administrators to conclude that it was worth institutionalizing. But educational politics often follow strange paths. Take Lido, for instance, where the environmental science project was applauded by board, students, and teachers but got increasingly squeezed out because of lack of support from a new principal and a lame-duck superintendent, and because field-sited projects had less appeal when new facilities became available. Or take Dun Hollow, where

TABLE 27. Synthesis of Early and Late Stages of Practice Mastery

Stage	Conceptualization of the practice	Cognitive activity	Instructional repertoire[a]	Concerns[b]
1. Preimplementation	Undifferentiated	Simulated conceiving, planning, activity, and management sequences	"Untested."	Information (SoC): Characteristic effects, requirements for use
2. Initial use	Disjoined, unconnected components	Multiple discrepancies between predictions and observation of outcomes	Confrontation—many prior algorithms not effective. Multiple demands; apparently disjointed, irreconcilable with own teaching. Reversions to prior repertoire when possible	Personal-ego concerns (SoC): Professional adequacy—evaluation of peers Control of classroom Reconsideration of incentives
3. Stepwise and disjoined use	Whole reduced to 2–3 parts, with hypothesized simple causal relationships between them	Focus on 2–3 macrocomponents; trial and error to determine constraints, erratic predictive accuracy	Mechanical use (LoU) Running stepwise through basic steps Reversions to earlier practice	Minimal management (SoC): Achieving mastery of 1 or 2 components while keeping basic order, maintaining goal direction in other activities
4. Initial coordination	Some functional relations perceived between subparts, and between parts and whole	Components still disjointed, minimally coordinated; conceived of as chunks of activities and practices on same skill or at certain time of day	Mechanical mastery—more ease in getting through routines, linking these routines to other ongoing classroom work Close to LoU "routine use"	Management (SoC): Get ahead of basic organization of program Scheduling, pupil management, anticipating next frames, providing for difficulties
5. Coordinated practice	High differentiation and coordination; details of program are related across components and to whole	Conceiving new combinations of elements in practice; reorganizing specific parts and correctly predicting effects of use	Coordinated work; inserting and linking parts according to contingencies Introduction of parts of program to other skill areas or activities	Consequence (SoC): Assuring optimal organization, monitoring student process; trying to increase achievement level
6. Refinement and extension	Extensions of schemata (concepts of instruction) to include other components of one's own practice, and to other, as yet untried, practices	Conceiving alternatives; can integrate components into this practice from another ongoing practice	Refinement; initial tryout of integrations, extensions from other sources Close to LoU "refinement" and "renewal"	Maintenance and extension; keeping basic level of efficiency while incorporating new parts and discarding or recombining others; getting management in place for more elaborate practice Close to (SoC) "refocusing"

[a] LoU = Levels of use of the innovation (Hall et al., 1975; Loucks et al., 1975).
[b] SoC = Stages of concern (Hall, 1976; Hall & George, 1978).

teachers experimented thoroughly with an Eskimo studies project and judged it unfit for districtwide diffusion, only to see the superintendent recommend expansion of the project. Or take Astoria, where the decision to institutionalize a kindergarten screening project was made for 92 district schools *before* teachers (in Mitchell school, our focus) found the project so inappropriate that they simply farmed out segments of it to aides in a pull-out format.

This decoupling between the mastery or endorsement of users, on the one hand, and the (usually) administrative decision to continue or discontinue an innovation only says that substantially varying criteria are being used by different actors.

Operationalizing Stabilization of Use

Let us try to examine more systematically the relationship between stabilization of use and continuation of the innovation. What constitutes stabilization of use? Up to now, we have come closer to equating user practice mastery with stabilization by suggesting that when users get on top of the project, it settles down. Even later user-initiated changes in an integration or extension mode are usually made, we said, from a solid base of instructional control over classroom life. But we do have instances where user mastery was relatively high, but the program remained unsettled (e.g., Plummet, Perry-Parkdale, and Carson). So user practice mastery was probably contributing to program stabilization and vice versa, but not determining it. In other words, there must be sources of stabilization of use other than practice mastery. What might they be?

In our explanatory analysis (Chapter 6), we try to identify and account for several sources of ultimate stabilization, including administrative constraint, input shifts, personnel changes, and program expansion. Our task here is more descriptive. We want to specify a generic factor that adds to the final estimate of stabilization of use that part of the equation not covered by user practice mastery. We shall call this factor *program settledness* to indicate that core components of the innovation are no longer being added, deleted, or transformed. In causal terms, we are saying that the several sources listed above eventually induce higher or lower program settledness. This global factor, when combined with user practice mastery, gives us a composite index of stabilization of use.

How did our field sites perform on each of these constituent measures (practice mastery and program settledness) and on the composite stabilization index? Table 28 shows the relative estimates, taken from the 12 causal networks and from the survey measure of levels of innovation use (LoU).[27] Table 28 has some valuable information. First, the overall levels of stabilization of use are moderate to good overall. Practice mastery brings the general stabilization level slightly up and program-settledness estimates bring it slightly down, suggesting that users settle down before programs do. Also, except at the low-stabilizing sites, the two indices (mastery and settledness) are usually at the same level, suggesting that they are related.

---

[27]Recall that for many field-study measures, there was parallel survey measurement for the full study population from which the field study sample was drawn.

TABLE 28. Stabilization of Use, as a Function of Practice Mastery
and Program Settledness[a]

Sites	Estimate of program settledness	Estimate of user practice mastery	LoU rating[b] (N of users)	Stabilization of use
Astoria (NDN)	High	High	Routine (4)	High
Tindale (IV-C)	High	High	Refinement (1) MD (8)	High
Calston (NDN)	Mod–high	Mod–high	Mechanical use (1) MD (2)	Mod–high
Perry-Parkdale (NDN)	Moderate	High	Routine (2) Refinement (1)	Mod–high
Lido (NDN)	Moderate	High	Routine (1) Integration (1) MD (1)	Mod–high
Burton (NDN)	Moderate	Moderate	Routine (1) MD (3)	Moderate
Banestown (NDN)	Moderate	Moderate	Mechanical use (2) MD (1)	Moderate
Masepa (NDN)	Moderate	Moderate	Mechanical use (3) Routine (1) MD (3)	Moderate
Carson (IV-C)	Low–mod	Mod–high	MD	Moderate
Plummet (IV-C)	Low–mod	Mod–high	Refinement (2) Integration (1) MD (1)	Moderate
Dun Hollow (IV-C)	Low	Low	Mechanical use (2) MD (1)	Low
Proville (IV-C)	Low	Low–mod[c]	MD	Low

[a] All data in the table come from the later implementation period.
[b] LoU was measured in two ways: (1) a "high-fidelity" measure that automatically gave low levels of use when the user was carrying out a version of the innovation "unacceptable" to the developer; and (2) a more relaxed version, called *practice-related mastery*, where the measure dealt with the user's actual level of skill in using the local version of the innovation, even if it had been adapted "unacceptably." This table uses the second measure. MD = missing data.
[c] Estimate for teachers.

Sometimes, this relation is very close. For example, one of the final three users at Calston remained uncomfortable with the program, variously using and suppressing parts in a process that translated into uneven practice mastery. There was a very similar phenomenon at Burton. At Banestown, the practice was complex, and we came upon users when they were just beginning to get it under firm control. In these cases, mastery and program settledness were inseparable. But there was sometimes no relationship at all. For example, program settledness at Astoria owed virtually nothing to user practice mastery and came largely from some early and major amputations of the core program components. And at Masepa, program *unsettledness* resulted from the addition of new components in the classrooms of *experienced users,* whereas uneven skill mastery came from the addition of *new users* to the project.

How does the survey measure levels of innovation use (LoU) line up with our estimates of stabilization of use? At first glance, not too badly; there are no aberrant instances. But there are lots of missing data. And we do not find a linear relationship between LoU and stabilization. We can also see some anomalies. For example, the "routine" users at Astoria were really using only a few particles of the original innovation. The same was true at Burton. At Masepa, we judged two of the three "mechanical use" teachers to be chiefly making refinements and extensions, and we thought the user judged to be "routine" was in trouble all three times we observed her. As noted earlier, these judgments may have depended heavily on *which parts* of the new practice teachers were working with when observed or interviewed. Finally, users at Dun Hollow appeared to us to have so thoroughly revamped the practice that they were in the opposite situation from users at Astoria; disjointed use resulting from major refocusing. The Dun Hollow finding may account for the—possibly misleading—levels-of-use assessment of "mechanical use," suggesting that users were in the initial phases of use. In sum, it looks as if, minimally, a close check of the components in use should accompany the levels of use measure, in order to protect its internal validity. In addition, it seems that a context-free index of practice mastery pays a price in intelligibility.

Stabilization of Use and Program Continuation

Let us try to look more systematically at the relationship between stabilization of use and the prospects of continuation of the innovation. Table 29 arrays our 12 field sites according to the extent of stabilization of use, then displays other continuation-relevant data in the following columns.

At first glance, no sharp relationships stand out. However, the data are instructive. Let us begin with the fourth column, "Likelihood of continued use."[28]

Continuation was likely in fewer than half the cases (five). There are four "uncertain" sites and three low/nil ones. Overall, the picture is not rosy.

Did the high-likelihood sites have anything in common? At first blush, perhaps they were the extremes in actual practice change: Masepa, Carson, and Tindale had high change in user practice, and Astoria and Burton were low. But Plummet was also a high-change sit and Lido a low-change site, and both were unsure of the future.

Were the stabilized sites more likely to continue than the poorly stabilized ones? Yes, at the extremes, but not at all in the middle range.

The third column tells us that in 7 of the 12 cases, users wanted—mostly or unequivocally—to continue. But at only 4 of these sites were their wishes likely to be fulfilled. So positive user attitudes may enhance, but do not deliver, a high likelihood of continuation. On the other hand, users' *not* liking the innovation looks like a slightly better predictor. Still, it seems that teacher preferences are not decisive, at least when it comes to ensuring continued use at a site.

Nor does the longevity of a project ensure its future. Setting the second column against the fourth, we see (somewhat ominously) that the youngest innovations (Astoria and Burton) are assured of at least another year at the same

---

[28]What follows is an abridged version of a more thorough analysis in the technical report (pp. 206–209).

TABLE 29. Relationships between User Practice Stabilization and Local Continuation

Extent of practice stabilization/Sites	End of year	Users' attitudes toward continuation	Likelihood of continued use[a] (same level or better)	Prime factors contributing to high or low likelihood of continuation
High stabilization				
Astoria (NDN)	1	Positive	High	Project mandated Heavy local transformation for good fit
Tindale (IV-C)	3	Mostly positive	High	Local mandate well enforced Procedures codified User satisfaction
Moderate–high stabilization				
Calston (NDN)	2	Mixed[b]	Low	Budget crisis—staff cuts, reassignments
Perry-Parkdale (NDN)	3	Mostly positive	Uncertain	Staff turnover Uncertain funding
Lido (NDN)	4	Mixed[b]	Uncertain	Lower administrative support Lower priority (new facility now available) Users' discouragement
Moderate stabilization				
Burton (NDN)	1	Positive	High	Parts of project written into curriculum Heavy local transformation, good user fit
Banestown (NDN)	2	Positive	Uncertain	Budget crisis Staff reduced, reassigned
Masepa (NDN)	3	Mixed	High	Project mandated Strong logistical support Improved pupil performance
Carson (IV-C)	3	Mostly positive	High	Procedures codified, routinized Project mandated Widespread local support
Plummet (IV-C)	4	Positive	Uncertain	Likely staff turnover Lower district support
Low stabilization				
Dun Hollow (IV-C)	3	Negative	Low	User and principal dissatisfaction No strong local advocate
Proville (IV-C)	4	Negative	Nil	Other central office priorities; no advocate Project discontinued User and principal dissatisfaction

Note. From Miles & Huberman (1984). Reprinted by permission.
[a]Researcher assessment, usually pooled from interview data and site report tables.
[b]Some wanting to continue, others not.

level; whereas the veterans (Lido, Plummet, and Proville) are either uncertain or on their way out. But the remaining sites line up to suggest that project length of use predicts continuation.

Now to the meatiest column, the fifth. We have listed prime factors in roughly estimated order of magnitude. Also, for the most part, these items are low-inference. They come directly from users' responses and were pooled to make a site-level judgment. What do they say about the determinants of continuation at the 12 sites?

When the likelihood of continuation is *low* or *nil* (Dun Hollow and Proville), we find two cases of dissatisfaction with the practice on the part of both principals *and* teachers, lowering building endorsement, along with the absence or disappearance of an energetic local advocate. There is one case of external turbulence: budget cuts, with resulting reductions or reassignments of project staff.

When continuation is *uncertain,* we also find external turbulence from immediate or threatened budget cuts (two cases), plus lower administrative support (two cases) and staff turnover (two cases), the latter being the result of lower funds or reduced local backing. At Banestown, there was another wrinkle. In one of the three schools studied, nonproject staff (other teachers) found the project to be a "space invader" and did not accommodate to it, with the tacit backing of the principal. So it seems that we can expect less continuation when most of the people doing it or administering it do not like it, when other key actors (other teachers, and other central-office staff) do not support it, or when there is heavy external turbulence. If we look for one overarching contributor to uncertain continuation, it would clearly be lack of sustained *administrative support.* When budget crises strike, central office administrators have several options, one of which is cutting a new project back or out. But there is always the option of cutting *elsewhere,* which, in these cases, was not exercised. Why not—especially since the central office staff were usually the chief advocates of these innovations? There seem to have been several reasons. These advocates had moved on to other priorities (Perry-Parkdale), had doubts about the project (Dun Hollow and Plummet), had ridden the innovation to a promotion elsewhere (Proville) or were themselves unable to reverse the course of events (Calston and Banestown). At Calston, the central office advocate was herself knocked out of the central office as a result of budget cuts. At Banestown, there was an unwritten code that special projects went first when money was short. But the central office "champion" of the project managed, via some fancy item-budgeting and reassignments, to keep the project alive at slightly below its former level of operation. So sustained central-office support seems to matter.

If low likelihood of continuation is associated with low building-level endorsement, and uncertain continuation with lack of sustained administrative support, what does the support and endorsement picture look like at the five high-likelihood sites? Overall it looks good. The Tindale users were satisfied. The project at Carson had broad-based support. The people at Masepa obviously liked the improved pupil performance that they were getting.

Astoria and Burton introduce us to one likely reason for good building-level support: The project was transformed to ease local constraints, thereby gaining users' endorsement in particular. At both Astoria and Burton, users got to pick and choose among the project components for the most congenial, least locally disruptive segments. The Astoria users kept the testing component and threw out almost everything else. The teachers at Burton picked off some supplementary exercises and materials. As we shall see in the next section, when we trace the changes made in the innovation, administrators often bartered such discretionary use in return for user endorsement of the project.

At these five sites where continuation was highly likely, there was also more explicit evidence of administrative-level support: administrative fiat and administrative codification. The project was mandated or otherwise literally written into local regulations and procedures. So we have direct or inferred user and administrator endorsement *together with* administrative fiat—an unbeatable combination of muscle and commitment. Also, when we look underneath the shroud of mandates and pressures exerted directly on users by administrators, we can see a less dramatic but probably more compelling indicator of project continuation. At Tindale, for example, new teachers were given a highly specific curriculum guide for the reading program, including worksheets and suggested units, materials, pretests, and summative tests. At Masepa, all new teachers in the district underwent training in the ECRI program. At Carson, the project had an operating manual and standardized profiles and educational plan forms. There was a "community resource manual" available to present and future project staff. Two things were happening here. First, the project was becoming codified and standardized, so that new users could pick up where the old users left off. As a teacher at Carson put it, the project had been "routinized": it was on the way to being a part of the local landscape, a taken-for-granted fixture. Second, these measures were not inconsequential. Writing a project into the curriculum, fitting it into the yearly administrative and budget cycle, arranging for training for all new district staff, and taking out the practices that the innovation replaced were all steps taken to firmly *institutionalize* the project.[29] As a Tindale teacher put it with resignation, "It's here to stay." Undoing these measures would be cumbersome (i.e., would call for substantial organizational and classroom changes). So we have come full circle in the innovation process, so that routinized projects become the baseline against which the "demand characteristics" of a newer practice—what it requires from the site—will be measured.

Finally, it is important to point out here that we are looking at the *end* of a causal chain. That is, although administrative fiat and codification substantially determine continuation, they themselves are the product of several prior or coterminous factors. In causal terms, you have to *get to* such support in order to enhance continuation, and our chart does not tell us *how* apparently secure sites got there and insecure sites didn't. For that, we need the more explanatory analysis of how stabilization of use is accomplished, which appears in Chapter 6 with our explanations of institutionalization.

[29]This process of "routinization" as a composite indicator of institutionalization was first conceptualized and studied by Yin *et al.* (1978).

Conclusions

Most users at the field sites attained good practice mastery, within 18 months for the complex projects, and within 5–6 months in the case of the "downsized" projects. Later energies were thus channeled into refining, debugging, and extending core components.

In this later phase, users reported a sense of achieved efficacy. By then, they spoke of being comfortable ("secure," "relaxed") with the practice, technically on top of it; of feeling confident and in control ("getting it to go *my* way"); and of feeling gratified by signs of success, notably their pupils' responsiveness.

Users also got a more differentiated and integrated fix on the project by dint of gradually making it work consistently and predictably. Understanding the innovation meant learning what could be *done* with it.

For complex projects, by midway in the second year, the project was easier to do, went more quickly, had predictable effects, and, overall, "worked" progressively better. Most time was being spent on six types of task: *reaching up* (taking on more demanding segments), *debugging* outstanding flaws, *refining and codifying, integrating* these new materials into existing ones, *adapting* the practice to ongoing changes in the pupil population, and *extending* the innovation to other activities.

Later problems and concerns shifted from the self to the pupils and the task, a shift that is in keeping with other research. As one teacher said, "I was a lot more off myself and on the kids." Still, users at several sites complained of waning energy, of disenchantment and discouragement. New, more instutional concerns surfaced: the priority of the project, poor functioning of a part or the whole, lack of support from staff outside the project, and worries about whether the promised results could be delivered.

It appeared that user practice mastery and/or the relative settledness of the innovation did not ensure project continuation. Whereas later project "stabilization" was estimated as moderate-to-high at nine sites, in only five cases was the outlook good for continuation at the same level or better. The key predictors of continuation were teacher and administrative support, low environmental turbulence, and clear indications that the project was getting locally "routinized," that is, was being built into training and budget cycles and becoming codified in the form of teachers' guides and prototype materials.

CHAPTER 5

Transformations over Time

By way of providing an advance organizer for this section, we refer back to the conceptual flowchart (Figure 1, p. 11) that oriented our initial fieldwork. For now, our focus is on the fourth column, the "cycle of transformations." The notion here, derived from psychological and sociological theory and highlighted in the recent Rand Corporation study of federally sponsored educational innovations (Berman & McLaughlin, 1974–1978), is that innovations enter an environment that they change and by which they are in turn altered. As we saw in the preceding chapter, users, administrators, and even program developers bend *innovations* to match local characteristics and constraints. The reshaping goes on throughout the implementation process and varies notably with the scale or the scope of the project, the degree of latitude given users to make changes, and the perceived results of initial use.

But innovations are also, by definition, carriers of practice change. A user may trim a new curriculum unit or pick selectively from it, but whatever is used will constitute a change to some degree in ongoing classroom *practice*. Some innovations, in fact, are heavily teacher-transforming. One project in our sample, the integrated language-arts program at Masepa, fit this description. Teachers reported that they had altered their daily classroom organization, their core curriculum, their relationships with their pupils, and even their vision of themselves as teachers. As one teacher said, "On balance, it's a complete change from what I was doing." Most informants at Masepa said that they had never dreamed their instructional repertoires and routines would be so thoroughly taken apart and reconfigured.

Figure 1 also shows that the dynamics of reciprocal change included changes in *organizational* rules, norms, practices, and relationships. We saw innovations as changing organizations that would in turn adapt the innovations locally. These school-level changes would also result in classroom-level changes or would themselves be the product of revisions in user practices. We take up organizational-level change in detail in a following section (pp. 167 ff.). First we examine how the innovations themselves changed.

MODIFICATIONS IN THE INNOVATION

Introduction

Here we were interested in several questions:

1. In what ways did the innovations actually change over time? How extensive and how important were these changes?
2. What accounted for these changes? What factors seemed to be at work?
3. Could we develop a general explanatory model incorporating the various factors? If yes, how would it play out for the sites, or for clusters of sites?

Type, Extent, and Significance of Changes over Time

Mapping the *pattern* of innovation changes (additions, reductions, and reconfigurations) over time for the 12 projects was the first analytic task. We needed also to estimate the *extent* of change (the number of components changed) and the *importance* of the changes (details, ancillary segments, and core segments).[1]

According to final estimates—at the end of three years, or at the close of data collection at the sites with shorter implementation histories—over half the sites (7) had dropped or changed from one-third to two-thirds of the key components to "unacceptable" versions. One-fourth had made such changes in more than two-thirds of the key components. The remaining two sites (Masepa and Tindale) had changed little. They were implementing "ideal" revisions of the developer's practice and were the heavily "policed" projects that we will discuss later.

So there were numerous and consequential changes. We also saw more attrition with time: Of the seven sites with shifts from initial implementation to later use, five entailed reductions in the number of acceptable components. The remaining two (Banestown and Proville) began with substantial reductions, then gradually restored some core components as the school staff got more on top of the new practice.

Our site-level analysis of the extent and importance of changes shows five sites with "significant" changes, four with "moderate" changes, and three with "minor" changes—again, a picture of substantial local adaptation. By way of anticipating the scenarios we will recount later, here is a thumbnail sketch of what happened at the five sites with farther-reaching changes:

1. *Astoria* (NDN): The program, poorly fitted to ongoing grade-level and classroom organization, was converted to a pull-out format staffed by aides and parent volunteers.
2. *Burton* (NDN): The project called for wide-ranging changes in instructional formats, levels of pupil responsibility, and out-of-school contacts

---

[1]Details on the substance and methods are in the technical report (Huberman & Miles, 1983b, pp. 218–219).

that school staff were unable or unwilling to make. With administrative permission, they ignored the components asking for such changes.

3. *Carson* (IV-C): The individualized education project made heavy demands on staff time, the available resources, and record keeping; it was progressively stripped down and simplified, with much of the individualization lost.

4. *Plummet* (IV-C): The initial project had to be massively revamped, through curricular and instructional changes, to accommodate the incoming student population.

5. *Proville* (IV-C): Very little was done to follow through on the initial design; only a skeleton program was executed, then discontinued.

Even the projects making what we estimated to be "moderate" changes turned out to have reductions or reconfigurations in core components. For example, one of the major objectives at the Calston (NDN) site was to enhance pupils' appreciation and mastery of literature. By the third year, at least one of the three remaining teachers was using the literature segments of the program only as "rewards" for good behavior. At Banestown (NDN), the program called for the selection of underachieving pupils with grade-level aptitudes, to come to a pull-out lab in three- to five-week cycles. But about a third of the pupils were at sub-95 IQ levels, and all stayed in the lab a full year.

From a strictly local perspective, all these changes—including the significant ones—were logical, if not inevitable. At their best, they took account of local characteristics and constraints, sometimes prolonged the life of the program, provided better access to funds and materials, and increased administrative support.

At their worst, the changes flowed from teacher or administrative resistance that was poorly founded, or from simple convenience. In some cases, the moderate to high changes were productive, enhancing the innovation's impact on students (Plummet, Banestown, and Perry-Parkdale). But in others, a moderate to high degree of change closed out the possibility of student impact (Burton and Proville). In two "well-policed" sites with minor changes (Masepa and Tindale), the impact was high; at the third (Dun Hollow), minor changes were irrelevant to the impact of a poorly designed, resisted program.

In short, neither "fidelity" nor "adaptation" necessarily makes for student impact. The question is whether a program is well designed in the first place— and whether the adaptations made strengthen or weaken that design.

Were there between-program differences in the type of modifications made over time? Site-level analysis[2] shows here that the NDN *projects* experienced heavy cuts at the start, most of which were maintained or intensified over time (Astoria, Burton, Lido, and Perry-Parkdale). The remaining three projects (Banestown, Calston, and Masepa) appear to have gone through a shakedown cycle, then to have restored some of the initial design characteristics. So, contrary to much theory and some conventional wisdom

[2]See the technical report (pp. 218–219) for details.

about the timing of change, the bulk of the local NDN sites in our sample were making major changes *before* or *at the start* of program execution, then settling into a substantially reduced format with some later restorations.

A *IV-C* analysis yields a slightly different pattern. Proville aside, there were few initial reductions of any importance—a natural result of the developmental nature of the IV-C grants. By the second year, however, there was some heavy remodeling at Carson, at Plummet, and allowing for the difference in scale, at Dun Hollow. Proville appeared to be getting on its feet by making partial restorations. Overall, these sites seem to have made more swings and lurches than the NDN sites, whose progression was more linear. As a set, the IV-C projects had less definition; they were often more shadowy to users, who had an unclear idea at the outset of what the project entailed, beyond a general concept.[3] IV-C site personnel discovered and shaped the project as it unfolded to a greater degree than did the NDN personnel—who, reacting to a more clearly defined product, often picked and chose segments to fit their instructional or organizational styles. But there was still a high modification rate in three of the five IV-C innovations in relation to the original design. An analysis over time tells us that the IV-C projects had slightly more, and later, reconfigurations than did the NDN innovations. The maverick IV-C case was Tindale, which began with a tight, well-designed product whose faithful execution was consistently enforced at the two target schools.

The most common form of reconfiguration across innovations appears to have been organizational: changing program formats (Astoria and Plummet); revising program cycles and record-keeping procedures (Banestown and Carson); and shifting pupil selection (Banestown and Perry-Parkdale). When the project was more classroom-contained, there were shifts in instructional resequencing (Dun Hollow and Tindale). But sometimes reconfigurations were simply the product of additions mixed with reductions. For example, at the Masepa site, teachers began—first tentatively, then more brazenly—to discard segments of the new, highly regimented, comprehensive language-arts program, which they replaced with some of the materials and activities that the innovation was meant to supplant. When this happened, teachers at Masepa gave one of the following reasons:

Reducing
1. Lack of time to carry out the program as designed
2. Need to unload materials judged to be boring or inappropriate in class
3. Incompatibility of program segments with one's own instructional style
4. Deletion of components felt to be overly taxing
Adding
5. Supplementation of the program where it was judged to be thin
6. Restoration of activities or materials that teachers enjoyed working with or felt had "worked for me" in the past

---

[3]This was also true of the NDN projects, but to a lesser extent, and for different reasons. The "outsideness" of NDN projects could result in user unclarity and confusion, as we have already seen—even though the project was a well-defined package.

Changes at the other sites with classroom-contained innovations (Burton, Calston, Lido, Dun Hollow, and Tindale) were similarly justified. To give a more concrete sense of why these kinds of changes were made, here are some excerpts from Masepa interviews:

1. *Reductions for lack of time.* "There have to be shortcuts. . . . There are just too many things to do to be able to do them all at once. . . . We let the girls ease into it." (Local trainer)
2. *Deletion of boring or inappropriate segments.* "Those kids hated it. They got so sick of the same directives over and over again. The next year, I stopped following all those steps. Everyone around here is cutting corners. . . . They would have revolted if I hadn't cut it down. We started to have more fun." (Sixth-grade teacher)
3. *Deletion of uncongenial segments.* "I can't imagine doing that (write-a-story) stuff every day. I'd go crazy . . . and I don't go in for all that record-keeping stuff." (Second-grade teacher)
4. *Deletion of overtaxing segments.* "Can you imagine? Correcting 27 stories a day! . . . And all those timed practice trials! Why do they have to read it three times and time themselves?" (Fifth–sixth-grade teacher)
5. *Addition of "needed" components.* "There are a lot of things you don't get in. . . . I've had to add worksheets on adverbs, adjectives, and parts of speech. There's a lot that had to be added for me to be happy with it." (Sixth-grade teacher)
6. *Addition of strong or enjoyable units.* "I have an individualized reading program that I'm going to stick into this. I've been hesitating, but now I'm going to do it." (Sixth-grade teacher)

Factors Inducing Changes in the Innovation

Typically, the 12 innovations were not modified simply because local users wanted modifications, nor was goodness of personal fit the only or most salient reason. For one thing, the teachers made *substantial* changes only when they were authorized to do so, which was not always the case. For another, recall our earlier remark that program reconfiguration was sometimes the result of *structural incompatibility.* Working arrangements and regulations could not accommodate to the innovation, and so the innovation accommodated to them. In trying to get a census of all the factors operating at the classroom and school levels to induce modifications in the innovation-as-originally-designed, we found eight main "predictors" of change. Our list excludes what was sometimes a major contributing factor: external events over which the local actors had virtually no control, such as staff turnover or budget cuts. It's useful to note that at three highly turbulent sites (Banestown, Calston, and Perry-Parkdale), the innovation changes were only moderate; only at Plummet was there high turbulence and high innovation change, and the causal connection there was weak.

Table 30 shows the status of five of these eight change-inducing factors,

TABLE 30. Effect of Five Predictors on Changes in the Innovation[a]

Change sites	User fit[b]	Anticipated classroom change[b]	Anticipated organizational change[b]	Organizational fit[c]	Demand characteristics[c]
Significant changes					
Astoria (NDN)	Good	**High**	**High**	**Poor**	Strong
Burton (NDN)	**Fair**	**High**	High	Poor	Strong
Carson (IV-C)	Fair–good	High	**High**	Fair–good	Mod–strong
Plummet (IV-C)	Good	High	**High**	Good	Strong
Proville (IV-C)	Good	Low[d]	Mod	Fair	Mod
Moderate changes					
Banestown (NDN)	Good	Low	Low–mod	Good–**fair**	Small–mod
Calston (NDN)	Good	**Mod**	Low	Good	Small–mod
Lido (NDN)	Fair	Mod	Low	Good	Small–mod
Perry-Parkdale (NDN)	Fair–good	Low[d]	**Mod**	Good	Mod–strong
Minor changes					
Masepa (NDN)	Fair–**poor**	High	Mod	Fair	Mod–strong
Dun Hollow (IV-C)	**Poor**	Low	Low	Good	Small–mod
Tindale (IV-C)	**Fair**	Mod	Low	Good	Mod

[a]Boldface indicates a strong predictor of ensuing changes.
[b]From informants' responses.
[c]Researcher's estimates.
[d]Program with few classroom-level components.

with the 12 sites arrayed by the relative significance of the changes. We have already examined the first four factors in our review of the adoption process; the fifth requires a brief introduction.

Demand Characteristics

In order to be implemented as designed, innovations make a number of demands on local settings. These can be logistical (provision for transportation); normative (more student responsibility); structural (redeployment of staff, curricular revisions); or political (support from central office staff or school board members). They may exert pressure at one or several levels: at the community level (multiplying contacts with and providing resources to schools); at the district level (changing regulations or evaluation procedures); at the school-building level (reassigning pupils and staff); and, obviously, at the classroom level. There can be up-front demands that need to be met before the program can be executed, as well as later demands when some features of the innovation clash with local practices and norms. Demands can be major or minor; they can require additional resources (in staff or materials) or resources reallocated from existing programs.

All too often, it seemed to us that before setting out, the local teachers and administrators had not made a thorough diagnosis of the demands implied in the adoption of a new program. They saw some problems and reacted to them with changes, but they missed many others. Maybe this sketchy diagnosis was salutary; some sites might not have gone ahead had they looked too closely at the structural and normative implications. But there was inevitably a day of reckoning when the programs came face to face with major local constraints. We have already seen that the NDN sites seemed to do much of their reckoning earlier than the IV-C sites. This is essentially what happened at Astoria and Burton, at an early date. Another example was Perry-Parkdale, where moderate-to-strong demand characteristics implied nontrivial organizational changes (e.g., coordinating schedules, lowering pupil supervision, cooperating with the community, and pulling pupils from academic activities), which resulted in an imperfect organizational fit that was not at first visible but later reduced the scope and the innovative bite of the career education program there.

Did any one of the five factors in Table 30 strongly predict the ensuing changes in the innovation? *Demand characteristics* were strong for significantly altered projects, but not weak for projects making minor changes. *Organizational fit* was poor for two of the high-change projects and fair-to-good for all those in other categories, but there was no perceptible covariation.

If we lump the projects making moderate and minor changes and contrast them with high-change projects, the degree of *anticipated organizational change* looks like a good predictor, covarying nicely. It's as if the innovation was altered—usually reduced—when the discrepancy was too great. Astoria was a good example of immediate alteration. At the four other sites for which this factor is in bold face as a strong predictor, there was a sleeper effect. Discrepancies surfaced during program execution and either led to on-the-spot program changes (Banestown and Plummet) or gradually wore down the protagonists at the site, who began to simplify, routinize, and depersonalize the more energy-consuming components of the new practice (Perry-Parkdale and Carson). Much of that energy had been consumed, of course, in *maintaining* the discrepancy between the customary organizational practices and the procedures used in the new practice. For example, here is a review of the reduction in energy investment at the Carson (IV-C) site, where a highly individualized instructional project was implemented:

> It was not just that individual teachers spent less time (a half or a third as much as before, some said) with individual students, but that home visits were eliminated, conferences were reduced in number, there was a tendency to encourage "batch"-type activities planned and executed by the coordinator, the high school program shifted toward course advising with fewer individual activities and trips, and questionnaires (a means, supposedly, of improving and steering the program) were typically not filled out by 20–30% of teachers ("too many questionnaires"). And there was regular griping about the forms for the program itself: "When it comes to bookwork, *let me teach*. I'm not a secretary." (Teacher at Carson)

When programs with few classroom-level components are deleted from Table 30, the degree of implied classroom-level change clearly distinguishes the programs that were significantly altered from the others. All things being equal elsewhere, when the demands of the program promised classroom transformation, the program was changed substantially. A good example is the Burton (NDN) site, where the teachers doing the IPLE curriculum *faithfully* were required to conduct simulations and theme-centered projects, to arrange for short internships in the community, and to bring external resource people into the classrooms. That was not what most of the teachers either had in mind or felt comfortable with. Their interest was in extracting short, easily organized, and "fun" fragments from the program to enliven the conventional lecture and discussion formats that they liked and did well. Duly authorized, this is what most did.

But note in Table 30 that the levels of implied classroom-level change are not uniformly *low* for slightly changing innovations, so the relationship is, at best, partial. This set of innovations does diverge from the others, however, in *goodness of user fit*, which is uniformly fair to poor. (A site-level estimate of "fair" fit usually meant that some teachers felt that the innovation "fit me like a glove," whereas others said that they were "being violated" in the ways they would have to work with and relate to their pupils.) We judged poorness of user fit to be a strong catalyst for local changes in these three projects, although such alterations were minor. For significantly or moderately changing innovations, the fit was either more congenial or, if not, had little effect on the degree of program change.

Table 30 tells only part of the story. The remainder is shown in Table 31, where we find the final three predictors of program change. Only one of these (*implementation readiness*) has been discussed earlier. Beginning with this predictor, there is a slight trend for unready projects to make significant changes and—looking back to the site-level data—to make them *early*, as we would predict. But the remaining cases do not fall into line; some high-change sites were ready (Astoria and Burton), and no low-change site was fully prepared at the start. There is strong evidence, however, that at three of the higher-change sites (Plummet, Proville, and Banestown), the program was full of bugs from the start and that this led to fairly drastic shifts in the characteristics of the program that was executed. In two cases (Proville and Banestown), the nature of the program change was that little of it was executed because little was ready to be executed. In the third (Plummet), far too little thought had been given to the characteristics of the incoming pupils, for whom the initial program design proved quite inappropriate.

Administrative latitude refers to the degrees of freedom given to the users for making discretionary program changes. Note that such latitude was typically high, especially for high-change projects. Note also that the two low-latitude sites experienced only minor changes in the innovation, so we have the rudiments of a linear relationship: more license to change produced more change, less produced less. Note next that we have more boldface type here than in any other column in Tables 30 and 31, which suggests that latitude was a decisive predictor of program change. And note finally that six of the eight cases where administrative latitude was judged a strong predictor are NDN

TABLE 31. Effects of Readiness, Latitude, and Scope on Changes in Innovations[a]

	Implementation readiness[b]	Administrative latitude[b]	Initial (pre-implementation) scale and scope of innovation[b]
Significant changes			
Astoria (NDN)	Adequate	Low-**High**[c]	Large
Burton (NDN)	Adequate	**High**	Small-moderate
Carson (IV-C)	Adequate-partial	**High**	**Large**
Plummet (IV-C)	Partial-**inadequate**	**High**	**Large**
Proville (IV-C)	**Inadequate**	High	Moderate
Moderate changes			
Banestown (NDN)	**Inadequate**	High	Small-moderate
Calston (NDN)	Adequate-partial	**Moderate**	Small
Lido (NDN)	Adequate-partial	**High**	Small-moderate
Perry-Parkdale (NDN)	Partial-adequate	**High**	Moderate
Minor changes			
Masepa (NDN)	**Inadequate**	Low	Large
Dun Hollow (IV-C)	Partial-adequate	**Moderate**	**Small**
Tindale (NDN)	Partial-adequate	**Low**	Moderate-large

[a]Boldface indicates a strong predictor for ensuing changes.
[b]Researcher's estimates from checklist.
[c]Low for central office, high for building principal.

sites. We saw earlier that NDN sites were places where changes in the program were often made early, either before program execution or in the first months. What seemed to be happening was that administrators were giving early and wide latitude to the users who were asking for it—possibly as a precondition to use in their classrooms. This was in fact the scenario at four of the NDN sites where administrative latitude was deemed important: Astoria, Burton, Lido, and, to a lesser extent, Perry-Parkdale, where local developers bargained with building administrators. Users spoke freely of these local agreements, sometimes invoking professional prerogatives.

The site-level data point to two new wrinkles. The Lido case points to a bargaining daisy chain from developers to central office administrators to building-level personnel. The developers gave a license to modify the innovations, possibly as a means of obtaining local adoption, possibly also to strengthen the project by promoting local adaptations. Such deals were struck at four of the sites (Burton, Calston, Lido, and Perry-Parkdale) as a precondition for adoption.

The excerpt from the Burton case report suggests a local strategy of administrative latitude whereby the first-year users got a license to modify a "pilot" innovation that would be subsequently revoked when the project was written into the curriculum. This happened at Burton, although only fragments of the original program were, in fact, institutionalized. There was a similar, somewhat more restricted, license given to teachers at Dun Hollow, but the project was dropped at the end of the pilot phase.

Table 31 shows two other profiles of administrative latitude. First, Masepa and Tindale were low-latitude sites. Administrators at the central office and building levels ran very tight ships. From a Tindale teacher:

> We *had* to succeed because the program wasn't leaving. If it didn't work, the people would have to leave instead. *We* were supposed to change.

And from a Tindale building-level administrator (department chair):

> If you want to depart from the guide, ask me and also tell me why you want to do it and how it will fulfill the guide's objectives. We (she and the department chair at the other adopting school) mostly decide "no" before teachers even ask to make changes.

The rationale at both sites was that (1) the program was designed to be effective, and (2) to get a fair trial, it had to be run faithfully. Later, when weaknesses or problems could be unequivocally pinned down, more latitude could be given to enable intelligent change.

But the fidelity emphasis didn't stop teachers from making surreptitious changes during the early years of implementation. At Tindale, there was fairly widespread collusion:

> You're doing A, I'm doing B, let's not tell anyone. Let's cover up. (English teacher)

At Masepa as well:

> I see teachers using textbooks all the time. Workbooks too. . . . They just don't talk about it much. (First-grade teacher, nonuser of the project)

Some teachers camouflaged the changes they made in the innovation:

> She added that if the English department chair happened to walk into her classroom . . . she was always prepared to shift back to what's in the curriculum and can "sing and dance" if necessary. (Tindale site report)

Others dug in their heels:

> In this program, you're like a robot. But I learned that, if I wanted to change something, I would just go ahead and do it. After a while, I saw that a lot of it was hogwash. I learned to cut corners and do it just as well. (Sixth-grade teacher at Masepa)

Finally, at Astoria, there was a slightly convoluted pattern of administrative latitude. The central office administrator demanded, but did not monitor, orthodox program execution. The vice-principal who was responsible for the classrooms involved not only authorized but actually designed the far-reaching modifications that made it possible to use the program locally. There is some (though weak) evidence that the two administrators agreed tacitly on this procedure.

We have been presenting "latitude" for most of our sites as a bargain struck explicitly or implicitly to avoid jeopardizing adoption and implementation. There is another plausible hypothesis: Perhaps administrators allowed users to modify the project characteristics as a sort of palliative after having constrained them to adopt the project. Recall earlier (p. 48) that pressure was the chief motive for adoption for about half the users. If this hypothesis is valid, we should find a strong relationship between latitude and levels of pressure to adopt. Figure 6 plots that relationship. We have three clusters: low latitude/ high pressure (Masepa, Tindale, Calston, and possibly Dun Hollow); high latitude/high pressure (Astoria and Banestown); and high latitude/low pressure (the projects in the lower right quadrant). For the high-pressure sites, latitude increases over time when initial latitude is low (note arrows).

Our hypothesis at first glance does not pan out; only Astoria and, to a lesser extent, Banestown had pressure to adopt associated with latitude to change. When we look more closely into these two cases, only at Astoria was there an explicit "payoff" of the kind we were hypothesizing. In fact, the overall plot seems to say that, at least initially, high-pressure sites allowed *little* latitude and low-pressure sites allowed a *lot* of latitude.

But there are lighter-handed or more liberal forms of pressure. At Astoria, the administrators (in this instance, the vice-principal) were saying something like this to users: "You have to do it, but first you can change it substantially." At 6 of the remaining 11 sites, the message (usually from administrators to teachers) was something like this:

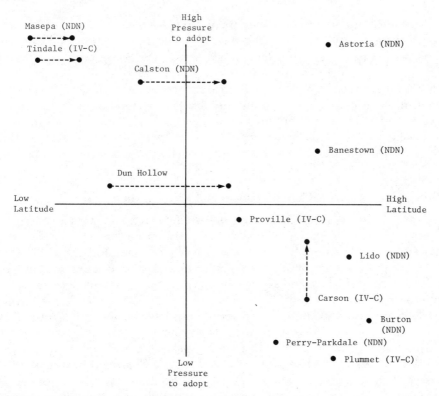

FIGURE 6. Relationship of pressure to adopt and degree of latitude given to users at 12 sites. Arrows signify evolution during later program implementation. (From Miles & Huberman, 1984. Reprinted by permission.)

> I'd like you to do this, at least on a trial basis. You can pick and choose or reconfigure it
> whenever you find it necessary. (Banestown, Burton, and Lido)

Or this:

> You're going to do this. Start out doing it like the developer wants it done. Later, you
> can make changes. (Dun Hollow, Calston, Masepa, and Tindale)

What about the other four sites? Three had the convictions of a minor crusade. The administrators were saying to the teachers something like this:

> Let's dive into this together and de-bug it as we go. (Carson, Perry-Parkdale, and
> Plummet)

Finally, at Proville, there was a message from the central office to principals like this:

> We want to try this and we want at least token collaboration from you.

So there is some support, though it appears in a nonblatant, smoothed-down form, for our guess that administrative latitude was in part the *quid* for the *quo* of the adoption decisions made and handed down from administrators to users.

Now let's return to the last column of Table 31. *Scale and scope of the innovation* affected the extent of local changes in the program but seldom stood alone as a strong predictor. For example, at Astoria, it was the *combination* of large scale, poor organizational fit, extent of building- and classroom-level change, and high administrative latitude that led to program modifications. Large-scale, organizationally demanding projects with less than adequate readiness brought on substantial change in the innovation (Carson and Plummet). Conversely, the smallest scale, relatively undemanding classroom-level project (Dun Hollow) changed little because there was effectively very little to change.

A General Model and Four Scripts

This succession of tables and charts has allowed us to tease out microlevel contrasts and clusters as we moved successively across the eight predictors of change in the innovation. We now piece these fragments together.

Figure 7 is an attempt at an integrated explanation. It looks at first like a forbidding maze of boxes and arrows, but it turns out to be simple enough if we read progressively across it. The *column headings* across the top take us through the adoption process (Column 1) to early, then later, program execution. The *second column heading* corresponds to the point of initial change—before implementation is under way. Then, with *Column 3*, early implementation, we see the next wave of changes. If we look down Column 3, there are four patterns of early implementation. At this point begin the four scenarios, labeled A through D. Each is shown separately as a horizontal progression ending at a common (modal) outcome for the 12 sites. Before we walk through the model, here are the four scenarios and the sites involved.

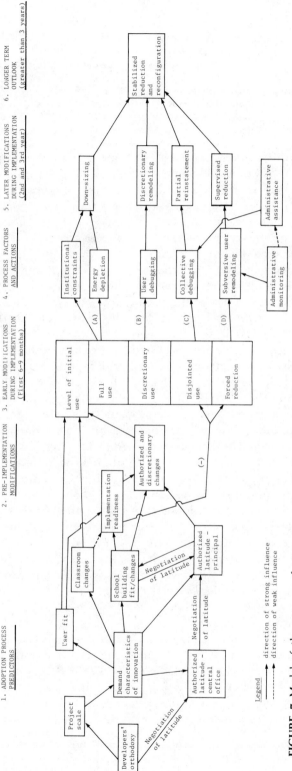

FIGURE 7. Model of the process of innovation change. Legend of scenarios: (A) Overreaching—Carson, Perry-Parkdale, Plummet; (B) Locally refitting—Burton, Calston, Dun Hollow, Lido; (C) Salvaging—Banestown, Proville; (D) Enforcing—Masepa, Tindale.

Scenario	*Progression of innovation changes*	*Sites*
A. Overreaching	Low → moderate-high	Carson (IV-C), Perry-Parkdale (NDN), Plummet (IV-C)
B. Locally refitting	High throughout[4]	Burton (NDN), Calston (NDN)
	Low → moderate	Dun Hollow (IV-C), Lido (NDN)
C. Salvaging	High → moderate	Banestown (NDN), Proville (IV-C)
D. Enforcing	Low throughout	Masepa (NDN), Tindale (IV-C)

This grouping is different from earlier ones. It focuses on what people at the sites were *doing* to the innovations, not on the magnitude of the changes made. Note also that a site is missing. Astoria does not fit conveniently into any family. Its script might best be called *surreptitious reconfiguring,* virtually all of it done at the preimplementation stage.

To run through the schema, we start at the *adoption process.* The path leading across the bottom set of boxes in Column 1 is, as we saw in Table 31, a decisive one. Some developers insisted on orthodoxy (e.g., Masepa and Tindale), which usually led to a decision in the central office to allow little local latitude. The principals passed on the order to the teachers. There was some allowance for minor changes owing to burdensome demands that could not be met (e.g., eliminating grades) and to an especially poor fit at the building level (e.g., time constraints from other commitments). On the other hand, when the developers negotiated liberally over components that could be locally dropped or altered (e.g., at Burton, Lido, and Perry-Parkdale), there was greater latitude given first by the central office, then by building administrators. In this second type of situation, the innovations were molded—usually by reducing their scope—to fit local characteristics. Perceived demands, teacher preferences, and complications at the classroom and building levels all led to a scaling down of the project. Sometimes, administrators and teachers negotiated the amounts and types of authorized changes (e.g., at Banestown and Calston); sometimes, the teachers got outright discretionary authorization to make changes (e.g., at Burton and Dun Hollow). If the classroom fit was poor and/or the teachers felt unready, they began to implement selectively the components that they liked, felt on top of, and could integrate into their standard repertoires. In a few cases, there was virtually no discernible negotiation phase (e.g., at Carson, Plummet, and Proville—all IV-C sites), and there was something of a rush into full program execution, which, when readiness was low, got the project into difficulty (Plummet and Proville) or which, even when readiness was stronger (Carson), slowed implementation somewhat.

As the schema in Figure 7 shows, changes in the innovation could come at two points, either *prior to execution* (Column 2: the arrows leading to authorized and discretionary change) or *during early implementation* (Column 3: the arrows leading from the predictors directly to levels of initial use). Sometimes, there were changes at both points, especially when administrative latitude was high. At Calston, for instance, there was first a cascade of negotiations between the

[4]Remember that this rating indicates that a high rate of initial changes was *maintained* throughout the period we studied.

innovation advocate in the central office and the building principals, then within-building discussions about the time to be given to the program relative to other commitments. When execution began, the project was both overly time-consuming and lacking in some core materials, so the teachers rapidly trimmed and reconfigured it.

The first segment of the Figure 7 schema (Column 1), leading to preimplementation changes, provides a general map of the predictors, their interrelationships, and their interaction with the sequence of local decision-making. The remainder (the scenarios in Columns 3-6) is more project-sensitive.

Scenario A: The "Overreachers"

To begin with the first family of sites, the flow of events can be summarized this way: The project was organizationally ambitious and entailed the creation of a new institutional subsystem and/or comprehensive role changes. The break with conventional schoolwide procedures (Carson) and norms (Perry-Parkdale) was substantial; in one case (Plummet), there was an entirely new institution. In short, the projects were demanding. Levels of readiness were partially to minimally adequate. The projects began full bore (few changes in the design) with a committed staff and strong administrator-teacher collaboration. There were shades of a crusade, with ambitious objectives for pupils (both cognitive and socioemotional) and interpersonally close teacher–pupil relationships.

During later implementation, the "overreaching" projects began to confront the problems resulting from their poor fit with organizational norms and procedures. At Perry-Parkdale, for example, the pressures for controlling and monitoring pupils began to set limits on nonacademic activities and on the amounts of responsibility given to pupils. And at Carson, the investment needed to maintain alternative modes of counseling, planning, and record-keeping was heavy. There were also shifts in pupil population, bringing more difficult or less enterprising students into the program. Energy and enthusiasm began to ebb, leading to pressures to simplify and lighten the procedures. These changes brought on a more consequential wave of changes in the innovation, involving more mechanization and structure that streamlined procedures and lowered personal involvement. The projects were "downsized," not so much in scope or size, but in the level of ambition and staff involvement. The changes were then stabilized; the innovation became more firmly institutionalized but paid a price. To some degree, the "soul" had gone out of the project in the process.

Scenario B: "Locally Refitting"

These projects shared several antecedent characteristics. Some began with poor user fit (Burton and Dun Hollow) or a moderate-to-large degree of implied classroom change (Calston and Lido). These were important features because the innovation itself was small-scale and run entirely at the classroom level.

The program was dropped into the classroom ·or added to an existing curriculum. Moreover, the teachers had been told explicitly, or had been led to believe, that they could make discretionary changes to facilitate their task and to give the project a good chance of success. The changes involved (1) picking and choosing promising segments of the program (Burton and Lido) or (2) trying out as much of the program as possible, then shedding parts that correlated poorly with the standard curriculum (Calston and Dun Hollow). In the latter case, building administrators leaned on users more heavily during the adoption phase. In the former case, users were in the driver's seat from the start.

The chronicle of program execution for "local refitters" was uneventful, compared to that for the overreachers. As discretionary use had been authorized, only parts of the new practice got into the classroom. At Dun Hollow and Lido, the developer's format was followed fairly closely, then subjected to more changes as the materials did not work, took too much time, or needed resequencing or shoring up. This was more the case at Dun Hollow, where teachers complained of a poor product from the start. At Lido, changes came later, partly as a result of organizational shifts at the high school that cut back on the more innovative features of the program. Similarly, teachers at Calston and Burton engaged in progressive debugging to get a good classroom fit. At all four sites, administrators looked on from afar, making few attempts to change the course of local modifications. As a result, users made idiosyncratic changes and the program began to look different in different classrooms. At the end of this process of discretionary remodeling, classroom use stabilized with moderate-to-high levels of change in the innovation.

Scenario C: "Salvaging"

The two projects in this scenario led more adventurous lives. Prior to program execution, they shared four features. First, both faced moderate demands. At Banestown, there were logistical problems around scheduling remedial lab sessions for eight classrooms. But the interpersonal and normative demands were more severe: sharing pupils and coordinating pupil work in a highly individualistic school, assuming that low-performing pupils could attain grade-level achievement, and creating an oasis that pupils would not like to leave. At Proville, there were primarily logistical problems: scheduling, transportation, and coordination of school–workplace activities. As a result, both innovations called for moderate organizational changes. Third, wide latitude was given to users by administrators. At both sites, central office administrators were active advocates of the project, which they sold to the local schools and executed as rapidly as possible. Too rapidly. At Banestown, users had strong personal commitment and administrative support but began with inadequate training, materials, skills, planning, and provisions for debugging. At Proville, the project was hastily thrown together by a newly appointed program director in a bare-bones version of the original design.

The arrow on Figure 7 from "implementation readiness" to "disjointed use" tries to chart this progression. At both sites, users tried to do as much of the project as they understood or had mastered, but this amounted to proportionately little. Lab teachers at Banestown spent the first four months, as one said, "just hanging in, trying to survive until June so we could work on it over the summer." We estimated that there were 7 of the 10 key components[5] missing or unacceptably used at Proville. Banestown was delinquent in 8 of its 11 core components.

The rest of the story is mapped on the schema. Administrators got more active and worked more closely with users to salvage the project. Some of the original design features were reinstated: Training, monitoring, and matching pupils to internships were handled more thoroughly at Proville; testing, record keeping, and coordination with classroom teachers were put in place at Banestown. But the settled-down version of both projects stayed a highly truncated version of the developer's model.

Scenario D: "Enforcing"

In the last two projects, orthodox versions of the practice were all but rammed into execution despite the complaints of poor fit and likely classroom turbulence on the part of high school English teachers at Tindale and primary-level staff at Masepa. Classroom-level changes were many and mountainous at Masepa, and the organizational demands were stiff: changes in scheduling, grading, pupil assignment, and instructional materials in all areas of language arts. The demands were less severe at Tindale, but there, team teaching was a stress for those used to self-contained classrooms.

The teachers at both sites felt unprepared, although many of the needed components were in place. The training was seen as inadequate, understanding was foggy, and the materials were either absent (Masepa) or too voluminous (Tindale). As a result, initial implementation fell somewhat short of the ideal. Components were cut short or cut out. Users were unable to do it all and, in some cases, didn't like doing any of it. Administrators monitored closely, trying to keep modifications to a minimum. By the second year, the teachers had achieved a tolerable level of instructional mastery but were now leaving out small segments that they found superfluous, offensive, boring, or ill designed. By the end of the second year at both sites, there was an informal assessment of the demerits of the program, followed by an implicit agreement that a few parts could be replaced by previous units or activities that teachers believed to be sounder. Surveillance continued, and mechanisms were put in place for periodic in-service training and for the development of materials. The final version was somewhat less than orthodox, but the developers kept it nearly standard, both by enforcing faithful execution and by introducing additional practices and instructional materials in succeeding years.

So there were at least four main roads to the stabilized use of innovations in our sample. All involved some reduction in original hopes; all involved reconfiguration as the innovation encountered users in their organizational context.

---

[5]This total includes additional key components identified by the researcher. If only the developer's list is used, four of seven components are unacceptable or missing.

Conclusions

As predicted, there were numerous changes in the 12 innovations during the course of implementation. Over half the sites changed from one-third to two-thirds of the core components, by reducing them, adding to them, or reconfiguring them with other parts of the users' repertoires. Longer projects showed more changes. The pattern at the NDN sites was one of early and fairly heavy reductions made before or during initial implementation. Changes at the IV-C sites were more irregular and tended to come later, but the overall magnitude of change was similar to that at the NDN sites.

In justifying the modifications made locally, users gave these explanations: reductions due to lack of time to do the whole project; deletion of boring, inappropriate, personally uncongenial, or overtaxing parts; and addition of "needed," strong, or enjoyable units.

Casting a wide net for the best predictors of degree of change made in the innovation, we isolated eight. Poor *user fit* was associated with minor changes. When there was high *anticipated classroom change*, people at the field sites tended to make significant changes in the innovation, often in the direction of paring it down to a less discrepant version. The same thing appeared to happen in case of high *anticipated organizational change* and poor-to-fair *organizational fit*. The gist here is that when working arrangements and regulations could not accommodate to the innovation, the innovation (at all but two sites) tended to be changed to fit. Organizationally speaking, two-thirds of the projects made moderate to strong *demands,* many of which were not visible at the outset. The organizational response to these demands sometimes, but not always, took the form of refashioning the innovation in order to weaken the demands.

Relating *implementation readiness* to magnitude of change showed that ill-prepared projects made significant and early changes. Also, in some cases, *largeness or smallness of innovation scale* went along with magnitude of change, with large-scale ventures making greater changes. Finally, *administrative latitude* proved a powerful predictor. When site personnel got greater license to make changes, they did just that, usually in the direction of watering down the more demanding—and potentially change-inducing—aspects of the project.[6] Sometimes, administrators and teachers negotiated amounts and types of authorized changes; sometimes, teachers got outright discretionary authorization.

We found four different scenarios for latitude giving and innovation change across our sites. One was inverse to the more typical high-latitude scenarios; we could call it *enforcing.* At two sites, administrators permitted few changes, supervising users closely and thereby delivering highly faithful, change-producing innovations in the face of initial discontent and passive resistance. The three other scenarios were *overreaching* (initially faithful, then

---

[6]Louis *et al.* (1981), working from a roughly similar data base, had findings that concur with both the substance and the implications here. In their study, greater adaptation of the original projects was negatively related to outcome levels; reducing the program scope, more particularly, led to reduced effects. In contrast to the Rand study (Berman & McLaughlin, 1974–1978), which has largely shaped policy thinking in the years since its publication, Louis *et al.* and we would caution against seeing "adaptiveness" as necessarily a positive feature of the innovation process.

highly cut-back implementation as local staff wore itself out); *locally refitting* (smaller scale innovations with wide latitude given users to make changes); and *salvaging* (ambitious, ill-prepared and roughly starting projects that were initially cut back, then progressively reinstated).

What sorts of transformations occurred in *users* during the implementation process? We turn next to this question.

CHANGES IN USERS' PERCEPTIONS AND PRACTICES DURING IMPLEMENTATION

Introduction

In our previous sections on early and later implementation, we reviewed in some depth how users learned and changed. Here, we work at a more general level, seeking answers to four questions:

1. In sum, *what kinds* of practice and perceptual changes took place in the course of carrying out an innovation?
2. *How much* change in the users occurred? What were the differences between the high- and low-changing sites?
3. *Why* did practice change occur? What were the chief predictors?
4. Was there a *progression* in the change process? Did some shifts in practice and attitude come before others?

Types of Reported Change

As we have seen, some innovations were giants and other midgets in terms of the changes they called forth. We had sites at which people spoke of being "transformed" and others where informants had to think long and hard to find something they were doing differently as a result of the new practice. Sites in the latter category had either substantially scaled down the innovation (for example, Burton) or discontinued it (Dun Hollow and Proville). Eventually, however, all informants at all 12 sites reported some personal changes arising in the course of project execution. Table 32 lists them, assigns them to one of several categories, and shows the number of sites at which at least one informant mentioned the item. Only the items mentioned at more than one site are shown.

Overview

Taken as a whole, the table yields a good vision of what users saw these innovations as accomplishing for them. There are some fairly distinct *leitmotivs*. Let's look first toward the pupils. The categories and items point to successful attempts to individualize and differentiate classroom or project activities, with greater latitude given pupils to organize and carry out their own work, and with a premium put on interpersonal closeness and trust. Both emotional and cognitive concerns were present. Second, if we look toward informants, they

TABLE 32. User Change during Implementation: Types and Items[a]

---

1. Changes in everyday classroom practices (Daily organization, routines)
   (5) More individualization, more sustained individual contact
   (4) Pupils more "in charge," self-directed, self-paced
   (3) Working with others, sharing pupils
   (3) Less time for other activities; other subjects driven out
   (2) More accountable to outsiders, more policed
   (2) Less structure, less prearrangement
   (2) More structure; regimentation
   (2) Multiple materials, no longer one text, manual, set of workbooks
   (2) No longer able to monitor whole class
   (2) Changes in scheduling
2. Repertoire expansion
   (3) Ability to individualize, differentiate
   (3) More "meat" in curriculum, more approaches to call on
   (2) Greater skill in diagnostic/testing procedures
3. Relational changes
   (4) Closer to pupils, more concern for pupils
   (2) Closer to other teachers (in team)
   (2) More egalitarian relationships with pupils
4. Better understanding, comprehension, of:
   (5) Actual ability/skill levels of pupils
   (3) Emotional problems of pupils
   (3) How the school system operates, who has power and influence
   (2) Principles and procedures for mastery learning
5. Self-efficacy
   (3) More resourceful, effective
   (3) More self-confident
   (2) Less energy, low investment, burnout
6. Transfer
   (3) More organized in general, better at planning
   (3) Using skills, procedures in other subject matters
7. Changes in attitudes
   (4) Able to trust pupils, less need for control
   (2) Can "share" pupils; don't need own class
8. Changes in professional self-image
   (5) Myself as a teacher

---

[a]Numbers represent number of sites where item was mentioned.

believed that they had become more instructionally skillful, especially in techniques for individualizing work with pupils. The general sense is of users as better *clinicians*: They could diagnose, treat, and plan more effectively. They also had a bigger bag of instructional tricks—new units, new sequences within existing units—some of which were transferable to other subject matters. Finally, innovating seems to have been an *accomplishment*, a means of showing oneself and others that these practices could be mastered, even under difficult conditions, possibly also at the cost of energy depletion. This fresco matches the type of projects that we found ourselves studying in the NDN and Title IV-C programs; they were predominantly *remedial* projects, with a pupil public that was variously underachieving, disaffected, deviant, and, as a result, *difficult* to handle and slow to change. So when changes *were* observed, they became a source of strong professional pride.

Now to survey the several categories of user change reported in the course of project execution:

1. *Changes in everyday classroom practices.* We saw earlier that new practices make *demands* on classrooms and schools, many of which surface gradually, such as changes in norms or institutional climate. Generally speaking, the users are aware at first of the changes in their everyday organization and routines. If we look at Table 32, some of these demands may appear to be trivial (using multiple materials) and others momentous (pupil self-direction), but appearances can be misleading. Working with multiple materials, for example, often meant jettisoning the teacher's manual, workbooks, and worksheets—leaving the user, as one put it, "all naked."

The changes were of several types: less group instruction, changes in monitoring and scheduling, a different mix of material covered, and a new division of labor between teachers. A salient theme, as mentioned above, was the shift from group- to individual-centered instruction. Many of these programs turned around mastery learning, diagnosis–treatment procedures, counseling, programmed instruction, and other modes of differentiated classroom work or field experience. Functioning in these new modes had multiple effects. A teacher at the Calston site reviewed some of them:

> I was able to get closer to the children. I was actually working with them. I wasn't just reading with a group and pulling out information from students one at a time. Also, I was no longer simply giving students assignments and sending them off to do some work. The individualization of the program has forced me to see what each child is doing specifically.

There were several consequences of decentralizing school or classroom life, many of them appearing in Table 32. For example, the pupils were more in charge of their own instructional pace and sequencing, which made them harder to monitor. Many teachers were uncomfortable with this, at least initially, saying "I don't really know what they can and can't do" (Masepa), or "Maybe they know what they're doing, but it doesn't feel right" (Calston). Also, self-pacing meant that pupils were making more, and more varied, demands on teachers—asking for new assignments, demanding corrections so they could move on to the next module, asking for reviews of difficult segments—that had previously been handled collectively, and at a time determined by the teacher. Many users came up with revealing images when talking about these changes— "like a treadmill," "can't get my wind," "relentless"—that suggested greater wear and tear and probably contributed to the later "routinization" and "streamlining" of these innovations that we reviewed in the previous section.

A related item: Doing the innovation sometimes meant doing *less* of another core activity, with no easy way of resolving the dilemma. At three sites (Calston, Masepa, and Dun Hollow), this was a major issue; "dropping in" or "adding on" a unit amounted to driving out another, and administrators wanted *both* in. Here was another decision point at which innovations were often truncated. And the process could sometimes be insidious:

> I used to do a lot more group work with conferences, games, and debates. Strange, I've forgotten I did all that. When I think about it now, I really miss it. (Teacher at Masepa)

Two other items on the list deserve a short comment. Some of the projects (e.g., at Tindale, Perry-Parkdale, and Plummet) involved teamwork, with new, sometimes threatening consequences: sharing pupils and being "onstage" in front of other teachers, while teaching and coordinating. Coordinating and being visible also made users more accountable to others, including both administrators and pupils:

> Most teachers wouldn't want it. Your neck is on the block. The successes and failures of the students rebound directly on you. You can't hide in the classroom. (Staff member at Perry-Parkdale)

2. *Repertoire expansion.* Changes in daily practice brought with them new skills and routines. As Table 32 shows, having to individualize led to greater skills in diagnosing and differentially instructing. Also, if the add-on and drop-in units drove out other segments, they also added to the instructional resource bank that users could draw from. As we saw earlier (see pp. 49 ff.), gaining access to new skills was one of the prime motives of users in deciding whether or not to volunteer for a new program. Innovating (with the attendant front-end training, the injection of new materials, and help in moving from collective to individualized classroom management) was an attractive way of expanding one's repertoire without having to go it alone, spend money, or cut into vacation time.

3. *Relational changes.* As the teacher at Calston noted, individualizing entailed closer contact with pupils. Users spoke of "knowing" their pupils better and, in some instances, of caring more about them. In terms of instructional treatment and subsequent pupil performance, this is a powerful formula: more individual work, tighter relational bonds, and tailored remedial materials. Relational changes were often noted in interviews:

> There's really more one-to-one contact. When you're conferencing, you're really *with* that child and he knows it. . . . You really get to develop warmer feelings with that child, and he really gets to show you that he's got that mastery level, and that makes him feel really good. (Teacher at Masepa)

Similarly, a teacher at Carson noticed that she had become "more sensitive to kids, more aware of them individually, more aware of how I affect them." She was doing "more mothering," just as the men at Perry-Parkdale found themselves doing more fathering. Note, however, that relational shifts could also affect the balance of power in the classroom or lab. At two sites (Perry-Parkdale and Plummet), users spoke of greater egalitarianism—and its limits. There is a nice vignette from Perry-Parkdale: A student complained to a staff member that he could learn just as well by taking various jobs as by doing the career education program. The staff member's response: "The hell with what you want. I'm 32, you're 17."

Finally, relational changes stemming from team teaching or from other forms of interuser collaboration were mentioned explicitly at two sites, Plummet and Tindale. But from an analyst's viewpoint, such outcomes were more widespread across our sites, and were sometimes negative. Some users came to dislike others (for instance, at Banestown and Perry-Parkdale), while at the same time getting closer to *other* colleagues. Cohesion was strong, with positive effects, at Carson, Masepa, and Lido but was not named specifically by informants.

4. *Better understanding and comprehension.* The items listed in this category in Table 32 are fairly straightforward. Installing a mastery learning program brought with it an understanding of its mechanics and assumptions. Doing individualized remedial work, usually connected with some diagnostic testing, gave users a far more precise fix on ability and skill levels than they had customarily had. "It [otherwise] would have taken me six months to see their weaknesses," said a teacher at Astoria, "and I'd have more doubts about how right I was." Note that this item was mentioned at nearly half the sites. A corollary item was the increased understanding of pupils' emotional problems (at Banestown, Carson, and Plummet) and the awareness both *that* and *how* ability and achievement levels are tied up with emotional problems. Some projects (Banestown and Carson) also brought teachers into contact with the dynamics of their pupils' home lives.

A final item is increased knowledge of school- or districtwide politics and economics. Users learned useful lessons from the pressures exerted on them to adapt, from rising and falling budgets, from the second-order effects of apparently innocuous changes in supervision or testing, from interpersonal warfare within the central office, and from the conduct of grantsmanship. It was a glimpse into a theater that many classroom-bound practitioners had never seen. Some—notably users with career shifts in mind—found it a valuable apprenticeship; others were turned off and gradually went sour on ambitious school-improvement efforts.

5. *Self-efficacy.* From both the pupils' and the teachers' vantage points, technical mastery of the program was an important reinforcer. As we saw earlier, the difficulties encountered by users in early implementation gave way progressively to the sense of "being on top of" the project and of "having a good handle on it." New routines emerged, unsteady segments got stabilized, and bugs were eliminated. Users began to play with the project, both in their heads and at school—varying components, trying out a new segment, integrating a piece from another subject matter. As Table 32 shows, the users remarked on their experience of mastery by feeling more resourceful, effective, and self-confident. This reaction was explicit at three sites and implicit at most others. In pooling the comments from site informants, the basic message reads something like this: "I can do it. I can *see* that I can do it, and so can the others. It's been a real challenge." In some cases, however (for example, Carson and Plummet), some users also felt burned out in the process.

6. *Transfer.* This category has two items in Table 32, both relating to what

we call *metaeffects* in our later discussion of program outcomes. First, executing these innovations seemed to help users get their instructional houses in order at three sites—Calston, Masepa and Tindale—all places implementing a structured, scripted program. There was even evidence at Tindale and Masepa that one of the private objectives of local administrators was to improve teachers' daily organization by inserting these projects into the schools. The line of thought went like this: "It'll help them get it together. . . . It's good for disorganized people like Mrs. X" (Masepa). And the gambit seemed to work. Users at Tindale spoke often of being "more organized" since they had begun work with the remedial curriculum. Users at Calston spoke of "having everything ready when you need it." Teachers at Masepa said that they had learned to plan more carefully. In all three cases, these habits carried over into other subject matters, along with some of the core program components (reinforcement, advance organizing, rapid error correction, and individualizing).

7. *Changes in basic attitudes.* The items in this category of Table 32 are interesting. Logically enough, how users felt about their work evolved from their trials and tribulations while doing it. Team teaching brought users at Banestown and Perry-Parkdale beyond the privatism ("my kids") that classroom-bound instruction usually imposes and nurtures. Similarly, individualization and pupil self-pacing or self-management demanded a less centralized, controlling mode of supervision; otherwise, users would have gone crazy monitoring 25 different schedules. So letting go was adaptive, but it wasn't easy. Here are two testimonies:

> I've learned to let go of the child. They play those games with me *and* with others. I've had to accept that . . . I've also had to trust the students more since they are working on their own. (Teacher at Calston)

> I just started into the KARE approach and went from day to day. KARE pointed me in that direction, and gradually I gained a different sense of control at off-campus sites. I was learning how to be flexible. (Teacher at Lido)

Occasionally, these accounts read like a pilgrimage. For example, a user at Perry-Parkdale recounted his experience of "trying to force students to do things," then of "laying back," worrying much of the time about whether his pupils were actually going to their job sites. Previously, he had worked in a classroom setting where everyone could be monitored. In addition, there were strong institutional pressures at these sites to account for pupils' time and performance and to control their behavior during the schoolday, even (or especially) if they were off-campus. Both factors contributed to uneasiness on the part of the project staff at all three sites involving nonclassroom, off-campus programs (Lido, Perry-Parkdale, and Proville). As the Perry-Parkdale staff member summed it up, "It's hard to swallow, not having control of the kids."

8. *Changes in professional self-image.* The logical next step in this progression is a change in users' vision of themselves as teachers. As the excerpts from teachers at Calston and Lido just suggested, some users found their way in the

course of implementation to a self-redefinition as a more "trusting" or less authoritarian practitioner. There were instances of this at these two sites and at Perry-Parkdale.

But there were other scenarios. At Plummet, at least two informants came to the realization that even a highly experimental, alternative high school might be unable to reach adolescents who were turned off or troubled, no matter how strong a teacher's commitment. Perhaps as a consequence, these users began to look elsewhere—possibly for a new role out of education. At Masepa, the script was still different. There, almost *all* informants had defined themselves as spontaneous, casual, or unstructured in their work prior to this program. They now found themselves running highly regimented, closely clocked, faintly military classrooms, with few opportunities for group work or changes of pace. And they were doing well—being amazed both at the performances of pupils and at their own metamorphosis. In a classic instance of dissonance reduction, they began gradually to redefine themselves as "pretty structured," and to transfer some of the same techniques to other segments of their teaching.

Anticipating our later treatment of the process or progression of practice and attitude change, we want to note two things here. First, practice and attitude changes followed logically from the demands of the project. This accounts, for example, for the recurrence of certain themes in the different categories of Table 32. For example, if we take the theme of "letting go," the progression seems to look like this:

Individualization/ → Pupil self-   → Inability to   → Development → Letting → Changed self-
pupil-centered-   pacing   monitor (in   of trust   go   image as
ness   Self-organi-   class, off-   a teacher
                       zation   campus)

Note that in order to simplify the progression, we have left out some steps. For example, pupil-centeredness also leads to relational closeness and to a better grasp of individual ability levels and emotional states. Trust then develops as a result of the bond between staff and pupils: "Trust violation" was a common *leitmotiv* at many sites. There was something like an implicit contract between the parties that pupils going off-campus would not "betray" their teachers in return for pastoral care. The same agreement obtained in classroom-bound projects: the pupils would complete their work and do the requisite exercises or mastery tests in return for individual help with difficult concepts or operations.

The second point follows directly. Trust and letting go are accomplishments; they come *after* cycles of early implementation—often after a few wild, overcompensating swings between blind confidence and total mistrust. They also assume some *evolution* on the part of pupils, who only gradually show themselves to be trustworthy as they, too, contend with the demands of the project and the institutional or personal stresses it exerts. The point is that changes in everyday classroom practices probably precede cognitive and relational changes, which, in turn, build gradually into shifts in attitudes and in the more basic constructs that make up users' operational philosophies.

How Much Change?

As we said in the introduction to this section, some projects transformed users, and others entailed minor tinkering with a curriculum or an instructional skill. Still others were in between. There is, however, still another category: projects that could have resulted in substantial practice and attitude changes but didn't. Typically, these were unsuccessful ventures, and ones that were disliked, either because of their poor design (Dun Hollow) or their purely opportunistic nature (Proville). But *not liking* a project, as was the case at these two sites, was not sufficient to avoid its change-inducing aspects. For instance, several users at Masepa and Tindale complained bitterly of the weaknesses and the arbitrariness of the new curriculum, but they admitted that they had been durably altered by it.

Before making and discussing estimates of the degree of which users' practices and perceptions were changed across the 12 sites, let us look briefly at three exemplars: a high-change site, a low-change site, and an unsuccessful site.

A High-Change Site: Masepa

For all users, the ECRI language-arts project was, as one put it, "the biggest thing I've taken on." The program involved a near-total organization of the classroom, highly scripted instructional sequencing that was hard to put in place, the integration of subject matters that had previously been taught separately, drastic decentralization of pupils' seatwork and evaluation, and abandonment of the customary teaching props: teacher's manual, workbooks, and worksheets. The first-generation users were amazed that they had actually waded in voluntarily; many used images such as "falling down and getting up" or "getting wiped out every day." Here is how it looked to one user:

> Think about how many patterns I've had up to this time. It's real hard for someone like me to catch onto this program, such a big shift. . . . It's a whole new philosophy. like that mastery idea with spelling.

In terms of reported changes in the course of implementation, there are six features that distinguished Masepa from the low-change sites:

1. The project *began with a vengeance.* The initial implementation required a new set of skills and routines that were highly discrepant from users' previous practice.

2. The reported changes were *pervasive.* All users mentioned changes in daily routines and in relations and understanding. At least three or four claimed changes in basic attitudes and constructs. All reported instances of repertoire expansion and transfer to the other subject matters.

3. Users took a *long time to settle down.* The third-year users still felt that they were not in control of the program, in part because new segments were added each year.

4. The project *consumed all available energy.* Users were not experimenting elsewhere and claimed the project was wearing them out.

5. When users talked about changes, a fair number of *negative changes* cropped up: loss of variety, sacrifice of favorite activities, uncertainty about success, and losing touch with certain pupils.

6. Teachers said that they had been *forced* to make as many and as drastic changes as they did. Without administrative pressures, far less of the project would have been executed.

A Low-Change Site: Burton

Recall that this was a drop-in social studies curriculum, from which teachers were allowed to pick selectively. Had the program been executed as designed, there would have been far-reaching changes in everyday classroom practice. To run through the six dimensions used above:

1. Three of the four users *began timidly,* with very modest changes in their habitual classroom routines. The project was substantially downsized prior to initial use.

2. Three of the four users had *trouble identifying any practice changes* during or after a full year of use. One said that he had used so little of the program that there was no possibility of an impact. The salient item was repertoire expansion; all the users felt that they had enriched their social studies curriculum.

3. Users had *little trouble getting on top of the project,* because they were making only minor changes.

4. All the users saw the project as a *small part of their yearly action.* More energy was being channeled elsewhere.

5. All the users *felt positively* about the few changes they had made, but these feelings were limp.

6. *Only one of the four users felt stretched by the experience.* The others had made discretionary changes that had reduced the gap between prior and ongoing practice. Administrators kept their hands off, on the premise that this was a trial year. If we contrasting Masepa with Burton, it looks as if more was changed when more was ventured.

A Negative Experience: Dun Hollow

Recall that this site was the locus of an Eskimo studies project dropped into two primary schools. Teachers complained from the outset that the units were poorly designed and hogged too much of the social studies curriculum. There were features consonant with both big-change and small-change projects, but the unique aspect was the shift from an early experience resembling the big-change innovations to a later configuration more like that at the Burton site:

1. The start-up was fairly *ambitious;* it involved a major reshaping of the social studies curriculum and some time-consuming exercises that the teachers had never tried.

2. The changes were, curiously, at *both* ends of the continuum. There were shifts in daily working arrangements and some strong attitudinal shifts, one of

which had to do with suspicion about any new innovations that might be paraded at the school.

3. It took *half a year* to master the project technically, mainly because of its design features (e.g., activities pegged at a higher cognitive level than pupils could handle).

4. A *lot of energy* was expended at first. The flow ran like this:

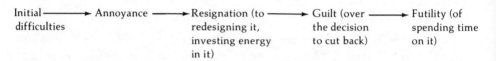

By the end of the year, the energy investment was almost nil.

5. The users had *nothing good* to say about the practice, apart from the validity of the initial concept (sensitivity to and familiarity with Eskimo culture).

6. As in the big-change projects, the users *felt pushed* beyond what they would have voluntarily taken on. But users also had misgivings about starting in with what they saw as a poor-quality project, not about the discrepancy between prior and anticipated experience.

By way of pulling together these strands, we summarize in Table 33.

Predictors of Practice Change

Up to now, our analysis has dealt with the features of practice change and with dimensions that distinguished between high-changing, low-changing, and negative experiences. Some of those dimensions look causal; discrepancies between past practice and the proposed new practice, for example, seem, logically enough, to have heralded higher magnitudes of practice change. We

TABLE 33. Exemplary Sites Showing Different Degrees of User Change

	High change	Low change	Negative change
1. Start-up discrepancy from usual practice	High discrepancy	Low discrepancy	Moderate discrepancy
2. Pervasiveness of change	High—all facets	Low—repertoire only	Low–moderate—routines and attitudes
3. Technical mastery	Slow in coming	Rapid	Slow, then rapid
4. Energy investment	Very high	Low	High, then low
5. Negative changes reported	Some	None	Many
6. Stretched—pushed beyond voluntary change	Yes—well beyond	No	Yes—at the start

Note. From Miles & Huberman (1984). Reprinted by permission.

TABLE 34. Reported Changes in User Practice and Perception

	Dimensions of change arising from implementation[a]						
Sites	Daily routines	Reper-toire	Relation-ships	Under-standings	Self-efficacy	Transfer	Basic con-structs, attitudes
Masepa (NDN)	X	X	X	X	X	X	X
Plummet (IV-C)	X	X	X	X	(X)	N/A	X
Banestown (NDN)	X	X	X	X	X	(X)	
Tindale (IV-C)	X	X		X	X	X	
Carson (IV-C)	X	(X)	X	X	X	N/A	
Perry-Parkdale (NDN)	X	(X)	X	(X)	(X)	N/A	(X)
Calston (NDN)	X	X	(X)	(X)	(X)		(X)
Lido (NDN)	X	X		(X)			(X)
Astoria (NDN)	X	X	(X)	X			
Burton (NDN)		X					
Dun Hollow (IV-C)	X-0	X-0					(X)
Proville (IV-C)	X-0				N/A	N/A	

Note. From Miles & Huberman (1984). Reprinted by permission.
[a] X = change claimed unambiguously by several informants; (X) = change claimed unambiguously by only one informant; X-0 = initial change, then reversion to initial practice; N/A = not appropriate/applicable; Blank = no unambiguous changes cited.

will try now to order some of these variables and to get a better look at these several influences.

We needed to order the 12 sites by magnitude of practice change. Using the field researchers' site reports, we made the estimate by noting the number of categories in which changes were reported and, within categories, the extent of the claim (e.g., noted by more than one informant). We then tried to separate trivial or short-term changes from more deep-seated or fundamental shifts, such as the transfer of innovation-specific skills to other areas, and shifts in core attitudes or constructs. Table 34 shows these estimates arrayed in the form of a Guttman scale, from which we made the estimates of change in Table 35.

Table 35 arrays the 12 sites by practice change magnitude and displays three kinds of predictors. First, we see three *baseline discrepancy indicators*: the degree of practice change required to implement as planned, the actual size or scope of the project, and the extent of classroom or organizational constraints on carrying out the practice as it looked just before starting in. (These variables were described and rated in the section on early implementation. In our "causal network" analysis [see pp. 189 ff.] we called these variables *implementation requirements*.) We tried a crude test of the predictive power of these indicators by scoring each one (minor/small/poor[7] = 1, moderate = 3, major/large/good[7] = 5), then summing them to make an *early-implementation-requirements* prediction index.

[7] Scoring reversed for classroom/organizational fit.

TABLE 35. Predictors of Magnitude of User Practice Change

Magnitude of change, by sites	Early implementation requirements				General attitude during implementation	Administrative pressure	
	Required practice change[a]	Project size/scope	Classroom/organizational fit	Index of early impl. requirements		Direct: strong-arming	Indirect: exhorting, reinforcing
High change							
Masepa (NDN)	Major	Large	Mod-good	14	Positive	High	High
Plummet (IV-C)	Mod-major	Large	Good-poor	12	Positive	Low	High
Moderate change							
Banestown (NDN)	Major	Small-mod	Moderate	10	Positive	Mod	High
Tindale (IV-C)	Major	Large-mod	Moderate	12	Positive	High	High
Carson (IV-C)	Major	Large	Moderate	13	Positive	Low	High
Perry-Parkdale (NDN)	Mod-major	Mod	Moderate	10	Positive	Low	Low-mod
Moderate-low change							
Calston (NDN)	Moderate	Small	Poor	9	Positive	Mod	Mod
Lido (NDN)	Moderate	Small	Moderate	7	Positive	Low	Mod
Small-no change							
Burton (NDN)	Minor	Small	Good	3	Positive	Low	Mod
Dun Hollow (IV-C)	Minor	Small	Poor	7	Negative	Mod	Low
Proville (IV-C)	Minor	Moderate	Moderate	7	Negative	Mod	Mod
Astoria (NDN)	Minor	Small	Good	3	Positive	Low	Low

Note. From Miles & Huberman (1984). Reprinted by permission.
[a]Discrepancy between users' customary instructional practices and those required to implement the innovation at the time of initial use.
[b]Good in the district, poor for needs of incoming students.

A second predictor was the general majority attitude *toward the innovation* during implementation, and a third was the degree of direct and indirect *administrative pressure* to maintain initial levels of change.

Let us now march deliberately through Table 35.

Magnitude of Actual Practice Change

Although our cutoff points are arbitrary, there is still some variance here, with the central tendency in the moderate-to-low range. Half the projects resulted in moderate-to-high change; the other half had more modest change. With a few exceptions, none of these innovations was revolutionary. On the other hand, we also had few placebos. We can also see that the between-program differences (NDN vs. IV-C) are not tied to magnitude of change.

The *required practice change* was, overall, considerable and did seem to covary with the magnitude of reported change during implementation. In other words, what an analyst might have expected to happen tended to happen, notably at the lower end of the scale. But how does it happen that most of the innovations were unrevolutionary in terms of the magnitude of user change but the degree of implied practice change was fairly high? One answer is that several of these projects (Plummet, Banestown, Perry-Parkdale, and Lido) took the users from their customary surroundings, usually the classroom, and put them in a new environment: an alternative school, a pull-out lab, a separate program, or a field site. This move called for some rapid adjustments, notably in the initial phases (thus, high practice change) but did not necessarily take users beyond changes in daily routines and basic instructional repertoire (thus, lower final magnitude). In fact, it may have been *easier* for users to contend with a new activity in a *new* environment than to have their habitual environment seriously shaken up, as was the case at Masepa, Tindale, and, to a lesser extent, Carson.

Project size or scope seems to predict the magnitude of practice change fairly well: Ambitious ventures and midget ventures mostly turned into large and small changes, respectively, in user practice. But some small ventures resulted in moderate change (e.g., at Calston and Banestown), if only because a modest *institutional* project could still be an ambitious *individual* project for those users most caught up in its implementation. One ambitious undertaking seems to have ended up with only moderate user-practice changes, even when the estimate of initially required practice change was high. This is the Carson case, and it seems, at first glance, anomalous.

Recall that Carson was the site of an ambitious individualized instructional counseling and prescribing project. If done as planned, the program would have markedly modified the teachers' role performance by putting them in a more differentiated, interpersonally closer relationship with their pupils, including contacts with the pupils' home lives. But there was a general drift over time at Carson toward a more streamlined, "routinized" version of the program, which, for some informants, took away its core.

The other deviant case is Proville, where a program of moderate scope resulted in little practice change. By and large, the program there was simply sabotaged by resisting principals and vocational educational teachers and weakly supported by its central-office advocate. In addition, though the program asked for role changes on the part of students and their support-staff mentors, it was progressively watered down.

Classroom and/or organizational fit problems seem to go moderately well with lower degrees of reported practice change in Table 35, suggesting that the constraints involved set a limit on the possibility of making, say, changes in relationships or basic attitudes. For example, Calston was constrained by the presence of an existing reading program, which vied for time and attention with the 4D reading project. Had the users been given their head, it is likely that the project would have brought on farther-reaching shifts in teaching repertoires, transfer to other subject matters, and a full understanding of the mastery learning concept.

But we also see deviant cases here: The user-transforming Plummet site started with many problems of fit (which had to be overcome through the energy of an ideologically committed staff); the IPLE program at Burton was largely a drop-in program, where administrative latitude for using only parts of the innovation was substantial, and the users used (and learned) little. Once again, we see that challenged users may be the highest changers.

Prediction Index

A score summing these three early-implementation-requirement variables does seem to correlate fairly well with the magnitude of practice change during implementation, especially in the lower part of the scale. The middle and upper regions have two slight anomalies. Masepa changed more than would have been predicted, and Carson, as we just saw, less.

General attitudes during use were too lopsided to discriminate between sites, except that users in two of the four nonchanging sites clearly disliked the projects, which (in part as a consequence of poor user support) ended up making few ripples in the stream of classroom life. Had we used a more differentiated scale, the results would have been more conclusive. For example, at the end of both the first and the second years, there was a vocal minority at all the higher-change sites (Masepa, Plummet, Banestown, and Tindale) who had serious misgivings about the project, especially at Masepa and Tindale, where administrators had strong-armed users into continuing. Users were uniformly content at the lower-change sites: Calston, Lido, and Burton. The message here may be that major practice changes are likely to have some kicking and screaming associated with them.

At first, *administrative pressure* does not seem to go coherently with magnitude of practice change. Strong-arming was effective at Masepa and Tindale, but ineffective at Dun Hollow and Proville. Did lack of strong-arming *increase* practice change at Plummet or Carson? It's difficult to know. But if we expand the notion to include *indirect* pressure or, put more generously, to include exhortation (encouragement with the expectation of follow-through on the user's part), things look different. Note that exhorting goes more with higher-changing sites; note also that the additive—or possibly multiplicative—effect of strong-arming plus exhorting is stronger at the higher-changing sites. So, to some extent, administrators seemed to be pushing up increments of users' practice change. When it *all* comes together—major implied practice change, major scope, minor fit problems, overall positive user attitudes, and a carrot-and-stick leadership—we get a Masepa; and when practically all these omens are reversed, we have a Dun Hollow or Proville. In policy terms, the major question here is whether some or most of these variables are *manipulable*, that is, can actually be put into operation in the course of the school improvement process. More on this later.

A Progressive Model

Let us now try, in one picture, to put all these pieces together. We have just seen that implementation requirements can, if imperfectly, predict the magnitude of practice change. Direct and indirect administrative pressure from principals and superintendents seem to contribute as well. Finally, some dimensions of user change seem to come later or to be more difficult to achieve than others, notably transfer of skills to other tasks, and core attitudes about children or one's role as a teacher. If we lay out all these variables over time, as a progression, the resulting network looks like Figure 8.

Conclusions

The implementation of these innovations produced substantial and fairly widespread changes in users' practices and attitudes, although there was variability among the different projects. Some were "teacher-transforming." Others were—or became—very modest efforts with correspondingly modest effects.

Users reported—and the researchers observed—eight types of changes attributable to the effects of the innovation:

1. Changes in users' everyday classroom practice
2. Repertoire expansion (e.g., ability to individualize)
3. Relational changes (e.g., better rapport with pupils)
4. Cognitive growth (e.g., better understanding of pupils' ability levels)
5. Self-efficacy (feeling more resourceful, instructionally effective)
6. Transfer of innovation-derived skills to other parts of one's instructional practice
7. Changes in attitude (e.g., more trusting of pupils)
8. Changes in professional self-image

Across the 12 sites, the drift of these changes was that teachers had become better clinicians, more instructionally skillful, able to better individualize and differentiate instructional treatments, and more interpersonally close to their pupils.

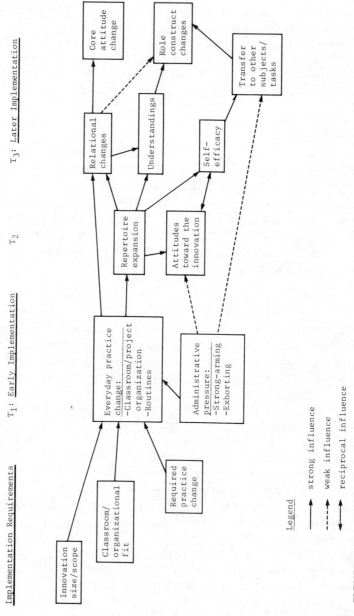

FIGURE 8. Causal flowchart tracing user practice changes. (From Miles & Huberman, 1984. Reprinted by permission.)

These practice and attitude changes followed directly from the demands made by the project; doing one-to-one remedial work, for example, usually led to the development of better diagnostic skills and individualized treatment on the part of teachers.

About half the sites reported moderate to high levels of user practice change stemming from the innovation. At the high-change sites, the projects began with a vengeance, induced pervasive changes (not only in daily routines but also in basic constructs), took a long settling-down time, consumed all available energy, caused negative changes (e.g., loss of variety and sacrifice of other, favorite activities), and did all this through administrative pressure. At the low-change sites, there was the inverse profile: timid beginnings, modest changes in daily routines, rapid practice mastery, minor energy expenditures, and little user sense of having been "stretched."

Several factors were found to predict the magnitude of practice change: *required practice* change, project *size* or scope, classroom and organizational *fit*, and administrative *pressure*. The combination of direct pressure ("strong-arming") and indirect pressure ("exhorting") seemed to deliver higher levels of user practice change in the course of implementation.

We were able to assemble these findings into an inclusive model of user-practice-change predictors and outcomes, with the more immediate outcomes (e.g., attitudes toward the innovation) building up to more consequential ones (e.g., changes in core constructs, transfer).

With this image of *user* change in mind, we now turn to *organizational* change.

TRANSFORMATIONS IN THE SCHOOL AS AN ORGANIZATION

Introduction

We have been examining the degree to which the innovations changed in the process of implementation, as well as the degree to which the innovation's users learned and developed at the same time. The third, associated aspect of changes during implementation involves the school as an organization. Schools are social systems; their constituent classrooms, with their operating practices, rules, and norms, and their working relationships among adults, make up a larger whole that forms a context for any innovative effort. And the local school is, in turn, embedded in the organization of the school district. It is logical to expect that that context itself may become transformed in some way: When innovation meets organization, organization may change along with the innovation and its users.

The programs we are studying, NDN and IV-C, have sometimes been charged with a "technological bias"—with simply encouraging schools to carry out "part innovation," developing or replacing new parts that do not function well in the "machine" called a school. With this bias, one assumes that the "receiving system"—the school—is somehow taken as given and is not itself subject to change and development. But we believe that view is too limited. NDN, in particular, and IV-C, to some extent, are programs that have been interested not just in getting new part-innovations in place, but in developing the capacity of the school for further problem solving, change, and innovation. Some NDN and IV-C innovations are quite substantial; implementing them and getting them into place on a continuing basis could be expected to alter the organization. At a minimum level, the simple addition of the innovation represents an organizational change of some degree. In addition, there may be more comprehensive, "metalevel" changes (for example, a climate more favorable to innovation) or side effects (for example, increased faculty cohesiveness) that constitute additional organizational transformations.

We believed that organizational changes might be visible at three different levels: *structure,* which includes rearrangements of persons, roles, groups, and resources; *procedures,* methods of all sorts for carrying out the work of the school; and *climate,* the attitudes, feelings, and relationships among persons. As we talked with and watched the people at our sites, we were interested in the following aspects of these features:

1. What they looked like, before and during the implementation process
2. How good or poor a "fit" the innovation was with these organizational features
3. What difficulties or problems the innovation posed for the organization
4. What sorts of changes were of a transitory, implementation-specific sort, and what changes were more durable
5. What the net extent or scope of the changes seemed to be
6. Which of the above (or other) factors might explain the amount and type of organizational change noted

Our field notes for each site were used to answer a series of research questions covering these issues.

The Extent of Organizational Change[8]

How typical was the organizational change at our 12 sites? Table 36 provides a summary look. At only two of our sites, Carson and Masepa, could it be said that the innovation was in place on a reasonably full-fledged, wide-scale basis, with accompanying changes in the organization. For five more sites (upper right of Table 36), the innovation was being used thoroughly and extensively (recall that the innovation's use was itself an organizational change), but with few associated organizational changes. For the remaining five sites, there was not strong evidence of full implementation or associated change. On balance, we cannot say that the implementation processes that we were examining had led to much organizational change beyond the specific

[8]Interested readers will find a detailed, site-level analysis, along with methodological indications of cross-site analytic procedures, in the technical report (pp. 279–281).

TABLE 36. Extent of Organizational Change

		Have organizational changes occurred beyond the innovation itself?	
		Yes	Few or none
	Yes	Carson Masepa	Plummet Perry-Parkdale Tindale Banestown Astoria
Is the innovation in place?	Partially, or on limited basis		Calston Lido Burton
	No		Dun Hollow Proville

Note. From Miles & Huberman (1984). Reprinted by permission.

innovations being put into place. Some illustrations from each of these three categories may be useful.

At Masepa, the innovation itself (eventually mandated for *all* teachers) transformed the teachers' prior classroom practice substantially ("On balance, it's a complete change from what I was doing") to an intensive, morning-long, integrated language-arts program covering reading, grammar, spelling, composition, and penmanship, which transformed the student role and the teachers' required responses:

> There's no way not to be ready. The kids are waiting . . . they know exactly what they want to do. They'll ask for assignments. (Teacher at Masepa)

And outside the classroom, the new language-arts program led to substantial organizational changes: integrated scheduling for all Grades 2–6 to permit cross-age grouping; tighter supervision ("On your evaluation form, you get docked if you haven't done everything"); and a good deal of mutual help among teachers:

> Teachers will come up to you at recess time and say, "Hey, I need thus and such." We share.

> We really do discuss things around here. You can get a lot of insight. . . . People talk about what they are doing. (Teachers at Masepa)

In Tindale, a substantial new English course sequence was in place in both district high schools. It was aimed at the needs of low-achieving students and was functioning well. The program required team teaching from teachers who had only been used to self-contained classrooms. That affected relationships:

> The program banded together people who didn't like it. If a team didn't work out, you made enemies. If it did, you made friends and improved relationships within the department. (Teacher at Tindale)

The teachers in the program were also closely monitored and evaluated; little deviation from the curriculum was permitted. Initially, this close supervision led to a good deal of fear and mistrust:

> At in-services, people looked at each other with distrust, but the "big brother" atmosphere kept people from even rolling their eyes at some bit of nonsense going on. (Teacher at Tindale)

But these changes (the fear and lack of trust were transitory, it turned out) did little to influence the Tindale high schools beyond the sheer fact of the program's presence in the organization. The program itself was a quasi subsystem; most of the teachers in the program did not teach other courses.

At Lido, a teacher already engaged in teaching a marine science program was able, with a principal's support, to get materials and funds for a new forestry and ecology course, through adopting an NDN innovation on environmental education. But only parts of the materials were used, and the courses involved shifted in student input:

> The course is all floaters now. It has become a holding bin as far as guidance is concerned because they know Eric and I are worried about discipline. He gets the aggressors . . . I get the burnouts. (Teacher at Lido)

With the departure of the supportive principal and the onset of budget cuts (organizational changes largely independent of the innovation), the users became discouraged about further innovation:

> My horse is tired, my saddle is slipping, and my lance is broken. I've applied for some industry positions, and I know I'm not the only one either. (Teacher at Lido)

There was little evidence that the program—itself only partially implemented—had induced any durable changes in the Lido district organization.

The Content of Organizational Change

If we keep in mind that organizational changes were not substantial at most of our sites, what sorts of changes took place? Table 37 arrays them for inspection. Several things seem evident. First, transitory changes in structure are quite rare, and procedural changes are diverse and scattered. Second, transitory climate changes during the early part of implementation seem to be negative, as might be expected when an imperfectly understood innovation, with its associated structural and procedural changes, encounters the existing order. Third, when we turn to durable changes, we note that the innovation itself is the most frequent form (five sites) of structural change in the organization; at another five sites, no durable organizational changes occurred at all, as we saw in Table 36. We should note in passing that, at four of the five sites where no durable organizational changes occurred, there were also no *structural* changes, even transitory ones, though there were sometimes transitory procedural and climate changes. Evidently, changing organizations means changing their structure. The fifth no-change site (Proville) had only one structural change (a new project director), which proved transitory.

Expansion to new users and scheduling shifts appear at three sites. The remaining changes involve new roles (e.g., helping teacher), new groups (e.g., an advisory committee), and physical space. Fourth, the most frequent durable change in the innovation itself[9] from a structural point of view entails changes in the population of students. We have already illustrated this in the Lido case; it is of more general interest that the other four cases (Perry-Parkdale, Plummet, Tindale, and Banestown) also involved shifts toward the recruitment or selection of lower-ability students. These shifts came in part from the fact that the innovations either were directly aimed at low-ability groups or were explicitly designed as alternatives to the conventional program; several had especially compassionate and supportive staff. On all counts, they tended to become a blend of a dumping ground and an oasis.

In some cases, the shift occurred because of "unrelated" changes, like the power struggle in the Banestown central office, which dictated the shift of the remedial lab's population toward younger students.

A fifth comment on Table 37 is that durable procedural changes were quite diverse. The tendency of the within-innovation changes, as we saw earlier, was clearly toward energy reduction and simplification. That tendency, perhaps, represents the dark side of routinization, appearing as the energy and excitement of the temporary implementation system wears off. Finally, the durable climate changes continue to be cast in good-bad terms, but the balance among them has shifted, so that collaboration, cohesiveness, and support now outweigh discouragement, resentment, and enmity—though the latter climate changes are by no means absent.

We have only two sites where anything like a metalevel, or second-order, shift occurred in attitude toward innovation itself. One was positive:

> At the central office level, the program is seen as a prototype, as a "springboard" for other classroom-based programs in remedial reading using individualized instruction and criterion-referenced testing. (Banestown site report)

This view was in part held from the beginning of implementation at Banestown, but it was certainly deepened by the experience.

At another site, attitudes toward future innovation became more wary:

> If we were to get involved with another program, I'd become more involved so that I could be in a better position to agree or disagree with teachers, or to say to the county office, "It's off. Something's wrong." (Administrator at Dun Hollow)

> It's possible they [the administrators] won't want to take a chance on another program. (Teacher at Dun Hollow)

Such shifts are often assumed to flow from innovative programs: Excitement and benefit supposedly induce favorable attitudes toward school improvement and so on, or poor experiences deepen school people's cynicism and future resistance. It is easy for school improvers to slip into implicit "magnification" of the potential impacts of their work, forgetting that life in schools goes on in its

---

[9] On pages 134–150, we have examined changes in the innovation itself in a good deal of detail. Here, we emphasize primarily those innovation changes that had strong organizational relevance.

TABLE 37. The Content of Organizational Changes[a]

Type of change	Transistory changes		Durable changes	
	Within the innovation	In the organization	Within the innovation	In the organization
Structure	Addition of project director. Evolving departments. Creation and dropping of advisory committee.	Change in locus of control, funding, and supervision.	Shift in student input (5). Reorganization: more department interdependence. Advisory committee. Team teaching.	Innovation itself (5): remedial lab, alt. school–work experience program, English curriculum, accountability system. None (5). Scheduling (4). Expansion of innovation to new users (3). Space for program (2). Creation of coordinator role. Creation of management committee. Creation of in-service committee. Summer-school version of program added. Increased team teaching. Creation of helping teacher role.
Procedures	Active, coercive student recruiting	Innovation lapsed, is discontinued.	Tighter supervision, control (2).	Innovation itself (5): pupil screening, referral/intake, teaming, pullout procedures.

Leadership providing support (emotional, material). Leader "consultation" with teachers. Nonusers help users with testing. Aides, parents help with instruction. Increased community contact.	Field testing of materials. Teachers exchange books. Other instruction displaced.	Student "batching." Routinization of forms/procedures. Charismatic leader more distant. Fewer staff meetings. Reduced student time in program. Staff reassignment. Selective use of materials.	More paperwork (2). Added student transportation (2). Teacher load reduction. Freeing time: substitutes, early dismissal. Dropping letter grades. More coordination among teachers. More teacher discussion of individual students. Specialist consultation for individual students. Loss of teacher control over student assignment.
Climate: Conflict (4): in teams between users, users-aides, departments. More cohesiveness (2), pioneer spirit, esprit. User resentment (2). Less cohesiveness. Tension, fear, mistrust.	User–nonuser conflict (2). User resentment of remedial lab. Ambiguity about management committee. Expectations for more upward influence violated, lower morale. Resistance by principals, then support.	Discouragement, burn-out, loss of interest (3). Collaborative, help-giving climate (2). Cohesivenss (2). Less cohesiveness. Overload. Development of friendships/enmities.	Resentment of paperwork (2). Wariness about innovation. More openness to innovation. Norm change: flexibility, colleagueship, el.-sec. interaction. None: climate still good. None: climate still bad. More administrative awareness of the innovation.

Note. From Miles & Huberman (1984). Reprinted by permission.
[a]Each item represents a change occurring at one site. Changes occurring in more than one site have numbers appended.

intense way, absorbing this or that specific innovative project with minimal disturbance. (Note, for example, that Louis *et al.*, 1981, found that well-run, comprehensive programs for getting schools to utilize new products were successful in doing that but failed to teach the schools to do routinely better problem-solving about the utilization of future products.)

So, although metalevel attitude shifts may have occurred at our sites, they were only rarely noted in our site reports. Other sorts of organizational changes were occurring that might represent "capacity" increases: new roles, new groups, more student-focused procedures, and supportive climate shifts. But we should remember that, by and large, such changes were limited to 6 of our 12 sites and were prominent at only 2.

What May Be Causing Organizational Change?

We wished to understand what might be causing—and blocking—organizational change at our 12 sites. To do this, we examined data for each site on a series of potentially explanatory factors that appeared in two general domains: the preexisting contextual features of the schools and their districts and features of the implementation process itself.

Contextual Features

Here we examined 11 factors,[10] as follows:

1. Environmental pressure: the degree to which local communities or state agencies were exerting influence relevant to the innovation
2. Demographic changes: shifts in community population and/or student input
3. Needy student population: presence of students with unsolved needs for which the innovation was a potential solution
4. Innovative history: whether district- and building-level actions in the past had been generally favorable or not to school-improving change efforts
5. Superintendent orientation: general operating style, level of activity, and endorsement of the innovation
6. Board attitude: whether the board was traditional or progressive, whether it was supportive of administrative initiatives or not
7. Fund-seeking history: the district's past success in attracting outside funds
8. Salience of program funds: how important or central the innovation-associated funds appeared to be in the case of this innovation; size of funding
9. Motivation for adoption: whether the innovation was chosen for opportunistic or problem-solving reasons
10. Central office advocates: whether district office persons existed who supported the innovation energetically

[10]For a comparative site-level display of these data, see the technical report (p. 289).

11. Climate of school: whether building-level norms favored collaboration and support, or isolation and low interdependence

These factors were chosen in the first instance through an inductive examination of the arrayed data for our 12 sites. But it is no accident that a number of them also appeared in the larger study and/or in prior research (for example, the opportunistic/problem-solving dimension was noted by Berman & McLaughlin, 1975, Vol. 3). The reader will also note that several of the factors are not purely "contextual" but reflect the interaction of the local context with the prospective innovation: This is true of Factors 1, 3, 8, 9, and 10. This interaction is not surprising; as Downs and Mohr (1976) have pointed out, the proper unit of study in an inquiry like ours is not the local setting or the innovation considered separately, but the innovation–organization pair.

Now, let us review the several contextual factors to see which conclusions are possible about the effects of context:

1. *Environmental pressure.* There were only five sites where environmental pressure was reported to be a salient contextual feature; they were somewhat more likely to be sites that experienced organizational change to some degree. At Carson, the influx of professionals into the rural community brought increased expectations for the schools, even pressure for reform. At Plummet, the forces were even more powerful: loss of state revenue because of dropouts; overload on the city's juvenile justice system; and the presence of strong community advocates for an alternative facility for "hard-core" students. At Banestown, the forces were more distal, coming from the state department of education's accountability pressure, which meant more monitoring of the schools and an accelerated search for new programs. Perry-Parkdale was required by the state department of education to develop an approved career-education program, but that pressure did not seem acute. The external pressures on Proville, though local, were not acute either; the recession was reducing the number of jobs outside the district available for students, and the high-technology employment environment led to a shortage of cheap labor for within-district jobs, which the proposed program could readily fill with students.

On balance, we might conclude that environmental pressure for change may have had a part in predisposing the districts toward innovations that would eventually lead to organizational change, but the case is not very compelling.

2. *Demographic changes* and 3. *Needy student population.* We can profitably discuss these two predictors together. They are, in effect, another form of environmental pressure, showing up in student inputs. Generally speaking, it appears that if a district was experiencing demographic shifts and/or had a specified, needy student subpopulation for which the innovation might be appropriate, organizational change was more likely. (Five of the seven organizationally changing sites had these properties, and only one of the low-changing sites had them. In fact, note that Calston, of the no-change sites, was implementing more of the innovation than the others.) The sheer presence of poorly achieving (Title I or

other) student populations was important at Masepa, Tindale, Banestown, Plummet, and perhaps at Calston (though the population there was gently characterized as "mixed"). Perhaps all this is obvious: Schools are "supposed" to be for students. But much slippage is possible between the presence of a needy student population and the installation of a change that represents some actual organizational change (let alone an impact on the students). We need to keep examining other predictors.

4. *Innovative history.* Here, we relied on interview data and the results of the Building Work Climate questionnaire in the general survey. A look at the site-level data suggests that innovative history is not a very strong predictor of organizational change: It is perhaps a necessary but not a sufficient condition. Although both of our sites (Carson and Masepa) with clear organizational change had moderate to high levels of recent innovation adoption and two of the modestly changing sites (Plummet and Perry-Parkdale) had a similar history, the picture from there on was mixed.

Three of the five modestly changing sites (Tindale, Banestown, and Astoria) had low innovative histories, both at the district and the building level. But at sites with limited innovation use and no organizational change, the picture does not support the idea that district and school innovative history will predict organizational change.

Perhaps more economically, all of the modestly changing programs except for Proville were "drop-in" ones with minimal organizational demands. It may be that programs of this sort induce little organizational change regardless, and past innovative history is simply irrelevant. Conversely, programs that are potentially organization-changing (subsystems or districtwide programs, as at Carson, Masepa, Plummet, and Perry-Parkdale) seem to require at least a moderate innovation history. Only Tindale was an exception.

5. *Superintendent orientation* and 6. *Board attitude.* Here too it seems sensible to discuss together the stances of those in the upper regions of the systems we were studying.

Once again, except for our changeful sites, Carson and Masepa, the picture is one of only moderate support for these items as predictors. At those sites, reformist, vigorous superintendents (or surrogates, as at Masepa) and a supportive, progressive board were at work. With less certainty, the modestly changing sites seemed to have superintendents whose style was not mentioned in the site report, but whose endorsement of the innovation was positive, along with (at Plummet, Perry-Parkdale, and Tindale) a reasonably supportive board (*supportive* meaning willingness to endorse administrative positions and policies). At the no-change sites, we note for Lido, Dun Hollow, and Proville that there was either a nonendorsing superintendent, a traditional or nonsupportive board, or both. Burton was a deviant case: The superintendent was active, change-oriented, and even Machiavellian (he introduced changes ranging from a management-by-objectives program to mandatory homework to a rotation of administrators into new positions, saying "Our greatest enemy is social inertia"), and the board was supportive and progressive. Here, too, we might speculate that because the innovation involved was small-scale (drop-in) in intent, larger contextual features of the superintendent's and the board's style did not matter as far as organizational change was concerned.

7. *External fund-seeking history;* 8. *Salience of program funds;* and 9. *Motivation for adoption.* To what extent did the districts' past track records in obtaining external funds (outside their local communities) result in more eventual organizational change? How salient was the existence of external funds? And did opportunistic (as opposed to problem-solving) motivation for proceeding with the project predict eventual organizational change?

Fund-seeking history as such seemed to show little pattern: Aggressive fund-seekers and those with suspicion of or a disinclination to attract external funding were found in all organizational change categories. Our sites ranged widely on this dimension.

Perhaps the issue is more whether external funds were *salient* or not in the decision to proceed. If we combine this factor with the next one, *motivation for adoption,* some regularities appear.[11] It is quite apparent, to begin with, that the high-changing sites were those where external funds were not especially salient, and the problem-solving motivation was strong; at Carson, there was interest, even passion, directed toward the innovation *before* funds were actively sought.

We can also see at the five modestly changing sites that problem solving was largely typical; even at opportunistic Perry-Parkdale, the need to develop a "capstone" for the existing career-education program was strong. And we can see that for those sites with more organizational change, the salience of funds (and their dollar amount) was larger. (Once again, we have to invoke the idea of the scale or scope of what was being attempted: The Plummet alternative school, the Perry-Parkdale EBCE program, and the Tindale curriculum for low-achieving adolescents were just *bigger* than the Banestown remedial lab or the Astoria readiness-assessment program.)

At the non-organizationally-changing sites, we note more opportunism and/or funds salience (even though, except for Proville, the scale of the innovations and the size of funding were small). The Proville brand of opportunism was perhaps the most extreme of any we encountered:

> Those who aspire to administrative ranks were commonly referred to as the "fair-haired boys." Typically, one is "brought into" the district office by a "friend" . . . "getting along" and "showing a 1000% loyalty" appear more salient than organizational effectiveness.
>
> Tweed [the superintendent] is referred to as the "godfather." . . . He was said to display a passion for soft money positions . . . so as to more easily move people in and

---

[11]We should note that deciding whether an adoption is "problem solving" or "opportunistic" is not the simplest of tasks. We settled for a "problem-solving" orientation when it appeared that the potential adopters really did have a problem in mind that was connected with the essence of the innovation (for example, Calston's severe reading problems and the properties of the Matteson 4D reading program), and for an "opportunistic" one when other, often equally urgent, issues were at stake (for example, the Dun Hollow superintendent's need to stay on the good side of the intermediate unit that had developed the innovation, or the Proville superintendent's wish to promote a loyal supporter into the central-office administrative ranks using the vehicle of district *and* external funds).

177

ple are described in terms of their relationship to Tweed: One is or is nan." (Site report)

trators bragged that their success rate for getting state IV-C , the best in the state. But that penchant was not the key issue: eurial Perry-Parkdale cared to some degree about the programs it was _____, funds for, and on a smaller scale, the Calston district was acknowledged to be the best in the entire city at getting extra funds. But the reading program that they chose brought them no dollars at all, just materials and in-service assistance that were previous, given citywide budget cuts.

So, the moral of Factors 7–9 may be that organizational change is more likely when problem-solving orientation is strong, and when the scale of the innovation is large enough to deserve substantial funding (say, $50,000 or more). Though throwing money at problems is not supposed to solve them, defining one's problem as solvable by a moderate (rather than a minimal) amount of money may induce organizational change (*if* opportunism is not the central feature of the quest).

10. *Central office advocates.* The striking thing here is that 10 of our 12 sites had central office advocates. Only at small-scale Lido, with its nonsupportive superintendent, and at Dun Hollow, with its ambivalent director of elementary instruction, did the innovation not have a friend in court. We conclude that we must look more carefully at what the advocates *did* during implementation, or to other factors, to explain differential amounts of organizational change.

11. *Climate.* Finally, did the preexisting climate of the adopting school make a difference in the final degree of attained organizational change? A scan of the site-level data suggests that it did: The two schools with clear organizational change were marked by norms supporting collaboration, cohesive relation-ships, and a reasonable tolerance of diversity. By contrast, the schools that showed minimal or no organizational change had norms supporting isolation and low interdependence. The deviant case among the nonchanging sites was Burton, where in one school of three there was reasonable collaboration, but no real organizational change. As the site report noted:

> With the possible exception of Mr. Joyce's high level of involvement with his law course and his desire to make it more activity-oriented, contextual factors within the buildings did not seem to play a part in the decision to experiment with this program.

(Joyce did *not* work in the building described by its principal as "cooperative.") And we should note that (1) all three schools at Burton were conservative in orientation; and (2) the innovation that they were considering was not especially organizationally demanding and was made even less so through administrative latitude.

Summary

Reviewing what we have learned about the effects of organizational context on a column-by-column basis, it seems fair to say that organizational change was more likely in settings where the *demographic mix* had shifted

recently, and where a *"needy" student population* existed; it was also possible th
environmental pressure from external agencies leaned schools toward eventually
changing their structure. Prior *experience with innovation*, by itself, was not
necessarily associated with larger degrees of organizational change, but if it
was associated with a *problem-solving* rather than an opportunistic orientation,
more change was likely. The *superintendent's and the board's attitudes* made a modest
positive difference; the presence of a *central office advocate* was typical, but it did
not guarantee organizational change. More crucial was the presence of a
problem-solving orientation, applied to a reasonably *large-scale innovation*, and supported by *moderate funding*. Finally, there is some evidence that a *cooperative, cohesive climate* made organizational change a more likely outcome.

A preliminary causal map assembling these propositions is shown in Figure
9. In effect, what seems to be happening is that *environmental pressure* (1),
demographic shifts (2), and the presence of *a needy student population* (3) in a district
with a positive *innovative history* (4) induce the choice of a *more ambitious innovation*
(6). Such innovations, in turn, require larger amounts of *funding* (7), which, *if*
accompanied by a *problem-solving orientation* (5) to begin with, induce organizational change (10). A *building climate* (9) that is cooperative also seems to support
organizational change. But funding, a problem-solving orientation, and climate
do not change the organization directly; they must operate through a set of
specific *implementation process features* (8), to which our discussion turns in the next
section.

To look at the low side: If problem-solving orientation (5) is weak (in effect
replaced by opportunism), a situation that at our sites was also accompanied by
low cooperation (9) at the building level, little organizational change occurs.
The money obtained simply goes toward organizational maintenance rather
than change. Or, further back in the diagram, if environmental pressure (1),
demographic shifts (2), and a needy student population (3) are low or lacking,

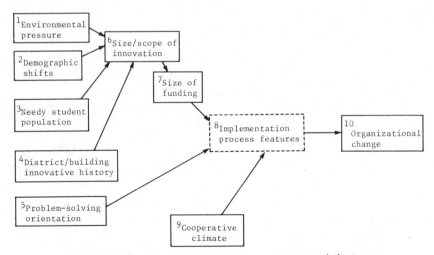

FIGURE 9. Contextual features causing organizational change.

179

choose a smaller scale innovation (6), with small funding (7)
ential for changing the organization.

n Process

l factors do not give us the whole picture. We need to examine
the po̲.̲.̲.̲ ̲ ̲ ̲ ̲ ̲ses for organizational change that come up during the implementation process. We identified 12, as follows:

1. Scope of intended change: the size of the originally conceptualized
   innovative effort. (This has already been alluded to above.)
2. Organizational fit: the degree to which the innovation was congruent
   with existing organizational arrangements:
   a. As anticipated before implementation.
   b. As noted actually, during implementation.
3. Administrative latitude: permission for users to adapt, alter, or selectively implement the innovation.
4. Administrative pressure: influence applied to induce implementation,
   exuding from central office personnel, the project director (if there is
   one), and the immediate school principal(s) involved.
5. Administrative support: help, assistance provided to users in aid of
   implementation (also from the three roles named above).
6. Organizational-level issues arising during implementation:
   a. Coordination: problems of linking, communicating, and keeping
      parts of system acting coherently.
   b. Autonomy: users' concerns about their own freedom of choice and
      action.
   c. Work load: users' concerns about added activities required by the
      innovation.
   d. Existing structure: problems arising from the innovation's interac-
      tion with organizational structure or procedures (cf. actual organiza-
      tional fit).
   e. Competition: issues involving win-lose struggle for scarce resources.
   f. Conflict: other situations involving incompatible goals, usually accom-
      panied by negative feelings.
   g. Power distribution: issues where the established set of influence
      relationships (formal and informal) comes into question, is seen as
      inequitable or undesirable.

Let's examine each of these causes in turn as predictors of organizational
change, by reviewing the site-level data[12]:

1. *Innovation size or scope.* Our discussion of funding has already prefigured
what we have to say here. There was a substantial range in size across the 12
sites—and the variable, by itself, is a rather good predictor. Our two high-

[12]Substantive and methodological details are in the technical report (pp. 301 ff.).

changing sites, Carson and Masepa, were both large-scope innovations. The ordering of the sites by innovation size within the next category, from Plummet to Astoria, is almost identical with their ordering on net organizational change. And in the zero-change category, there was only one deviant case, Proville, which is useful as an outlier (more on this later). In general, the Proville failure seems to have stemmed, as we have seen, from opportunism, weak program design, heavy principal and user resistance, weak assistance, and high administrative latitude. But for 11 of 12 cases, the general message is: more attempted, more gained.

2. *Organizational fit.* To what degree did the innovation look to respondents, and to us as site researchers, like a good or poor fit with the existing organizational structure and procedures? This question was assessed at the (recollected) point of adoption, and during implementation itself. At all sites but Astoria, a good to moderate fit was anticipated; in effect, school districts do not "look for trouble" in choosing innovations, it seems. Recall that the Astoria "adoption" occurred because of a systemwide mandating of the EPSF innovation, which was indeed inappropriate for the student population at Astoria and interfered considerably with existing curriculum, teaching methods, and time use. As we shall see, the immediately chosen palliative for this situation was that of allowing considerable latitude during implementation: The net *actual* fit turned out to be good.

Also, for only one site (Banestown) was the actual fit the same as that expected. For most others, the actual organizational fit was *poorer*. For some (Proville, Tindale, Lido, Perry-Parkdale, and Masepa), the difference was only a half step, but for others, it was more substantial. At Calston, the reading program that the central office coordinator and principals thought would be a simple drop-in supplement to the existing citywide reading program turned out to involve competition for resources (other schools had to give up precious reading materials) and to reduce the nonusing teachers' decision powers over student grouping. And it turned out that "supplementary" actually meant "extra" as far as the teachers were concerned. At Dun Hollow, another drop-in program "simply" involved the field testing of new social studies materials on Eskimos. But the materials were so incomplete that excessive teacher work time was involved, and the Eskimo work actually displaced other social studies content, to the teachers' distress.[13]

These five cases suggested a tendency to deny or to avoid possible organizational fit problems—the "Scarlett O'Hara" effect again. Proville's work experience program, if fully implemented, would have had substantial organizational change-stresses; it would have shifted the roles, the time use, and the reward systems for students, vocational education teachers, and school-district classified employees. But the scope of the program seemed unaddressed in the

---

[13]Plummet was a special case. Its actual fit with the high-school sending district was good. Its fit with the actual incoming student population turned out to be poor; the curriculum and the materials were simply inappropriate, a problem that set off a strong (and eventually successful) revision and reorganization effort.

planning and the early implementation. As it turned out, there were substantial problems: of 281 eligible students, only 16 had schedules that permitted their participation; principals were angry and cynical ("Just another dumb program they're shoving down our throats"), and vocational education teachers were furious:

> I just about threw the guy [the coordinator] out. He actually insisted he was going to take students out of my class. I told him he couldn't have them.

On balance, the fit issue as such does not seem to be a strong predictor of eventual organization change.

3. *Administrative latitude.* By *itself*, latitude seems to have predicted organizational change mainly at the ends of the organizational-change scale; for the sites from Calston to Proville, moderate to high latitude for a small-scope innovation practically guaranteed zero organizational change. And for the larger-scale innovations at Carson and Masepa, the latitude was moderate to low. But administrative latitude was so typical at the modestly changing sites, except for the vigorously enforced Tindale reading curriculum, that we do not have much predictive power in the mid-range.

4. *Administrative pressure.* To what degree did administrators in the central office, or working as project directors, or at the building level, exert pressure for implementation, either of the "strong-arming" or the exhortational variety? The general picture, as we saw earlier, was that a good deal of *central office* pressure was being exerted: Only at Plummet did we hear a user say,

> Mostly, I've been happy for the lack of interference, the fact that we've been allowed to operate autonomously. We've been allowed to experiment.

We should note here that (1) the Plummet staff was highly committed to the alternative-school enterprise they were running, and (2) they were receiving moderate to high pressure for implementation from their immediate superior, the school's director.

Second, where *project directors* existed (all for IV-C programs plus Perry-Parkdale and Lido), they, quite naturally, exerted moderate to high pressure for implementation. That is supposedly what project directors are hired to do. But when we get to *principals,* the picture is quite different. Only at high-changing Carson and Masepa did we find high principal pressure for implementation. There was moderate pressure at Astoria (to implement the revised, cutdown version of the innovation), at Calston, and initially at Lido. But elsewhere, the principal provided only low pressure (Banestown, Dun Hollow, and the new principal at Lido); provided none at all (Perry-Parkdale, Tindale, and Burton); or was more-or-less visibly *opposed* to implementation (Proville and the other school at Perry-Parkdale).

A cross-role look at the issue of pressure suggests that for *moderate- to large-scale innovations*, pressure was needed at at least two of the three levels (central office, project, and principal) in order for organizational change to occur. The only exception in six cases was Proville, where the negativism of the principals may have succeeded in canceling the pressure from above. For *small to small–moderate innovations,* failure to touch two of the three bases resulted in almost no change at all (Burton, Lido, and Banestown), and even where pressure was present at two of the three levels (Astoria, Calston, and Dun Hollow), the organizational changes were minimal because the scope was minimal to begin with.

5. *Administrative support.* The question of support presumably interacts with that of pressure. Here, we define support rather broadly as all assistance efforts except control (see p. 102): teaching/training, facilitation, solution-giving, resource-adding, advocating users' interest, feeding back formative data, and supporting and encouraging.[14]

Generally speaking, we note that *central office* support levels were high to moderate (eight sites), sometimes low (two) or absent (two); those of *program directors* moderate to high (except at our zero-change sites, Dun Hollow and Proville); and those of *principals* high only at high-changing Carson and Masepa (and at cooperative, conscientious Astoria).

We should take a moment to note that the conventional wisdom that identifies the principal as the main supporter or blocker of change efforts is cast into doubt in our sample. Although substantial organizational change did require principal pressure and support at both Carson and Masepa, the moderate organizational changes at Perry-Parkdale and Tindale and the minimal changes at Banestown proceeded essentially without the principals' being onboard. At Perry-Parkdale and Banestown, the innovation was isolated, sealed off to some extent from the normal flow of the schools involved. At Tindale, the high-school principal's role simply was defined as having nothing to do with curricular matters. And it is almost a toss-up at our nonchanging sites whether the principal's essential absence from the change picture was more or less critical than the fact that the changes were small-scope to begin with, or than the associated fact that latitude was typically high.

Looking across roles, we can see that organizational change was most likely when there was strong support from at least two of the three levels; that the picture for the sites with successful innovation but modest organizational changes shows that moderate to high support from one to two levels was necessary; and that the zero-change sites (except for Calston, at the top of that array) typically had minimal support. We also see here another explanation for the Proville debacle: Support was minimal at the levels of both the project director and the principal. (The combination of high pressure and low support seemed particularly resented by users, not only at Proville, but at one Calston school and at Dun Hollow.)

One other note: Considering the pressure and control exerted close to the programs involved, it appears that for *moderate to large innovations,* a combination of moderate pressure and high support (Carson, Plummet, Perry-Parkdale, Astoria, and early Lido) was more typically associated with successful implementation (and, for larger innovations, organizational change). Only

---

[14]Control was also defined on page 102 as a type of assistance, but we have broken it out separately here under the heading of "pressure."

Tindale departed from this pattern, and the high pressure for implementation present there had its side effects, including a "big brother" atmosphere:

> You don't criticize his [the central office advocate's] program and expect to survive here. (Teacher at Tindale)

> You go where you're safe and secure first [to peers] to gripe and complain. (Teacher at Tindale)

6. *Issues arising during implementation.* The issues noted up to now emerged inductively from the site analyses. We wondered whether any of them, or any combination, might be predictive of organizational change. Two generalizations seem founded.

First, the sheer number of organizational issues arising during implementation seems to have been a function of the innovation's size or scope; the moderate to large ones averaged 3.1 issues, and the small and small–moderate ones 2.2. For one deviant case, there was the moderate-to-large change at Perry-Parkdale, where the smoothly functioning program had few internal issues and had to contend only with issues in its environment: competition for students ("Students are *jobs*"), resources, space in the curriculum, and threats to existing high-school procedures. The other deviant case was the tightly managed Tindale project, where the only problems were those within newly implementing teams.

For small-scale innovations, there were also two deviant cases. Calston, the most-changing of our "least-changing" group, ran into unanticipated "fit" problems ranging from the loss of autonomy involved in giving up valued books, to overload ("There was just too much to do at the same time") and loss of decision power over student allocation. The numerous problems at Banestown seemed to stem mostly from the intra-central-office competition and conflict and the resulting coordination difficulties.

A second possible conclusion is that issues involving coordination, autonomy, and the relation of the innovation to the existing structure appeared somewhat more frequently as salient issues when a program was on the way to inducing organizational change of some degree: See the cases of Carson, Masepa, Plummet, and Perry-Parkdale, and compare these with all other sites.

But in addition, there seem to have been few organizational-issue correlates of final change; matters of work load, competition, conflict, and power distribution appeared at high-, modest-, and zero-changing sites alike. The five factors discussed earlier seem to have been more crucial.

Conclusions

In brief, we have learned in this section that innovations of larger *size and scope* are more likely to induce organizational change[15]; that administrative *latitude* tends somewhat to reduce such change; that both *administrative pressure*

---

[15]This general finding, along with the subfindings leading to it, mirrors closely those of the Louis *et al.* (1981) study.

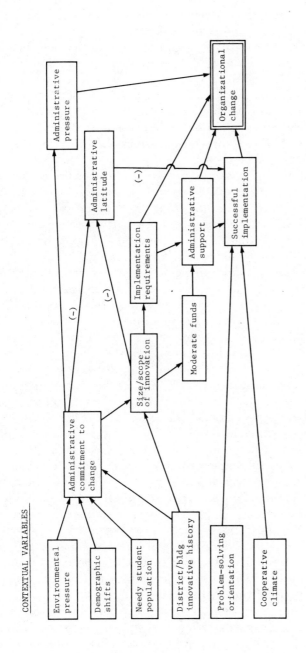

FIGURE 10. Contextual and implementation-process features causing organizational change.

and *administrative support* (typically from at least two mutually reinforcing levels) are needed (though the principal need not be the source); and that moderate pressure and high support from assisters close to the action (either as project directors or principals) seem an optimal balance.

How do these predictors affect the causal diagram that we began earlier? Figure 10 suggests a revised model that incorporates our findings.

Our explanation proceeds as follows. As we saw earlier, *environmental pressure, demographic shifts,* and a *needy student population* are associated with the *choice of a larger innovation.* But how do they cause that choice? We assume that they operate through heightened *administrator commitment to change,* which is also boosted by past *innovative history;* innovative history also increases the likelihood that larger innovations will be chosen.

Once a larger-scale innovation is chosen, its heavier *implementation require-ments* (note the larger numbers of implementation issues that we have found) dictate the need for greater *administrative support* of users; that support is also aided by the presence of the *moderate funds* that typically go with larger innovative projects. *Administrative support* (aided by a preexisting *problem-solving orientation* and *cooperative climate*) tends to result in reasonably full-scale, *successful implementation;* that, and the actual implementation requirements themselves, bring about organizational change. Such change, however, also seems to require *administrative pressure,* stemming from administrative commitment.

It also seems clear that when administrators have a lower commitment, *administrative latitude*[16] is typical; latitude tends to result in less complete, less successful implementation, and thus less organizational change.

If a smaller-scale innovation is chosen, that also seems to be associated with more administrative latitude; the resulting weaker implementation, along with the brute fact of smaller innovations' minimal implementation require-ments, results in fewer organizational changes.

There were two cases in which the "latitude" aspect of the model did not fit very well: Plummet and Perry-Parkdale, where there was relatively high latitude and also successful implementation. Both were relatively isolated subsystems within their districts, and it seems likely that, once the basic policy decision to implement them had occurred, the distal and local administrators provided latitude for a committed, professionalized staff to "do their thing" in the best way they knew how. So, for these cases, we must invoke one or two extra variables, something like "environmental buffering" and "staff profession-alism." Perhaps both stem from the fact that *new systems* were being created (Miles, 1980; Gold & Miles, 1981), less subject internally than our other sites to the constraints and pains of the existing order.

This concludes our discussion of transformations in the innovation, in users, and in the local organization. We now turn to the question of the *outcomes* of the implementation processes that we have been examining.

---

[16]Latitude and pressure are not necessarily opposed; we had many cases where both were moderate to high (Banestown, Plummet, Perry-Parkdale, Astoria, Calston, and Proville) at the central office level, at the local school level, or both.

CHAPTER 6

The Outcomes of School Improvement

Now we begin the end of our story. What were the ultimate outcomes of the school improvement projects that we have been studying? And what might explain the degree to which a site achieved stronger or weaker outcomes? In this section, we review the six outcomes that we analyzed and explain how the sites fared on them. Then we look at a series of "predictors"— factors in the innovation, the site context, and the implementation process—that might explain why particular outcomes were achieved. Then we proceed in more depth, outcome by outcome, searching for explanations for each one. The reader will encounter what feels like repetition, because the variables we have been discussing so far will be reinvoked in our search for confirmation and integration.

THE OUTCOMES

We originally thought (see Figure 1, p. 11) that school improvement efforts should reasonably lead to (1) institutionalization of the innovation; (2) to various gains and losses, both individual and institutional; and (3) to assorted side effects.

As our analysis proceeded, we developed a more differentiated list of outcomes, as follows:

1. *Stabilization of use:* the degree of practice mastery and "settledness" of the new practice in the users' instructional repertoire. We have already reviewed this outcome as the last stage of later implementation (pp. 124–131).
2. *Percentage of use:* the number of users in a school or district in proportion to the number of "eligible" or possible users. (This is, in effect, a measure of the spread or internal diffusion of the innovation: how widely it was being used by those who could potentially use it.)

187

3. *Institutionalization:* the degree to which the innovation was "built in"—incorporated into the ordinary structures and procedures of the school and its surrounding district. By this, we do not mean sheer "continuation," which might have occurred, for example, if a key administrator willed it—but the presence of indicators that the innovation had become organizationally routine.

These first three outcomes focus on whether the innovation was stable, widely used, and "built in." But the question still arises: What did the innovation *do* for people? To answer this question, we focused on three "impact" outcomes, as follows:

1. *Student impact:* achievement and affective and behavioral changes in the students as a result of exposure to the innovation.
2. *User capacity change:* changes in users' knowledge, attitudes, or skills that were of general professional value, beyond the immediate innovation's requirements. (The idea is of increased capability, strength, and development as a professional.)
3. *Job mobility:* the movement of school personnel to new positions, either inside their schools or districts (down, sideways, or up), to new positions outside their districts, or out of education altogether.

This last outcome may seem surprising. School improvement projects are supposed to improve schools, not to shift people into new jobs. We found, however (to anticipate our later discussion), that at least half the projects we were studying did have decisive effects on job changes. Some people "rode" the innovation to new and better positions, leaving a promising program behind; others had their sights raised and saw new opportunities; still others were "burned out" or became discouraged about their prospects and sought jobs elsewhere. Job mobility is an example of a frequent, but largely unremarked, outcome of school improvement projects. We should note, too, that it occurred at many sites for reasons *unconnected* with the improvement effort—such as fiscal crisis.

The assumption here, of course—which we endorse—is that these outcomes are generally desirable ones, and that a stronger showing is a more positive sign. But we shall also be demonstrating that job mobility in particular is not an unmixed blessing, and that low or negative outcomes can be, in the context, *also* desirable, in that the best local response to the innovation as it ultimately played out can be to abort it.

How did our sites fare on these outcomes? Table 38 displays the results of our analysis and provides a general overview. The table is deliberately arranged alphabetically within the IV-C and the NDN program sponsorships, rather than by magnitude of "total" outcome, because we do not wish to promote the idea that all six outcomes were equally important—and/or similarly high or low within a particular site. The outcomes cannot be simplistically added together to result in some general "goodness of outcome" score. However, in Chapter 7,

TABLE 38. Outcomes of School Improvement Effort, by Sites

Sites, by program sponsorship	Stabili- zation of use	Percentage of use	Institu- tionali- zation	Student impact	User capacity change	Job mobility
NDN Sites						
Astoria	High	Mod	High	Mod-low	Low-mod	Mod
Banestown	Mod	Mod	Mod	High	High	High
Burton	Mod	Low	Low	Low	Low-nil	Nil
Calston	Mod-high	Mod	Low	Mod	Low-mod	Mod
Lido	Mod-high	Mod	High-mod	Mod	Mod	Low
Masepa	Mod	High	Mod-high	High	High	Low-mod
Perry-Parkdale	Mod-high	Mod	Low	High	High	High
IV-C Sites						
Carson	Mod	High	Mod	Mod	Mod	Mod
Dun Hollow	Low	Low	Nil	Low-mod	Low-nil	Nil
Plummet	Mod	Mod	High	High	High	Mod-high
Proville	Low	Low	Nil	Low	Nil	High
Tindale	High	High	High	High	High	High

we will explore the degree to which the sites fell into general families, each with a roughly similar degree of success.

We will not dwell on this table here, since we will review each outcome in detail below and develop explanations for its degree of achievement. For now, it is perhaps enough to note that the outcome patterns across sites, and across program sponsors, are indeed diverse and nonmonolithic.

PREDICTING OUTCOMES

How could we understand what led to what at our sites, in a systematic way? Our solution was to elaborate for each site a "causal network" of 30 or so variables, with arrows between them showing what we inferred were causal influences (see Appendix C for a sample). We began this exercise with a common list of 31 variables (Table 2, p. 13), which we expected would make sense at each of our sites. In fact, we found (1) that 4 or 5 of the 31 were typically not in play at any given site; (2) that a few site-unique variables forcefully insinuated themselves; and (3) that, as we proceeded through the final cross-site analysis, 5 additional variables, such as "administrative latitude," emerged as important predictors.[1]

Figure 11 displays all these variables in one place, sorting them into blocks,

[1]The procedures used for identifying these variables, for mapping the site-level causal networks, and for comparing the networks across sites are described briefly in the original technical report (Huberman & Miles, pp. 317–319). The networks are, briefly put, a qualitative analogue of path-analytic modeling, using canons of inductive inference. The full set of procedures, including the decision rules and the step-by-step applications, is in our methodological sourcebook (Miles & Huberman, 1984, Section IV.J and V.H.).

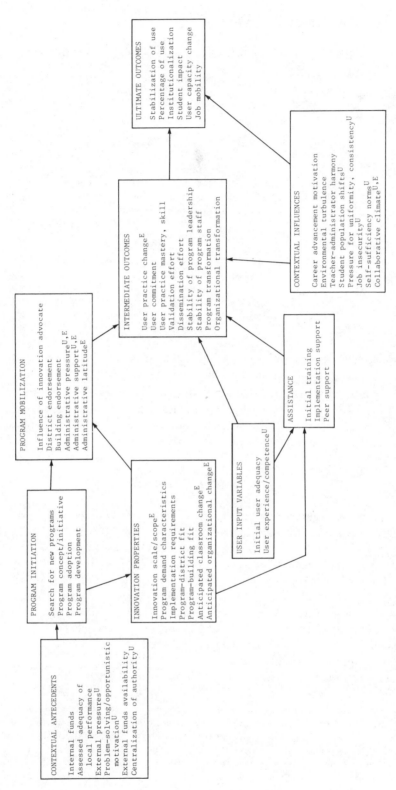

FIGURE 11. The school improvement process: Predictors and outcomes. U = variable unique to 2–3 sites in initial analysis; E = variable emerging as important during later analysis; variables without superscripts were defined as common to all (or nearly all) sites in initial analysis.

each with a general heading. The arrows show the general direction of influence between blocks. (Naturally, we found many specific instances of influence in other directions between specific variables, as well as within-box influences.)

In brief, the general idea is that *contextual antecedents* in the local district led to *program initiation* involving a particular innovation; the *properties* of that innovation, as well as the initiation process itself, led to a stage of *program mobilization.* The innovation properties set requirements for the sort of *assistance* needed, in tandem with the kind of *users* involved. The assistance, the properties of users, and program mobilization processes all led to *intermediate outcomes,* ranging from user commitment to organizational transformation. But those intermediate outcomes are not enough to account for the final or *ultimate outcomes;* those are influenced as well by local *contextual influences,* which naturally have a conditioning effect on the intermediate outcomes as well.

In the next section, we treat in succession each of the six ultimate outcome variables. First, we provide a general description of how much of the outcome was achieved at our sites; then, we do an analysis of what seems to have been "causing" or leading to the outcome. Usually, we give more emphasis, as Figure 11 dramatizes, to the later links in the chain, *intermediate outcomes* and *contextual influences,* rather than dwelling on variables early in the causal chain. Those earlier variables and their interactions have been discussed in the preceding chapters of this book.

STABILIZATION OF USE

Introduction

In our analysis of later implementation (pp. 114–132), we traced the process by which innovations stabilize locally. We focused there on the stages and the ultimate extent of user practice mastery, which we tied in with the relative "settledness" of the innovation—whether it was still undergoing sizable changes or was essentially in a refinement mode. Adding practice mastery to degree of settledness gave us a conceptually plausible and workable index of stabilization of use.

In the later implementation section, we also looked forward to the likelihood of continuation. It turned out there that stabilization of use may help but does not guarantee continuation, notably when users do not like the practice, administrators do not support it, or the money to maintain it disappears. In this section, we will look backward—to the constellation of factors that account for high and low degrees of local stabilization of use.

What It Took to Get Stabilized

In our first pass through the causal networks, as well as the explanatory text that accompanied them, we tried to determine which conditions had to be met for stabilization of use to occur. Looking at the networks, we extracted "streams" running from antecedent variables through mediators to our semifinal outcome indices, "user practice mastery" and "program settledness," and finally out to our dependent measure, "stabilization of use." This process usually involved some interpretation. For example, goodness or poorness of "user fit" prior to adoption was little help; we had to estimate whether initially poor fits were improved and initially good fits were maintained during program execution.

This initial scan turned up 11 potential predictors. In order to see how well they predicted stabilization of use, we arrayed the 12 sites according to the levels of stabilization that we had already estimated (pp. 126 ff.), and we summed the relative "values" of each predictor to get a rough prediction index.[2] It predicted the ends of the site distribution (highs and lows), but not the intermediate cases. It is likely that only *some* of the predictors actually affected stabilization in a direct way. It is also likely that their interactions—the order in which they occurred, as well as the mix of the directly and indirectly impacting ones—were an important set of clues in explaining outcomes.

We then used the following procedure to illuminate these empirically driven causal paths. First, on each causal network, we traced back the predictors from "stabilization of use" that lay *in a direct stream* (i.e., were connected by an unbroken stream of arrows). We also noted the predictors (boxes) that were *immediate* causes (that lay close to the "stabilization" variable on a direct path) and the ones that were more *remote* (further back on the direct path). We then identified the remaining predictors that were on the chart—but not connected to the "stabilization" box by any route. If you could not get from there to stabilization of use, we assumed weak or no directional influence. Finally, we noted predictors that were *missing* on the causal networks, which meant that the analysts had considered them inoperative as causal factors. In this instance, for 9 of the 12 variables we examined, there were causal paths— immediate or remote—on at least *one-half* of the causal nets.[3]

If we highlight variables with direct causal links on at least 8 of the 12 networks, we get the following list:

1. Overall assistance (11 sites)
2. User commitment/acceptance (11 sites)
3. Implementation requirements (11 sites)
4. District endorsement (9 sites)
5. User practice mastery (8 sites)
6. Program transformation (8 sites)

Scenarios Leading to High Stabilization

Conceptually, the strong predictor variables just listed sound reasonable. If an innovation is a fairly good fit with users' prior practice, has significant (nontrivial) implementation requirements, and is accompanied by district

---

[2]See the technical report (pp. 319 ff.) for more details.
[3]For a closer look at the methodology, see the technical report (pp. 322–323).

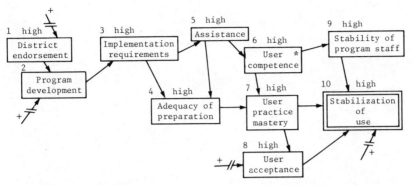

+Influence of other variables not discussed
*Site-specific variable

FIGURE 12. Practice mastery and stabilization of use: Tindale (IV-C).

endorsement, we might expect a gradual process of user mastery and adaptation of the innovation, accompanied by user commitment, and leading to stabilization. But how did the process actually work at the sites? Let's look at a few typical scenarios.

The High Road to Success: High Practice Mastery

Tindale was one of the high stabilization sites. It scored well on both the "practice mastery" measure and the "program settledness" measure. If we look at an excerpt from the causal network[4] the "practice mastery" process worked as shown in Figure 12. Note that all the boxes are rated "high." Tindale had everything going for it, including high adequacy of preparation (4), which was typically uneven or poor elsewhere. At first, the story here looks uniformly cheery: The district endorsed (1) an ambitious project (3), prepared and backstopped it well (4, 5), and produced skillful (6, 7), compliant (8) users whose stability (9) enhanced the project's stabilization (10). However, the script at Tindale had some pain in it: "User acceptance" followed a long period of low user commitment. Essentially, the users were constrained to use a widely disliked practice, but over time, and as a result of increasing skill, they came to accept and even like it.

An alternative path to skillful stabilization included user commitment earlier in the process. An except from the Perry-Parkdale causal network is shown in Figure 13. Again, the harbingers of stabilization were all good. The project was well endorsed (1) and well assisted (4, 5). Users liked it (6) and got better at doing it (7, 8).

There are three noteworthy points here. First, we found the combination of assistance, skill, and commitment to be *proximate* to stabilization at virtually all sites. These were the variables that lay closest to the outcome measured and

---

[4]In producing these excerpts, we typically took all the variables seen as immediate predictors of (that is, two steps prior to) the outcome being studied, plus other connected ones that were essential for telling the story.

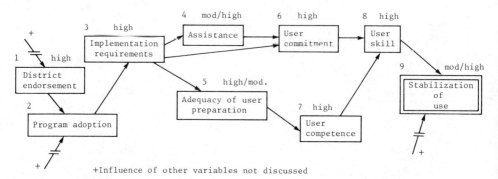

FIGURE 13. Practice mastery and stabilization of use: Perry-Parkdale (NDN).

appeared to be the most decisive in determining the ultimate level of skillful stabilization. If commitment and assistance were low (as, for example, at Proville and Dun Hollow), a more favorable but distant predictor, like high "district endorsement" or high "program–district fit," did not turn the situation around.

Second, note that commitment *followed* program adoption. We saw earlier (Chapter 4) that many users were lukewarm or wary about the practice initially and were seduced or strong-armed into program execution by enthusiastic administrators. Even users with more favorable initial attitudes, like those at Perry-Parkdale, had their doubts or came to the project more for career-related reasons than because of deep-seated commitment to the project's goals. But what happened? Users confronted a challenging practice that turned out to be more intractable than they had thought. They worked hard at it, receiving external and peer assistance. They gradually got on top of it. The *process* of effortful mastery of a professionally demanding project heightened commitment. Commitment was *achieved*; that is, it was not necessarily preexistent to program execution. For example, lukewarm or low levels of initial commitment were turned around at Masepa and Tindale by the challenge of the exercise, by the experience of craft mastery, and by the support provided by peers, administrators, and external consultants. In policy terms, this may mean that we have been wasting some of the time we have invested in assuring outselves that users want to do the new project. More energy should go into the follow-up support that can deliver users' commitment when it improves practice mastery.

This discussion brings us to the third point: the presence of latent variables. We realized during our analysis that some variables (for example, "implementation requirements" or "program demand characteristics") assumed the presence of latent or underlying variables (in this case, the latent variable of *"user practice change"* could be expected to follow when a program's requirements or demand characteristics were heavy). So better mapping of the "practice mastery" scenario should include this latent variable. It would go like this: The project makes demands in terms of the classroom-level changes needed to make it work. Users progressively meet those demands through the assistance-

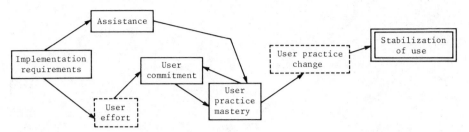

FIGURE 14. Practice mastery and stabilization of use: General model with latent variables.

supported process of practice mastery, and in so doing, they become more committed to the practice. We might note, for support of this scenario, that the levels of user commitment were lower at most of the sites with lower degrees of practice change (Astoria, Calston, Dun Hollow, and Burton).

Reflection also suggests adding another latent variable to the formula, *user effort*. As we saw in the analysis of early implementation (pp. 172 ff.), practice change seldom came cheap, without storm and stress. Part of the celebration of successfully making these changes seemed to result from the time and energy expended in achieving practice mastery. This is a staple of cognitive dissonance theory: Effort builds commitment, if only to justify to oneself *why* one has expended so much effort (Lawrence & Festinger, 1962), and greater effort, of course, usually improves performance. So a fuller model of skill-driven stabilization of use—and one that explains both high and low levels of stabilization—would look like the one in Figure 14.

Tindale Revisited: Program Settledness

We said that Tindale achieved high stabilization because it performed well on both practice mastery and program settledness. How did it achieve program settledness?

The answer is simple: enforcement. The pathways are shown in Figure 15.

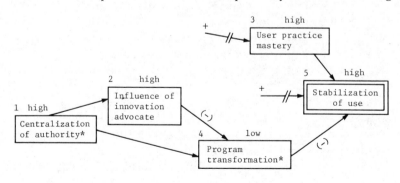

+Influence of other variables not discussed
*Site-specific variable

FIGURE 15. Program settledness and stabilization of use: Tindale (IV-C).

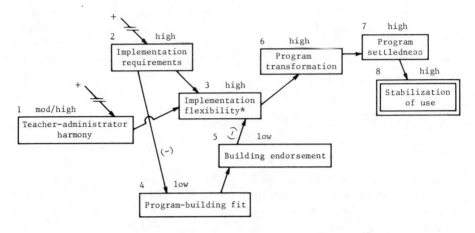

+Influence of other variables not discussed

*Site-specific variable

FIGURE 16. Program settledness and stabilization of use: Astoria (NDN).

We have described this "enforcement" scenario in our analysis of changes made in the innovation (pp. 134 ff.). We noted, however, that only two sites (Tindale and Masepa) followed this pattern.

The flow is straightforward. Given strongly centralized authority (1), the innovation advocate's influence (2) was high in restricting program transformation (4).[5] That low latitude, along with user practice mastery (3), accounted for stabilization (5).

Stabilization through Administrative Latitude

For another (and more frequent) script, let us look at the other high-stabilizing site, Astoria (Figure 16). At Astoria, we can see that the program settled down (7) essentially because administrators, who had good working relations (1) with users, gave users "implementation flexibility" (3) in carrying out a demanding (2), poorly fitting (4) program. The program was substantially transformed (6) in the process of becoming stabilized.

As we looked at other moderate- to high-stabilizing sites, this pattern recurred; it was virtually identical at Calston and Burton, and it was similar at Carson. The program settled down because administrators let users reduce the discrepancy between ongoing school-level and classroom-level practices and the demands of the innovation—by changing the innovation. So program transformation is the way many schools "metabolize" innovations. The underlying variable, as we have already noted, is *administrative latitude*. Note, by the way, that program stabilization at Tindale and Masepa can be seen as the product, in part,

---

[5]Here, as with our original causal networks from which these excerpts were drawn, the symbol (−) refers to *inverse* causal relationships, where high X causes low Y and vice versa. *Direct* causal relationships have no sign attached.

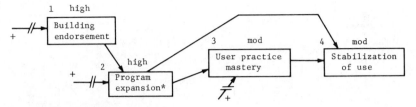

+Influence of other variables not discussed
*Site-specific variable

FIGURE 17. Moderate practice mastery and stabilization of use: Masepa (NDN).

of *low* administrative latitude, which must be accompanied by plenty of assistance and administrative pressure.

Scenarios Leading to Lower Stabilization

Up to now, we have looked at higher stabilization scenarios. How about the less successful cases? Were they less successful because the same variables rated "high" on the strong stabilizers were rated "low"?

Lower Stabilization from Moderate Practice Mastery

For several low-stabilizing sites, the answer seems to be "no": practice mastery was moderate, not low. This was true for Dun Hollow, Masepa, and Banestown.[6]

Masepa and Banestown had something thematically in common: *new* inputs (of users or of students). But they meant something different at each site. At Masepa, the input of more and more users destabilized the successful program somewhat, as shown in Figure 17. As the program was seen to succeed and gained building endorsement (1), more users were brought aboard (2) so that the *site*-level assessment of practice mastery (3) had to include *recent* users, who were often foundering on components that the third-year users had well under control.

There was a similar pattern at Banestown, where we watched users only 18 months into the execution of a sophisticated, individualized instruction program in a novel (pull-out) setting. Had we picked up this site in its third or fourth year, the skill mastery would have been higher. As it was, the causal flow illustrates two streams found elsewhere (e.g., at Masepa). The first was a "demands-to-assistance" stream. Higher implementation requirements depressed preparedness and led to assistance from without and within the district, bringing on at least moderate stabilization. The second stream might be called "district endorsement to assistance." Here, the central office administrators backing the project got it out of serious trouble by providing assistance

---

[6]Dun Hollow had "moderate" practice mastery mainly because the users dealt with the project by doing, revising, and then discarding it; a better judgment on "practice mastery" might be "not applicable."

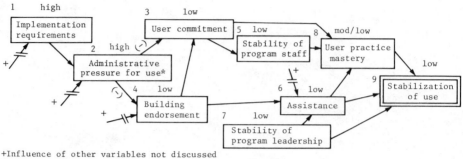

+Influence of other variables not discussed
*Site-specific variable

FIGURE 18. Lower practice mastery and stabilization of use: Proville (IV-C).

in the form of encouragement, consultants, and/or materials. The two streams highlight two facets of the implementation process that we mentioned earlier: (1) initial levels of assistance matter less than later levels, and (2) levels of district endorsement have practical consequence not only during adoption but also further down the line.[7]

The Lowest of the Low

At the extremes, we did see the linear relationship that we proposed between predictors and stabilization of use. If, at Tindale, all the key antecedents of practice mastery were high, contributing to high stabilization of use, at Proville the same antecedents were rated low, and they acted to bring on lower stabilization. Compare Figure 15 (Tindale) with the practice mastery stream at Proville (Figure 18). Here nothing worked "right." A demanding innovation (1), pushed by the administration (2), encountered resistance (4) and weak commitment (3) at the building level. Instability of the program staff (5) and the leadership (7) enfeebled assistance efforts (6), and mastery (8) was minimal. The innovation withered away.

Lower Stabilization of Use from Lower Program Settledness

We saw that program settledness feeds overall stabilization of use either by suppressing program changes (e.g., at Tindale) or by allowing discrepancy-reducing ones (e.g., at Astoria). What keeps programs from getting settled?

In some cases, the answer is the same as for practice mastery: Inputs changed. Input instability could take multiple forms: internal reorganization (Plummet), the introduction of new components of the innovation (Masepa), and even simplification of the project (Carson).

But let us look more closely at the dynamics of lower program stabilization. Figure 19 shows the sequence at Carson. As in the three other cases of discrepancy reduction (see Figure 16 and discussion), the institutional task here

---

[7]For a fuller analysis of the Banestown causal flow, see the technical report (pp. 331–332).

was to achieve program stabilization by *changing the innovation* to improve its local fit, thereby gaining building endorsement. Here the program's demands (2) resulted in poor fit (3) and, for later users, in low building endorsement (5). So the accommodation process began, facilitated by some of the organizational transformations (4) that the project had wrought (e.g., increased interpersonal trust and improved communication). Users, with the tacit consent of administrators, began watering down and otherwise streamlining the program (6). Building endorsement (5) improved, as did, presumably, later program–school fit (not shown on the figure). Though these changes reduced the impact of the project, they improved its stabilization (8). As we saw earlier (e.g., at Astoria and Burton), this was a common trade-off: more rapid program settledness (9) for less program impact. Unfortunately, external support (7) at Carson was weak, which kept the building endorsement (5) lukewarm and made the streamlining process more stressful. Essentially, however, the building endorsement problem was resolved.

If that problem is *not* resolved, projects get into trouble, notably in terms of program stabilization. Note from Figure 19 (Carson) that the district endorsement was high, but that it did not deliver high building endorsement. The same problem was present at Dun Hollow, Perry-Parkdale, and Proville—all cases where ultimate program survival was tenuous. At Perry-Parkdale, the endorsement of the principal was lacking. At Proville, there was low endorsement by both the principal and the teachers. At Dun Hollow, project teachers were unhappy, and building administrators backed them implicitly. So program stability—and beyond this, institutionalization—are unlikely if the building-level actors, including nonusers, are actively nonsupportive, whatever the amount of district-level support. Central office administrators can get an innovation *adopted*, as we saw in the adoption section (Chapter 4, pp. 54 ff.), but they cannot ensure its *survival* without obtaining building-level support. The

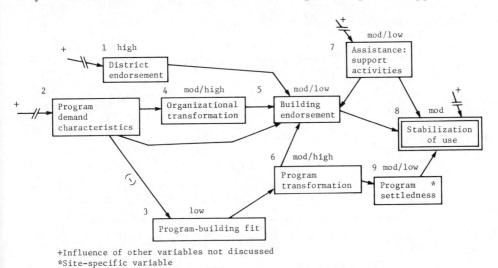

+Influence of other variables not discussed
*Site-specific variable

FIGURE 19. Lower stabilization of use from program unsettledness: Carson (IV-C).

price of that support is typically the innovation transformation required to produce a better program–building fit.

If that price is not paid, we find innovations that are gradually orphaned, as administrators turn elsewhere and hand off the project to lukewarm users, so that there is no remediation activity and the project—Proville is a textbook example[8]—is left to rot.

Conclusions

Stabilization of use was a compound of practice mastery and program settledness. Overall, we had 10 sites that worked their way to moderate to high levels of practice mastery and program settledness.

An analysis of the 12 cases, using the causal network for each, showed that there were several avenues to both higher and lower stabilization of use. Higher mastery usually resulted from the provision of adequate initial preparation and follow-up assistance, along with strong local endorsement, all of which translated into users' acceptance of or commitment to the project, and into users' technical mastery of its core components. The thumbnail scenario was as follows: Users confronted a challenging new practice that turned out to be more intractable than expected. They worked hard at it, receiving peer and external *assistance*, and gradually *mastered* it, thereby heightening their *commitment*. Lower assistance, both initial and ongoing, tended to depress levels of practice mastery and commitment.

Higher program settledness was helped but not assured by skillful execution. Rather, it resulted chiefly from *building-level endorsement* and *limitation of changes* in pupil or program characteristics. Endorsement often came from resolving the problem of *building-level fit*, which was often done by *transforming the innovation* to make it more amenable institutionally. Closely policed innovations also settled down (few changes were authorized), and gradually, sometimes grudgingly, they got the building-level endorsement that assured settledness.

PERCENTAGE OF USE

How widely had the innovations we studied diffused within the buildings where they were being used, and within and their surrounding districts? And what might account for that spread?

Introduction

Working from interviews, documents, and the results of the survey data, we established for the school buildings and the districts that we were studying just how many current users there were, and what the possible "eligible" population of users might be. Were all the potential users involved with the innovation, or only a fraction?

---

[8]The causal network for Proville, showing the same variables at work but with low ratings leading to low stabilization of use, is discussed in the technical report (pp. 335–336).

Percentage of Use: The Outcome

In surveying our different sites as of the end of the 1980 school year, four clusters emerged clearly.[9] Carson, Masepa, and Tindale were all sites where the percentage of use was *substantial;* all or many teachers in the school and the district were eligible to use the innovation, and all or many were doing so. Our second category included Plummet, Perry-Parkdale, and Banestown. They had full *in-building* use, but more *limited district* use. All were somewhat isolated programs: an alternative school, a work experience program, and a remedial laboratory, in which all (100%) of their staffs were by definition using the innovation.

Our third category was *moderate to full* use for a *specialized population.* The Astoria EPSF screening program, though mandated districtwide, had only kindergarten and first-grade teachers as eligible users. The Calston 4D reading program dealt only with intermediate teachers in elementary schools where the principal had shown active interest (23 of 25 principals rejected the innovation, and no one was going to force it on them). The Lido environmental studies program, though nominally "interdisciplinary," involved use only by science teachers in the district's single high school.

And finally, we had three sites where the percentage of use was *minimal:* A fifth or less of the eligible teachers in the building and the district were using the innovation in Burton, Dun Hollow, and Proville (where, indeed, the percentage of use was zero, following discontinuation—"The VIP program is dead").

What Caused Differences in Percentage of Use?

We can see from site-level analysis that time *alone* was not a sufficient explanation of increasing diffusion through a building or a district. In Banestown, it only took $1\frac{1}{2}$ years to get all the "eligible" users of the remedial lab onboard; in Astoria only 1 year was involved following the mandated adoption and the flexible implementation of EPSF. On the other side of the continuum, we see that 4 years at Lido did not achieve use by all the eligible users, even within the confines of one small high school. Three years of scattered effort at Proville failed to get a resisted program durably in place; at its height, we should note, the innovation reached only 40 of the proposed 100 students.

We can also see that program sponsorship tells us little: The substantial IV-C implementations at Carson, Tindale, and Plummet were offset by the minimal ones at Dun Hollow and Proville. Similarly, we see high percentages of use under NDN sponsorship at Masepa, Perry-Parkdale, and Banestown, and lower percentages at Lido and Burton.

To get a fuller picture of causation, we need to turn to our causal networks.

Recurrent Predictors of Percentage of Use

We begin, here again, by mapping the predictors.[10]

To summarize what we found: It appears that a higher percentage of use is

---

[9]Details of this analysis are in the technical report (pp. 338–340).

[10]For details, see the technical report (pp. 341–345).

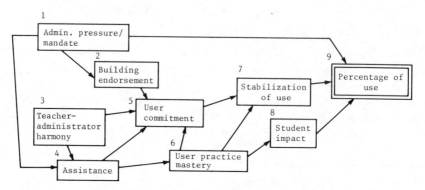

FIGURE 20. Factors predicting percentage of use.

more likely at sites where there is *administrative pressure* to implement (with or without a systemwide mandate), coupled with sustained *assistance* to users, who, along with their principals, are *committed* to the innovation, endorsing it. The assistance, in a positive climate (*teacher–administrator harmony*) and with continued use, tends to lead to greater *user mastery, stable use,* and higher *student impact.*[11] Given all these circumstances, the innovation tends to be used by many or all of the potential users in the school and the district. If the circumstances are weak or absent, less extensive implementation is typical. To those wishing for a rational approach to innovation, what could be more fitting? The picture is one of reasonableness and coherence.

These findings can be displayed in the derived causal model shown in Figure 20. The model suggests several main routes to high percentage of use. One, at the top, involves direct exertion of administrative influence (1, 9); another emphasizes commitment development and stabilization of use (2, 5, 7, 9); and the third uses assistance (4) to develop commitment (5), practice mastery (6), and student impact (8), along with stabilization of use (7). But this model is a "smoothed" one, drawing from separate variables across 12 idiosyncratic networks. We need to see how the process actually worked at particular sites, and whether there were "families" of sites showing characteristic causal patterns—and whether they resemble the paths suggested here.

Scenarios Leading to High Percentage of Use

Did the high-percentage-of-use sites fall into a common scenario? Roughly speaking, Tindale and Masepa did—and it was rather like the outline above. First, the Tindale excerpt is shown in Figure 21. This net excerpt resembles the proposed model reasonably well. We can see both the commitment development (2, 3, 4, 6, 8) and the practice mastery (7, 8, 9, 10, 11) streams as leading to

[11]Student impact did have an immediate causal influence on the percentage of use at the high-percentage-of-use sites Carson, Tindale, Plummet, and Perry-Parkdale, and a remote influence at Masepa. In striking contrast, the variable had *no* causal connections at any of the other, lower-percentage-of-use sites: the idea of student impact (high or low) was, in effect, decoupled from how widely the program was used across the school or the district.

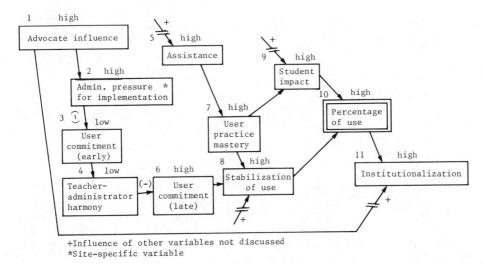

+Influence of other variables not discussed
*Site-specific variable

FIGURE 21. Commitment and practice mastery as routes to high percentage of use: Tindale (IV-C).

stabilization of use and student impact, thence to high percentage of use. Note that initial administrative pressure (2) dampened user commitment (3) and jeopardized teacher–administor harmony (4); efforts to restore harmony then led to increased user acceptance (6). But the mastery stream was probably more critical. We added the institutionalization (11) variable here because it figures in some scenarios to follow. Note that advocate influence did induce administrative pressure but did not operate directly on percentage of use, though it was a force for institutionalization.

The network at Masepa was also a reasonable analogue of our proposed model, though it turned out to be considerably more complex.[12] But high percentages of use could come about through simpler means, with minimal attention to practice mastery as such. That picture appeared at Carson, also a high-percentage-of-use site (Figure 22).

At Carson, the fate of the program was strongly influenced by the humanistically oriented superintendent (1, 2). The program did not require substantial gains in user skill, so early preparation (4) served to increase commitment (5), as did the shared ideology (2); committed users achieved impact (6), which, along with the superintendent's strong influence (1), resulted in the decision to mandate the program (7), thus boosting its official percentage of use (8) to 100%. Institutionalization followed.

The scenario at Banestown was even more stripped-down (Figure 23). Here a high percentage of use (8) was achieved essentially through the decision making and influence of the innovation's main advocate (2) in the central office. Users got district-level assistance (3) and achieved adequate practice mastery (6) through continued peer assistance (5), resulting in moderately stabilized use (9)—but all that was decoupled from the basic decision to use the innovation, a

[12]For details, see the technical report (p. 348).

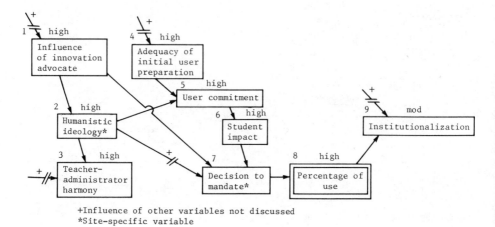

+Influence of other variables not discussed
*Site-specific variable

FIGURE 22. Administrative pressure and commitment as routes to high percentage of use: Carson (IV-C).

pull-out remedial reading program operating at its maximum scope in the schools involved. It could be argued, of course, that for a larger-scope innovation, or minus the assistance and stabilization, the central office edict would not have sufficed—an argument that we can test later by looking at a site (Proville) where precisely that happened.

Scenarios Leading to Low Percentage of Use

In general, with a number of bendings and qualifications, the model we have proposed seems plausible. For innovations that require considerable user skill, all three streams (pressure, commitment, and mastery) probably need to be present; for undemanding ones, administrative action alone can probably prevail. But for a good test of the model, we should look at sites where the percentage of use was minimal or was operative for a special population—to see whether the streams we have noted were *not* followed (more precisely, had "low" values on the variables involved).

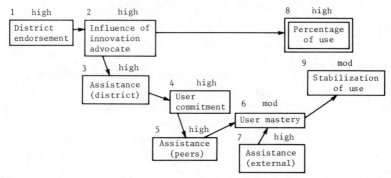

FIGURE 23. Administrative influence as a route to high percentage of use: Banestown (NDN).

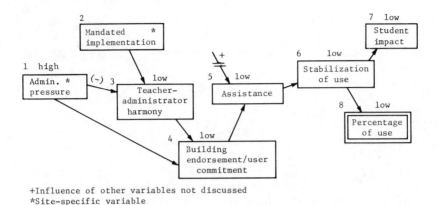

+Influence of other variables not discussed
*Site-specific variable

FIGURE 24. Administrative pressure, lack of assistance, and low commitment as routes to low percentage of use: Proville (IV-C).

The most extreme case to make this test on is Proville. The network extract is shown in Figure 24. The clear moral is that pressure to implement unaccompanied by assistance or means to induce commitment is unlikely to achieve more than minimal percentage of use. At Proville, the administrative pressure (1) simply alienated principals and teachers (3), who never developed commitment (4). They never asked for assistance, and little was forthcoming anyway (5) because the central-office program coordinator had other, more important fish to fry. The destablized innovation (6) died on the vine. (We might note that in the one high school at Proville where the principal pushed the idea and got assistance to the users, the program flourished briefly.)

At Dun Hollow, another low-percentage-of-use site, there was hardly any administrative pressure beyond an acceptance of the external developer's wish to field-test the innovation. Later, building endorsement dropped substantially. Lack of assistance led to weak commitment and destabilization of the program staff.User mastery was high but was self-developed and was connected from the percentage-of-use outcome. It looks as if a minimum of administrative pressure is needed along with commitment-developing and stability-assuring mechanisms. We can see this need illustrated a bit more clearly in the case of Burton (Figure 25), where users had full administrative latitude. They could try as much or as little of the legal education program as they liked, as it was a "pilot year." The latitude (1) enabled users to revamp the program (2), mainly by selecting a few parts that they liked and discarding the rest—even those that the developer considered essential. That transformation both dampened their commitment (4) and made user mastery (6) minimal, which was already low because no centrally provided assistance was given, and because the local norms discouraged peer-provided assistance (3). Naturally, stabilization of use (5) and resulting percentage of use (7) were minimal. Expect little, get little.

Scenarios for Moderate to Full Use (with a Specialized Population)

We will not present net excerpts here, since they represent an intermediate case between the high and low sites that we have been reviewing. In brief, the

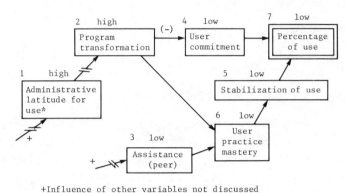

FIGURE 25. Administrative latitude and program transformation as a route to low percentage of use: Burton (NDN).

implementation at Astoria showed that a mandated program, especially in a centralized system, could achieve a full percentage of use for a limited population (first-graders), if at least moderate levels of assistance and commitment were present (aided here by strong teacher–administrator harmony) and some (not extreme) administrative latitude was offered.

The picture at Lido involved all the variables of our model, minus administrative pressure, but with administrative support and external assistance. Users used the latitude that they had to select from the innovation what they needed to buttress an ongoing environmental education program, to which they were committed.

Finally, the Matteson 4D reading program at Calston achieved user commitment and mastery through assistance, with only moderate administrative pressure. Commitment and mastery led to moderate-plus stabilization and low to moderate student impact. But the issue of percentage of use was completely disconnected from such matters, depending entirely on the instability of program staff and leadership that ensued from the citywide fiscal crisis.

Conclusions

For innovations that require at least a modicum of user skill, it looks as if high percentages of use can be assured by maintaining some administrative *pressure* for implementation, providing *assistance* sufficient to enable *user practice mastery* and *student impact*, and supporting the development of *user commitment*. Assistance can be less crucial for innovations that ask less of users. But *teacher–administrator harmony* is important to facilitate the process of commitment development and stabilization.

Administrative pressure *by itself* gets nowhere, judging from our classic Proville case. The barriers of teacher–administrator conflict, user noncommitment, and lack of skill are too substantial. Administrators can get away with mandating an innovation and achieving higher percentages of use only if reasonable attention is given to the development of commitment and of skill.

Not surprisingly, if pressure, commitment, and mastery are all low, low percentages of use are guaranteed.

When administrators—with or without pressure—give users latitude to adapt the innovation, much depends on what the latitude is used for. If it is used to reduce the load on users in a laissez-faire fashion, low percentages of use are likely. But if users already have a reasonable commitment to the innovation (as at Perry-Parkdale and Plummet) or to some other program that the innovation can further (as at Lido), then latitude giving can feed program development and increase the percentage of use.

INSTITUTIONALIZATION

Introduction

As we have indicated, we defined *institutionalization* as the presence of organizational conditions that signal *routinization* of the innovation. In short, we looked for structures, procedures, and organizational sentiments that were indicators of the innovation's being "built into" the school and the district. Such organizational conditions would transcend mere continuation, which might occur simply because a principal or a key user liked the innovation or found it more convenient than an alternative practice.

Degrees of Institutionalization: Examples

At field sites, we looked for organizational conditions supporting institutionalization, asking informants not only if the innovation would be around in the following and subsequent years, but *why* they thought so. In addition, each analyst filled out a standard checklist chart. A sample chart, showing the *moderate* degree of institutionalization at the Banestown site, appears in Table 39. The conceptualization underlying the chart was drawn from Yin *et al.* (1978). In brief, we were looking for a series of *supporting conditions* related to current operations (such as whether competing practices had been eliminated); for the completion of important *passages* (such as moving from soft to hard money, or getting the use of the practice written into job descriptions); and for the survival of the innovation through several organizational *cycles* (typically occurring during a school semester or year and including movement through new budgets and new personnel).

The analyst also commented on and amplified the chart with an accompanying text. For example, at Banestown, the analyst noted that, though the remedial lab had proved to be a better solution to needs than the existing practices (Title I aides or in-class work) and thus had good support both from teachers and from the central office, other signs were not good. For instance, the district budget line for the catch-up lab was still drawn fron soft money; supervisory responsibility for the program had shifted and might shift again; and the lab did not have a "firm institutional status." Still the analyst was more optimistic than the chart suggests, emphasizing the central office administrators' and users' belief in the demonstrated need for the project and the strength

TABLE 39. Institutionalization, Banestown Site

	School level	District level
Supporting conditions		
Is a core (vs. peripheral) application	Present— temporary	Promised
Operating on regular, daily basis	Present— temporary	Present— temporary
Provides benefits, payoffs to users	Present— looks permanent	Present— looks permanent
Competing practices eliminated	Dubious—weak	Dubious—weak
Receives support from:		
Administrators	Present	Present—partially soft
Users/staff	Present	Present
Clients (pupils, parents)	Present	Present
Other: external $, laws, etc.		
Passage completion		
Goes from soft to hard money	Absent	Absent
Job description becomes standard	Dubious	Dubious
Skills required are included in formal training prog.	Absent	Absent
Organizational status is established part of regulations	Absent	Absent
Routines established for supply and maintenance	Present— temporary	Present— temporary
Cycle survival		
Survives annual budget cycles	Absent	Absent
Survives departure or introduction of new personnel	Promised	Promised
Skills are taught in successive cycles	Present— temporary	Present— temporary
Achieves widespread use throughout organization	Present— temporary	Present— temporary
Survives equipment turnover or loss (includes materials)	NA	NA

of their support. He noted the existence of similar labs at four other schools in the county ("Cutting off the lab at the elementary school would jeopardize the institutional rationale at the middle school"). The analyst also invoked "local habits of innovating. . . . New practices are hard to get started, but once they get started, they are even harder to discontinue," and he quoted a key user, a lab teacher:

> They would keep it going unless something really wrong would happen. That's the way it is around here. Things keep going as long as there aren't big waves.

Finally, the analyst pointed out that recent budget cuts had not eliminated the lab at another school, and that the two lab teachers there were on the county payroll and would almost surely not be fired. The text concludes:

The most likely prediction is that the labs are high on the list of projects to be supported once core classroom practices have been assured. The labs would be sacrificed before funds for teachers or core equipment or instructional materials. Beyond that, the labs are high on the list of priorities for "special programs."

If we turn to a site that showed *high* institutionalization, the picture on the site chart is quite different. For example, at Tindale, the analyst, without exception, gave a rating of "Present, looks permanent" to each cell of the chart. The text justified the ratings. The analyst pointed out that the Tindale reading program had "replaced the old basic English curriculum and functions like any other curriculum in the school." All users interviewed saw the program as "built in," and "some had never known it not to be." Though continued in-service training was not contemplated formally, there was a "large core of users who may be called on to aid the new teacher in the program." The ultimate measure of institutionalization, ironically enough, appears in this sentence: "In several years, it will be revised, just as all other curricula are revised on a regular basis."

Finally, let's turn for one more example to a site where institutionalization was essentially *absent.* At the Burton site, the central-office social studies coordinator defined the IPLE legal education unit as "experimental" and gave teachers a license to "pick and choose" at will from the IPLE materials. In practically all cells of the chart, the analyst gave a rating of "absent." The only weak exceptions were that one user (of four) was using the materials fairly regularly and said that they "vastly improved teaching" and were "highly beneficial to kids." A few students said that they liked the exercises, and the social studies coordinator was supportive.

The chances for institutionalization looked very slim. In particular, the community-based and other experiential activities of the program were a very poor fit with users' usual practices. But ultimately, whether the IPLE materials would ever be institutionalized depended on the curriculum review committees. One user noted:

If the revision work is done by an IPLE supporter or two, then IPLE would get built in. If it's not done by a supporter, IPLE would be used less, much less. Teachers are free to use as much of a revised curriculum as they want or need.

The Extent of Institutionalization

Table 40 arrays our 12 sites according to degree of institutionalization; it is drawn from the site-specific charts and the accompanying text, like those we have just reviewed. There is plenty of variation. We have 3 sites with high institutionalization, 3 more with high to moderate, 1 moderate, 3 low, and 2 where the only conceivable rating was "nil." If we note that a rating of "moderate" institutionalization was given when the typical cell entry was "present," but "temporary" or "uncertain," it seems fair to say that only the top 5 sites should be considered reasonably well institutionalized.

We can see also from Table 40 that *program sponsorship* (IV-C or NDN) was no guarantee of high, nor of low, institutionalization. And it seems clear that the "crunch" conditions for institutionalization were more frequently to be found in

TABLE 40. Institutionalization at the School and District Level, by Sites[a]

		Supporting conditions	Passage completion	Cycle survival	Other supporting conditions	Overall rating
Plummet (IV-C)	School	▲	▲	▲	State daily attendance funds.	High
	District	▲	▲	▲		
Tindale (IV-C)	School	▲	▲	▲	Changing student population increases need for program.	High
	District	▲	▲	▲		
Astoria (NDN)	School	?	▲	▲	District mandate.	High
	District	▲	▲	▲		
Masepa (NDN)	School	▲/△	△	▲	District mandate.	High–mod
	District	▲	△	▲		
Lido (NDN)	School	▲	▲	▲/—	Community, board interest.	Mod–high
	District	▲	▲	▲/—		
Carson (IV-C)	School	△/?	△	▲?/?	District mandate. Received dissemination grant for next year.	Mod
	District	▲/△	▲/?	▲?/?		
Banestown (NDN)	School	△/?	?/—	▲?/—	Strong central office commitment.	Mod
	District	△/?	?/—	▲?/—		
Calston (NDN)	School	△/?	?/—	?		Low
	District	—	—	—		
Perry-Parkdale (NDN)	School	△/?	—	—	Dissemination funds anticipated.	Low
	District	△/?	?/—	—		
Burton (NDN)	School	△/—	—	—	"Pilot" year; program may go into curriculum.	Low
	District	—	—	—		
Dun Hollow (IV-C)	School	?/—	—	—	Field testing; future use uncertain.	Nil
	District	—	—	—		
Proville (IV-C)[b]	School	?	—	?		Nil[b]
	District	?	—	?		

[a] ▲ = present, looks permanent; △ = present, looks temporary; ? = dubious, weak, uncertain; — = absent.
[b] Innovation currently discontinued. For comparison, these estimates are for the preceding year.

the *passages* and *cycles* sections: Even some low-institutionalizing sites had "supporting conditions" in place. A look at the site charts showed that "benefits to users," "operating on a regular, daily basis," and "support from clients" were present at Carson, Calston, Burton, and Perry-Parkdale, though they had few or no items present in the "passages" and "cycles" lists. In short, favorable present operations were no substitute for organizational routinization.

Explaining Institutionalization

What might account for the differing degrees of institutionalization at our sites? Our first step was to examine the 12 causal networks, looking at variables that immediately preceded institutionalization, plus those that were more remotely connected.[13]

To summarize: It appears that higher institutionalization was likely when there was *administrative pressure* to implement the program, no *serious resistance* (seen in low building endorsement or weak user commitment), and a reasonable degree of *teacher–administrator harmony.* If implementing the program resulted in some degree of *organizational transformation,* did not have serious *assistance* gaps, and ended with use by a fairly large *percentage of eligible users,* who along with program leaders *remained* in the situation, then stronger institutionalization was likely. If those who owned and managed the innovation decided to disengage, other, positive factors (e.g., building endorsement, user mastery, and stabilization of use) made little difference.

Once again, however, this is a smoothed set of findings, drawn from ratings across the 12 sites. To illustrate the institutionalization dynamics clearly, we need to look at more specific causal pathways as they played out in particular sites.

Scenarios Leading to High Institutionalization

It developed that our 12 sites fell into four families or "scenarios" for institutionalization: Two were high and two were low institutionalizers. The two routes to high institutionalization we called *mandated, stable use* and *skillful, committed use.* Let's illustrate and discuss each.

Mandated, Stable Use

Altogether, four of our sites (Tindale, Astoria, Carson, and Masepa) followed this general scenario. The prototypical example is Tindale. The network excerpt is shown in Figure 26. Here, a powerful central-office administrator (2), the director of curriculum and special projects, working from a centralized power base (3), put considerable pressure on users (5) to implement the new locally developed reading program. Initially, this pressure lowered users' commitment (8); they resented and feared the pressure. But substantial assistance (1) was supplied, which increased users' practice mastery

[13]For details on substance and methods, see the technical report (pp. 362–365).

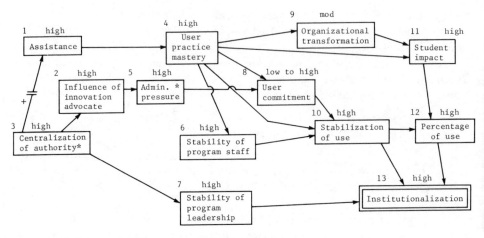

+Influence of other variables not discussed
*Site-specific variable

FIGURE 26. Mandated, stable use as a route to institutionalization: Tindale (IV-C).

(4) a good deal and subsequently their commitment (8). In addition, modest organizational rearrangements (9), including revised scheduling, pupil rotation, and teacher teaming, were made, increasing student impact (11). User mastery and commitment, along with stability of program staff (6), led to stabilized use (10), which both increased the percentage of use (12) and led to institutionalization (13). Stability of the program leadership (7) also aided institutionalization. The general picture is one of administrative decisiveness, accompanied by enough assistance to increase user skill, ownership, and stable use in the context of a stable system.

The three other sites sharing this scenario varied in particulars, of course, though all entailed a mandated use of the program. At Astoria, the mandate flowed even more directly from centralized authority, and stability was achieved through program simplification rather than through user mastery.[14] In a matter-of-fact exercise of central power, the central office advocate was able to directly mandate the use of an early-childhood screening program that fit the district's needs well. Both factors led directly to institutionalization. It did not matter that users recieved only moderate assistance, had low practice mastery, and felt few benefits or much commitment. The centrally mandated institutionalization could even survive the departure of its original advocate.

The Astoria experience was a "front-end" mandate. At both Masepa and Carson, a demanding innovation was tried out with substantial assistance for some time with one or two generations of users, then mandated at the "back-end" for all. The patterns were generally similar. At Carson, the exercise of power was moderated by the consent of the governed. The vigorous, charismatic superintendent infused his strongly humanistic ideology into the district, which led to strong user commitment to the individualized educational pro-

[14]For details, see the technical report (pp. 367–368).

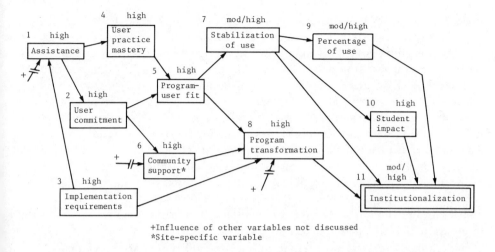

FIGURE 27. Mastery and commitment as a route to institutionalization: Lido (NDN).

gramming plan that they had developed. The program's success, along with the ideology itself and the direct influence of the superintendent, led to the decision to mandate the program for all. This decision automatically increased not only percentage of use but also institutionalization, which was also supported by high to moderate levels of district and building endorsement, and by the organizational transformations (e.g., increased communication and trust) that the innovation had carried in its wake.[15]

The picture at Masepa was similar, with an even stronger emphasis on the development of user commitment through serious effort, administrative pressure, assistance-aided skill development, and continuing district and building-level endorsement. Here, too, the mandate came late in the game, after the innovation had expanded to more and more users and had demonstrated its value in terms of student impact.

Skillful, Committed Use

A second scenario leading to moderate to high institutionalization appeared at Lido, Plummet, and Banestown. The element of mandating was absent. Under these circumstances, it appeared more essential that both skills, and commitment be present. Note, for example, that either or both could be and were absent in the "mandate" scenario (e.g., Astoria and Carson). The picture for Lido is shown in Figure 27.

The causal flow looks like this. The KARE environmental studies program had demanding implementation requirements (interdisciplinary, field-oriented "hands-on" learning by students) that led to initial assistance (1) that was strong enough to increase both user practice mastery (4) and commitment (2). User commitment also enhanced and was enhanced by community support (6) for the

[15]Details on this case are in the technical report (pp. 368–369).

program's presence in a local park site donated to the school district. Increasingly good program–user fit (5) led toward stable use (7), a higher percentage of use (9) as added teachers got involved, and student impact (10) (in this case, increased motivation and academic self-concept). All three led to institutionalization (11).

The KARE program was also the subject of considerable program transformation (8), taking the form of elaboration and development of the larger environmental-science program of which it was a part. That program development, aided by community support (6) and the implementation requirements (3), also aided institutionalization. The general thrust was one of a voluntaristic (nonmandated) development of user mastery and commitment as a route to program development and stabilization, thence to institutionalization.

The story at Banestown was quite similar. There too, assistance, both at the district and at the within-user-team level, led to increased commitment to the innovation (Catch-up remedial-reading lab) and to skill in its use; there too, considerable program transformation led to stability and student impact. The effect on institutionalization were strong enough at Banestown to overcome the potential destabilization of program leadership and staff threatened by a possible loss of funding.

The third site where a skill and commitment scenario occurred was Plummet. It differed from Lido and Banestown in having a strong organizational-transformation component, along with powerful external community support, but it was otherwise a close analogue.[16]

Scenarios Leading to Low Institutionalization

We were able to sort the remaining five sites into two families, which we called *vulnerability* and *indifference*.

Vulnerability

At Perry-Parkdale and Calston, the innovative programs were quite vulnerable to environmental turbulence. They had no organizational structures to protect them when funding crises struck or advocates departed. So even though user mastery, commitment, and stabilization of use were moderate to high, there was little guarantee of durability.

This picture becomes very clear if we look at an excerpt from the Perry-Parkdale network (Figure 28). The temporary funding of the program (2), a work-experience program for what turned out to be disaffected students drawn from two high schools, increased its vulnerability (1), already high because the students, out in the community on their own, could easily behave like "assholes" and embarrass the staff. In effect, the program was competing not only for funds but for students (6). This competition reduced building endorsement (5), specifically that of the principals. The program's staff tended to withdraw,

---

[16]For details, see the technical report (pp. 371–372).

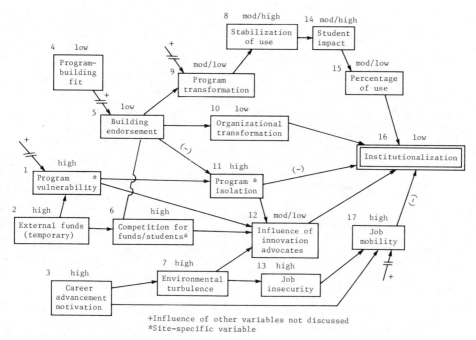

FIGURE 28. Vulnerability as a route to low institutionalization: Perry-Parkdale (NDN).

working in isolation (11); this withdrawal reduced their effective influence (12) and that of the central office advocates. Though the program itself was altered (9) to meet the principals' objections, there was very little alteration in the surrounding district *organization* or that of the high schools (10). The program's isolation, the lack of organizational supports, and the lowered power of the program advocates all weakened institutionalization (16), even though the program was being used stably (8) with good student impact (14), though for only a small percentage of students (15). Institutionalization was even further weakened by the career advancement motivation (3) of key central-office people and principals, which induced much turbulence (7) within the district. The job mobility (17) of key program staff was, as a result of these and other factors, also high. Overall, we have a picture of a strong, promising innovation that was insufficiently protected through strong links to its enviroment, so that turbulence, the movement of key people, and the negative attitudes of powerful principals could wreak havoc.

The story at Calston was less complex but equally bleak. A well-stabilized reading program, Matteson 4D, was seriously jeopardized institutionally because no organization transformation at all had occurred, so that the program's continuation depended solely, as the site analyst noted, on whether the present users would continue in their jobs. But it seemed that they would not; Calston was threatened with a severe fiscal crisis that knocked the central office advocate out of her job and threatened the jobs of a principal and some users.

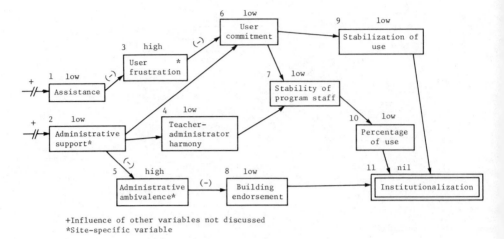

FIGURE 29. Indifference as a route to low institutionalization: Dun Hollow (IV-C).

Indifference

The weakest institutionalization occurred at three sites (Dun Hollow, Proville, and Burton) when the administrators, in particular, showed by their behavior that they were essentially indifferent to the fate of the innovation; they did little either to assist the users to develop mastery and commitment or to stabilize use. A prototypical case is Dun Hollow (Figure 29). Though the administrators at Dun Hollow had been perfectly willing to "volunteer" some teachers to field-test the new curricular materials for Eskimo studies, they provided little or no support (2); moreover, the assistance from the developer (1) was weak. The frustrated users (3) had little commitment (6) to the materials; this lack of commitment and the poor relations with the administrators (4) engendered by weak support lost one teacher to the program (7) and put the participation of the two others in doubt. The use of the program was unstable (9) and was limited to a very small percentage of the eligible users (10); institutionalization (11) was weakened on both counts. Administrative indifference showed up further as ambivalence (5) about whether the materials deserved curriculum incorporation; that ambivalence translated into weak building endorsement (8). The net result: a rating of "nil" for institutionalization.

The story at Proville was, if possible, one of even deeper indifference. The CEP work-experience program had been an opportunistic vehicle for the superintendent to bring a protégé into the central office, and to attract additional outside funds. But the protégé was quickly loaded with other tasks and eventually found greener job pastures elsewhere. His successor struggled anew with the task, but also got competing assignments. So there was no one to counter the resentment and resistance of the principals and the vocational education teachers who had been pressured to implement a program that they found undesirable, and there was no one to provide the assistance that might have bridged the gap. As noted earlier, the program was simply left to rot.

The Burton picture was more constructive, but almost as unavailing. There, the central office administrator's *de facto* indifference was benign; it was masked under the heading of "experimental," "pilot" use of the IPLE legal education materials for possible later curriculum incorporation. Building principals, in their usual role at Burton on curriculum matters, were uninvolved. Only weak assistance was provided, and the "pick-and-choose" license given to users meant that the least demanding IPLE materials were tried out. There was little user commitment, less mastery, and minimal impact on students and the organization. Even if IPLE materials were somehow written into the curriculum the next year, the "pick-and-choose" norm would still apply.

Institutionalization: An Epilogue

Institutionalization is an outcome of school improvement efforts that can be assessed rather cleanly by what happens later on. As of June 1980, we assessed the likelihood that each of our 12 innovations had been "built in" enough to ensure its continuation. As noted, we believed that durability was likely in about half the cases.

Looking at our June 1980 data, we assembled specific predictions for each site. What would happen the next year, or the year after? Was our understanding of institutionalization adequate to such a task of forecasting? In the spring of 1981, a year later, we reported our predictions back to each of our 12 sites, asking them to tell us whether our guesses had been correct. Table 41 reviews the predictions made and includes the institutionalization ratings presented earlier in this section. Then it displays the actual course of events at the 12 sites.

We also asked the site personnel to give their reasons for the course of events that had occurred, as well as getting them to check the validity of *our* reasons. The last column of Table 41 shows the site personnel's explanations of the institutionalization outcome. First, we show their spontaneous explanations, in order of priority; then we display their reactions to *our* explanations, focusing only on those that they agreed were of relevance. Whenever their and our explanations coincided, the material is in bold face type.[17]

What can we conclude from Table 41? First, it is clear that the accuracy of our predictions was moderate to high for all sites; we were never badly off.

Second, we should take a look at the degree to which our explanations coincided with theirs (bold face type). This occurred for 53 of the 92 causes given (58%). The proportion of agreement did not differ for the sites with moderate, moderate to high, or high accuracy, so we must conclude that some causes had differential weighting or importance. A good example is Banestown, where our accuracy was only moderate, mainly because we expected continuation in at least one middle school in addition to elementary-school use.

[17]It should be noted that the table does *not* contain those of our explanations that the site personnel dismissed as wholly or partly irrelevant. On the average, about a third of our explanations were treated this way.

TABLE 41. Institutionalization: Predictions and Actuality

	Rating of institution-alization	Our prediction re institutionalization for 1980, 1981, 1981–82	Site report as of Spring 1981	Our predictive accuracy	Explanations by site personnel[a]
Plummet (IV-C)	High	Program will continue as durable part of district setup for '80–'81, '81–'82.	Continued '80–'81; operational for '81–'82, but may be shut down thereafter, under close board scrutiny.	High–mod	**District financial problems;** other school closings; lower cost-effectiveness of program; board racism; director has new supervisor; **staff and leadership instability; need for program; state funds, stable, impactful program.**
Tindale (IV-C)	High	Level will remain high; some efforts to modify or reduce program.	Level remains high in spite of staff change; only minor program changes.	High	Teacher ownership, **central office and principals' support,** close supervision by dept. heads, **curriculum incorporation; organizational changes not easily reversible;** materials availability; student impact.
Astoria (NDN)	High	Will continue as routine though nominal implementation; further program changes likely.	Institutionalized in nominal form; simplifications made in record keeping.	High	**System mandate; preparation for fall use under way, May '80;** user endorsement of testing aspect; satisfaction with present implementation level; **resistance to full implementation (poor fit);** low implementation pressure; resignation of advocate.
Masepa (NDN)	High–mod	Will remain at focal school, and for district, in Grades 3–7 for '80–'81; some modest program changes by individual teachers.	Remained at focal school and in district Grades 3–6 (or 3–8) for '80–'81. Some program changes by individual teachers.	High	**Board mandate 3–7. In-service training** for untrained teachers. **Resistance from some teachers,** mandate withdrawn, Grades 2–7; teachers discontinued. **Central office and school board support.**

Lido (NDN)	Mod-high	Program will be maintained but scaled down in hours (esp. extracurricular ones); same number of pupils.	Continued at slightly scaled-down level (extra-curricular time, some projects).	High	**Instructor time**; site distance; budgetary control, student demand for courses not increased or decreased; **community, board support; built into courses; meets need; disagreement between lead user and principal.**
Carson (IV-C)	Moderate	Program will continue in approx. present form during '80–'81 and for '81–'82. Status for '82–'83 uncertain.	Program continued '80–'81; less emphasis on field trips. Will continue, approximately same form, '81–'82; '82–'83 less certain, but probably will continue, possibly in altered form.	Mod-high	**Supt.** and principals' stability and **endorsement** (mixed); teacher stability and endorsement (mixed); active new coordinator (helps, causes resentment also); active steering group; parental support. **Dissemination funds require program in place. Role ambiguity for new coordinator. Program routinization** (manual, etc.).
Banestown (NDN)	Moderate	Program will be durably incorporated into 3 elem. schools, 2 middle schools; central office will call for line-item support for lab teachers, and for stab. of program Grades 3–7.	In 3 primary schools, middle schools unsure. Service extended to 2nd-graders. In district budget.	Moderate	**Administrative support**; teacher commitment; lab teachers freed of other tasks (except in middle school) because of **budget cuts; student impact;** community support. **Need for upper-grade follow-up to DISTAR program.**
Calston (NDN)	Low	Continued use is user-dependent; if they stay, program will continue; if they leave, replacements will not cont.	One user using in each of 2 schools; replacements not using.	High	No training time for replacements by peers or **outsiders** or principal. Previous user coping well. **Principals supportive; self-training** by previous users.

(continued)

TABLE 41. Continued

	Rating of institution- alization	Our prediction re institutionalization for 1980, 1981, 1981–82	Site report as of Spring 1981	Our predictive accuracy	Explanations by site personnel[a]
Perry–Parkdale (NDN)	Low	Transitional year '80–'81; program then will phase out.	Transitional year (fewer students and staff), '80–'81. Will continue $\frac{1}{2}$-time basis, '81–'82.	Moderate	**Tight funding; loss of external funds, de-clining enrollments/cutbacks; weak endorsement by central admin.; support** by other central admin., **weak endorse-ment by principals, counselors, teachers; possibility of dissemination funding; program meets needs; pro-gram well implemented and stabilized.**
Burton (NDN)	Low	Innovation's topics, activi-ties, and materials will be written into soc. studies curric., but program as whole will not be adopted.	Topics, activities, materials written into individual curriculum, and into guides for civics, gov't., history and law—but not as broad district policy for social studies.	High–mod	**Planned to do this** ('79–'80); program is poor fit to schedule; **little time free for** evaluating program; **current users on curric. revision committee; freedom for teachers to adopt portions; no rewards** for taking more responsibility: **success, user satisfaction.**
Dun Hollow (IV-C)	Nil	Will not be incorporated into curric.	Not incorporated, though some parts included as supplementary material.	High	Contact with prior curriculum decisions, **not written into curriculum; materials poor, inappropriate, lengthy, time-consuming; little support from principals.**
Proville (IV-C)	Nil	Program will not be con-tinued in any form origi-nally contemplated; will be discontinued.	Program ended. Some staff used ideas in their objectives.	High	**Loss of funds;** changing priorities, new supt. and board; **weak endorsement; no org'nl changes** to support; shift to decentralization.

[a]Items in boldface had been part of our analysis.

Though we accurately noted budget cuts as a cause of possibly lowered institutionalization, we did not understand that the ax would differentially fall on the middle school programs—even though we, like the site informants, thought that the need for the program in those schools would continue.

Or note Perry-Parkdale, where our analysis—largely confirmed by site people—led use to predict a program phase-out. In fact the program hung on by its fingernails; central office support and the hope of future money had more weight than we had thought.

Occasionally, we were surprised, as by the board's willingness in "gung-ho" Masepa to back off from its mandate of the ECRI program of Grades 3–7 when some teachers complained. But it is consistent with our understanding of Masepa that given this freedom, only two (seventh-grade) teachers decided to exercise it and not use the program.

On balance, however, we understood our sites well enough to make good predictions. That our causes and those offered by site personnel did not overlap tightly suggests, as we might have expected, that a matter as complex as the institutionalization of innovations is multiply caused, perhaps overdetermined. All we need to do is have a good handle on some—perhaps half—of the key causes. That is probably enough for predictive confidence.

Conclusions

We found that about half our sites succeeded in institutionalizing their innovative programs reasonably well, moving them through the "passages" and "cycles" of routinization carefully enough that stable continuation was likely. It was clear that satisfactory *current* operations and support were not enough: Sites with strong institutionlization had made clear organizational changes— mandating the innovation, building it into the curriculum, and changing working procedures or structures—that were relatively irreversible.

An examination of predictors showed us that good institutionalization requires *administrative pressure*, accompanied by lack of serious *resistance* and a reasonable degree of *teacher–administrator harmony*. Thus, we are not speaking of tyrannical operations but of firmly pursued ones. Strong institutionalization means *organizational transformation*, as we have just noted, accompanied by a reasonable amount of *assistance*, enough to bring about *stabilized use* by a large *percentage of users*. It also helps if there is *personnel stability* on the part of both users and administrators.

We found that institutionalization scenarios played themselves out in four different patterns. The strongest (appearing at four sites) was that of *mandated, stable use*, where there was an explicit systemwide commitment to continued use of the innovation, as well as provisions to stabilize that use. Without such a commitment at the system level, we found a second scenario (at three sites) in which strong assistance and support combined to develop *user mastery and commitment*, thence stability and moderate to high institutionalization.

It was also clear that institutionalization could fail, either by vulnerability (two sites), where the administrators had not done enough to guard the innovation against resistance or environmental turbulence, or by indifference (3 sites), where they simply did not care enough to supply the assistance and protection that the innovation needed if it was to survive.

Finally, we found that using our assessment of the degree of institutionalization, we were reasonably able to predict the course of events at the site *vis-á vis* the continuation of the innovation one year later. Predictive success occurred even when our explanations did not coincide with those of site personnel.

STUDENT IMPACT

Introduction

So far, we have looked at the innovations' stability at our sites, how widespread their use was, and how firmly built in they were. But these aspects do not necessarily bear directly on another question: What difference did the programs we studied make in the behavior, the knowledge, and the attitudes of their end consumers, students? No matter how fully and stably implemented an innovation is, it may or may not improve student attitudes and performance. Student performance is usually claimed to be the "bottom line" of school improvement. The idea that such a claim is often rhetorical, and the fact that our conceptual framework examined other important outcomes as well, do not obscure the importance of student impact.

Our assessment of student impact was quite variable across sites. For some sites, we had detailed interview and questionnaire responses from users, administrators, counselors, parents, and students themselves, along with "hard" test scores and even a comparison group or two; for others, we had little but unsupported—though usually convergent—opinion. There was the additional problem that some programs aimed high, contemplating changes in everything from student achievement to improved self-concept, while others were much more modest, hoping only for reading-skills improvement or "environmental awareness." So our picture of what these programs accomplished locally is not always crystal-clear. By and large, however, we had robust evaluative data (test scores and/or fairly rigorous external evaluations) for 7 of the 12 sites, notably for the sites that turned out to have high levels of student impact.[18]

In this section, we first review the nature and the extent of student impact across the 12 sites (both direct and metalevel, plus side effects), then look at the factors predicting that impact. We conclude, as before, with some typical scenarios leading to high or low student impact.

[18]We should remind the reader that all the NDN innovations we studied had passed through the validation process operated by the Joint Dissemination Review Panel, which meant that if implemented reasonably faithfully and thoroughly, they were expected to have predictable and positive student impact.

Types and Extent of Student Impact

Our cross-site analysis[19] took into account the *objectives* of the innovative program involved; the *direct* outcomes (both positive and negative, seen by the stakeholders including users, administrators, counselors, parents, evaluators, and students themselves); and what we called *metalevel outcomes and side effects*. A metalevel outcome was one congruent with the program's purposes, but affecting more-general aspects of students' functioning. For example, the Matteson 4D reading program at Calston caused the *direct* outcome of improved reading skills, which was a directly contemplated objective. But the fact that the program contained much provision for student independent work, on a variety of interesting materials, resulted in a *metalevel* outcome: more self-direction on the part of students. Side effects were not easily separable from metalevel effects but usually had more of an unintended flavor. We noted, for example, the alienation of students in the Perry-Parkdale work experience program, who enjoyed the program's concreteness and relevance but thereby came to dislike their regular high school's courses and activities. This example also illustrates the fact that we looked for both positive and negative effects on students.

Our 12 sites were ordered by the approximate degree of student impact. A rating of "high" was given when it appeared that (1) the program was achieving most of its aims; (2) it had also achieved other positive metalevel and side effects; and (3) these judgments were corroborated, either through repeated responses from one role incumbent, through cross-role verification, or through the availability of evaluation data. Weaknesses in any of these three criteria lowered the ratings.

A review of these data suggests several generalizations. First, positive effects dominated—even at sites where there was considerable user dissatisfaction or even resentment (for example, Proville and Dun Hollow). By and large, when asked about outcomes, site personnel noted the good things. It's of some interest that the sites (Perry-Parkdale, Tindale, and Masepa) where more negative effects were noted were also the ones where much was being attempted: a thoroughgoing work-experience program, a comprehensive reading curriculum that ramified into math and science, and a demanding, comprehensive reading program. We shall see shortly that such programs also tended to develop more capacity in users. For now, we note that attempting more may have laid the program open to achieving some unintended negative results as well.

Second, the presence of metalevel outcomes and side effects was typical of our sites; only in Dun Hollow and Burton (both sites with sharply limited use and low stability of use) were there none. Evidently, it is unwise to restrict our attention, as many evaluators do, to the intended, "concrete," first-level or direct effects of innovative programs. Nearly all of the nondirect effects could be deemed educationally significant, from "improved attitude toward school"

---

[19]For details, see the technical report (pp. 382–386).

and "increased attendance" to "more expressive, independent behavior" and "more on-task behavior."

Third, it may be that programs with highly differentiated objectives, such as those at Masepa, Perry-Parkdale, or Carson, were more likely to show high impact, if only because the program personnel, evaluators, and researchers were more likely to look for results on the whole range of objectives. The sites with more limited hopes, such as Proville, did not inspire such close scrutiny. The question of differentiated objectives is, of course, allied with the issue of innovation size and scope, "demandingness," and the like.

Finally, it turned out that program sponsorship (NDN or IV-C) made no consistent difference as far as student impact was concerned.

Let's turn to the question of what might have caused differences in the amount of student impact.

Factors Causing Student Impact

As in the preceding sections, we reviewed the 12 causal networks, working backward from the "student impact" box, and looking for variables that were directly connected (within two steps) or more remotely causal.[20]

To summarize briefly: It appears that high student impact was more likely when *user commitment* was high, when *program transformation* either was held to a minimum or was used to correct an initially overambitious start, and when strong *assistance* took place, resulting in *practice mastery* and *stabilization of use*. The presence of *administrative pressure* was a remote cause of student impact—but only, it appears, when it translated into willingness to restrict program transformation, to supply strong assistance, or to do both.

In particular, it's clear that high student impact was likely when the innovation was large, was possibly poorly fitting, and was revamped but not substantially downsized (the "overreaching" scenario at Perry-Parkdale and Plummet; see also the moderate impact at "overreaching" Carson). It is also clear that high student impact could come when program transformation, possibly with poor fit, was kept to a minimum through enforcement (Tindale and Masepa). On the low end, a poor fit with plenty of accompanying transformation (the "latitude" strategy) guaranteed a reductive "refitting" or "salvaging" scenario with little impact (Astoria, Proville, and Burton)—especially if assistance was weak.

We need now to look at how the high, moderate, and low student-impact scenarios play themselves out at our sites.

Scenarios Leading to High Student Impact

Our high-impact sites clustered into two scenarios: (1) *enforced, supported mastery* and (2) *stabilized mastery*.

---

[20]This exercise is shown and discussed in the technical report (pp. 387–390).

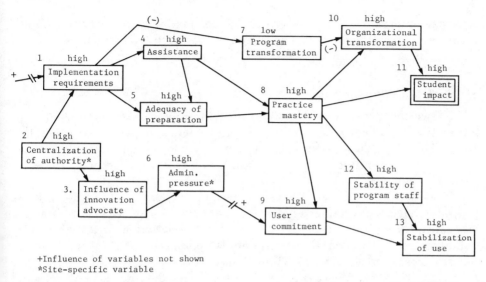

FIGURE 30. Enforced, supported mastery as a route to high student impact: Tindale (IV-C).

Enforced, Supported Mastery

Once again, Tindale is a textbook exhibit. The network extract is shown in Figure 30.

At Tindale, the centralized authority (2) accruing to the innovation's central-office advocate (3) enabled the mandating of a very demanding, comprehensive program for reading, math, and science for low-achieving students. The "enforcing" mode, with strong pressure to implement (6), led at first to low, then higher, user commitment (9). The program's demanding requirements (1) led to careful assistance (4) and good initial user preparation (5), both of which developed strong user practice mastery (8)—another source of increased user commitment. But the mastery stream was not the sole cause of high student impact (11). The enforcing mode meant that program transformation (7) was kept to a minimum; users were closely policed ("Changing an activity is a venial sin, but changing an objective is a mortal sin," one teacher noted). The bargain struck in exchange for fidelity was that needed organizational changes (10) in scheduling, pupil rotation, and team teaching were carried out, which added to student impact. Note that the stability of program staff (12) and stabilization of use (13) were *results* of skill and commitment, not the converse. This carefully managed process of change essentially worked through the avenues of commitment and mastery.

The story at Masepa was essentially similar. High student impact was achieved through strong user commitment and assistance-developed practice mastery, and program transformation was kept to a minimum, in part because the developer insisted on a faithful replication of the ECRI reading program. The main difference from Tindale was that user commitment came via the early success of a pilot experiment, with close teacher–administrator collaboration that generated strong user effort. The mandating of the program did not occur until late in the game and, incidentally, was itself fed by clear evidence of student impact.

Stabilized, Committed Mastery

Altogether, six sites—Perry-Parkdale, Banestown, and Plummet, (all high-impact sites) and Lido, Carson, and Calston (moderate-impact sites)—went this route. The key variables were practice mastery and stability, accompanied by strong user commitment. Let's look at how these were assured at Perry-Parkdale (Figure 31).

The Experience-Based Career Education program at Perry-Parkdale proved to have heavy implementation requirements (1), which called for ample assistance (2) and also exerted pressure for the selection of a high-quality volunteer staff (5), and for careful initial preparation (3), which further buttressed staff skills. The heavy implementation requirements ("Here your neck is on the block. Most people wouldn't want it") induced, as at Masepa and elsewhere, a good deal of user commitment (4). That heightened user practice mastery (7), already boosted by assistance (2) and by the strong professionalism of the staff (5). Transformation in the program itself (6) stayed low because of user commitment (4) to the spirit of the innovation and the staff ability (5), and this fidelity contributed considerably to program stabilization (8), already doing well because of practice mastery (7). Student impact (9) was the consequence of such stable, skillful use.

Similar courses of events occurred at Banestown and Plummet. At Banestown, active central-office assistance for the Catch-up remedial-lab users boosted user commitment and skill, both of which had been threatened by a too-rapid early implementation. Once commitment and skill were in place, active peer assistance among users developed practice mastery still further, as they revamped the program moderately to achieve stabilization.

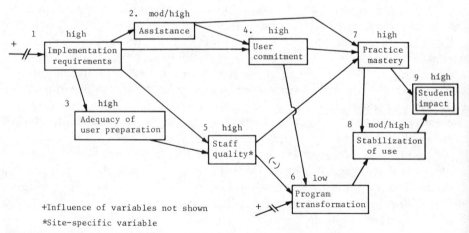

FIGURE 31. Stabilized, committed mastery as a route to high student impact: Perry-Parkdale (NDN).

The Plummet picture was, as at Banestown and Perry-Parkdale, one of close cooperation among a committed set of users who were also volunteer staff with high professionalism.

Commitment was also heightened by strong implementation requirements. The "innovation" was a complete school, and the staff members were given much discretionary latitude to develop and redesign it. The resulting practice mastery, developed with peer support in the caldron of the new alternative school, led to stabilized use and strong student impact.

It is worth noting that these three cases were all somewhat "set off" from their surroundings, operating as subsystems with a life of their now, and that they developed strong internal loyalties and mutual support. They were "apart together" and used that fact to their advantage—and to the advantage of their students.

We should note that the "stabilized, committed mastery" scenario did not always work as well as in these three cases. For example, at Carson, the decision to mandate the program brought in many new, less committed users, and the program was considerably simplified ("watered down," some said). That transformation, together with sketchy assistance, led to only moderate stabilization of use, and to moderate student impact.[21] Generally, we have the same scenario here as at more successful sites, except that the key causes of student impact were moderate.

If we look for a moment at Calston and Lido, our other two moderate-impact sites, the stable and committed mastery scenario was also operative. Both were trying small-scale, less demanding innovations. At Calston, user commitment was only moderate, even with good front-end assistance that increased initial practice mastery. The Matteson 4D reading program was moderately refashioned to fit the realities of the city's existing comprehensive reading program. This adaptation and weak ongoing assistance resulted in only moderate student impact.

At Lido, good early assistance and community support led to strong user commitment for the KARE environmental-education program, and to practice mastery. Use stabilized well, but the reality was that the KARE approaches and materials were such a small part of the larger environmental-education program that it was hard to get more than moderate student impact.

Scenarios Leading to Low Student Impact

We found two scenarios here, with two sites each: *weak commitment* and *program blunting*.

Weak Commitment

The clearest exhibit of weak commitment was Proville. The excerpt is shown in Figure 32.

At Proville, the work-experience program was mainly a vehicle for career advancement (1); the program's developer rode the innovation into a central

[21]For a detailed analysis, see the technical report (pp. 395–396).

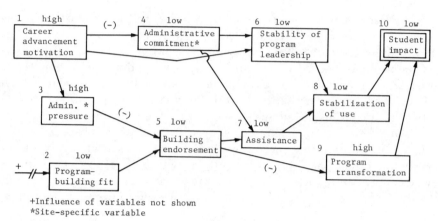

+Influence of variables not shown
*Site-specific variable

FIGURE 32. Weak commitment as a route to low student impact: Proville (IV-C).

office job and had little continued commitment (4) to it. The program also had a poor fit with the high schools' programs (2). This, along with the super-intendent-induced pressure for implementation (3), led to much resentment and low building endorsement (5). In short, neither the program's advocates nor its users had any real commitment to it. Weak commitment on both sides led to weak assistance (7) and to considerable sabotaging and skeleton-izing of the program (9), which along with weak stabilization of use (8)—itself caused by career-driven leadership changes (6)—meant that student impact (10) was essentially nil.

The Dun Hollow story was also marked by low commitment. The superin-tendent and the principals agreed casually to the field testing of the new Eskimo-studies materials "to stay on the good side" of the intermediate unit that was developing them. But they supplied no support, and users had little commitment to what proved to be a time-consuming exercise with little apparent future in the district.

Program Blunting

We use the term *program blunting* to refer to scenarios (Burton and Astoria) where the main causal thrust came from the latitude that users had to transform a poorly fitting program so substantially that student impact was minimized. Let's look at Astoria (Figure 33). Here, the districtwide mandate (2) for use of the early-childhood screening and skill-development program meant that certain demand characteristics (3), notably the kindergarten emphasis on the requirement for scheduling flexibility, made for a poor program–building fit (4), already potentially poor because of the heavy program requirements (1). The teachers had to take time not only for the initial testing, but for daily remedial work with individual students. But as we saw earlier, much latitude (5) was granted by the central office advocate. This restored the teacher–administrator harmony (6) that had been threatened by the innovation. Working closely together, the vice-principal and the teachers devised a "flex-

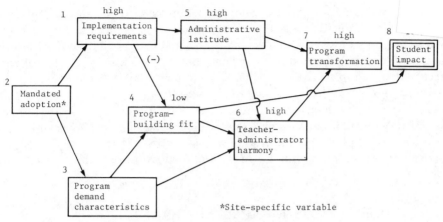

FIGURE 33. Program blunting as a route to low student impact: Astoria (NDN).

ible" implementation plan that farmed out the testing to aides, parents, and the vice-principal herself, and that discarded the remedial teaching of many skills. In short, program transformation (7) was substantial, so the program could not be expected to have the impact (8) that its original developers had expected.

The scenario at Burton was similar, though there was no mandate. The central office advocate considered the IPLE program to be in a "pilot" year, when users could "pick and choose" promising aspects of the program and then, supposedly, build them into the curriculum. But users quite naturally shied away from the more demanding or adventurous components (e.g., the emphasis on activistlike community experience and more student-directed learning activities). Yet, these very aspects of the program were central to the IPLE program's success, so the student impact was minimal.

Conclusions

Though our measurements of student impact were uneven across sites, we found that five of our sites had reasonably strong student impact, as measured by interrole agreement and—when available—by test results on the achievement of program objectives, as well as on more general positive "metalevel" and side effects. Another three sites showed moderate impact; the remaining four sites were moderate or low.

The main factors explaining student impact were *user commitment*, along with strong *assistance* that led to *practice mastery* and *stabilization of use*. The most frequent scenario (six sites), "stabilized mastery," stressed these factors. Two other sites added the feature of "enforcement," with the extra feature of administrative pressure and the restriction of undesirable changes in the innovation. The low-impact sites suffered either from low commitment or from what we called *program blunting*—reducing the thrust of the innovation so far that its effects were trivial.

Essentially, we found that developing committed, stable, and skillful use of a good-quality innovation was the critical predictor of student impact. If people learn to use the innovation well and routinely and feel committed to it, positive results will occur—provided institutional unrest or friction is low. It's of some interest that this picture is considerably simpler than the one that we have drawn for some of the preceding outcomes (e.g., institutionalization). The message is not, however, a narrow one of "fidelity at all costs." Some considerably revamped innovations worked well—provided the changes were made in the service of the innovation's chief goals, rather than for organizational or personal convenience. Commitment and competence can drive productive adaptation.

USER CAPACITY CHANGE

Introduction

Capacity change was an outcome variable that emerged progressively in the course of data collection, as teachers told us that carrying out the innovation was bringing a host of by-products in its wake. The skills involved in technical mastery of the new practice often appeared to translate into instructional or classroom managerial changes in *other* subject matters, or in routine tasks. Looking for a blanket term to cover these shifts, we chose *user capacity change* to indicate such a heightening of school-based professional ability.

Separating the part of capacity change clearly attributable to the innovation from the part extending beyond the practice was a delicate operation; it was usually a distinction that our informants found hard or irrelevant to make. By the same token, it was hard for us to unravel "process changes" from the "outcomes" that we are handling in this section. For instance, capacity changes usually came in the form of "enablers": To successfully implement an individualized remedial-skills program, the teachers had to learn how to work with one or two pupils at a time, while keeping the remainder of the group on task. Learning to do this is a legitimate instance of capacity change; it outlives and extends beyond the innovation, yet it is also, more narrowly, a precondition for the successful implementation of a specific practice. But determining just when such a change occurred—during or near the end of a given year—was usually impossible. The more important point is that, at the majority of the sites, there *were* such changes reported at levels that we determined as being moderate-to-high.

Essentially, we wanted to know not only which changes occurred, but also *where* such change occurred, *how* "high"-capacity change sites were different from "low" sites, and *why* these differences occurred. This section will run succesively through these topics.

As we proceed, we shall try to weave in several findings from earlier sections, notably from the section reporting on the changes in users during implementation. In fact, we can lead off profitably by reproducing the summary flowchart from the "user change" section (p. 166) and appending to it our "capacity-change" outcome measure (Figure 34).

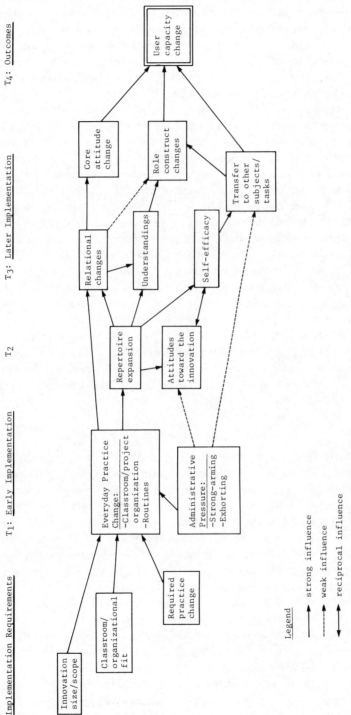

FIGURE 34. Causal flowchart tracing user practice changes as antecedents of user capacity change.

As the figure shows, the innovation sets off project-specific changes in instructional and organizational routines, which gradually translate into new understandings, feelings, relationships, and transferable skills, the sum of which is a more general increment in professional capacity. Also, some of the important predictors of capacity change appear here: the size and scope of the project, the local fit, the required practice change, and what we have called, perhaps uncharitably, *administrative pressure*.

The general message of the "user change" section as that greater practice change occurred when more was attempted, that is, when the innovation made strong demands on the users to change their customary instructional practice in order to implement the program successfully. These demands resulted from ambitious (big and/or complex) projects that were poor local fits, forcing the users to swim in new waters. Users were, in turn, encouraged, often prodded, and usually helped by local administrators who were anxious to obtain outcomes that were more than trivial or incremental. As these new skills were mastered, they acted both to deliver project-specific outcomes and to generate the kind of second-order outcomes that we have labeled *capacity changes*. Finally, we noted that many of the higher change-inducing projects addressed a hard-to-change or even a hard-to-reach pupil population, which often had the effect of calling forth great effort and commitment on the part of users. As we said earlier, the more ventured, the more gained. In other words, when users pushed themselves or got pushed beyond their customary instructional practices, they stretched their minds and their repertoires. The policy question here is how practice-stretching can be facilitated and sustained below tolerable thresholds of pain and uncertainty. Some of the answers are provided in the section on assistance (pp. 88–113).

Types and Degrees of Capacity Change

Essentially, the cross-site portrait has already been painted in the user change section. Table 32 (p. 152) reports on the types and items of practice change, and Table 34 (p. 161) shows a rough, Guttmann-like scaling of the 12 sites according to the pervasiveness or the extent of practice change. When we moved out to the end of the experience and asked users to think in particular about the second-order effects of implementation—the ones that had affected other parts of their instructional practice—and then rescaled the 12 sites, the results were similar. We came up with a rough ordinal scale moving from "low"-capacity change to "high"-capacity change. The types of capacity change fell into the categories that we had generated for Table 32 in the user change section: changes in dialy routines, in general instructional repertoire, in relationships, in understandings and feelings, in other segments of one's work, and in basic constructs and attitudes. But there were some shifts in emphasis and some new instances. Let us do a brief census of the instances of capacity change, keying them to the sites and to the different "scenarios" that we evolved (see pp. 144 ff.) in trying to account for the later history of changes in the innovation.

Table 42, the result, contains some useful information. Above all, it fleshes out precisely what "user capacity change" is made up of. Reading down the chart also brings home the point that innovations, whatever their objectives for pupils, can be vehicles for some farther-reaching professional and instructional changes on the part of teachers. All these items can be seen as a sort of value-added increment over and above improved pupil performances or attitudes; the chart shows, too, how diverse such increments can be.[22] In part, this finding should not be surprising. Recall that when we assessed users' motives for adopting the innovation (see Table 8, p. 48, and the discussion, p. 49), the incentives for professional growth outnumbered those of attaining desired pupil outcomes. In short, the innovations were perceived in part as opportunities for capacity enlargement. In Table 42, it appears that there was, in fact, a substantial payoff for users at 7 of the 12 sites and at least some user-centered rewards at 9.

How do the relative rankings of the 12 sites jibe with the estimates made in the "user change" section, notably in Table 34 and Table 35 (pp. 161 and 162)? Fairly well. Banestown, Tindale, Perry-Parkdale, Lido, and Astoria are at a slightly higher notch on the user capacity scale, but the rank orders have not changed substantially. How do we account for these shifts? First, they resulted from a greater number of second-order outcomes being reported when users were asked or probed specifically about this topic—something we did far less of during our assessment of user change during implementation. Either these changes came later, or users were more loquacious about them.

Also, there are some *new items*, the ones highlighted in bold face type. They sound two themes: a career-crystallizing theme and a "cosmopolitanizing" theme. First, working through the innovation helped users to better channel their future energies by showing them how they coped in previously unknown roles. For instance, a teacher at Perry-Parkdale moved into a modified counseling role in the career education program, enjoyed it, and then left the program to do full-time pupil counseling. At Banestown, the main lab teacher acquired specialized skills that she pursued further in a degree program; she then attempted to get a supervisory assignment. The second theme, cosmopolitanizing, turns around contacts made outside the local school district. Users at Perry-Parkdale met people and observed practices elsewhere in the state in the course of disseminating the career education project. The chief user of the environmental education project at Lido became a local expert. These items helped to boost the user capacity-change ratings and rankings at those two sites over the estimates made of practice change during implementation.

Finally, while we are at the descriptive level, a scan of the final column of Table 42 is instructive. To recall our several scenarios of the changes made in the innovation (pp. 144 ff.), the higher-capacity-change sites were primarily

---

[22]Note that Table 42 is cast in positive terms. Though we saw in Chapter 5 that there were a few sites with negative implementation experiences, notably Dun Hollow and Proville, there was little evidence of durable capacity *decreases*. We did encounter instances of increased wariness toward innovations and/or cynicism about improvement efforts but they were rare.

TABLE 42. Instances of Capacity Change, by Sites

Capacity-change rating/Sites	Instances mentioned by informants[a]	Innovation change scenario[b]
High capacity change		
Masepa (NDN)	Better understanding of learning process.	Enforcing
	Better fix on actual achievement levels.	
	Better organized ("It's shaped me up").	
	Better rapport with pupils.	
	Understanding, application elsewhere of mastery learning principles, techniques.	
Plummet (IV-C)	Stronger commitment to "alternative" systems.	Overreaching
	Better rapport with students and staff.	
	Better understanding of students and of student-tailored curricula.	
	Sense of increased "professionalism."	
	More knowledgeable about changing individuals and institutions.	
Banestown (NDN)	More capable in individualizing instructional treatments.	Salvaging
	More knowledgeable about tests and testing.	
	Transfer to other tasks (at other $\frac{1}{2}$-time post).	
	Better mastery of school curriculum.	
	Better understanding of emotional problems of pupils and their effects on performance.	
	Better at teamwork.	
	More resourceful, i.e., more instructional materials at hand or in one's repertoire.	
	Crystallizing, helping to orient career plans.	
Tindale (IV-C)	Better organized.	Enforcing
	More information-sharing with colleagues.	
	Greater interest in low-ability pupils.	
	Increased skills in reading-related instructions.	
	Transfer of remedial approach to other parts of one's practice.	
Perry-Parkdale (NDN)	Better at collaboration with colleagues.	Overreaching
	Expanded, more realistic view of teaching lower-achieving students ("Be tough . . . some kids are unreachable").	
	Improved managerial skills.	

(continued)

TABLE 42. Continued

Capacity-change rating/Sites	Instances mentioned by informants[a]	Innovation change scenario[b]
High capacity change		
Perry-Parkdale (NDN)	**Crystallizing, orienting career plans.** **"Cosmopolitanization"** (meeting people, oberving practices outside the district).	
Moderate capacity change		
Carson (IV-C)	Closer rapport with pupils. More knowledgeable about pupils' home life. Increased understanding of pupils ("You see them in a totally new light"). "Better in the classroom." More institutionally savvy.	Overreaching
Lido (NDN)	Increased hands-on teaching capacity. Increased interdisciplinary skills. **Better able to interact with other environmentalists in other schools.** More expert in town council.	Locally refitting
Low–moderate capacity change		
Calston (NDN)	Closer rapport with pupils. Providing a wider range of instructional activities. Better planning, organizational skills.	Locally refitting
Astoria (NDN)	Better testing procedures; better understanding of specific areas of weakness. Revisions in lesson plans for other subject matters.	(Not cataloged— closest script is "locally refitting")
Low–nil capacity changes		
Burton (NDN)	Larger stock of resource materials.	Locally refitting
Dun Hollow (IV-C)	Possibly less stereotyping of minority group.	Locally refitting
Proville (IV-C)	None reported or observed for teachers.	Salvaging

[a]Mentioned by more than one informant at sites with more than three informants; mentioned by one informant, with no contradictory evidence from others, at sites with two or fewer users. Items in boldface are *not* mentioned in user change section, Table 32.
[b]See Section on "changes in the innovation," especially pp. 144 ff.

those with an "enforcing" and "overreaching" script, whereas the lower-change sites were mostly "locally refitted." This finding makes good sense. *Enforcement* scenarios involved ambitious classroom-level changes that the administrators sustained through a mixture of close monitoring and assistance. The *overreachers* did precisely that. Although they fell short of their goals, they still went full-

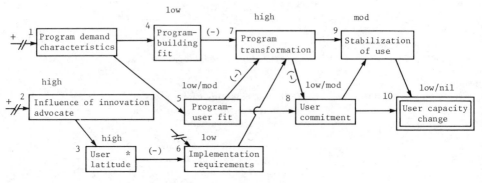

FIGURE 35. Downsizing as a route to low capacity change: Burton (NDN).

bore for at least several months beyond their and the school's conventional practices and, in so doing, appeared to enlarge local capacities. By contrast, the *local refitters* were mostly sites where an initially ambitious project was whittled down to a far more modest, less user- and school-discrepant version that effectively reduced the possibility of second-order outcomes like the capacity changes we are after in this section. For somewhat different reasons, Calston, Astoria, Burton, and Dun Hollow were low-enforcing, underreaching sites, and their teacher-centered outcomes were correspondingly meager.

Scenarios Leading to Low Capacity Change[23]

Moving beyond descriptive analysis, we naturally want to know what else distinguished the low-capacity-change from the high-capacity-change sites. In other words, how can we *predict* degrees of user capacity change, and what do such predictions tell us about ways of increasing the impact? In part, Figure 34, at the start of this section, supplies some of the answers. But we suspect that such a general model undercomplicates the real-life phenomena at our field sites. There are probably several paths to both low and high user-capacity change. To find them, we need to analyze the 12 casual networks. Our low-changing sites had two basic profiles, a "downsizing" or "midgetizing" profile and a "fouling-up" profile. Let's look at them in turn.

Downsizing

Figure 35 shows part of the causal network for Burton, with a "downsizing" scenario. Most of the boxes, ratings, and streams are virtually identical to those at Astoria and—if we take higher ratings into account—close to those of the Calston network.

The display tells a relatively simple story. The project, if implemented

---

[23]Here, for clarity and contrast, we change our ordinary sequence and start with the "low" scenarios.

faithfully, was demanding (Box 1) and would call for substantial changes that fit poorly at the building level (4) and with the teachers' usual repertoires (5). The innovation advocate (2), a central office administrator, wanted to get the project adopted, so he gave the teachers discretionary latitude (3) to use as much of it as they liked, which, in turn, lowered the stringency of the implementation requirements. All the arrows then point to the "program transformation" box (7); the innovation was downsized to far more modest proportions—most teachers used only snippets of it—which heightened a generally low commitment to the practice (8) on the part of users. The project became moderately stabilized (9) in the course of the year, but its impact on users (10) was virtually nil.

Fouling Up

There was another way to get low user-capacity change, to which we gave the unlovely label of "fouling up." The two prime cases, Dun Hollow and Proville, had similar networks; an excerpt from Dun Hollow's is shown in Figure 36. This is a still shorter story: A poorly designed and moderately demanding project (1) resulted in a poor program–user fit (3). Initial preparation (4) in the face of substantial implementation requirements (2) and ongoing assistance (5) were poor, further increasing user resentment (6) and further depressing user commitment to the project (7). Gradually, the project withered away after some futile attempts at recasting it. User capacity change (8) was therefore slight. The key here seemed to be the lack of both front-end and ongoing support. Such support might have enabled adaptive improvement in what was essentially a poor-quality innovation. Also, if we look back at the Burton network, "user commitment" is beginning to loom large as a predictor of capacity change.

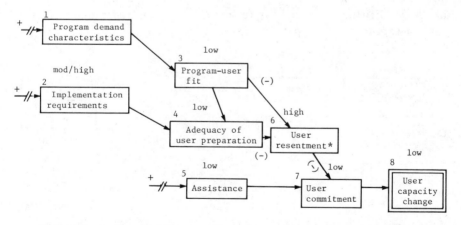

+Influence of other variables not discussed
* Site-specific variable

FIGURE 36. Fouling up as a route to low capacity change: Dun Hollow (IV-C).

Scenarios Leading to High Capacity Change

Now, let's contrast these two profiles with those of the five high-capacity-change sites. We found two scenarios, one common to all five sites, and another subscenario characterizing only Masepa and Tindale. We also unearthed a subtheme affecting the levels of user capacity change at Perry-Parkdale and at a "moderate" change site, Lido.

Achieving Major Practice Change

The common scenario here furnishes a nice contrast with the "low"-change sites and, in so doing, strengthens its explanatory power. Here is the causal flow, using Tindale data (Figure 37). The upper stream shows how "fouling up" can be avoided. The project was demanding (Box 1), but the local administrators delivered adequate assistance (3) both to increase the initial levels of user preparation (4) and later levels of user skill (6), which then led to stabilized use (9) and to user capacity change (10) as a result of the successful implementation of the demanding new practice. Elsewhere (e.g., Banestown, Masepa, and Plummet), initial user preparation was poor, but *later assistance* from within and outside the school assured practice mastery.

The lower stream of Figure 37 has a little more drama. The bulk of the users—as contrasted with the "pioneers" who developed the innovation—did not like the project (5), in part because of its poor fit (2) with their customary practices and operating philosophies. This dislike led to friction between users and administrators (7). Gradually, however, users got better at doing the program (6) and came to appreciate its merits, so acceptance (8) grew. The practice settled down (9), preserving the initial change gradients. Elsewhere (e.g., Plummet, Perry-Parkdale, and Banestown), the initial levels of commitment were higher and led equally to the "stabilization" and the "capacity change" boxes. It looks as if the royal road to coping successfully with demanding, ill-fitting projects has to include ongoing assistance and at least minimal acceptance on the part of users.

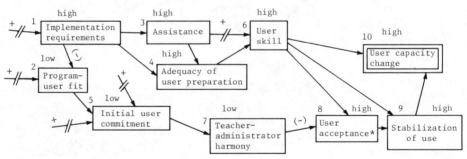

+Influence of other variables not discussed

*Site-specific variable

FIGURE 37. Achieving major practice change as a route to high capacity change: Tindale (IV-C).

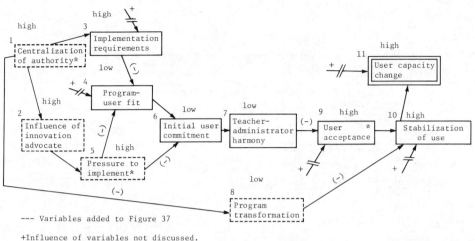

FIGURE 38. Enforcement of major practice change as a route to capacity change: Tindale (IV-C).

Enforcing

The second subscenario for high-capacity-change sites is also a mirror image of most of the "low" sites. In contrast to liberally "downsizing" the projects, the story at Masepa and Tindale was that of *enforcing* major practice changes. Let us go back to the bottom stream of the Tindale network (Figure 38), adding to it these "enforcement" variables. The message here is that centralization of authority (Box 1), along with the accompanying power and drive of the central office administration, acted to keep the change gradient high by making sure that the project was not downsized or otherwise transformed (8), while at the same time providing the assistance (see Figure 37) that contributed to stabilization of use (10). That high change gradient, stabilized, left the users with a new set of skills and constructs. It is likely that, left to their own devices, users would have implemented less and would have had correspondingly fewer capacity gains. As uncomfortable as we may feel about the enforced maintenance of major practice change, it appears, under certain conditions, to be a good vehicle for getting the kinds of teacher capacity change that we displayed in Table 42.

Cosmopolitanizing

We mentioned earlier a final *leitmotiv*, a subtheme in the prediction of user capacity change. This one is shown in Table 42 in the boldface items for Perry-Parkdale and Lido. The innovations brought the users into wider contact with people and practices outside the local school system, from which users learned and extended their own capacities. These contacts also, incidentally, opened doors to future career shifts. The causal stream for both Perry-Parkdale and

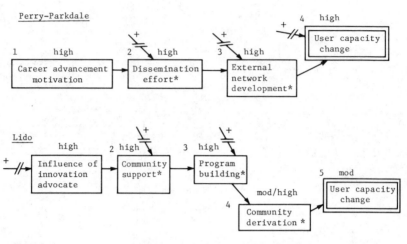

⁺Influence of variables not discussed

*Site-specific variable

FIGURE 39. Cosmopolitanization theme: Perry-Parkdale (NDN) and Lido (NDN).

Lido is shown in Figure 39. The excerpts are fairly self-explanatory. Dissemination effort (2) brought the users at Perry-Parkdale into wider contacts (3), and the effort itself entailed the development of new skills (4) (of presenting the practice, marshaling evidence in its favor, preparing new users, and so on). Similarly, the innovation advocate at Lido (1), with community support (2), extended the environmental science project into the community (3, 4), where he became a local expert and, via that expertise, also developed dissemination and problem-solving skills (5) in a new context.

Conclusions

Let us try to tie these different strands together. At 7 of the 12 field sites, we found moderate to high levels of user capacity change in the form of new skills, constructs, and attitudes derived from the innovation and applicable beyond it. When the 12 sites are scaled by degree of capacity change, the profiles are similar to those obtained for practice changes during implementation, although some new themes appear (e.g., career crystallization and cosmopolitanization). In addition, the profiles bear a relation to the four scenarios described in the section on changes in the innovation. The high-capacity-change sites were more likely to be "overreachers" or "enforcers"; the low-capacity-change sites tended to be "local refitters."

The low-capacity-change sites typically turned out that way as a result of making sizable *changes* in the project, of delivering *inadequate assistance*, and of failing to ensure *user commitment*. The high-change sites maintained ambitious changes by providing *assistance* and by gaining at least local *acceptance* of the project. In two high-change cases, close *administrative monitoring* had the effect of preserving initially high levels of practice change and thereby of producing capacity growth on the part of the implementing staff.

A final ingredient is the enhanced capacity achieved when the project staff *disseminate* the new practice outside the local school system.

JOB MOBILITY

Introduction

As we saw in the analysis of four informants' motives and attitudes (pp. 44 ff.), about 40% of the users and 50% of the administrators had career plans tied in with the adoption of the innovation. Administrators, in particular, had designed personal trajectories that turned around solidifying a recent promotion or getting ready for a new one. We also noted that in some cases (e.g., Proville), administrators rode the project to a job elsewhere and, in so doing, destabilized it, sometimes mortally. But when career motives were *absent* (e.g., at Dun Hollow), the project often lacked the requisite energy to get it through difficult moments and to assure its future.

Looking out the back end, we naturally wanted to know whether and when people got where they wanted to go. How much job mobility occurred? And was it related to the innovation, or only adventitious? Were there sites with similar events occurring between an initial career-advancement motive and an ultimate move to another job? Did these things *not happen* at places where people *did not* get the career shifts they were seeking?

Timing and Extent of Job Mobility

Our first task is a descriptive one. Looking across the 12 field sites, we need to find out *how many* key actors made innovation-linked job shifts, *when* these shifts occurred, *where* the people were coming from and going to, and, finally, how *job mobility profiles varied* by site and by program (NDN vs. IV-C).

We have tried to pack all that information into a single summary chart. Table 43 arrays the projects by *program type*, then shows for each project the *number of key actors involved*, the *job mobility shifts at three moments in the life of the project* (its creation, during or at the end of the first year of implementation, and beyond the initial year), *whether these shifts were innovation-related*, and, in the final coumn, a *site-level estimate* of job mobility. Note that the cell entries tell us where users and administrators were coming from and going to, much as we tracked individuals' contemplated trajectories in the section on user and administrator motives for adoption.

Our first observation is that there was a moderate amount of moving around related to the innovation (63 moves for our 12 sites, of which 83% were clearly innovation-related). Activity was high at the *outset*, when the project created new, often upwardly mobile roles. This was when a fair number of teachers moved into project-related administrative slots. Activity was also high during *later* implementation, when administrators moved out and up or simply

TABLE 43. Job Mobility at Sites, by Time Period

Sites	No. key actors involved[a]	T₁—Creation/initiation of project	Innovation-related?[b]	T₂—Early implementation (1st year)	Innovation related?[b]	T₃—Later implementation	Innovation-related?[b]	Overall mobility rating for site[c]
Astoria (NDN)	5	1 cent. office (C.O.) admin. strengthens new role	▲	1 bldg. admin. moves *up*; 1 C.O. admin. moves *out* and *over*	▲ ▲	NA	NA	Moderate
Banestown (NDN)	6	1 aide moves *in* and *up* to teacher status; 1 teacher moves back *in*; 1 teacher prepares for move *up*; 1 C.O. admin. positioned for move *up*	▲ ▲ ▲ ▲			1 tchr. moves back *down*; 1 tchr. moves *over* to desirable post	— —	High
Burton (NDN)	9	1 C.O. admin. strengthens role	▲			NA	NA	Nil
Calston (NDN)	7	1 tchr. prepares for move *up*; 1 C.O. admin. extends authority; 1 bldg. admin. strengthens position	▲ ▲ ▲			1 C.O. admin. moves *out* and *down*; 1 tchr. (librarian) moves *out* and *over*; 1 tchr. in process of moving *out*	— ▲ ▲	Moderate
Lido (NDN)	5					1 bldg. admin. moves *out* and *up*	▲	Low

Site	No.								Rating
Masepa (NDN)	13		▲	1 tchr. moves up to supervisory role	▲	1 tchr. moves up to supervisory role · 1 C.O. admin. retires · 1 proj. admin. moves *out*	▲ · — · —		Low–moderate
Perry-Parkdale (NDN)	10	3 tchrs. move *in* from less desirable jobs · 1 tchr. moves *in* and up to admin. post	▲ · ▲	1 C.O. admin. moves *out* and (tries to go) *up*	◢	1 tchr. moves *out* and *over* · 1 tchr. moves *out* and back *down* · 1 proj. admin. moves *out* and *up* · 2 bldg. admins. move *out*, 1 moves *up*	▲ · — · ▲ · —		High
Carson (IV-C)	27	2–3 tchrs. move *out* · 2–3 tchrs. move *in* · 1 bldg. admin. strengthens role	▲ · ▲ · ▲	1 teacher moves *out* · 1 bldg. admin. moves *out*	— · —	1 tchr. (prog. coord.) moves *out* · 1 bldg. admin. moves *out* and *over* · 1 bldg. admin. moves *up* · 1 tchr. moves *in* and *up* to prog. coord. role then moves *out* and *up*	— · ◁ · — · ▲		Moderate

(continued)

TABLE 43. Continued

Sites	No. key actors involved[a]	T₁—Creation/initiation of project	Innovation-related?[b]	T₂—Early implementation (1st year)	Innovation related?[b]	T₃—Later implementation	Innovation-related?[b]	Overall mobility rating for site[c]
Dun Hollow (IV-C)	7	1 regional admin. extends role	▲			NA	NA	Nil
Plummet (IV-C)	6	1 tchr. moves *in* and *up* to admin. role; 5 tchrs. move *in*	▲ ▲	4 tchrs. move *up* to supervisory role	▲	1 bldg. admin. moves *out*; 1 tchr. moves *out*	▲ ▲	Moderate–high
Proville (IV-C)	14	1 tchr. moves *in* and *up* to admin. post	▲	1 C.O. admin. moves *up*; 1 tchr. moves *in* and *up* to admin. post	▲ ▲	1 C.O. admin. moves *out* and *up*; 1 tchr. moves *in* and *up* to proj. admin. role	▲ ▲	High
Tindale (IV-C)	14			1 tchr. moves *up* to bldg. admin. post	▲	1 bldg. admin. retires; 1 C.O. admin. moves *out* and *up*; 3 bldg. admins. move *up*	— ▲ ▲	High

Note. Adapted, with permission, from Miles & Huberman (1984).
[a] People in key roles connected to the project for whom job mobility was possible.
[b] ▲ = yes, clearly; ▲ = possible, in part; — = no; NA = not applicable.
[c] Researcher estimate based on proporation of actual job moves to total of key actors, with higher weighting for moves by people immediately responsible for, or crucial to, the innovation (e.g., project director).

up within the district, and teachers associated with the project took their places. How many people actually moved up? If we take the full number of innovation-related job shifts (63), 12 entailed teacher promotions to administrative slots,[24] and 10 involved administrators' moving higher. That number amounts to 35% of the innovation-related job shifts.

While we're counting noses, there seemed to be more innovation-related job mobility at the five IV-C sites (37 moves or positioning for imminent moves) than at the 7 NDN sites (29). The final column in Table 43 confirms this trend. Dun Hollow excepted, all IV-C sites had moderate to high moving around, whereas the NDN sites were more diverse. The most likely cause lies in the genesis and scale of the projects. The IV-C innovations were generated locally and almost invariably created new coordination and supervisory roles. Also, three of the five were large-scale projects. By contrast, most of the NDN projects were add-ons or drop-ins to existing organizational arrangements (Perry-Parkdale being an obvious exception) and, in four of the seven cases, modest ventures overall.

Note that some job mobility (14 moves, or 18% of total) was *not* related to the innovation. Such mobility was of two types: (1) project staff were planning to leave or to retire or were moved elsewhere independently of the project; and (2) environmental turbulence, usually in the form of sudden budget cuts, ejected people from the project, usually into unwanted jobs. More on this latter type in a moment.

Low-Mobility Sites

At 4 of the 12 sites, we found little or no evidence of innovation-related job mobility: Burton (NDN), Lido (NDN), Dun Hollow (IV-C), and, at a somewhat more active level, Masepa (NDN). Looking over the data, our best explanation has three parts. First, in all cases—with the possible exception of a building principal at Lido—neither users nor administrators were trying to change jobs at the time of adoption. Second, these were relatively tranquil places. There was little environmental turmoil, no fiscal crisis to "RIF" (reduction in force) people out of innovation-related jobs, and no major turnover in project staff and leadership (although, here again, Lido lost a key innovation advocate). Third, in three of the four cases—the exception being Masepa—the innovation itself was of modest proportions. The smallness of scale meant that no new supervisory, assistance-giving, or dissemination positions were created for people to move into or to use to prepare for a move elsewhere. Modest scope also meant that practice change was limited, which, in turn, gave users and administrators few opportunities to revise their existing roles or to construct new ones.

Sites Where Mobility Occurred

In the eight remaining cases, the career moves were clearly tangled up in the fate of the innovation locally. At the grossest level of analysis, we have four

---

[24]Included here are the promotions of high-school teachers to department chairs.

families: (1) *casualty cases* (sites where job mobility was unwanted and came as the result of environmental turbulence; both Banestown and Calston were examples); (2) *raw opportunism* (sites in which career motives prevailed from the start and were satisfied; Proville was the clearest cut instance); (3) *success-driven advancement* (sites where the innovation was mandated; Astoria, Carson, and Tindale were examples); and (4) *win–lose* scenarios (sites in which career shifts resulted from *both* user-perceived success and job instability; Perry-Parkdale and Plummet were examples). Let us run briefly through these four scripts.

Casualty Cases

The innovations at both Banestown and Calston were hobbled by budget crisis. Both projects had been doing well. The users had worked their way, with some pain, to smoother program execution. There was evidence of improved pupil performance. The Banestown administrators had been gearing up for districtwide use the following year.

The later causal flow for Calston is shown in Figure 40. The district had to make drastic budget cuts (1), which were made first in the newer or experimental programs. In the ensuing turbulence (2), staff were reassigned (4). Calston lost all but one of the original users, along with its chief innovation advocate (3), the curriculum coordinator.

The Banestown network is identical, except that the "internal funds" box follows from "environmental turbulence."

In both cases, however, it is worth noting that the *level* of implementation—the numbers of staff and pupils engaged in the project—dropped only slightly during the following year. And—an interesting wrinkle—for some actors, career plans were not compromised. One Banestown user who was reassigned got her own classroom far sooner than she had expected. The central office staff kept their own and their protégés' platforms intact for later administrative leaps. Only one actor was frozen in a full-time slot that she did not want. So forced mobility was not always a disaster for career progression.

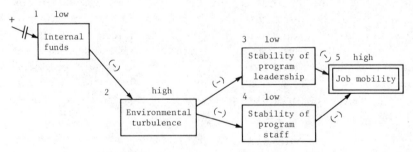

+Influence of variables not discussed

FIGURE 40. Job mobility as casualty: Calston (NDN). (From Miles & Huberman, 1984. Reprinted by permission.)

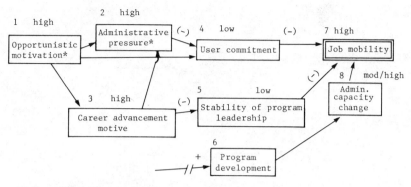

+Influence of other variables not discussed
*Site-specific variable

FIGURE 41. Job mobility as opportunism: Proville (IV-C).

Raw Opportunism

Proville has the dubious distinction of being alone in this category. At other sites, the career motives were equally strong, but they usually translated into a strong and relatively long commitment to the project's success. At Proville, however, one of the innovation advocates rapidly rode the project into the central office and then promoted a friend, who then moved on to a state-level administrative slot. These advancements seemed to be part of a local tradition of coopting protégés into an "old-boy network" via the creation of administrative posts through soft-money grants. The causal network excerpt is shown in Figure 41. Local principals and teachers saw the central office as cynically opportunistic (1) and reacted negatively (4) to the proposed project, which was forced (2) on the local high schools. Then, the chief project adminis-trator jumped ship at the end of the initial year (5, 7), bringing on a protégé who rapidly did the same. The paradox was that the project design was probably a good one, meeting a local need and stretching the high schools' capacity. But the initial local resistance, together with indifferent leadership, first slowed and then gradually eroded the project.

Note finally the arrow leading to job mobility (7) from administrative capacity change (8) and program development (6). The script here was more socially redeeming. In the course of program development, the administrators tried out and then exercised administrative skills that they could then take elsewhere, presumably to apply to other program-development efforts. We found this phenomenon elsewhere as well (see below).

Success-Driven Advancement

These three projects (Tindale, Astoria, and Carson) were probably the most appealing. They succeeded, their users and administrators were pro-

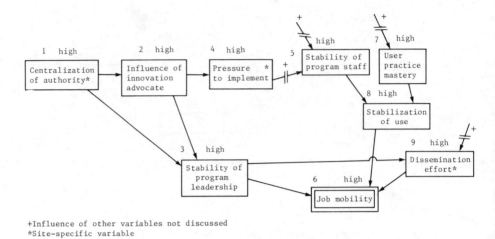

+Influence of other variables not discussed
*Site-specific variable

FIGURE 42. Job mobility as success-driven advancement: Tindale (IV-C).

moted, and, from all available evidence, career advancement motives were muted, if not absent, at the outset. Good works paid off.

First, let's look at Tindale, where the remedial reading project was successfully executed and institutionalized (Figure 42). We can note, as at Astoria, the pressures exerted from a centralized, district-level administration (1), especially when the administrators were advocates (2) of the innovation. Advocacy and authority make a strong tandem. As Henry Adams wrote, "Power, when wielded with abnormal energy, is the most serious of facts."

Still, up to now, we could be at Astoria or even at Proville. What was different here was that staff and leadership functions remained stable (5, 3), and practice mastery (7) and ultimate user commitment (not shown in the figure) were high. The success of the project and its leadership stability (3) led to wider dissemination (9), which created opportunities for visibility and—why not?—new jobs (6).

Users moved into building-level administrative slots at Tindale and elsewhere; one of the department heads moved into the central office; and the central office administrator got a more appealing job in another district. No one, however, cried foul. The inference is that upward job mobility was merited in the sense of being "earned" by hard work, and was seen as a legitimate payoff for successful program execution. Also—a difference from Astoria and Proville— the core staff remained, and former staff members moved into new leadership roles, so the project never broke stride locally.[25]

If we survey the network from Carson,[26] some of the same ingredients that we saw at Tindale are here: strong advocacy, local commitment, successful use, and administrative constraint. As at Tindale, career advancement motives surfaced after successful local use and brought on personnel shifts. In this case,

[25]We should also note that nondisruptive mobility seemed to be occurring at Masepa. See Table 7 (pp. 46–47).
[26]Not shown here; see the technical report (p. 426).

the high-school principal moved to a larger district (where he could specifically apply what he had learned at Carson), and the program coordinator moved up to a statewide job in instructional TV.

At both Tindale and Carson, then, we seem to have had an *emergent*, rather than a preexistent, career advancement motive. But we should be careful here. Just because the career shifts happened while we were watching the site does not mean that they either originated or crystallized with this innovation. The evidence is stronger that these shifts were contemplated for some time, and that the project accelerated or matured them. People acted, in part, on the strength of their local success, which may have opened doors elsewhere. But they had probably been ready to act before then. For example, feeding back on our causal network, a user at Tindale put the reading program in this perspective:

> I'm not certain that all the job mobility was a direct result. . . . It definitely helped one career in particular, but other aspects helped job mobility or caused job mobility for the people involved.[27]

The picture at Astoria was generally similar to that at Tindale and Carson, though the link between the success of the mandated project and the job change of involved administrators was less clear.[28]

Win–Lose Scenarios

Our third family of job mobility cases put together the upbeat features of success-driven mobility and the sad endings of the casualty cases. Plummet and Perry-Parkdale fit this description and had similar causal networks. Perry-Parkdale's appears in Figure 43. We recognize from Calston and Banestown the ominous stream from low internal funds (2) to environmental turbulence (3) to job insecurity (5) (at casualty sites, no one had enough advance warning to be insecure about his or her job before losing it), and finally to—for the most part, unwanted—job mobility (7). Perry-Parkdale lost two of its three staff members that way, and institutionalization (10) was thereby weakened.

On the other hand, the stream leading from user practice mastery (6) to user capacity change (8) to job mobility (7) looks more like the "redeeming" path at Proville and the scenario at Tindale. Through progressive mastery, users and administrators developed new skills that they were interested in using elsewhere—preferably, but not necessarily, at a higher level. One user at Perry-Parkdale, for instance, came via the program to a more clearly defined career focus (counseling) and left the project to move that way. But another left because there was no money to support his staying.

Another already-traveled route to job mobility is shown in the stream from dissemination effort (4) to external network development (9) and ending at job

---

[27]Similarly, the Carson program coordinator had had prior experience in educational TV, and she was in part motivated to take the state-level job because she lived in the capital and could avoid the commute to Carson. The Carson success was certainly a feather in her cap, however.
[28]See the technical report (pp. 423–424).

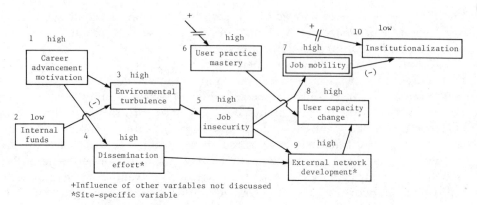

+Influence of other variables not discussed
*Site-specific variable

FIGURE 43. Job mobility as a win–lose scenario: Perry-Parkdale (NDN).

mobility (7). As at Tindale, the dissemination function built into IV-C projects gave administrators a good opportunity to self-advertise for potential job openings. But the project as a whole, both at Plummet and at Perry-Parkdale, was weakened by these imminent and actual departures, just as the "casualty cases" had been. As the program director at Perry-Parkdale put it to express his uncertainty, "Things are in a plasma state."

An added note: The causal network for Plummet (not shown) explicitly mentions burnout as a contributor to transfers out of the project. There were similar signs, though implicit ones, at Carson and Perry-Parkdale. What we probably have here, once again, are *multiple* or *cumulative effects* bringing on job mobility. Users or administrators grow *and* reorient *and* sometimes get exhausted in the course of program implementation, often coping with environmental turbulence. The dissemination effects increase their visibility and the scouting for other jobs; they think of moving out and, if possible, of moving up somewhere else.

Sometimes, though not in the majority of cases, people got where they wanted to go. Administrators, not surprisingly, fared better at this than did teachers. But in most cases, the movement of key people destabilized and hurt the very program that they had worked to build up. Only at Tindale and perhaps at Masepa did all the ingredients come together, so that the career progressions of the project staff and director actually reinforced the innovative project locally. The Tindale scenario (Figure 42) seemed to include most of the facilitating factors that we saw at other sites, while excluding the inhibiting factors we found at the "casualty" sites. In this sense, Tindale may have been a policy-relevant illustration of how career progression can be coupled with stability of staff and leadership.

It could be argued, of course, that mobility that disrupts local programs may contribute to another educational enterprise. For example, the Carson principal will probably replicate the IPA program in his new job. Nevertheless, it's important to maintain precious social capital. On balance, one would wish for school improvement programs that could accommodate individuals' needs for career advancement without destabilizing the local gains achieved.

Conclusions

We found a moderate amount of innovation-related job mobility, which typically took place at the creation of the project and during later implementation. About a third of these moves were upward, with teachers moving into supervisory and administrative slots and administrators moving higher in the hierarchy. There was markedly more innovation-related mobility at the IV-C sites than at the NDN sites.

Looking more closely at the eight sites with moderate to high levels of job mobility, we found four families: *casualty cases*, where most shifting, triggered by unexpected budget crises, was not innovation-related; *opportunism*, where upward mobility was at the root of the project; *success-driven advancement*, where the project staff were promoted as a result of successful implementation; and *win–lose* scenarios, which combined the features of the success-driven advancement and the casualty case. The key institutional task was enabling nonexploitive job mobility without destabilizing the project.

CHAPTER 7

Why School Improvement
Succeeds or Fails

INTRODUCTION AND OVERVIEW OF FINDINGS

Having examined each of the outcomes separately, noting the clusters of variables preceding and determining the levels of outcome, we are now ready for an integrated look at all six outcomes and their chief determinants. Collating this material will also help us to pull together the strands of earlier chapters. The overarching question here is whether there are general outcome patterns and, if so, whether they have the same or similar antecedents. If no clear patterns emerge, are there distinct "families" of sites, each with a specific outcome profile and the same causal trails leading there?

To recapitulate briefly the main points of this section, we found four patterns corresponding roughly to different levels of outcome: (1) high outcomes resulting from enforced and stabilized use of the innovation; (2) moderate–high outcomes as a result of high practice mastery and lower institutional settledness; (3) moderate–low outcomes resulting from program "blunting" or "downsizing"; and (4) low outcomes as the fruit of administrative and teacher indifference.

We should also note at the start that these were interrelated, but not nuclear, families. That is to say, each member case within a family was more like the others in that family than those in other families, but there were still differences within the families—differences in the level of outcome (e.g., "moderate" for some, "moderate–high" for others) and differences in the ratings and the configuration of determinants. At no two sites did we have precisely identical causal nets with identical ratings and paths. We did, however, have reasonably strong overlap on most ratings and on most causal pathways within each of the four families that we identified. In brief, our sites sorted themselves into meaningful clusters that make sense, illuminating what makes for "success" and "failure" in school improvement. We put these two terms in quotation marks to indicate their problematic nature. To take only one example: For a school to stabilize and institutionalize a poor-quality innovation could hardly be called "successful" school improvement. Broadly speaking, we use "success" to mean stable, built-in, widespread use of a well-designed innovation that had a positive impact on students and teachers. "Failure" was more complicated, as we shall see.

LEVELS AND PATTERNS OF OUTCOME

The easiest way to begin is to array the outcomes of the 12 field sites in a "horserace" grid, stretching from winners to losers. This is another version of Table 38 (p. 189), where we introduced the outcome measures and the relative performance at the 12 sites. Table 44 translates the ratings into symbols, weights and sums them, and connects each site to the four "scenarios" we developed in the section on changes in the innovation (pp. 144 ff.). Note that the rudimentary "summed scale" does not include the "job mobility" outcome, which cannot be scaled normatively. More (or less) mobility is not in any clear sense "better," in the way that higher student impact or stronger institutionalization is better for schools. For example, job mobility could help a school by making its accomplishments more visible to the world—or by exporting its poorer staff. Or it could weaken a school through loss of expertise—or by damaging its reputation. It all depends on who leaves, and on what their roles in the school were.

The first thing that jumps out of the table is that, indeed, some sites have done well and others dismally. Tindale has a "perfect" score, with Masepa and Plummet close behind, after which there is more unevenness. Then, beginning with Calston, further down the list, we reach the moderate–low sites and then hit the lowest performers. If we look more closely for patterning between the two extremes, it looks as if a subset of higher- but not highest-scoring sites— Plummet, Banestown, and Perry-Parkdale—has stronger outcomes in the individual or classroom-centered domain (student impact and user capacity change) than in the institutional domain (institutionalization, percentage of use); these sites also have a higher incidence of job mobility.

There is also an obvious relationship between the levels of outcome and the four scenarios in the final column, which we evolved in discussing changes in the innovation. Aside from "salvaging," it appears that the higher levels of desired outcomes go with the "enforcing" and "overreaching" scenarios, and the lower levels with "refitting." This finding tells us that we have to stand back from the thicket of ratings and their multiple determinants to keep in mind what was *happening* at these sites in the course of project execution. By simply clustering causal paths and outcomes that have similar magnitudes and links, we run the risk of ignoring the dynamics of each case. Causality is always *local*. Only by cycling back to the cases can we assess the true comparability of the sites within a cluster.

The scenarios give the first clue to the grouping of sites indicated by the

TABLE 44. Performance of 12 Sites on Outcome Measures

Group/site	Stabilization of use	Percentage of use	Institutionalization	Student impact	Capacity change	Summed scale of Cols. 1-5	Job mobility	Innovation change scenario
1. Tindale (IV-C)	▲	▲	▲	▲	▲	15	▲	Enforcing
Masepa (NDN)	△	▲	▲/◢	▲	▲	13.5	△/△	Enforcing
2. Plummet (IV-C)	▲	△	▲	▲	▲	13	△/▲	Overreaching
Banestown (NDN)	▲	△	▲	▲	▲	12	▲	Salvaging
Perry-Parkdale (NDN)	▲/◢	△	△	▲	▲	11.5	▲	Overreaching
Carson (IV-C)	△	▲	▲	△	△	11	▲	Overreaching
3. Astoria (NDN)	▲	▲	▲	▲/△	△/△	11	▲	Not ascribed—closest is refitting
Lido (NDN)	▲/◢	▲	▲/◢	▲	◢	11	△	Refitting
Calston (NDN)	▲/◢	▲	△	▲	◢/△	9	▲	Refitting
Burton (NDN)	▲	△	△	△	▲/—	5.5	—	Refitting
4. Dun Hollow (IV-C)	△	△	—	▲/△	△/—	4	—	Refitting
Proville (IV-C)	△	△	—	△	—	3	▲	Salvaging

[a] ▲ = high (3); ◢ = moderate (2); △ = low (1); — = nil (0).
[b] Outcome themes: (1) High outcomes from enforced, stabilized use; (2) Moderate-high outcomes from high mastery and low settledness; (3) Moderate-low outcomes from program blunting/downsizing; (4) Low outcomes from indifference and discouragement.

numbers 1 to 4 in the first column, and listed on the bottom of the chart under "outcome themes." To begin with Group 1, Tindale and Masepa were sites with ambitious projects executed under conditions of strong administrative pressure and equally strong administrative assistance.

Group 2 comprises sites that "overreached" in the sense of attempting practice changes beyond their initial capacity or readiness. The overreachers tended to reduce the scope of change later in the life history of the innovation, whereas "salvaging" entailed a gradual reinstatement of core components that were abandoned in the feverish initial phase. In both cases, we have attempts at ambitious practice change: the chart tells us that these sites did well in terms of student impact and user capacity change and less well (except for Plummet) in terms of institutionalization and percentage of use.

A glance at the outcome profile for Group 3 shows its heterogeneity; the outcomes were moderate to low, but idiosyncratically so. As the scenario and outcome themes suggest, these were places where initially ambitious projects at the classroom or school levels were blunted or downsized, a phenomenon we have analyzed earlier. Downsizing was more strongly characteristic of Astoria and Burton than of Lido and Calston, but in all cases, the users were given and took advantage of wide latitude to trim and reshape the projects locally. Note that this set is composed solely of NDN projects; we will have more to say about this shortly. The basic theme here is that aiming initially or eventually for a modest change will get you just that, and sometimes less than that.

Earlier, we have often paired the two remaining sites in our discussion of dysfunctional paths to gloomy outcomes. What the members of Group 4 (Dun Hollow and Proville) had in common was that both were "failures," programmatically speaking. Institutionalization was nil; impact was low. Poorly designed projects died—or were killed—through attrition and lack of commitment.

Now let's look in greater detail at the four groups.

HIGH OUTCOMES FROM ENFORCED, STABILIZED USE

Throughout this study, we have highlighted successful implementation at some places where administrators exerted strong and continuous pressure on users. Tindale and Masepa were not the only sites where administrative muscle was used; we saw such pressure during the "adoption" phase at virtually all the sites, and outright mandating at Carson and Astoria as well, yet the outcomes were lower there. What made Tindale and Masepa different and accounted for their higher performance on the outcome measures?

Figure 44 tries to answer the question by laying out the key predictors and outcomes in a composite causal network. The relatively small number of boxes with broken lines (see the legend) suggests that these were very similar cases. Let us walk through the figure.

At both Tindale and Masepa there was good program–district fit and strong district-level endorsement (2), with much of the endorsement and the resulting program adoption and development (4) stemming from the influence of central office administrators (3). The fit and the endorsement at Tindale

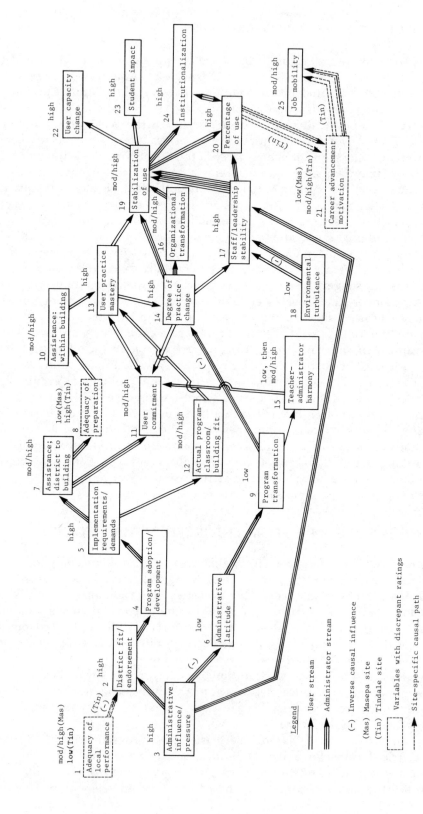

FIGURE 44. Group 1: High outcomes from mandated, stable use.

Legend

→ User stream

⇒ Administrator stream

(-) Inverse causal influence

(Mas) Masepa site

(Tin) Tindale site

⬚ Variables with discrepant ratings

--→ Site-specific causal path

1 Adequacy of local performance — mod/high(Mas) low(Tin)

2 District fit/endorsement — (Tin)(-) high

3 Administrative influence/pressure — high

4 Program adoption/development

5 Implementation requirements/demands — high

6 Administrative latitude — low

7 Assistance; district to building — mod/high

8 Adequacy of preparation — low(Mas) high(Tin)

9 Program transformation — low

10 Assistance; within building — mod/high

11 User commitment — mod/high

12 Actual program-classroom/building fit — mod/high

13 User practice mastery — high

14 Degree of practice change — high

15 Teacher-administrator harmony — low, then mod/high

16 Organizational transformation — mod/high

17 Staff/leadership stability — high

18 Environmental turbulence (-) — low

19 Stabilization of use — mod/high

20 Percentage of use — high

21 Career advancement motivation — low(Mas) mod/high(Tin)

22 User capacity change — high

23 Student impact — high

24 Institutionalization — high

25 Job mobility (Tin) — mod/high

were heightened by the fact that the reading program there addressed the problem of declining reading scores (1). At Masepa, there was no strong problem-resolution issue; the ECRI program simply looked good to the initial users and local administrators, and it had been well marketed.

What happened next is what set these sites apart from others. As the bottom region of the network shows, administrative influence and pressure (3) were exerted in the form of low latitude (6) given users to make changes (9) in the project as originally designed. This was where the enforcement theme came into play. The users' initial reaction was negative; they felt "policed" and "professionally violated." The result was the initially low degree of administrator–teacher harmony (15).

The hallmark of these sites was the friction between administrators and users got resolved, whereas at the low-outcome sites such interrole friction festered long enough to depress the levels of desired outcomes. The upper region of Figure 44 shows how conflict resolution was achieved. The program, once adopted or developed (4) required important shifts (5), both within the implementing classrooms and in organizational working arrangements. The central office administrators furnished initial assistance (7), in order to heighten users' technical preparation (8); the chart shows that Tindale provided more of such assistance and to better effect than did Masepa. But follow-up assistance (7) from the central office was high at both sites. This, combined with fairly strong within-building support (10), both between users and from building administrators to users, increased user commitment (11) and user practice mastery (13), which also fed one another. It also helped that the implementation requirements (5), although they demanded practice and organizational shifts, were not incompatible with ongoing arrangements; the innovation–classroom and innovation–building "fit" (12) was good in both cases, thereby facilitating user mastery (13).

These middle boxes are the crucial ones. Users needed ongoing assistance in the form of materials, training, and consultation, and they got it, both from the district and from the building. Assistance heightened commitment and more important, improved practice mastery. Mastery of a complex, difficult practice led to major practice change (14), which generated further commitment (11), as did reduced friction between teachers and administrators (15). The cycle of mastery → practice change → commitment meant eventually that the teachers came over to the administrators; in return, the administrators continued to provide ongoing assistance and even gave the users a bit more leeway to make changes in some of the project components.

The rest of the story is fairly straightforward. On its way to being institutionalized (24), the project called forth changes in scheduling, record keeping, curriculum, and materials that translated into organizational transformations (16). As the practice, its users, and the working conditions surrounding it all settled down into a stable pattern of use (19), the teachers consolidated their practice changes in the form of expanded repertoires and capacities (22) and further increased student impact (23), which, in these two projects, was high, sometimes dramatically so. Stabilized use, success with students, and new organizational arrangements codifying the innovation all worked in the direction of institutionalizing the innovation (24) and preserving, or even extending, the number of users (20). Finally, administrative and user staffing both remained stable (17), and there were no external or internal crises (18) to disrupt local use. At Tindale, the success of the practice led to new career options (21). Senior administrators moved on, and users moved up into their slots in the job mobility profile (25) that we called *success-driven advancement*. The important thing to note is that these shifts did not destabilize the project, either at Tindale or at Masepa, where retirement and relocation among key administrators also went smoothly, with few transitional ripples.

The policy-relevant message from these high-outcome sites is that significant practice change can be achieved through benevolently authoritarian forms of management, provided that administrative commitment remains stable, that continuing external and internal support are delivered, that working arrangements are modified to accommodate the new practice, that the fiscal and political environment is neutral or benign, and that care is given to the replacement of key actors. (It also helps to have a product of high quality—but this was the case in 10 of our 12 projects, and several of those 10 produced lower-grade outcomes.) Finally, as we shall see shortly, there are *several* ways to high outcomes; enforcement is only one of those paths.

Figure 44 contains two streams that we have drawn differently, to show that the key variables for users were usually not the same ones as for administrators. For the administrators, the key tasks are finding or developing a practice with a good local fit, getting it adopted, providing ongoing technical and institutional support, and getting the practice stabilized, extended to a wider public of users, and "routinized" in such a way as to incorporate the project into the existing training, budget, and policy cycles. In this first scenario, there is the additional administrative task of keeping the project intact, both in terms of its core components, and through preserving the magnitude of practice change that the innovation required of its users.

The users have other fish to fry. What matters to them are the demands made by the innovation on their current skills and on the way they run their classrooms; the initial and ongoing assistance they have available; the degree to which they feel committed to the practice as they get on top of it; the possibility of settling down into a phase of masterful, impact-producing use; and the likelihood of deriving some skills and materials that are transferable to other parts of their yearly repertoire. The successful projects in this group were clearly the ones in which *both* agendas, those of administrators and those of teachers, were met, often because there were mechanisms for containing and resolving the conflict between the administrative diktat and users' professed autonomy.

MODERATE-HIGH OUTCOMES FROM HIGH MASTERY AND LOW SETTLEDNESS

As a set, the second cluster of sites (Plummet, Banestown, Perry-Parkdale, and Carson) achieved well, but not as well as the enforcers. In particular, these were places where the users excelled and the student impacts were strong, yet where such positive individual and classroom-level outcomes did not translate into equally high institutional outcomes. Why not?

Figure 45 lays out the progression of determinants, using most of the same variables as in Figure 44. Let us go quickly through this scenario and then contrast it with that at the "enforcement" sites.

The first antecedent variables set a different tone from the first outcome pattern. Here, we have more of a problem-solving impetus; both Banestown and Plummet were facing crises, and Carson and Perry-Parkdale evolved practices that met fairly strong local needs. In all four cases, the local performance was judged to be suboptimal (1). This need set the stage for administrative pressure (3) to adopt or develop a program (5) whose characteristics matched the district's needs (4).

There was, however, a second impetus in this group of projects: career ambitions (2), on the part of both administrators and teachers. These projects were not, as at Proville, simple vehicles for promotion, but they seemed to attract people with interests in moving in, moving up, or moving someone else up. Ultimately, these career-centered motivations weakened the projects, but initially, they provided energy and muscle.

The projects in this group were demanding (6), less in their institutional ramifications than in the efforts that they required of users. Preparation, both technical and political, was adequate (7), as was central office assistance (8) in the initial year. In practice, however, users found that the innovations were problem-prone and that their fit with local conditions was poor (9). The program was too fluid at Banestown; the users floundered. The staff at Perry-Parkdale and Carson struggled feverishly to make the practices work without undue overload. The lack of match between the program characteristics and the students was nearly catastrophic at Plummet. Poor fit had two important consequences. First, users sought, and got, authorization from project administrators (12) to make changes in the project (11). Although these changes sometimes reduced the scope and the bite of the innovation, notably at Carson, the degree of practice change (15) remained high, in part because the users were thrust into organizationally novel roles: a new pull-out remedial lab at Banestown, an entirely new institution at Plummet, an autonomous program spanning two high schools at Perry-Parkdale, and a major counseling function added to instructional roles at Carson. Poor fit (9) also triggered within-building assistance (10), which, in turn, heightened user commitment (14) and practice mastery (17). In effect, the sites in this group ranked highest in lateral assistance. The institutional response to "overreaching" was, from the start, mutual help, which often lent a "crusading" flavor to the implementation process, notably at Plummet and Carson. These were the sites at which the users worked hardest—and did so under relatively *little* administrative pressure. The fruit of that work was high practice change (15), strong practice mastery (17), and, through stabilization of the technical aspects of the innovation (20), high student impact (22) and user capacity change (21) notably in terms of user attitudes and relationships. The people at these sites had learned to look at

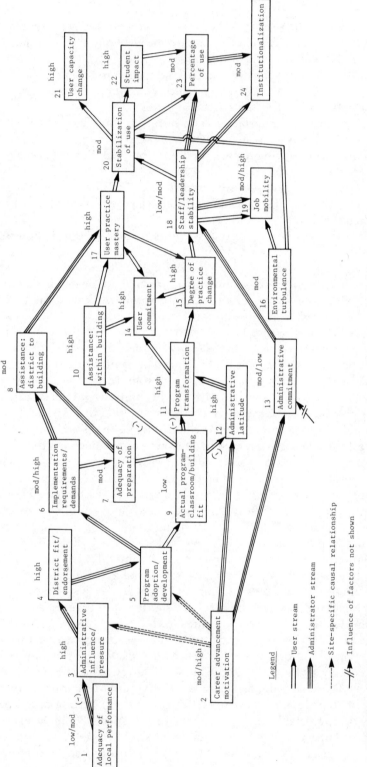

FIGURE 45. Group 2: Moderate–high outcomes from high mastery and low settledness. (From Miles & Huberman, 1984. Reprinted by permission.)

themselves and their pupils differently, whereas users at the "enforcement" sites felt technically, instructionally, and managerially stronger.

The assistance–mastery–commitment cycle was the sunny side of these sites and accounted for the strong individual- and classroom-level outcomes, but there was also a more shadowy side. For users, poor local fit, together with the continuous adaptation of the project and high degrees of practice change under conditions of uncertainty, produced attrition. At Perry-Parkdale and Plummet, there were clear signs of burnout. At Banestown, users began to look tentatively elsewhere. At Carson, users responded to role overload by watering down the innovation. Attrition, combined with the relative success of the practices, also revived or crystallized career advancement motivations. Near the end of our field research, users began to leave the projects (19)—many left the site altogether. The lowered staff stability (18) lowered the stabilization of use (20) and the percentage of project users (23). At the same time, three of these four sites were hit with budget cuts (16), as a result of which some users— notably at Banestown and Perry-Parkdale—were thrust back into conventional classroom slots. These are the "win–lose" scenarios we sketched in the section on job mobility. The success of the project helped some achieve their career goals, but environmental turbulence sacrificed others to unwanted re- assignments.

Administrators also began disengaging. What these four projects had in common, along with the Lido site, is that later administrative commitment (13), at the project, building, or central office level, either waned or was directed elsewhere. The reasons were several, and they varied by site: changes in administrative authority (Banestown and Plummet); central office turnover (Perry-Parkdale); or the departure of key innovation advocates (Carson, Lido, and Plummet). But there was also the nagging sense at all the sites in this group that key building and district administrators, or even project directors, were on the make, and that the incipient success or turbulence were signals to move— up, if possible. Looking back at Masepa and Tindale, in the enforced, stabilized use cluster, most of the career shifts either were promotions *within* the project (e.g., at Tindale, from users to department heads or from department heads to building- and district-level slots connected to the innovation) or were *career-innocent* (e.g., at Masepa, retirement and change of residence when a husband was reassigned). But in our "overreaching" group, on the other hand, the trend was toward career shifts *out of the project*—often out of the district—either for more opportunistic reasons or because of environmental turbulence. In either case, leadership stability was weakened (18), with attendant effects on job mo- bility (19), on stabilization of use (20), on the numbers of users (23)—which, typically, dropped or remained roughly constant—and, even more consequen- tially, on the level of institutionalization (24). Because these innovations succeeded and the core users remained, short-term continuity was assured. But the mixture of environmental uncertainty and fickleness or turnover on the part of key administrators undermined the institutional routinization required for longer-term survival.

This group of projects illustrates the fact that new practices can be introduced and consolidated without heavy administrative strong-arming, and that at the outset career-driven motives can accelerate adoption. The necessary conditions appear to be administrative flexibility, strong lateral assistance, and adaptive program transformation that resolve poor local fit while preserving significant practice change.

The problem appears to be that as users achieve masterful ownership of the practice, some burn out and others revive career ambitions. Nor do career-driven administrators appear to build a lasting commitment to projects that they sponsor or lead, so that success *or* turbulence is a prompt to move on. Although the stakes they pull up unsettle the rest of the enterprise, the school improvement effort stays reasonably well in place on the strength of its achievements.

Finally, the respective user and administrator "streams" show once again that different role incumbents have different agendas. In this project group, the administrator stream moves in two directions. First, it addresses the resolution of local problems by championing projects with a good district-level fit. That role calls for meeting the implementation requirements with preimplementation assistance and at least minimal follow-up support. In parallel, there is the career advancement stream that drives, at least in part, local adoption and the kind of administrative flexibility that enhances the change of success. However, that stream also flows into more opportunistic waters, so that sometimes later commitment may wane, leadership stability may weaken, job mobility increase, and the scope and durability of the practice become uncertain.

The user stream, by contrast, is closer to that of the "enforcement" group. Users focus on adequate preparation, local workability, and the assistance and program transformations needed to achieve practice mastery. This focus, in turn, produces desirable local effects: significant practice change, user commitment, technical stabilization, student impact, and user capacity change. But given untoward contextual features, the same causal chain can spell trouble. Poor fit, high program transformation, and a high degree of practice change can also deplete users, who, when caught up in career mobility or local turbulence, can destabilize the projects when they leave.

MODERATE-LOW OUTCOMES FROM PROGRAM BLUNTING AND DOWNSIZING

Group 3 (Astoria, Lido, Calston, and Burton) is more of a mongrel than the others. This shows up immediately in Table 44, where the outcome patterns are revealed as various. Only Lido and Calston seem to belong in the same ballpark, and Burton seems to be in another, lower league. Still, these sites share some common features that make them a coherent cluster. For one thing, their outcomes were modest—in the case of Burton, very modest. More usefully, their outcomes were modest for the same reasons: Innovations that were not major ventures to begin with were still further reduced in scale and scope, so that major change was ruled out and the outcomes were correspondingly limited. The reductions took place at the instructional level. Users, given near-discretionary latitude by administrators to make changes, locally refit the innovations and, in so doing, stabilized them as minor add-ons or drop-ins. The refitting was done by unbundling external (NDN) projects and using only those components that were congenial to personal teaching styles, and that called for few changes in ongoing instructional routines. There was one additional thread that tied this group together and connected it thematically to Group 2: For three of the four sites, later administrative leadership was low. Key innovation advocates at the building or district level backed off, left, or were reassigned.

Nevertheless, this was a group with different tales to tell. Figure 46 assembles those tales in one place and indicates the between-site differences.

Let us walk through Figure 46, stressing the features common to the majority of the sites in this group. First, there was no major problem-solving incentive at these sites, although Calston was after higher reading scores when it adopted the Matteson 4D program. Nor was there a strong career-advancement motif. People may have had an eye out for occasions to facilitate a career move, but they were not zooming in as intensively as were the personnel in the "overreaching" group or at Proville (see below). Otherwise, the first phase resembled that in Groups 1 and 2: strong central office influence and pressure (2), except at Lido; good district fit and strong endorsement (1), leading to program adoption (3).

As a set, these sites adopted modest add-on and drop-in products, but if used as designed, they could have been moderately demanding (4). The Calston reading project called for within-classroom differentiation and stringent record-keeping. The innovations at Burton and Lido would have put the teachers in unfamiliar and unconventional instructional roles. At Astoria, to use the early educational skills project as designed would have entailed major curriculum and scheduling changes. The key variable cluster, especially for Burton and Astoria, starts here. Anticipated and actual poor fit (5, 9) induced users to seek latitude from administrators (8) to trim or reconfigure the innovation, both before actual program execution and once the work was under way. The latitude was forthcoming, and so was high program transformation (12), typically in the form of reducing the program components, so that the degree of practice change was, at best, modest (15). Because these were "downsized" versions of an already modest innovation, institutionally speaking, practice mastery (14) was achieved without much stress, and the practice itself settled down fairly quickly (16). But its settling into a small-scale, unthreatening enterprise meant that there was no substantial impact either on students (21) or on the users themselves (20). Still, because many or most of the potential users were participants in the project, the percentage of use (19) was moderate overall and usually improved the chances for institutionalization (22).

The user stream in this downsizing–refitting scenario was new in several respects. Unlike their role in "enforcement" sites, users took control over the projects and, in so doing, "blunted" them in the sense of reducing possible impact. Note, however, that user ownership need not necessarily translate into lowered practice change. For example, strong commitment and good within-

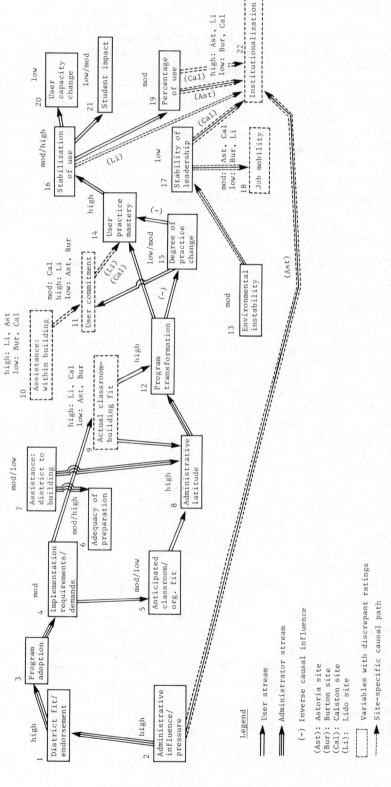

FIGURE 46. Group 3: Moderate-low outcomes from program blunting and downsizing. (From Miles & Huberman, 1984. Reprinted by permission.)

staff assistance brought the users at the "overreaching" sites to maintain a high level of practice change and to achieve local impact. As Figure 46 indicates, there was also high peer assistance, user commitment, and practice mastery at Lido, in a pattern akin to that of the second group. But the remaining sites showed a different pattern for the assistance–mastery–practice change-commitment cycle. The critical difference was that practice change, which could have been high at Lido and Calston, was only moderate to low—because program transformation had sapped its demands. As for Astoria and Burton, commitment and mastery were low to begin with, even though Astoria's within-building mutual assistance was strong.

The best way to read the remainder of the figure is to follow the administrative stream. District administrators tended to stand back once the program was adopted. Note that district-to-building assistance (7) was not strong, but it probably did not have to be in the initial phase, because these small-scale projects could manage with brief initial preparation (6). As the figure shows, the administrators "helped" most by granting the latitude to make changes (8). At Burton, it was the central office administrator who authorized discretionary changes, but elsewhere, authorization came from building administrators.

We pick up the administrative stream later on, with a key tandem of variables, environmental instability (13), and stability of leadership (17). At only one site, Calston, was there outright environmental turbulence, in the form of budget cuts that knocked the key innovation advocate out of the central office and thereby weakened institutionalization. Elsewhere, however, there was also movement. The changes in principal, school building, and student population demoralized the users at Lido and reduced the scope of the project. The archdiocese at Astoria reassigned both the key innovation advocate in the central office and the vice principal leading the team of users. By contrast, Burton was calm. So, at three of the four sites, there were leadership changes (17), which translated in two cases into a high incidence of job mobility (18) and into less secure institutionalization (22) at Calston and possibly at Lido. As the figure shows, institutionalization at Astoria was helped by outright mandating (2), despite low levels of impact.

FAILING: LOW OUTCOMES FROM INDIFFERENCE AND DISCOURAGEMENT

Dun Hollow and Proville were both sites where innovations "failed." The quotation marks indicate an important qualification: Though institutionalization was judged to be "nil" at both sites, there is good reason to think that the innovations were of poor quality and *should* have been dropped. Still, we must note (1) that coherent implementation efforts might well have salvaged the innovations and (2) that a good deal of energy was wasted at both sites.

Although Burton (in the blunting-downsizing cluster), for example, had few commendable impacts, the respondents felt that a few segments of the social studies curriculum might get written into the high-school curriculum, and most users expected to be implementing *some* facet, however trivial, of the project the following year. By contrast, Dun Hollow was considered locally to be a pilot project that had failed; there were no formal plans for continuation the following year. Similarly, the vocational educational project at Proville was considered "dead" by the end of our fieldwork; a very minor segment had been incorporated into a special-education project addressing a different student population.

Figure 47 displays the common routes to failure, using the same core variables as for the three previous groups. Although most of the ratings and causal paths were the same for Dun Hollow and Proville, many of the contextual features were different and warrant between-site distinctions. In effect, just as there are different ways to succeed, there are also different ways to fail.

In capsule form, the scenario at Proville is spelled out in the bottom stream of the figure. The central office administrators and their protégés advanced their careers (2) via the innovation, by pushing the project (1), by assuring its endorsement (3) and development (4), then by half-heartedly administering it (13) while they lobbied for promotions within and outside the district. Absences of and changes in leadership (17) led to desired job changes (22) at the price of project failure; institutionalization (20) was nil.

That, however, is not the whole story. Let us go through the flowchart: At both sites, central office administrators pressed for district-level approval (3) and development (4) of the project. In both cases, the motives were opportunistic: career-centered in the case of Proville and political at Dun Hollow, where the superintendent sought to improve relationships with a regional center disseminating the innovation. Note, however, that both projects were of potential interest to the district (3), although they were demanding (5) locally. The vocational educational program at Proville, if run correctly, would have called for coordination among teachers, employers, and trainers around pupil scheduling and academic work. The Eskimo-studies project at Dun Hollow was an integrated social studies unit requiring teachers to create much of their own material and to integrate it into the regular syllabus. Unfortunately, the users at both sites got little assistance (7) and were ill prepared (6).

Stopping here a moment, we should note that "adequacy of preparation" was a more crucial variable at these sites than elsewhere, but for different reasons. It was not only that the users were technically underprepared—as, for example, at Masepa or Banestown. Pedagogically, both practices were manageable. Rather, the project itself was faulty: ill designed for the target grade levels at Dun Hollow and very sketchily thought out at Proville. Note that the local-development aspect of IV-C programs, in effect, permits either adequate or poor design. The Tindale program was very well thought through; the Carson one was carefully but too ambitiously done; and Plummet developed a design that proved to be very poorly fitted to the actual incoming student population. Proville and Dun Hollow seem to have been at the bottom of the IV-C barrel.

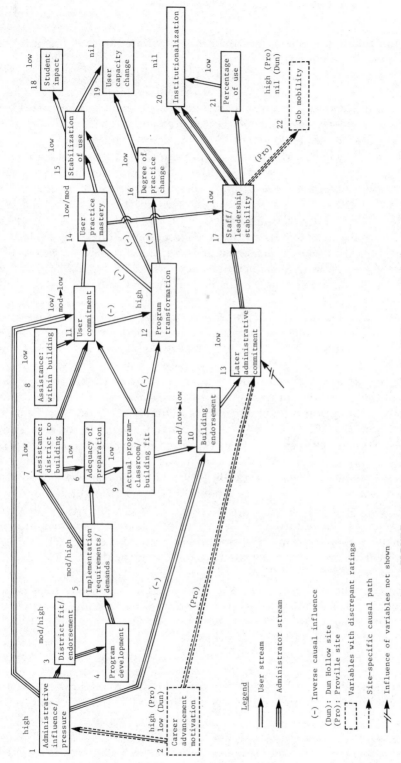

FIGURE 47. Group 4: Low outcomes from indifference and discouragement.

Legend

↑ User stream

⇈ Administrator stream

(–) Inverse causal influence

(Dun): Dun Hollow site
(Pro): Proville site

- - - Variables with discrepant ratings

▲ Site-specific causal path

↛ Influence of variables not shown

1 high — Administrative influence/pressure

2 high (Pro) low (Dun) — Career advancement motivation

3 mod/high — District fit/endorsement

4 — Program development

5 mod/high — Implementation requirements/demands

6 low — Adequacy of preparation

7 low — Assistance: district to building

8 low — Assistance: within building

9 low — Actual program-classroom/building fit

10 mod/low→low — Building endorsement

11 low/ mod→low — User commitment

12 high — Program transformation

13 low — Later administrative commitment

14 low/mod — User practice mastery

15 low — Stabilization of use

16 low — Degree of practice change

17 low — Staff/leadership stability

18 low — Student impact

19 nil — User capacity change

20 nil — Institutionalization

21 low — Percentage of use

22 high (Pro) nil (Dun) — Job mobility

Less thought went into them. Less expertise gravitated toward them. In many respects, they were lemons.[1]

We should also note that both projects began with lukewarm support. User commitment (11) was low to moderate at the outset, largely because of heavy-handed administrative pressure to implement (1), and also because the innovations were poorly designed and created problems of coordination and overload at the classroom or building levels (9). In addition, building administrators, especially at Proville, had also been pressured and were skeptical (10), both of the merits and of the motives for implementing the project. Although we had other sites with moderate to low building endorsement on the part of either the principal and/or other teachers not involved in the project (e.g., Perry-Parkdale and Banestown), the initial levels of user commitment were higher. Here, there were underdesigned or poorly designed innovations, forced on lukewarm users and principals who were suspicious of the project's origins and who realized when they started in that the projects were full of bugs. It was not an auspicious beginning, and things got worse when the needed assistance (7, 8) was weak.

At several points in this volume, we have stressed the importance of user commitment, in itself and as a function of user practice mastery. In all cases, when initial commitment was low, it tended to be boosted by the presence of district-level and peer assistance, by the experience of mastery and the resulting change in practice, and by gradually improving classroom or building fit. As the level of commitment rose, so did further practice mastery and, ultimately, stabilization of use. This was essentially the pattern for outcome Groups 1 and 2. In Group 4, on the other hand, the levels of commitment declined rapidly. At Dun Hollow, the users tried to revamp the Eskimo project on the run, jettisoned much of it in frustration, and either left the project altogether or reduced its use drastically. At Proville, the teachers stayed briefly with the practice, felt it was more trouble than it was worth, and opted out. Mapping this progression on Figure 47, we have poor fit (9) and lowered commitment (11), with both of these producing program transformation (12), increasingly in the direction of erasing the project from use. Practice mastery (14) was weak as a result of frustrated attempts to make the project work (Dun Hollow), or because of outright desertion (Proville). Low mastery, coupled with program reduction and desertion (12), produced low practice change (16) and low stabilization of use (15), which further depressed student impact (18) and user capacity change (19). There was simply too little going on to have any meaningful effect. As staff left the project (17), the number of users dropped (21), and the probability of institutionalization (21) became—probably fortunately—remote.

Given such poor starting conditions, it is difficult to see how that chain of events could have been broken. One possibility would have been to offer bet-

---

[1]The "guaranteed" quality of NDN projects does not, of course, guarantee easy implementation, which, as we have seen (e.g., at Masepa), can be replete with poor initial preparation and lack of resources and materials. But the NDN projects' soundness held up better when they came under fire than did these two poorly designed IV-C projects.

ter assistance and to encourage peer support, with the possibility that the innovation's design could have been improved through user feedback. But as Figure 47 shows (7, 8), neither district-level nor lateral support appeared. External technical assistance at Dun Hollow was sporadic and inefficient, and the building-level norms seemed to work against lateral assistance. At Proville, district administrators were busy elsewhere or were too unstable in their roles (17) to stay abreast. The users were scattered throughout four participating high schools, with little opportunity to collaborate.

The low level of administrative assistance betrayed the lack of administrative commitment (13) in the later stages of the project. There was simply no local advocate sufficiently committed or even sufficiently *present* to keep the projects alive. This indifference also meant that district-level administrators were unwilling or unavailable to counter the passive (Dun Hollow) or active (Proville) resistance of building administrators, which, in turn, suggested to the central office that it was better to let the projects die than to waste energy on them (see the arrow from Box 10 to Box 13). And die they did, in both cases from the discouragement and desertion of users (11) and, at Proville, from leadership shifts (17) and the attendant job-hopping of ex-project administrators (17, 22). In a sense, these two "failure" cases can be seen as a successful effort by users to protect their schools against poorly conceived ideas.

Looking separately at the user and the administrator streams is especially instructive here. It is clear that the users did not get the enabling conditions they needed to survive and succeed, unlike the users in outcome Groups 1 and 2. To cope successfully with poorly designed, demanding, ill-fitting practices, these users needed responsive assistance and follow-up support both from the district and within the building. Neither was forthcoming here. We also saw earlier that commitment is a key item and gets built through practice mastery leading to practice change, through assistance and a strong administrative presence—all of which were lacking or low here. Administrators who, especially in the later phases, were absent (Group 4), inconsistent (Group 3), or overly permissive (Group 3 again) set the stage for lower stabilization of use, lower student impact, and lower user capacity change.

Following the administrator stream shows us that pressure exerted for purely opportunistic reasons or in defense of an ill-prepared product gets innovations in trouble right off the bat with users and building principals. When unreasonable pressure is combined with indifferent monitoring of and ministering to the project, administrators are likely to get even lower local commitment and endorsement, both of which sap the energy required of users to get on top of the practice and to deliver its potential outcomes. When administrators turn away from innovations, by busying themselves elsewhere or by jumping ship, users are likely to respond in kind, and the result is lowered chances of project continuation. The most favorable reading of the situation is that the "wisdom of the user" has prevailed.

So there are several routes to school improvement, played out by the different, sometimes colliding, agendas of administrators and users.[2] That only

---

[2]For conclusions to this section, see the overall conclusion section (pp. 271–278).

two of our cases turned out to be wasteful of energy and deadening to hopes is encouraging. It appears that if administrators maintain serious commitment to change, are not afraid to exert direct influence, use their power to protect the innovation from opportunistic adaptation, and, above all, supply a steady flow of support, success is likely. But they alone cannot ensure success. Users need to help each other, to enhance their mastery of the innovation, to change their usual classroom practice—become *stretched*—and to sustain and develop their commitment in the process. Above all, working connections, problem-solving abilities, and conflict-management skills between users and administrators are essential for the people in these two worlds of innovation to complement each other's efforts productively. Finally, it is clear that if good-quality, nontrivial innovations enter this process—or get developed during it—they can have a significant impact on both pupils and teachers.

CHAPTER 8

What Have We Learned?

Summary and Integration of Findings

Our travels on the implementation voyage with our 12 sites have led us to some conclusions that we consider well founded. We believe that our sites are a good sample of schools and districts that have been carrying out innovation-based school-improvement programs under the aegis of the National Diffusion Network and Title IV-C, and we believe that we got close enough to the realities of those programs and the people doing them to understand what happened in them over time, and why.

This chapter reviews our conclusions, clustering related findings and making some general comments. We reference the sections from which the findings are drawn. A concluding section recasts the findings in terms of the dilemmas faced during school improvement.

OUR FINDINGS IN REVIEW

Settings and Actors

Educational innovations, as exemplified in the NDN and IV-C programs, appeared to be adopted or developed in districts with reasonable environmental stability and at least a "moderate" past interest in new programs. The implementing schools, on the other hand, were more traditional. Much of the district-level dynamism for school improvement came from the central office administrators, often coordinators or assistant superintendents for curriculum and instruction, who kept their eyes open for promising practices outside the district or energetically promoted a local product. The central office administrator thus became the prime advocate of the new practice, often reaching directly into the schools to implement it and thereby leaving the building principals to play a secondary role. (See pp. 32–42.)

Motives and Attitudes toward Adoption

The innovations were adopted as the result of multiple, sometimes tangled, motives. Nearly half of the users adopted the new practice because of

271

administrative pressure, but their attitudes toward it were usually neutral to favorable, especially when the innovation was central or salient. When the pressure was lower, users often invoked motives of professional growth; the practice might build up their instructional repertoire, help them in other aspects of their teaching, put them in contact with specialists, and stretch them beyond what they were currently doing. In brief, there was less user interest in innovation-specific benefits than in second-order rewards.

Administrators, who live in a different institutional world, were more interested in improving classroom-level instruction or schoolwide management, but they also liked the added funds and resources made available by externally assisted projects. It is noteworthy that in only a few cases did adpotion result from a percieved problem to which the innovation was seen as a solution, either by users or by administrators.

In roughly half the cases, the incentives for adoption were tied up with career plans for moving in, over, up, or away or, alternatively, for consolidating one's position. In the later phases of thes innovations, too many career-driven incentives crippled a project, but too few deprived it of the necessary energy to follow through to stable continuation. Sometimes, career incentives surfaced later in the life of the project—notably at the sites where implementation was successful. But *unwanted* job mobility could also occur as a result of unexpected budget and personnel cuts. (See pp. 43–57 and 241–251.)

Initial Perceptions and Assessments

The 12 innovations studied here, ranging from reading programs to career education and a complete alternative school, are representative of those supported by NDN and IV-C. About half were aimed at low-ability students, both elementary and secondary programs were included, and most were nontrivial, with moderately demanding implementation requirements.

These innovations posed problems initially for their target users, who sized them up as complex, hard to do, unclear, and flexible—sometimes too flexible. The classroom fit was seen as only fair; the users felt the new practice would make demands calling for substantial changes in the ways they managed their yearly work.

By contrast, most of the administrators saw the practice initially as relatively simple, straightforward, and manageable, and they anticipated that varying amounts of organizational change would result from adoption. There was a tendency for administrators to overweight the merits and to minimize the drawbacks of the practice, and to be ready to jump in with the intention of setting things right as problems arose. (See pp. 58–71.)

Early Implementation

Following on these perceptions, it appears that users made better predictions than administrators. Initial use was nearly always rough; few sites experienced a smooth early period. At the classroom level, teachers complained of day-to-day coping, unsuccessful attempts to "make it work like it's supposed to," continuous cycles of trial and error, inability to get through daily or weekly segments, and the sacrifice of other core activities. Surprisingly, the degree of preparedness was an influential but not a decisive predictor of smoothness of early use. In terms of preparedness, the smooth-starting sites were helped by the provision of resources and materials—a key provision, since so many of these innovations were materials-centered. The rough-starting sites were hurt by lack of user commitment to and understanding of the practice, by insufficient or unavailable materials, and by inadequate skills and training. Still, training was less crucial than prior experience—both its amount and its appropriateness to the demands of the innovation.

In terms of desirable outcomes, smooth early use was a bad sign. Smoothly implementing sites seemed to get that way by reducing the initial scale of the project and by lowering the gradient of actual practice change. This "downsizing" got rid of most headaches during the initial implementation but also threw away most of the potential rewards; the project often turned into a modest, sometimes trivial, enterprise. By contrast, most of the initially rough-implementing projects, including those that later produced the strongest outcomes, remained ambitious, change-inducing, and ill-fitting, all of which made for difficult initial use, but could deliver significant practice change.

To a large extent, the basic tension in school-based innovation was that of hanging on to the initial magnitude of practice change in the midst of poor local fit and general system stress. This tension involved the users of the innovation, but it also related closely to what administrators did when a change-bearing project upset local practices and procedures. The administrators who responded favorably—and rapidly—to users' requests to make changes in the innovation often consented implicitly to a watering down of the project, and thereby to far more modest results. Those who held out for fidelity to the original model were sometimes initially cast in unpleasant authoritarian roles, but they were able, under certain conditions, to deliver more sizable results. (See pp. 72–87.)

Assistance

Large-scale, change-bearing innovations lived or died by the amount and quality of assistance that their users received once the change process was under way. More help was forthcoming when the projects were more ambitious; smaller-scale ventures required and got less internal or external aid. The forms of assistance were various. The high-assistance sites set up external conferences, in-service training sessions, visits, committee structures, and team meetings. They also furnished a lot of ongoing assistance in the form of materials, peer consultation, access to external consultants, and rapid access to central office personnel. Even close relatives helped out a good deal, often by handholding and talking through difficulties. Although strong assistance did not usually succeed in smoothing the way in early implementation, especially for the more demanding innovations, it paid handsome dividends later on by substantially increasing the levels of commitment and practice mastery. (See pp. 88–113.)

Transformations in Innovations over Time

As the new practices were executed, they were modified. From the moment of initial use to the end of data collection, over half of the sites changed from one-third to two-thirds of the core components of the innovation-as-designed, by variously reducing them, adding to them, or reconfiguring them; the main trend was toward attrition. Whether and how much an innovation was changed depended on the intensity of the demands it made locally and, in response to that intensity, on the micropolitics of the schools. A poor innovation–classroom fit led users to ask building administrators for authorization to make changes. A poor innovation–building fit led principals to do the same at the central office.

At least four different scenarios were played out in this process. There was first an "enforcement" scenario, in which administrators held out for and got faithful execution of a large-scale, demanding practice, but provided generous amounts of supportive within-district assistance. Next, "overreaching" innovations began with a faithful version that they were forced to cut back considerably as problems multiplied and the local staff wore out. In the "salvaging" scenario, projects that were ambitious but ill prepared locally were cut back initially, but some of the original components were instated later on. Finally, smaller-scale innovations could be "locally refitted" by successive changes that tended to deplete the original substance of the new practice. (See pp. 133–150.)

Change in Users' Practices and Perceptions

In the course of consolidating a new practice, there were often substantial and widespread changes in the users' practices and attitudes: changes in everyday classroom routines and expansion of instructional repertoires, changes in interpersonal ties, cognitive growth, shifts in attitudes toward pupils or peers, shifts in professional self-image, and transfers of innovation-specific skills to other parts of the user's practice. The users in this sample typically saw themselves as having become better "clinicians"—more instructionally skillful, and better able to diagnose problems and to differentiate instructional treatments—and as being interpersonally closer to pupils.

About half the sites reported moderate to high levels of user practice change stemming from the innovation. At the high-change sites, the projects began with a vengeance, users reported pervasive changes (not only changes in routines but also changes in core constructs), users took a long time to settle down with the project, the innovation consumed all the available energy, and negative changes were also reported (e.g., loss of variety and the sacrifice of other, favorite activities). The low-change sites had the reverse profile: timid beginnings, modest changes in daily routines, rapid practice mastery, the innovation perceived as a small change in the yearly cycle, few negative feelings about the practice, and the sense, on the part of users, of not having been stretched by the experience. (See pp. 151–166.)

Most of these new skills, constructs, and attitudes derived from experience with the innovation, and were often applicable beyond it. They were maintained or extended during later use. Places with few of these *user capacity changes* turned out that way by allowing sizable and project-reductive changes, by failing to deliver adequate assistance, and by failing to ensure user commitment. The high-change sites, by contrast, maintained the initial levels of practice change by providing good assistance and by gaining local acceptance. In one family of sites, strong administrative and peer assistance helped to maintain strong practice change, which then translated into gains in general capacity. In another family, strong practice change and the resulting capacity growth came from administrative strong-arming coupled with consistent assistance. (See pp. 230–240.)

Transformations in the School as an Organization

The innovations in the NDN and Title IV-C programs studied did not seem, in the main, to bring about many organizational changes beyond those associated with introducing and institutionalizing the new practice itself. But there were exceptions. They seemed to occur in the presence of outside pressure for change, demographic shifts, a needy student population, and a recent history of district-level innovativeness. These were the pre-conditions for the choice of a larger-scale project, with some stiff implementation requirements in terms of the school-level changes needed to execute the project successfully. Local administrators, especially in the central office, were highly committed and delivered the necessary assistance, aided in part by the funding that came with the larger-scale innovations. The assistance was appropriately problem-centered and was built in a cooperative institutional climate. As the project was successfully implemented and extended, the school-level structure and the working procedures shifted to accommodate to the requirements of the practice. Making that shift successfully, however, called for sustained administrator pressure, stemming from administrative commitment. When the commitment was lower, there was less administrative pressure, and more latitude was given to users, with the result that implementation was less thoroughgoing and organizational change was correspondingly weaker. (See pp. 167–186.)

Later Implementation and Stabilization of Use

Gradually the users and their innovations settled down. Firm practice mastery usually came within 18 months in the case of the complex projects, and within 6 months in the case of the "downsized" innovations. Most of the later implementation time was spent on reaching up (taking on more demanding segments), debugging outstanding flaws, refining and codifying weekly routines, integrating new materials into existing ones, adapting the practice to ongoing changes in the pupil population, and extending the innovation to other activities. Users also worked their way through to a more differentiated and integrated understanding of the innovation by making it behave consistently. (See pp. 114–121.)

It was typical to achieve at least a moderate degree of stabilization, but there were various ways of getting there. The most common path was through technical mastery of the practice, which resulted from adequate initial preparation and—especially—follow-up assistance, plus strong local endorsement in the building and the district, along with users' commitment to the project. Such commitment was often the *result* of practice mastery rather than its antecedent. In capsule form, what happened in the higher-stabilizing schools was that users confronted a new practice that turned out to be even more challenging and demanding than they had expected. They took on the challenge, struggled, received support from their peers and from sources outside the school, and gradually got on top of the innovation, heightening their commitment as the effort they had expended bore fruit. When the assistance was less frequent, not sustained, or of a single type, there were markedly lower levels of commitment and practice mastery.

By itself, however, practice mastery did not ensure stabilization of use. That also came from stablilty in pupil and program characteristics, staff and leadership stability, and building-level endorsement. Endorsement was sometimes hard to get, especially as the innovations often complicated institutional life for people who were not direct actors. The core task here was to negotiate a better innovation-building fit without throwing out the change-carrying features of the project. (See pp. 191–200.)

Achieving Widespread Use

An important objective in the innovation process was extending a new practice to the full pool of eligible users in the school and district or, alternatively, achieving full use for a specific target group. Most sites came out with at least moderate levels of local diffusion. They did it essentially by maintaining administrative pressure on users during implementation while furnishing within-building and district-to-building assistance that, in turn, led to stronger user commitment, user mastery, and impact on students. Administrative pressure by itself—the administrator as thug—got nowhere; the users remained uncommitted, minimally skillful, and locked into a teacher–administrator disharmony that eventually did the project in. (See pp. 200–207.)

Impact on Students

The innovations were meant, in the first instance, to enhance pupils' performance and performance-related attitudes. It is clear that both externally developed (NDN) and locally developed (IV-C) innovations could achieve such gains. The evidence here is compelling, if not fully robust, that the impacts were substantial at about half our sites and moderate at several others. The higher-impact sites got there in one of two ways: via "stabilized mastery" (strong user commitment, fed by good assistance leading to practice mastery and stabilization of use) or via "enforcement" (administrative pressure, leavened by good district-to-school assistance, and little latitude given users to make changes in the innovation). By contrast, low student impact resulted from low user commitment and/or "program-blunting," that is taking out the more ambitious or demanding components and thereby trivializing the potential effects. (See pp. 222–230.)

Institutionalization

To maintain both the impact on students and widespread use, the innovations needed to shed their novelty or experimental status and become a durable feature in the local landscape. Effective current operations were not enough. Durability occured when the innovation successfully completed important passages (such as the transition from soft to hard money) and when it survived organizational cycles (such as yearly budget cycles and personnel turnover). At about half our field sites, the new practices got durably built into the district administration and curriculum.

Strong institutionalization seemed to require some administrative pressure, lack of serious local resistance, and at least minimal teacher-administrator harmony. It also thrived on staff and leadership stability, organizational transformations that rooted the new practice in local structures and procedures, and levels of assistance adequate to bring about stabilized use by a large percentage of the eligible users. One path to high institutionalization stemmed from administrative mandate; another went via strong user commitment and practice mastery. Low-institutionalizating sites were characterized either by vulnerability (administrators did project the new practice against internal resistance or external turbulence) or by indifference (administrators did not work hard to supply local assistance and protection; users disbanded). (See pp. 207–222.)

Looking across Outcomes

Most site personnel were interested in optimal results: good stabilization of use, widespread use, strong impact on students, user capacity changes, and institutionalization. Two of our sites did especially well and two miserably, and most lay in between. A prominent—but not the only—way to high outcomes on all these dimensions involved enforced, stabilized implementation. Local administrators used muscle along with tutoring and tenderness. They knew the projects well, tolerated few changes in the original design, provided good and timely assistance, got the users to accept or to become committed to the practice, maintained a steep gradient of practice change, ensured staff and leadership continuity, and protected the innovation from external turbulence.

A second high-outcome scenario called for commited users and supportive administrators to embark on a venture that went beyond their initial capacities. Users were thrust into new roles or new organizational settings and gradually worked their way—drawing heavily on peer assistance—to high practice mastery, strong commitment, and substantial student impact. In some cases, however, these strong classroom-level and individual-level outcomes did not translate into equally strong institutional outcomes. That occurred when users wore out, when both users and administrators were riding the innovation to new jobs, and when external turbulence was high. As the project staff and leadership turned over or redirected their energies, there was a drop in the levels of institutionalization and internal diffusion.

Moderate-to-low outcomes acorss the board were associated with sites where project "downsizing" or "blunting" occurred. Although these innovations were not major ventures, they tended to become further reduced in scale and force when the program-classroom fit was low and users asked for, and got, latitude to make changes. The ultimate level of practice change was modest, as were the levels of practice mastery and stabilization of use. Most other outcomes were insubstantial. Institutionalization was further compromised by later instability in leadership—when the key innovation advocates backed off, left, or were reassigned—and by some enviromental uncertainties as well.

Finally, failure to achieve any substantial outcomes was the result of local indifference and discouragement. Adoption stemmed from largely opportunistic motives. The innovations, although demanding, were poorly prepared, were ill fitting locally, and gained at best lukewarm support from users and building administrators, who had been pressured into doing the project. There was little later administrative commitment to provide assistance, or to look toward local institutionalization. Users responded to the poor design, poor local fit, and lack of support by discarding much of the practice, or by simply opting out, so that the project was discontinued, perhaps fortunately. Still, there was little effort to salvage or to improve the innovation, and much energy was wasted. (See pp. 252–270.)

SCHOOL IMPROVEMENT: SOME BASIC DILEMMAS

Our findings can be viewed integratively as the story of what happens when school personnel face key dilemmas in their day-to-day work. A dilemma requires a choice between two competing "goods," which set up a tension that must be resolved one way or another.[1] The people we studied faced countless dilemmas as they worked to improve their schools—some explicit, clear, even rationally considered, and others vague, fuzzy, and intuitively approached. Here, we focus on six core dilemmas that seemed to recur at our sites. In some cases, we can suggest the conditions under which one horn or the other of a dilemma may be "right," but in others, we will have to content ourselves with pointing to the dilemma as a crucial agenda for administrators and users, who will have to—as they always do in any case—make their own resolutions.

Fidelity versus Adaptation

Should innovations be "done right," carefully, according to the spirit and letter of their developers' intents? Or should they be adapted to fit local

---

[1] For additional discussion of the idea of dilemma resolution in educational improvement, see Miles *et al* (1978) and Miles (1981).

realities, to permit an even fuller and better implementation? At our sites, adaptation always took place—but it was sometimes constrained by administrators' stout refusal to permit adaptations that would weaken or water down the innovation. Enforcing fidelity for substantial, good-quality innovations really paid off— if it was accompanied by effective assistance. When adaptation went too far because of administrative "latitude," what often occurred was blunting or downsizing, trivialization, and weak student impact. Only at the sites where there was strong user commitment (and perhaps some degree of protection from environmental pressure through the creation of a "subsystem") did substantial adaptation *improve* the innovation. As Fullan and Pomfret (1977) and Berman (1981) have pointed out, user-oriented adaptation may be more necessary for complex, less clearly structured innovations that demand a strong user commitment to inquiry, learning, and revision. The basic choice for administrators and users remains: How far do we protect the innovation from damaging changes, and how far do we creatively fit it to local realities?

Centralized versus Dispersed Influence

Should central office and building administrators unabashedly exert direct influence, make demands, and press for implementation? Or should more weight be given to the knowledge and the professional expertise of teachers— who after all, are centrally responsible for delivering the innovation to students? We found that "enforcement" scenerios could be quite effective—*if*, as we suggested, the "muscle" was accompanied by "tutoring and tenderness." We also found that teachers—without pressure from above—were quite capable, given district-level assistance, of providing further assistance to each other, and of struggling through to the mastery of demanding innovations, and to student impact, growing professionally in the process. The underlying issue here is perhaps *commitment*. Administrative pressure without support and commitment simply leads to teacher resistance and failure; user influence over implementation without commitment to the spirit of the innovation leads to blunting or downsizing. But note that strong administrative influence need not mean low user commitment—that can be developed during supported implementation.

The worlds of administrators and users are very different. Many studies (see Miles, 1981) have shown that decisions in schools are "zoned": Some belong to administrators , others to teachers. There are "influence discontinuities." The question is whether to place the implementation of a school improvement effort squarely in the administrator's zone or in the teacher's zone. Straddles will probably run into difficulty.

Coordination versus Flexibility

Should the work of educational improvement be carried out in an interdependent, "tightly coupled," carefully designed way? Or is it more important to leave the users latitude, flexibility, room for more flexibility? This dilemma is *not* the same as that of centralized versus dispersed influence: It is possible to have centralized systems that allow much local flexibility (cf. Astoria in our study) or dispersed-influence systems that have close coordination among peers (cf. Masepa in our study). We found that efforts to develop cooperation, coordination, and conflict resolution across the differing worlds of administrators and users were often critical to successful implementation—*and* that it was often important to lay off from close supervision, giving dedicated professionals the chance to invent, adapt, and extend. Many of our administrators acted as if they believed the innovation would be easy, simple, and possible to coordinate without tears; users knew better. The basic tension remains: How closely knit should the implementation effort be, and how much local variation, autonomy, and creativity should be present? (Too much flexibility can mean lower percentages of use and weaker institutionalization, by the way.)

Ambitiousness versus Practicality

Should innovations be taken on that are demanding, far-reaching, stretching, and pervasive—even if they may induce stress and possible failure? Or should schools choose smaller-scale changes that can succeed and make a more modest but also a more predictable difference? Most of the innovations that we studied were nontrivial in original concept. At first, they looked hard and demanding to most users. If the ambitiousness was maintained, organizational change was more likely, and users often were stretched, grew, and became much stronger as teachers—but they also ran into stress and burnout. Ambitious efforts sometimes fell into our "overreaching" scenario, where cutbacks had to be made later on, or "salvaging" operations, where sadder but wiser people picked out pieces of the innovation from the wreckage of their original hopes. There is a case for practicality. But overemphasis on it, resulting in fatally "smooth" early implementation, got our sites little. The question remains: How high should sights be set—and what are the costs in personal stress, failed hopes, and eventual cynicism about future change efforts that one is willing to risk? Attempt more, get more. But "more" can mean more negative effects as well. One of the clearly important adjuncts of the decision to go the ambitious route is *sustained assistance;* without it, large-scale programs will simply backfire or wither.

Change versus Stability

Ultimately, should schools try to improve at all? The question may seem foolish or the answer self-evident: "Of course" changes for the better are to be desired. But change can also be disruptive and wasteful of resources; it may be far more important at any given point for a school to be doing a good job with familiar, well-tested instructional practices that have stood the test of time. Innovations always disrupt people's working lives to some extent.

We found that successful implementation required a careful, sometimes alternating attention to both horns of this dilemma. For example, implementing a change that was more than trivial usually required up to 18 months of sustained effort before something like "settledness" and user mastery had stabilized. The problems of achieving that stability, and of maintaining the stability of *personnel* needed for continued effective implementation, had to be kept in view by both users and administrators. Effective change requires a stable platform—though the platform itself may be transformed gradually during the process.

Career Development versus Local Capacity

This dilemma is especially ironic and painful. At our sites, it was often those people who were most successful with an innovation who were most likely to get or to seek a job somewhere else—away from the classroom or in another district. The local effort was weakened by their departure. Initially, career development interests often strengthened the "bite" of an innovative effort—but they often served later on to destabilize it.

If we look at the dilemma the other way, a primary emphasis on "local capacity" means a thoroughgoing implementation and a strengthening of the local school and district—but at the possible price of slowing down or hampering professionals' natural needs to grow, develop, and extend their horizons. Some of our sites managed the tension effectively by supporting internal, nondisruptive career moves—but many did not. The question is how to avoid the "failures of success," so that innovative efforts do not become automatically self-limiting.

Lists of dilemmas like these can promote the idea that all is a trade-off, and that everything "depends." Life is not so ambiguous, in fact. Most of our sites were successful in resolving these dilemmas productively; they achieved moderate to strong positive outcomes. That finding stems, we think, from the fact that administrators and teachers, though they live in different worlds and have different agendas, can, under the right circumstances, complement each other's efforts productively. Administrators who are committed can push, protect an innovation from casual adaptation, and supply supportive assistance. Users can follow their own professional growth motivation to master the innovation, help each other, extend their own classroom practice, and deepen their commitment. If administrators and users can work successfully together to meet their differing agendas, using good-quality, substantial innovations, there will be clear student impact. Schools can, it seems, improve, and we can now see more distinctly just how they do it.

References

Berman, P. Educational change: An implementation paradigm. In R. Lehming & M. Kane (Eds.), *Improving schools: Using what we know.* Beverly Hills, CA: Sage, 1981.

Berman, P., & McLaughlin, M. W. *Federal programs supporting educational change.* Santa Monica, CA: Rand Corporation.

Vol. 1. *A model of educational change.* R-1589/1-HEW, 1974.

Vol. 2. *Factors affecting change agent projects.* R-1589/2-HEW, 1975.

Vol. 3. *The process of change.* R-1589-HEW, 1975.

Vol. 4. *The findings in review.* R-1589/4-HEW, 1975.

Vol. 5. *Executive summary.* R-1589/5-HEW, 1975.

Vol. 6. *Implementing and sustaining Title VII bilingual projects.* R-1589/6-HEW, 1976.

Vol. 7. *Factors affecting implementation and continuation.* R-1589/7-HEW, 1977.

Vol. 8. *Implementing and sustaining innovations.* R-1589/8-HEW, 1978.

Blake, R. R., & Mouton, J. S. *Consultation.* Reading, MA: Addison-Wesley, 1976.

Crandall, D. P., and associates. *People, policies and practices: Examining the chain of school improvement.* Andover, MA: The Network, Inc., 1983.

Douglas, J. D. *Investigative social research: Individual and team field research.* Beverly Hills, CA: Sage, 1976.

Downs, C. W., Jr., & Mohr, L. B. Conceptual issues in the study of innovation. *Administrative Science Quarterly,* 1976, *21,* 700–714.

Fullan, M. *The meaning of educational change.* New York: Teachers College Press, and Toronto: OISE Publications, 1982.

Fullan, M., & Pomfret A. Research on curriculum and instruction implementation. *Review of Educational Research,* 1977, *47*(1), 335–397.

Goetz, J. P., & LeCompte, M. D. Ethnographic research and the problem of data reduction. *Anthropology and Education Quarterly,* 1981, *12*(1), 51–70.

Gold, B. A., & Miles, M. B. *Whose school is it anyway? Parent-teacher conflict over an innovative school.* New York: Praeger, 1981.

Hall, G. The study of individual teacher and professor concerns about innovations. *Journal of Teacher Education,* 1976, *27*(11), 22–23.

Hall, G., & George, A. A. *Stages of concern about the innovation: The concept, verification, and implications.* Austin: University of Texas R & D Center for Teacher Education, 1978.

Hall, G., Loucks, S. F., Rutherford, W., & Newlove, B. Levels of use of the innovation: A framework for analyzing innovation adoption. *Journal of Teacher Education,* 1975, *26*(1), 52–56.

Heck, S., Stiegelbauer, S., Hall, G., & Loucks, S. F. *Measuring innovation configurations: Procedures and applications.* Austin: University of Texas R & D Center for Teacher Education, 1981.

Huberman, A. M., & Miles, M. B. Deriving valid meaning from qualitative data: Some techniques of data reduction and display. *Quality and Quantity,* 1983, *17,* 281–339. (a)

Huberman, A. M., & Miles, M. B., with Taylor, B. L., & Goldberg, J. A. *Innovation up close: A field study in 12 school settings,* Vol. 4 of D. P. Crandall and associates, *People, policies and practices: Examining the*

283

chain of school improvement. Andover, MA: The Network, Inc., 1983. (b) (Referred to in the text as the *technical report.*)

Lawrence, D. H., & Festinger, L. *Determinants and reinforcement: The psychology of insufficient reward.* Stanford, CA: Stanford University Press, 1962.

Lippitt, G., & Lippitt, R. *The consulting process in action.* La Jolla, CA: University Associates, 1978.

Loucks, S. F., Newlove, B., & Hall, G. *Measuring levels of use of the innovation: A manual for trainers, interviewers and raters.* Austin: University of Texas R & D Center for Teacher Education, 1975.

Louis, K. S., Rosenblum, S., & Molitor, J. A. *Strategies for knowledge use and school improvement.* Washington: National Institute of Education, 1981.

McLaughlin, M. W. Implementation as mutual adaptation: Change in classroom organization. In W. Williams & R. F. Elmore (Eds.), *Social program implementation.* New York: Academic Press, 1976.

Miles, M. B. The development of innovative climates in educational organizations. *Tijdschrift voor Agologie,* 1972, *1,* 16–33.

Miles, M. B. Innovation from the ground up: Dilemmas of planning and implementing new schools. *New York University Education Quarterly,* 1980, *11*(2), 2–9.

Miles, M. B. Mapping the common properties of schools. In R. Lehming & M. Kane (Eds.), *Improving schools: Using what we know.* Beverly Hills, CA: Sage, 1981.

Miles, M. B., & Huberman, A. M. *Qualitative data analysis: A sourcebook of new methods.* Beverly Hills, CA: Sage, 1984.

Miles, M. B., Sullivan, E. W., Gold, B. A., Taylor, B. L., Sieber, S. D., & Wilder, D. E. Planning and implementing new schools: A general framework. In *Final Report, Part I: Project on Social Architecture in Education.* NIE-G-74-0051. New York: Center for Policy Research, 1978.

Mulhauser, F. Ethnography and policy-making: The case of education. *Human Organization,* 1975, *34,* 311–315.

Nash, N., and Culbertson, J. (Eds.). *Linking processes in educational improvement.* Columbus, OH: University Council for Educational Administration, 1977.

Paul, D. A. Change processes at the elementary, secondary and post-secondary levels of education. In N. Nash & J. Culbertson (Eds.), *Linking processes in educational improvement.* Columbus, OH: University Council for Educational Administration, 1977.

Runkel, P. J., Wyant, S. H., Bell, W. E., & Runkel, M. *Organizational renewal in a school district.* Eugene: Center for Educational Policy and Management, University of Oregon, 1980.

Schmidt, W. H., & Johnston, A. V. *A continuum of consultancy styles.* Los Angeles: University of Southern California, School of Public Administration Working Papers, 1977.

Weick, K. Educational organizations as loosely coupled systems. *Administrative Science Quarterly,* 1976, *21,* 1–9.

Wilson, S. The use of ethnographic techniques in educational research. *Review of Educational Research,* 1977, *47,* 245–266.

Wolcott, H. Criteria for an ethnographic approach to research in schools. *Human Organization,* 1975, *34:* 111–128.

Yin, R. K., with Quick, S. K., Bateman, P. M., and Marks, E. L. *Changing urban bureaucracies: How new practices become routinized.* Santa Monica, CA: Rand Corporation, 1978. R-2277/NSF.

Zaltman, G., Duncan, R., & Holbek, J. *Innovations and organizations.* New York: Wiley, 1973.

Data Collection Effort and Methods, by Site

Site	# site visits	Total days on site	# phone contacts Inter-views	# phone contacts Updat-ing	# formal, informal inter-views	# obser-vations	# docu-ments col-lected	# pages tran-scribed field notes
Astoria	7	4½	8	9	20	3	5	112
Banestown	4	9		6	47	7	8	408[a]
Burton	3	6		3	31	8	20	148
Calston	3	7	3	5	16	2	2	134
Carson	3	8		15	70	17	81	364
Dun Hollow	3	6		8	27	6	20	170
Lido	3	5		2	22	5	13	92
Masepa	3	9		7	46	10	6	370
Perry-Parkdale	3	7		5	60	11	49	301
Plummet	4	11	1	6	24	8	22	231
Proville	4	8	1	5	28	0	10	158
Tindale	4	9		8	49	8	23	225

[a]Combined notes of two researchers.

Sensitizing Codes and Operational Definitions

SENSITIZING CODES

Innovation Properties	IP	3.1
IP: Objectives	IP-OBJ	3.1.1
IP: Organization	IP-ORG/DD, LS	3.1.1
		3.1.1
IP: Implied changes—classroom	IP-CH/CL	3.1.4
IP: Implied changes—organization	IP-CH/ORG	3.1.5
IP: User salience	IP-SALIENCE	3.1.2
IP: (Initial) user assessment	IP-SIZUP/PRE,DUR	3.1.3, 3.4, 3.5
IP: Program development (IV-C)	IP-DEV	3.1.1, 3.3.3, 3.3.4
External context	**EC (PRE) (DUR)**	**3.2, 3.3, 3.4**
EC: Demographics	EC-DEM	
In county—school personnel	ECCO-DEM	3.2.3, 3.3, 3.4
Out county—nonschool personnel	ECEXT-DEM	3.2.3, 3.3, 3.4
EC: Endorsement	EC-END	3.2.3, 3.3, 3.4
In county—school personnel	ECCO-END	3.2.3, 3.3, 3.4
Out county—nonschool personnel	ECEXT-END	3.2.3, 3.3, 3.4
EC: Climate	EC-CLIM	3.2.3, 3.3, 3.4
In county—school personnel	ECCO-CLIM	3.2.3, 3.3, 3.4
Out county—nonschool personnel	ECEXT-CLIM	3.2.3, 3.3, 3.4
Internal context	**IC (PRE) (DUR)**	**3.2, 3.3, 3.4**
IC: Characteristics	IC-CHAR	3.2.2, 3.4, 3.5
IC: Norms and Authority	IC-NORM	3.2.2, 3.4.3, 3.5
IC: Innovation history	IC-HIST	3.2.1
IC: Organization procedures	IC-PROC	3.1.1, 3.2.4, 3.3, 3.4
IC: Innovation–organization congruence	IC-FIT	3.2.2
Adoption Process	**AP**	**3.2, 3.3**
AP: Event chronology—official version	AP-CHRON/PUB	3.2.4, 3.3.1
AP: Event chronology—subterranean	AP-CHRON/PRIV	3.2.4, 3.3.1
AP: Inside/outside	AP-IN/OUT	3.2.5
AP: Centrality	AP-CENT	3.2.2
AP: Motives	AP-MOT	3.2.6

AP: User fit	AP-FIT	3.2.7
AP: Plan	AP-PLAN	3.3.3
AP: Readiness	AP-REDI	3.3.4, 3.2.1
AP: Critical events	AP-CRIT	3.3.1
Site dynamics and transformation	TR	3.4
TR: Event chronology—official version	TR-CHRON/PUB	3.4.1, 3.4.2, 3.4.3
TR: Event chronology—subterranean	TR-CHRON/PRIV	3.4.1, 3.4.2, 3.4.3
TR: Initial user experience	TR-START	3.4.1, 3.4.2, 3.4.3
TR: Changes in innovation	TR-INMOD	3.4.1
TR: Effects on organizational practices	TR-ORG/PRAC	3.4.3
TR: Effects on organizational climate	TR-ORG/CLIM	3.4.3
TR: Effects on classroom practice	TR-CLASS	3.4.2
TR: Effects on user constructs	TR-HEAD	3.4.2, 3.4.3
TR: Implementation problems	TR-PROBS	3.4.1
TR: Critical events	TR-CRIT	3.4.1, 3.4.2, 3.4.3
TR: External interventions	TR-EXT	3.4.3
TR: Explanations for transformations	TR-SIZUP	3.4.1, 3.4.2, 3.4.3
TR: Program problem-solving	TR-PLAN	3.4.1, 3.4.2, 3.4.3
New configurations and ultimate outcomes	NCO	3.5
NCO: Stabilization of innovation—classroom	NCO-INNOSTAB/CLASS	3.5.1
NCO: Stabilization of user behavior	NCO-STAB/USER	3.5.2
NCO: User first-level outcomes	NCO-USER IOC	3.5.4
Positive and negative	NCO-USER IOC/+,−	
Anticipated and unanticipated	NCO-USER IOC/A,U	
Combinations (when appropriate)	NCO-USER IOC/A+, A− U+, U−	
NCO: User metaoutcomes	NCO-USER META	3.5.4
Positive and negative	NCO-USER META OC/+,−	
Anticipated and unanticipated	NCO-USER META OC/A,U	
Combinations (when appropriate)	NCO-USER META OC/A+, A− U+, U−	
NCO: User spinoffs and side effects	NCO-USER SIDE	3.5.5 (3.5.2)
Positive and negative	NCO-USER SIDE OC/+,−	
Anticipated and unanticipated	NCO-USER SIDE OC/A,U	
Combinations (when appropriate)	NCO-USER SIDE OC/A+, A− U+, U−	
NCO: Classroom institutionalization	NCO-INST/CLASS	3.5.5
NCO: Stabilization of innovation—organization	NCO-INNOSTAB/ORG	3.5.6
NCO: Stabilization of organizational behavior	NCO-STAB/ORG	3.5.7
NCO: Organizational institutionalization	NCO-INST/ORG	3.5.8
NCO: Organizational first-level outcomes	NCO-ORG IOC	3.5.9
Positive and negative	NCO-ORG IOC/+,−	
Anticipated and unanticipated	NCO-ORG IOC/A,U	
Combinations (when appropriate)	NCO-ORG IOC/A+, A− U+, U−	
NCO: Organizational metaoutcomes	NCO-ORG META	3.5.9
Positive and negative	NCO-ORG META OC/+,−	
Anticipated and unanticipated	NCO-ORG META OC/A,U	
Combinations (when appropriate)	NCO-ORG META OC/A+, A− U+, U−	
NCO: Organizational spinoffs and side effects	NCO-ORG SIDE	3.5.9 (3.5.7)
Positive and negative	NCO-ORG SIDE OC/+,−	
Anticipated and unanticipated	NCO-ORG SIDE OC/A,U	
Combinations (when appropriate)	NCO-ORG SIDE OC/A+, A− U+, U−	

NCO: Institutional expansion	NCO-INNOGRO/ORG	3.5.8
NCO: Organizational reduction	NCO-INNODWIN/ORG	3.5.8
External and internal assistance (separate codes for external, peer, administrative)	ASS	
ASS: Location	ASS-LOC	3.6.1
ASS: Rules, norms	ASS-RULE	3.6.1
ASS: Orientation	ASS-ORI	3.6.2
ASS: Type	ASS-TYPE	3.6.3
ASS: Effects	ASS-EFF	3.6.4
ASS: Assessment by recipients	ASS-ASS	3.6.5
ASS: Linkage	ASS-LINK	3.6.6
Emerging causal links	CL	
CL: Networks	CL-NET	N.A.
CL: Rules	CL-RULE	N.A.
CL: Recurrent patterns	CL-PATT	N.A.
Within site	CL-PATT/LS	N.A.
Intersite	CL-PATT/OS	N.A.
CL: Explanatory cluster (researcher)	CL-EXPL	N.A.
(respondent)	SITECL-EXPL	N.A.
Queries	QU	
QU: Surprises	QU-!	N.A.
QU: Puzzles	QU-Q	N.A.

OPERATIONAL DEFINITIONS OF SENSITIZING CODES

Innovation Properties—IP

Objectives: IP-OBJ	Goals, purposes, and problems addressed as defined by developer or in project literature.
Outcomes claimed: IP-OC	Changes, gains, or other benefits to pupils, teachers, staff, or school at large as claimed by developer or in project literature.
Organization: IP-ORG/DD, LS	Details on materials, staffing, space utilization, scheduling, grouping of pupils, pedagogical approach, or instructional theory as defined by developer or in project literature (D/D) or as locally designed (LS).
Implied changes— classroom: IP-CH/CL	Local site perceptions of changes and magnitude of those changes from existing conditions if new practice or program were implemented as "officially" described. This includes (a) changes in classroom organization (see IP—Organization for components), and (b) changes in attitudes, relationships, and operational philosophy.
Implied changes— organization: IP-CH/ORG	Local site perceptions of changes and magnitude of those changes from existing conditions if new practice or program were implemented as "officially" described. This includes (a) changes in administrative arrangements, also including budgeting, authority, planning, and monitoring, and (b) changes in relationships, relative power or privilege, institutional "climate" or press, both internally and in relation to key external persons, officials, groups, agencies.
User salience: IP-SALIENCE	Aspects of the new practice or program seen as critical, controversial, meaningful by teachers, administrators, and support staff; indications of consensus or divergence on these aspects.
User assessment: IP-SIZUP/PRE,DUR	User and administrator assessment of *implementation facility or difficulty,* including (a) complexity, clarity, facility of objectives or procedures; (b) relative latitude/prescriptiveness; and (c) amount of necessary assistance at front-end and/or ongoing. This includes judgments of merit/demerit of innovation.
Program development (IV-C): IP-DEV	Events and activities relating to the planning, developing of the program *after funding is received,* including curriculum development, staffing, organizational arrangements.

External context—EC

Demographics: EC-DEM	Characteristics of the community and district that are identified by informants as influencing adoption and implementation, including SES and ethnic composition, community wealth, rural/urban/suburban character.
Endorsement: EC-END	Pre- and post-adoption stance toward or assessment made of the practice or program by school board, district office, PTA, and other key community persons and agencies (e.g., local newspaper).
Climate: EC-CLIM	Attitudes toward and relations with local school on the part of key community figures and agencies, including central office, which are identified by informants as influencing adoption and implementation, including (a) openness of experimentation/conservatism; (b) quality and intensity of school–community relations; and (c) indices of general community support for school operations.

Internal context—IC

Characteristics: IC-CHAR	Descriptive features of the school identified by respondents as influencing adoption and implementation, including (a) prior experience and training of staff; (b) dominant teaching styles and types of classroom management; and (c) pupil, SES, and ethnic composition, achievement levels, prior experience with similar innovations.
Norms and authority: IC-NORM	Social-organizational features of the school that are identified by respondents as influencing adoption and implementation, including norms (notably norms relating to risk taking, social networks, tolerance of diversity, collaborativeness), authority, and power structure.
Innovation history: IC-HIST	Experience of school over previous 3–5 years with introduction of new practices or programs, including (a) number and type of programs; (b) comfort with, or perceived ease in, process of innovation implementation; (c) satisfaction with previous changes; and (d) presence of problem-solving or capacity-building mechanisms (e.g., lighthouse groups, planning commission, self-diagnosis procedures).
Organization procedures: IC-PROC	General arrangements for organizing classroom and schoolwide work, which may be independent of the innovation.
Innovation–organization congruence: IC-FIT	Indices or events suggesting the degree to which properties of the school are consonant with characteristics of the innovation.

Adoption process—AP

Event chronology— official version: AP-CHRON/PUB	Event history through adoption as recounted in public documents or orally by district and school administrators, developers, early adopters, internal liaison or "delegate" staff among teachers and support personnel. Chronology includes significant events, backers and opponents, other key actors, stance of opinion leaders and gatekeepers within the school, rationale for adopting the practice or program, decision process (persons involved within school, mode of decision).
Event chronology— subterranean version: AP-CHRON/PRIV	Event history through adoption as recounted either by public, promotional or delegated persons (see AP-EC/PUB) or by individual users, nonusers, and other respondents, which suggests (a) a consensual but different scenario, or (b) varying accounts of the same events. Chronology includes significant events, backers and opponents, other key actors, stance of opinion leaders and gatekeepers within the school, rationale for adopting the practice or program, decision process, etc. (See AP-EC/PUB)
Inside/outside: AP-IN/OUT	Indices that the source of the practice or program (outside/inside district or outside/inside school building) was influential in the adoption process.
Centrality: AP-CENT	Degree of priority, commitment, centrality of new practice or program to teachers, administrators, and support staff, eventually pupils, as compared to ongoing, routine activities or to other innovations (in preparation or operation).
Motives: AP-MOT	Manifest and latent reasons given by teachers and administrators for adoption, including (a) "legitimated" personal or institutional improvement; (b) response to external, institutional, classroom pressures or problems; (c) personal agendas; and (d) response to sanctions for nonadoption.

Adoption process—AP (*Continued*)

User fit: Perception by teachers of congruence between *personal* goals, theories
AP-FIT of instruction or learning and congenial ways of working with pupils, and goals, theories, implicit or explicit working arrangements contained in new practice or program.

Plan: Components and perceived adequacy of plan for implementation,
AP-PLAN including provisions for training, monitoring, debugging, support.

Readiness: Perception of institutional and personal capacities or willingness to
AP-REDI implement new program in form adopted. Subcategories include commitment, understanding, materials and equipment, skills, time allocation, organizational backup.

Critical events: Recollected incidents or moments that are judged as critical in
AP-CRIT determining the outcome of the adoption process, including crises or conflicts, key decisions, or interventions.

Site dynamics and transformations—TR

Event chronology— Event chronology during initial and ongoing implementation, as
official version: recounted by users, administrators, or other respondents.
TR-CHRON/PUB

Event chronology— Event chronology during initial or ongoing implementation, as
subterranean version: recounted by users, administrators, or other respondents, which
TR-CHRON/PRIV suggests (a) a consensual but different scenario from the public version or (b) varying accounts of the same events.

Initial user experience: Emotions, events, problems or concerns, assessments made by
TR-START teachers and administrators during first 6 months of implementation.

Changes in innovation: Reported modifications in components of the new practice or program,
TR-INMOD on the part of teachers and administrators, during initial and ongoing implementation.

Effects on Indices of impact of new practice or program on (a) intraorganizational
organizational practices: planning, monitoring, and daily working arrangements (e.g., staffing,
TR-ORG/PRAC scheduling, use of resources, communication among staff), and (b) interorganizational practices (e.g., relationships with district office, school board, community, and parent groups).

Effects on Indices of impact of new practice or program on institutional norms
organizational climate: and interpersonal relationships, including effects on power and
TR-ORG/CLIM influence, social networks, institutional priorities for investing time and energy.

Effects on Indices of impact of new practice or program on regular or routine
classroom practice: classroom practices (instructional planning and management).
TR-CLASS

Effects on Indices of effects of new practice or program on teacher and
user constructs: administrator perceptions, attitudes, motives, assumptions or theories
TR-HEAD of instruction, learning or management (e.g., professional self-image, revised notions of what determines achievement or efficiency, other attitudes toward pupils, colleagues, other staff members, stance toward other innovative practices).

Implementation problems: Difficulties or concerns relating to implementation at the personal,
TR-PROBS classroom, organizational, or extraorganizational levels, including reasons given for presence of difficulty or concern.

Critical events: Observed or recollected incidents or moments that are judged as
TR-CRIT critical in determining the direction and the outcome of implementation, including crises, conflicts, moments of decision, departures and arrivals, and interventions.

Site dynamics and transformations—TR (*Continued*)

External interventions: Contacts or interventions during implementation that are judged to be
TR-EXT   decisive or influential and that involve parties external to the school
                           building, excluding external agents.

Explanations   Explanations by respondents of the reasons for which events occurred
for transformations: or effects observed during the implementation phase.
TR-SIZUP

Program problem-solving: Plans or strategies devised for changing or improving the practice,
TR-PLAN   solving problems in relation to its implementation at either the
                           classroom or the organizational level.

New configurations and ultimate outcomes—NCO

Stabilization of   Degree to which new practice or program has "settled down" at
innovation—classroom: classroom or operational level, notably (a) the number and type of
NCO-INNOSTAB/CLASS   segments being or likely to be modified, but also including, (b)
                              characteristics of the stabilized practice, and (c) depiction of the process
                              of modification of those segments or components.

Stabilization   Degree to which user (teacher) behavior has "settled down" at
or user behavior: classroom or operational level relevant to the innovation, including
NCO-STAB/USER   indices of instructional planning and management being or likely to be
                              modified.

User first-level   Perceived or observed outcomes (summative effects) at the classroom
outcomes: level that are directly related to the objectives or prescribed outcomes
NCO-USER lOC   of the new practice or program as specified by the developer or user.
                              These outcomes may be attitudinal (e.g., changes in pupils' self-
                              concept or motivation) or behavioral (e.g., changes in pupil perfor-
                              mance or in teacher diagnostic practices). They may be judged
                              positively (as personal or classroom gains, strengths, advantages,
                              effort well spent) or negatively (as losses, weaknesses, drawbacks,
                              underrewarded effort) and may be anticipated or unanticipated.

User metaoutcomes: More widespread or superordinate outcomes (summative effects) of
NCO-USER META   the new practice or program as perceived or observed at the classroom
                              level. These outcomes relate to (a) increases or decreases in user cog-
                              nitions or capacity (e.g., deeper understanding of learning or instruc-
                              tional processes, increases or decreases in classroom management
                              skills) or to (b) changes in attitude (e.g., professional self-concept,
                              stance toward staff coordination activities). These outcomes may be
                              judged positively or negatively and may be anticipated or unan-
                              ticipated.

User spinoffs and   Perceived or observed outcomes of the new practice or program that
side effects: are unofficial or unintended (unrelated to specific or general outcomes
NCO-USER SIDE   as specified in or deduced from developer's or user's description of the
                              innovation). From the user's perspective, these outcomes may be
                              judged positively or negatively and may be anticipated (e.g., promo-
                              tion) or unanticipated (e.g., closer collaboration with a colleague).

Classroom   Indices of regular or routine use of the new practice or program, in-
institutionalization: cluding scheduling, materials, lesson or activity plans, formalized
NCO-INST/CLASS   arrangements with colleagues.

Stabilization of   Degree to which new practice or program has "settled down" at the
innovation—organization: administrative or organizational level, including (a) characteristics of
NCO-INNOSTAB/ORG   the stabilized practice; (b) segments being or likely to be modified; and
                              (c) depiction of the process of modification.

New configurations and ultimate outcomes—NCO (*Continued*)

Stabilization of organizational behavior: NCO-STAB/ORG	Degree to which administrative behavior and/or daily working arrangements pertinent to the new practice or program have "settled down" at the institutional level, including indices of institutional planning, operations, or communications in the process of modification or likely to be modified.
Organizational institutionalization: NCO-INST/ORG	Regular or routinized indices of incorporation of the new practice or program in institutional functioning, including fixed scheduling in the curriculum, budget provisions, plans for continued backup, support by external agencies (e.g., central office).
Organizational first-level outcomes: NCO-ORG IOC	Perceived or observed outcomes (summative effects) at the organizational level that are directly related to the objectives or prescribed outcomes of the new practice or program as specified by the developer or administrator. These outcomes may be operational (changes in working arrangemnts) or attitudinal (changes in stance toward working arrangements connected with it). They may be judged positively (as administrative and organizational gains, strengths, advantages, efforts well spent) or negatively (as losses, weaknesses, drawbacks, underrewarded efforts) and may be anticipated or unanticipated.
Organizational metaoutcomes: NCO-ORG META	More widespread or superordinate outcomes of the new practice or program as perceived or observed at the organizational level. These outcomes relate to increases or decreases in organizatinoal capacity or climate (e.g., improved capability to administer other innovations, increased tension between teaching and administrative staff). These outcomes may be judged positively or negatively and may be anticipated or unanticipated.
Organizational spinoffs and side effects: NCO-ORG SIDE	Perceived or observed outcomes of the new practice or program that are unofficial or unintended (unrelated to specific or general outcomes as specified in or deduced from the developer's or administrator's description of the innovation). From the administrator's perspective, these outcomes may be judged positively or negatively and may be anticipated (e.g., increased visibility in the district) or unanticipated (creation of cliques among teachers).
Institutional expansion: NCO-INNOGRO/ORG	Evidence of the expansion of the practice either within the adopting school, within other schools in the district, or outside the district.
Organizational reduction: NCO-INNODWIN/ORG	Evidence of the contraction or reduction of the practice from either the original set of users or from the set estimated at the point of implementation when stabilization occurs.

External and internal assistance—ASS

Location: ASS-LOC	Positions of and relationship between assisters and receivers in the school, including (a) physical position (outside/inside); (b) social position (status, power); (c) technical position (credibility, source, type, and degree of expertise); and (d) interpersonal position (networks of association), indication of the influence of position on assistance given and received.
Rules, norms: ASS-RULE	Perceived agreements, constraints, codes of conduct within the school that regulate the seeking and providing of assistance.
Orientation: ASS-ORI	Focus (content/process) and definition (expert/facilitator) of assister intention, role as perceived by receiver (coercive, reeducative).
Type: ASS-TYPE	Type and format of assistance provision, including technical, practical, psychological, administrative, political.

External and internal assistance—ASS (*Continued*)

Effects: ASS-EFF	Perceived or observed effects of assistance on implementation, both positive and negative, anticipated and unanticipated, direct (problem resolution) and indirect, or more general (e.g., increased professional confidence).
Assessment by recipients: ASS-ASS	Assessment of assistance provided, including pertinence, adequacy, responsiveness, legitimacy, usefulness.
Linkage: ASS-LINK	Indications of assistance provided from more than one source, including (a) degree of perceived integration or coordination and (b) perceived effectiveness of combined assistance.

Emerging causal links—CL

Networks: CL-NET	Functional grouping of persons, both formal and informal, within the school and between the school and external institutions or persons who influence the shape or direction of implementation.
Rules: CL-RULE	Consensual, dominant, or pervasive ways of perceiving how and why ongoing work and interpersonal relations are carried out, understandable or legitimated.
Recurrent patterns: CL-PATT/LS CL-PATT/OS	Recurring descriptions, remarks, explanations, interactions, or activities, either reported or observed, in direct relationship to the new practice or program but not deliberately or operationally included in its components.
Explanatory cluster: CL-EXPL SITECL-EXPL	Factors or features directly related to adoption or implementation of the new practice or program and observed or hypothesized to affect the shape, direction, or magnitude of its effects, as judged by the field researcher (CL-EXPL) or a respondent (SITECL-EXPL).

Queries—QU

Surprises: QU-!	Material from interviews, observations, documents that is striking or unexpected in light of other materials from the site.
Puzzles: QU-Q	Material from interviews, observations, documents, etc., that either (a) cannot be accounted for; (b) needs closer analysis; or (c) contradicts other materials or emerging hypotheses.

Example of a Causal Network with Associated Text

INTRODUCTION: LOOKING FOR EXPLANATIONS

In addition to describing what happened to a given project, we want to know *why* the process of implementation took the form it did. To get at the reasons, we have constructed a "causal network" for each of the 12 sites studied.

The causal network tries to put on one page the main factors and the ways they influenced each other during the life of the project—or, in our case, up to June 1980, when we completed our fieldwork. There are two kinds of factors in the network. The first kind is *general* factors, ones that seemed important at all 12 sites to explain the pattern of events and outcomes. There are also factors *unique to a given site*. For example, in the causal network for Perry-Parkdale (Figure C-1), "internal funds" (Box 4) is a general factor, whereas "search for add-on funds" (Box 6) is a factor unique to Perry-Parkdale; it is marked with an asterisk.

At first glance, the boxes and arrows probably look more like a Rube Goldberg machine or a maze than a coherent network. But we think the reader will find that it is relatively easy to follow, using the explanatory text that accompanies it. We believe that a more simplified figure wouldn't really do justice to the real complexities behind any attempt to change educational practices. As the figure shows, there are nearly three dozen key factors at work, and any single factor may influence several others.

HOW THE NETWORK IS ORGANIZED

The network runs as follows: The beginning or *antecedent* factors are at the left of the page. They give way to *intermediate* or intervening factors, which usually come later in the story of the innovation; these variables cover most of the page, from numbers 6 through 29. The *outcome* factors are on the far right.

The arrows from one box to another mean that the boxes are linked causally—that the box where the arrow begins has "caused" or "led to" the box where the arrow ends.

Each box also has a rating (high, moderate, or low). For instance, Box 3, "Search for programs," is high because active searching for a good career-education program was going on. The active search led to the choice of a program that was a good "fit" to the

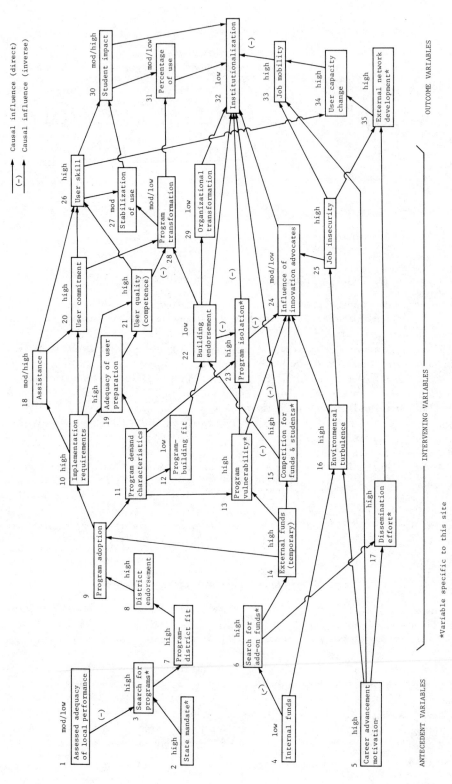

FIGURE C-1. Causal network for Perry-Parkdale CARED program. (From Miles & Huberman, 1984. Reprinted by permission.)

needs of the district, so Box 7 ("Program-district fit") is also rated high. Note that there are no ratings for Box 9 ("Program adoption") and Box 11 ("Program demand characteristics"). That's because these boxes are "yes/no" rather than being a measure of the *degree* or *level* of something.

When an arrow goes from a "high" box to a "high" box, there is no sign above the arrow; the same is true when a "low" goes to a "low." In both cases, the causal influence is *direct*. But when "high" goes to "low" and vice versa, there is a (—) sign above the arrow to show that the influence is *inverse*. For example, the arrow from Box 4 to Box 6 has a (—) sign, meaning that low amounts of internal funds led to high amounts of searching for add-on funds. A high-to-low sequence appears between Box 23 and Box 32: A high degree of program isolation led to a low degree of institutionalization (which was, you will note, also caused by many other factors).

READING THE NETWORK FOR PERRY-PARKDALE

If one reads along from left to right, the sequence is roughly as follows.

The first three antecedent variables (1, 2, and 4) worked out this way. The state mandate (2) for well-planned career education programs, together with the assessment of local performance as less than adequate (1), led to a search for new programs (3), which proved to be a good fit (7) with district characteristics, and hence to district endorsement (8), and to adoption of the program (9).

But these were not sufficient causes of adoption. Inadequate local funds (4) to cover existing programs led to a ceaseless search for add-on funds (6) as almost a "way of life" for the district. That search led to getting temporary external funds (14) for a three-year period; they were the other basic cause of adoption (9).

The program, when adopted, proved to have substantial implementation requirements (10), which dictated the need for assistance (18) and also exerted a good deal of pressure for careful selection of high-quality staff (21), and for careful preparation (19) of them to carry out the program. The heavy implementation requirements (10), and to some degree the assistance provided (18), induced a good deal of user commitment (20) and, in turn, user skill (26), which was also high because of staff quality (21). High user skill, in conjunction with the fact that the program was quite well stabilized (27) by late 1980, brought about a reasonable degree of student impact (30).

That stream of causality refers essentially to internal program dynamics. What was happening at the *district and building* levels?

Moving back to program demand characteristics (11), we note that certain aspects of the program (such as its removing students from high-school control and from high-school courses and activities) caused a poor fit between the program and the sending buildings (12). That poor fit led to lack of endorsement (22) from building principals, counselors, and teachers. This poor endorsement was further weakened by the presence of competition for funds and for students (15), induced by the fact that the external funds (14) were temporary in nature.

Temporary funding, together with the program's demand characteristics (11) (for example, the students were visible to employers, had to be responsible, and could easily behave like "assholes"), also made for a good deal of program vulnerability (13). As a consequence, the staff tended to operate the program in a rather isolated fashion (23), and to buffer it against the consequences of vulnerability when the immediate environmental endorsement (22) was weak. Certain program demand characteristics (11), such as the intensive time block, reinforced isolation (23) as well.

An added set of causal variables was also in play. The career advancement motivation (5) of key central office staff and principals operated to induce a good deal of turbulence (16) in the district. This turbulence effectively reduced the influence of those who were advocating the innovation (24); for some advocates, influence was further weakened by job insecurity (25).

So although the program was transformed and altered (28) to some degree to meet the objections stemming from low building endorsement (22), achieved a modest increase in the percentage of use (31) for a while, and was, as we have seen, proving reasonably effective with students (30), these factors were not enough to ensure the program's institutionalization (being built into the system) (32).

Rather, the weak building endorsement (22), the program's isolation (23), the competition for funds and students (15), and the weak exercise of influence by the innovation advocates (24) resulted in weak institutionalization (32). So, it seems likely, did the departure of program staff, whose job mobility (33) was driven by both career advancement motivation (5) and job insecurity (25). It also seems likely that the very user capacity development (34) induced by experience with skillful use of the program (26), enhanced by the external network of contacts (35) generated through the dissemination effort (17), also contributed to the decision of staff members (and, it seems, possibly the director) to move on.

Taken as a whole, these explanations seem baroque and complex. But there is fairly clear evidence that each causal link worked as described. The chart will look less complicated if one notes that the chart contains four basic streams: the *program development* stream across the top, the *building/district* stream in the middle, the *career* stream near the bottom, and the external *dissemination/networking* stream last. In many respects, the final outcomes can be seen as stemming from conflicting pressures across the streams.

Index

Site	Innovation type	Implementation req'ts	School level
NDN			
Astoria	Add-on	Moderate	Kdg.
Banestown	Pull-out	Moderate	3–6
Burton	Add-on°	Low–mod	9–12
Calston	Drop-in	Moderate	4–8
Lido	Add-on°	Moderate	K–12
Masepa	Drop-in	High	K–9
Perry-Parkdale	Subsystem	Mod–high	9–12
IV-C			
Carson	Add-on	High	1–12
Dun Hollow	Add-on°	Low–mod	1–6
Plummet	Subsystem	High	9–12
Proville	Pull-out	Low–mod	12
Tindale	Drop-in (quasi subsystem)	Mod–high	9–12

°These innovations could also be (and were) treated as displacing existing practice.